Callings

Callings

TWENTY CENTURIES

OF CHRISTIAN WISDOM

ON VOCATION

edited by

William C. Placher

William B. Eerdmans Publishing Company
Grand Rapids, Michigan / Cambridge, U.K.

Wm. B. Eerdmans Publishing Co.
2140 Oak Industrial Drive N.E., Grand Rapids, Michigan 49505 /
P.O. Box 163, Cambridge CB3 9PU U.K.

Printed in the United States of America

12 11 10 09 08 07   8 7 6 5 4 3 2

ISBN 978-0-8028-2927-6 (paper)
ISBN 978-0-8028-3048-7 (cloth)

www.eerdmans.com

In memory of
Carl H. Placher
1903-1966

Contents

Contents

2. Called to Religious Life:
Vocations in the Middle Ages, 500-1500

3. Every Work a Calling:
Vocations after the Reformation, 1500-1800

Contents

Contents

4. Christian Callings in a
Post-Christian World, 1800-Present

Acknowledgments

Excerpt from Ignatius of Antioch used by permission of Westminster John Knox Press.

Excerpt from "The Martyrdom of Saints Perpetua and Felicitas" reproduced by permission of Oxford University Press.

Excerpts from Palladius, *The Lausiac History,* from the Ancient Christian Writers, No. 34, translated and annotated by Robert T. Meyer, Ph.D., copyright © 1964 by Rev. Johannes Quasten and Rev. Walter J. Burghardt, S.J., and Thomas Comerford Lawlor, Paulist Press, Inc., New York / Mahwah, N.J. Used with permission of Paulist Press. www.paulistpress.com.

Excerpt from *Sayings of the Desert Fathers,* translated by Benedicta Ward, copyright © 1980. Reproduced by permission of Routledge/Taylor & Francis Books, Inc.

Excerpt from *Confessions of St. Augustine* by St. Augustine, translated by Rex Warner, copyright © 1963 by Rex Warner, renewed © 1991 by F. C. Warner. Used by permission of Dutton Signet, a division of Penguin Group (USA) Inc.

Excerpt from *The Rule of St. Benedict* by Anthony C. Meisel, copyright © 1975 by Anthony C. Meisel & M. L. Del Mastro. Used by permission of Doubleday, a division of Random House, Inc.

Excerpt from *Chronicles of the Crusades by Joinville and Villehardouin,* copyright © 1963 by M.R.B. Shaw. Reproduced by permission of Penguin Press.

Excerpts from Bonaventure, *The Soul's Journey into God, The Tree of Life, The Life of St. Francis,* from The Classics of Western Spirituality, translated by Ewert Cousins, preface by Ignatius Brady, copyright © 1978 by Paulist Press, Inc., New York / Mahwah, N.J. Used with permission of Paulist Press. www.paulistpress.com.

Acknowledgments

Excerpts from Mechthild of Magdeburg, *The Flowing Light of the Godhead*, from The Classics of Western Spirituality, translated by Frank Tobin, copyright © 1998 by Frank Tobin, Paulist Press, Inc., New York / Mahwah, N.J. Used with permission of Paulist Press. www.paulistpress.com.

Excerpt from *The Treasure of the City of Ladies* by Christine de Pisan, copyright © 1985 by Sarah Lawson. Reproduced by permission of Penguin Press.

Excerpt from *The Mission of Joan of Arc*, copyright © 2001. From *Medieval Hagiography* by Thomas Head. Reproduced by permission of Routledge/Taylor & Francis, Inc.

Excerpt from Thomas à Kempis, *The Imitation of Christ*, translated by Harold C. Gardiner, copyright © 1955 by Doubleday, a division of Random House, Inc. Used by permission of Doubleday, a division of Random House, Inc.

Excerpt from Martin Luther, *Address to the Christian Nobility of the German Nation*, is reprinted from *Three Treatises by Martin Luther*, copyright © 1960 Muhlenberg Press, admin. Augsburg Fortress. Used by permission.

Excerpt from Martin Luther, *Gospel for the Early Christmas Service*, is reprinted from *Luther's Works*, vol. 52, edited by Hans J. Hillerbrand, copyright © 1974 Fortress Press. Used by permission of Augsburg Fortress.

Excerpt from Martin Luther, *Trade and Usury*, is reprinted from *Luther's Works*, vol. 45, edited by Walther I. Brandt, copyright © 1962 Fortress Press. Used by permission of Augsburg Fortress.

Excerpts from Martin Luther, *Whether Soldiers, Too, Can Be Saved* and *Sermon on Keeping Children in School*, are reprinted from *Luther's Works*, vol. 46, edited by Robert C. Schultz, copyright © 1967 Fortress Press. Used by permission of Augsburg Fortress.

Excerpt from Ulrich Sadler, *Cherished Instructions on Sin, Excommunication, and the Community of Goods*, reproduced from *Spiritual and Anabaptist Writers*, edited by George Huntston Williams. Used by permission of Westminster John Knox Press.

Excerpt from John Calvin, *Institutes of the Christian Religion*, reproduced from *Calvin: Institutes of the Christian Religion*, edited by John T. McNeill. Used by permission of Westminster John Knox Press.

Excerpt from Ignatius Loyola, *The Spiritual Exercises* from *The Spiritual Exercises of St. Ignatius* by Anthony Mottola, copyright © 1964 by Doubleday, a division of Random House, Inc. Used by permission of Doubleday, a division of Random House, Inc.

Excerpt from *The Life of Saint Teresa of Ávila by Herself*, copyright © 1957 by J. M. Cohen. Reproduced by permission of Penguin Press.

Excerpts from Sor Juana Inés de la Cruz, *Reply to Sor Philothea*, reprinted by permission of the publisher from *A Sor Juana Anthology*, translated by Alan S. Trueblood, pp. 210-19, 223-26. Cambridge, Mass.: Harvard University Press, copyright © 1988 by the President and Fellows of Harvard College.

Acknowledgments

Excerpt from Søren Kierkegaard, *Fear and Trembling*, copyright © 1983 Princeton University Press. Reprinted by permission of Princeton University Press.

Excerpt from *Strange Freedom: The Best of Howard Thurman on Religious Experience and Public Life* by Earl Fluker, © 1998 by Walter Earl Fluker and Catherine Tumber. Reprinted by permission of Beacon Press, Boston.

Excerpt from *The Cost of Discipleship* by Dietrich Bonhoeffer reprinted with permission of Scribner, an imprint of Simon & Schuster Adult Publishing Group, copyright © 1959 by SCM Press Ltd.

Excerpt from *Waiting on God* by Simone Weil, copyright © 1966 Librairie Artheme Fayard. Reproduced by permission of Routledge/Taylor & Francis Books, Inc.

Excerpt from Dorothy L. Sayers, "Vocation in Work," in *A Christian Basis for the Post-War World*, ed. A. E. Baker, copyright © 1942 by SCM Press. Reprinted by permission of SCM Press.

Excerpts from *No Man Is an Island* by Thomas Merton, copyright © 1955 by The Abbey of Our Lady of Gethsemani and renewed 1983 by the Trustees of the Merton Legacy Trust, reprinted by permission of Harcourt, Inc.

Excerpt from Karl Barth, *Church Dogmatics*, copyright © T&T Clark, a Continuum imprint.

Scripture quotations taken from the New Revised Standard Version Bible, copyright 1989, Division of Christian Education of the National Council of the Churches of Christ in the United States of America. Used by permission. All rights reserved.

Preface

The idea for this book, and for me to edit it, emerged from a series of rich conversations with Dorothy Bass, Chris Coble, Craig Dykstra, Kim Maphis Early, and Mark Schwehn. Behind those conversations lay the exciting work of the Programs for the Theological Exploration of Vocation. Without that background, the generous support of the Lilly Endowment, and the encouragement of Jon Pott of Eerdmans, the book would never have happened.

Mark R. Schwehn and Dorothy C. Bass are editing a companion volume that assembles a complementary but quite different selection of texts on vocation. *Leading Lives That Matter: What We Should Do and Who We Should Be* gathers selections from beyond the Christian theological tradition that is the focus of *Callings*, including fiction, poetry, letters, memoirs, and other forms of literature by both Christian and non-Christian authors. The editors of *Summoning* share my conviction that encountering ideas from the past can illuminate our reflection in the present, and their book includes texts from the ancient world as well as from the very recent past. Unlike *Callings*, however, their book is arranged topically rather than historically. In light of the richness of the questions at the heart of both books, I look forward to the cross-referencing and interdisciplinary conversation that the books may together foster. Moreover, I am grateful that each book may offset some weaknesses in the other.

The most obvious weakness of *Callings* is that it includes no texts from the last fifty years. I could plead that some more contemporary material appears in *Summoning,* but that book is nothing like a continuation of this one. Truth is, the last fifty years include so many important trends — including changes in Catholic thought after Vatican II and a greater inclusion of the voices of women and people of color — that attempting to represent them would have vastly lengthened an already long book and given it a historically unbalanced shape. So it stops well short of the present.

Its ending point is not this book's only limitation. For a range of times, places, and traditions I could not find readings that seemed accessible to contemporary readers or could not secure the permission of copyright holders for the texts I wanted to use; no doubt the fault often lay with my not knowing where to look. But I decided my first responsibility was to find texts from the history of Christianity that would get people today thinking about vocation, even if that meant giving too much attention to periods where I could find a number of fascinating pieces and not enough attention to periods where I feared the texts I located would have had only historical interest. I have tried to gather texts with my likely audience in mind, an audience more apt to be thinking about choosing a profession than, for instance, surviving a famine. For millions of people, I realize, surviving famine is a more pressing concern, but they are an unlikely audience for a book like this one — whose audience, however, may include people with gifts that could someday improve the world's prosperity and justice.

Terry Archambeault, Dorothy Bass, Mike Eikenberry, Amy Huffaker, Wayne Lewis, Nick Myers, Elly Schroeder, Martha Schwehn, and Anne Sutherland provided a most helpful test audience. Rich conversation with Lewis Galloway and the Lake Fellows and other young staff members of Second Presbyterian Church in Indianapolis helped me rethink some important issues. Debbie Polley was, as always, the ideal interlibrary-loan librarian.

I could not have finished without the help of Nicholas Myers, a gifted Wabash student and my research assistant for the project. He not only did most of the work but was the first and most helpful reader of everything I wrote.

My father got his first full-time job when he was eighteen, teaching all eight grades in a one-room schoolhouse. During the rest of his career, he at various times taught everything from kindergarten to graduate school, and he thereby taught me, along with much else, what it means to have a vocation as a teacher. So this book is dedicated to his memory.

Feast of Ignatius of Antioch, Bishop and Martyr W.C.P.

Introduction

I don't know Who — or what — put the question, I don't know when it was put. I don't even remember answering. But at some moment I did answer Yes to Someone — or Something — and from that hour I was certain that existence is meaningful and that, therefore, my life, in self-surrender, had a goal.[1]

DAG HAMMARSKJÖLD
Secretary-General, United Nations, 1953-1961

"What are you called to do with your life?" "Do you have a vocation?" Put like that, these may seem strange questions, not the sort of thing we would ordinarily ask. We may not even be sure what they mean. Yet many of us worry about finding a direction or purpose or meaning for our lives. We wonder if the bits and pieces of our struggles, disappointments, and successes will add up to a significant whole. "Call" and "vocation" are categories the Christian tradition has long used to address such issues.

"Vocation" is just a Latin word for "calling" — the two words are more or less interchangeable. To tell the truth, neither one has a clear definition these days. When I was in high school, "vocational education" meant courses in auto shop and typing, for people who weren't going on to college.

---

1. Dag Hammarskjöld, *Markings*, trans. Leif Sjoberg and W. H. Auden (New York: Alfred A. Knopf, 1966), 205.

1

"Vocation," I suppose, just meant "a job," and so these were classes for people going straight from twelfth grade to full-time work.

By contrast, people preparing for ministry or priesthood often get asked if they have "a call." For some, it's an embarrassing question. They think that the pastorate or priesthood may be what they're supposed to do with their lives, but that word "call" suggests some kind of voice from heaven that corresponds to nothing in their experience. Perhaps it evokes memories of an old Bill Cosby routine about Noah's ark, in which a deep bass voice calls out from above, "NOAH! NOAH! THIS IS THE LORD, NOAH!" Cosby, a nervous grin on his face, looks upwards and says, "Yeeeah! Riiiight!"

Is that what it means to have God call you? Could most of us imagine such a strange event happening to us?

Down the centuries, Christians have looked for definitions of "vocation" somewhere between the trivial sense of "just a job" and the hard-to-believe image of a miraculous voice from heaven. *Central to the many Christian interpretations of vocation is the idea that there is something — my vocation or calling — God has called me to do with my life, and my life has meaning and purpose at least in part because I am fulfilling my calling.*

On much else concerning vocation, Christians have regularly disagreed. They have debated questions like these:

- Is what God wants me to do simply that I should live as a Christian? Or is my job my vocation? Or does my calling have at least as much to do with being a spouse, a parent, a good citizen, or something else?
- How do I know what I'm called to do?
- Is there one right answer to the question of my calling?
- Are there jobs it is wrong for a Christian to do?
- Can I make a mistake, and not do what God has called me to do? If so, what are the consequences?
- Can my vocation change?
- Can those who do not believe in God have vocations? Can there be a calling without someone who calls?

The answers to such questions have remained in dispute, and the following pages record some of the disputes. Christians will read them looking for what their own tradition has to say about vocations; non-Christians may also find it helpful to explore, by way of comparison with their own tradition or untraditional searches, how Christians have thought about issues of concern to any human being.

Amid all the controversies Christianity has preserved the fundamental idea that our lives count for something because God has a direction in mind for them. I recently heard the pastor of one of the wealthiest congregations in America addressing a class of graduating college students. "By nearly all the criteria by which our culture measures success," he said, "most of my congregation is spectacularly successful. They make more money than they know how to spend. They have the most prestigious job titles. You read many of their names in newspapers and magazines — they're famous. But as their pastor I know how many of them are *desperately* unhappy." Therefore he warned those graduating seniors: "Be careful about following the path to 'success.' You can arrive at the goal and find only emptiness."

If the God who made us has figured out something we are supposed to do, however — something that fits how we were made, so that doing it will enable us to glorify God, serve others, and be most richly ourselves — then life stops seeming so empty: my story has meaning as part of a larger story ultimately shaped by God.

But how can we discern such a call? To the occasional saint, the call apparently does come as a voice from heaven, but most people figure out, usually as part of a community, how God is calling them through prayer and meditation, inward reflection on their own abilities and desires, and looking out at the world around them and its needs. God calls you, the contemporary preacher and novelist Frederick Buechner has written, to "the kind of work (a) that you need most to do, and (b) that the world most needs to have done. . . . The place God calls you to is the place where your deep gladness and the world's deep hunger meet."[2] To believe that a wise and good God is in charge of things implies that there is a fit between things that need doing and the person I am meant to be. Finding such a fit, I find my calling.

Looking back to the wisdom of the Christian tradition can help us think about these issues better. The past does not always have the right answers, but its answers are often at least *different* from those of the present, and the differences cause us to question our own previously unexamined assumptions. Why do we think X when people used to think Y? After traveling in other countries, we come back to our own with new questions. But the past too is a different country, and, voyaging in it, we gain richer perspectives on our own time.

But great Christian thinkers can offer us more than just interesting alternatives. The twentieth-century theologian Karl Barth (a selection from

---

2. Frederick Buechner, *Wishful Thinking: A Theological ABC* (New York: Harper and Row, 1973), 95.

whose work appears at the end of this volume) once explained that he read Paul's letters in the New Testament primarily because "Paul knows of God what most of us do not know, and his letters enable us to know what he knew."[3] Many of the saints and teachers quoted in this book knew things about Christian vocation that most of us do not know. Reading selections from them can help us know what they knew. In all manner of ways — on social equality or on the role of women, for instance — many of them were narrow-minded or just wrong. But on how to follow our callings, they have something to teach us.

What Does the Bible Say?

Christians usually look for answers to our questions about faith and life first by turning to the Bible. But Scripture does not provide a clear, straightforward account when it comes to questions about vocation. Right at the start, for instance, if offers two very different pictures of the meaning of human work. In Genesis the Lord puts Adam in the midst of a beautiful garden "to till and keep it" (Gen. 2:15). Even in a good creation there is work to be done, and human beings are to find meaning and fulfillment in serving God's pleasure by doing it. In contrast, after Adam and Eve eat the fruit of the tree of the knowledge of good and evil, work comes as punishment: Adam will now eat only "in toil" and "by the sweat of your face" (Gen. 3:17, 19). It distorts the biblical message to take either one of these stories by itself and ignore the other. This complexity in the Bible, moreover, parallels a complexity we encounter in our own experience — work can be both blessing and curse, the task that fulfills us and gives our lives meaning in the service of God or the burdensome job we endure to put food on the table for our families.[4]

More generally, when the Bible talks about "call" or "vocation," it characteristically means a call to faith or to do a special task in God's service. In the Old Testament, God calls the first Israelites, the prophets, and rulers to do his will. In the New Testament the word *klēsis* ("calling," from the Greek verb *kaleō*, "to call," used eleven times, mostly in letters by Paul or authors in-

---

3. Karl Barth, *The Epistle to the Romans,* trans. Edwyn C. Hoskyns (London: Oxford University Press, 1968), 11.

4. "Man's life is built up every day from work, from work it derives its specific dignity, but at the same time work contains the unceasing measure of human toil and suffering." John Paul II, *Laborem exercens: On Human Work* (Washington: United States Catholic Conference, 1981), 3.

fluenced by him) consistently refers to God's call to a life of faith.[5] Paul assures the Thessalonians, "We always pray for you, asking that our God will make you worthy of his call" (2 Thess. 1:11). Reminding the Corinthians that God makes use of foolishness and weakness, he writes, "Consider your own call, brothers and sisters: not many of you were wise by human standards, not many were powerful, not many were of noble birth" (1 Cor. 1:26). In both cases the "call" was to come, be a Christian.

Some scholars therefore argue that the initial call to faith or calls to a special mission are the *only* biblically warranted meanings of the word "call." But it is always dangerous to argue that something did not exist just because the historical record does not mention it. The Bible, after all, focuses on the stories of people for whom God had a special task, not the more "typical" farmers or potters, husbands or wives, or parents, so it is hard to be sure whether the biblical authors would have thought of their more ordinary roles in life as callings. Colossians insists, "whatever your task, put yourselves into it, as done for the Lord and not for your masters" (Col. 3:23). This passage does not use the word "call," but it certainly invites Christians to think of any task as work done in the Lord's service. Here, as on other issues, the Bible gives us complex answers, and, in trying to understand them, it makes sense to ask how wise Christians down the centuries have interpreted them and understood what Christian faith means by vocation or calling.

Four Historical Periods

The ways in which Christians think about vocation have changed radically, in part because society has changed. For example, most of us in prosperous societies today have many choices of careers, but in most times and places the vast majority of people have had few options. A peasant's son became a peasant; a goldsmith's son joined the goldsmiths' guild. Daughters had even fewer choices. Even at the top of society, in the Middle Ages the king's eldest son became king, the next perhaps a bishop, the third likely joined the army, and the king's daughters were married off to strengthen key alliances. There could be interesting exceptions, but for most people it just wouldn't have made sense to ask, "What are the career choices you are considering?" So whatever "vocation" meant, it did not usually mean choice of jobs.

5. Karlfried Froehlich, "Luther on Vocation," in *Harvesting Martin Luther's Reflections on Theology, Ethics, and the Church*, ed. Timothy J. Wengert (Grand Rapids: William B. Eerdmans, 2004), 123.

Any broad categories oversimplify, but there are roughly four broad periods in Christian history when "calling" has had different meanings. Even the words used sometimes mark the differences.

Calling to Christian Life in the Early Church

For the first several hundred years of Christianity, Christians were a minority, rapidly growing in size but often at risk. Many Christians joined the church as adults, and their decision often meant a break from family and previous way of life. Their response to their call (in Greek, *klēsis*) made them automatically outsiders to most facets of society, uncomfortable with its standard forms of entertainment, unable to share much of its social life. Persecution of Christians was sporadic and usually localized, but in the Roman Empire, where most Christians lived, refusal to perform the sacrifices of the imperial cult was technically illegal. Even if the risk was usually small, being a Christian meant the possibility of arrest, torture, and death. Thus the fundamental vocational questions for Christians or potential Christians were initially, first, should I be a Christian? and, second, how public should I be about my Christian faith?

In the fourth century, after the Emperor Constantine became a Christian, Christians (still for some time a minority in the Empire) faced a different problem. Christian faith no longer risked torture; it could even provide a convenient way to get ahead in society. New converts flooded into the church. How could Christians preserve a sense that Christianity involved a cost, took a risk? What were Christians called to do when it seemed pretty easy just to be a Christian? Some of them went to the desert to be nuns and monks, and found their callings in lives of radical self-denial that preserved the dramatic challenge of Christianity.

Religious Vocations in the Middle Ages

For roughly a thousand years in the Middle Ages, by contrast to the situation of the early church, the vast majority of Christians grew up in the church, surrounded by other Christians. Whether to be a Christian was scarcely a real issue for them. But what kind of Christian should they be? Some felt called to be priests, monks, nuns, or friars. Indeed, for medieval Christians "having a vocation" (in Latin, *vocatio*) meant almost exclusively joining the priesthood or some monastic order. Thus the central vocational

6

choice for Christians was — should I stay a part of my family, marrying, having children; or choose the priesthood or the "religious" life in a convent or a monastery or as a wandering friar ("religious" usually meant "monastic")?

The Reformation and Seeing Every Job as a Vocation

Around 1500, however, many European ideas about vocation began to change, for both secular and religious reasons. On the secular side, the increasing complexity of society offered many people more choices. A peasant could run off to a rapidly growing city and find a new job. Someone with a bit of money could invest it in looms to produce cloth or a ship to go off on a trading expedition and grow rich off the profits. The adventurous and the desperate could set off for a new life in the Americas. On the religious side, even before the Reformation, adherents of the "New Devout" and other such groups were experimenting with ways to live a life particularly dedicated to their faith while holding a secular job or getting married. "We are not Religious [i.e., not nuns or monks]," one wrote, "but we mean to live in the world religiously."[6]

With Protestants, traditional categories underwent even more radical transformation. Martin Luther proclaimed "the priesthood of all believers" and, like most other Protestant pastors, got married. Thus among Protestants, everyone was a priest, and pastors increasingly lived more like everyone else. One could be called to a life of preaching, but alternatively to government, commerce, crafts, farming, or anything else — and preaching was as compatible with marriage as was any other calling.

In 1 Corinthians, Paul had written that Christians should remain uncircumcised if they had not already been circumcised and, if they were slaves, worry about how to be a good Christian as a slave rather than try to gain their freedom. He summarized his argument by declaring, "Let each of you remain in the *klēsis* in which you were called" (1 Cor. 7:20). In his German translation of the Bible, Luther at that point translated *klēsis* as *Beruf*, the ordinary German word for an occupation. (A standard German application form would say, *Name, Vorname, Beruf* — Last Name, First Name, Occupation.) Thus for Luther your "calling" was first of all your job (though he acknowledged that marriage and parenthood were also callings).

6. *De coercendis inconstancie filii*, quoted in Francis Oakley, *The Western Church in the Later Middle Ages* (Ithaca: Cornell University Press, 1979), 131.

Most Protestants followed Luther's example. "Our savior Christ was a carpenter," the seventeenth-century English Puritan Thomas Becon reminded his readers. "His apostles were fishermen. St. Paul was a tentmaker." Such were their initial callings or vocations.[7] Where Luther emphasized remaining in the calling to which you were called, his successors opened up the possibility that a good Christian might change callings during the course of life. But the basic idea remained: your job was your vocation, and thus everyone, not just priests, nuns, and monks, was called by God to their particular work.

Vocations in a Post-Christian Age

In the last two centuries, patterns of thinking about Christian vocation have continued to change. Since the Second Vatican Council in the 1960s, Catholic thought has shared the previously Protestant idea that any job can be a vocation. In more economically advanced countries, at least, most people have lots of choices of job or career. Even the "normal" pattern of a family — father and mother married for a lifetime, several children — is no longer the way most people live. New options in work and family life offer great freedom, but they also impose significant burdens. "What does God want me to do with my life?" becomes an even harder question.

Moreover, many people grow more nervous about identifying "vocation" with "job" or "career." An idea that seemed liberating to many of Luther's contemporaries has come to seem to some more like a burden. Furthermore, even when we have learned to dismiss many of the ideas of Karl Marx, we can recognize that he had some valid points when he talked about "alienated labor" in the modern world. The shoemaker of several hundred years ago made shoes for friends and neighbors, and brought all the skills of a craft to making them well. The modern assembly-line worker too often anonymously adds a particular bolt to a product for an unknown customer, a task in which one cannot really excel. The work does not seem to belong to the worker. It is hard to feel pride in one's work in such an "alienated" situation, and thus somehow also hard to feel "called" to such a job. Nor is the problem confined to factory laborers. Lawyers and businessmen working without ever meeting their clients, accountants moving money around to fit

7. Thomas Becon, "Thomas Becon Catechism," in *Works* (Cambridge: The Parker Society, 1844), 1:398; quoted in Paul Marshall, *A Kind of Life Imposed on Man: Vocation and Social Order from Tyndale to Locke* (Toronto: University of Toronto Press, 1996), 34.

the rules of tax law, and many others may feel just as alienated in their work.[8]

Many of us today also live much of our lives after retiring from our "job." We are apt these days to be more aware of the severely disabled and others who cannot hold a job at all. Does someone without a job not have a calling and thus not have a meaningful life? At a different extreme, some careers seem so to dominate people's lives as to leave us worrying if the idea of *job* as vocation is not a danger to our roles as spouses, parents, free creatures of God. Should our jobs consume our whole lives?

For these reasons and others, some contemporary theologians have grown suspicious of the very idea of "vocation." In recent years many Christians in Europe and North America have also come to feel — perhaps this is true for the first time since Christianity's first few centuries — that they do not live in a Christian society. Hence, some writers talk about our time as "post-Christian." It is not just that our neighbors may be Muslim or Hindu or atheist or vaguely "spiritual" but not Christian. The values of our culture seem to have so much to do with acquiring the lifestyles of the rich and famous. Advertising surrounds us with images of sexual pleasure and material wealth. "What is God calling me to do?" or "How can I pick up my cross and follow Jesus?" — these seem ever stranger questions. Trying to live as a Christian pushes upstream against the dominant values around us. We do not face the threat of martyrdom, but it is possible to see a connection between our time and the earliest centuries of Christianity, when Christians were outsiders in a world dominated by non-Christian values and assumptions. *Simply living as Christians* could be our calling too.

Learning from the Past

One reason to read passages on vocation from the history of Christianity is thus to encounter a range of different options. For Christians "vocation" does not have to mean "converting to Christianity" or "becoming a monk" or "finding a job" — it does not have to mean *any* one thing. The study of history frees us up by offering a wide range of ways in which past Christians have found that God was calling them, so that we do not feel that following the Christian tradition leaves us only one choice.

Beneath all these variations — from the *klēsis* to a Christian life in the

---

8. See William F. May, *Beleaguered Rulers: The Public Obligation of the Professional* (Louisville: Westminster John Knox Press, 2001).

early church, to the *vocatio* to a religious life in the Middle Ages, to Luther's *Beruf* and beyond — Christians in all times and places have struggled to figure out, "Is there something God wants me to do with my life? What is it? How can I be sure?" Yet a few other differences between past and present are also worth noting.

The most dramatic contrast to emerge when reading texts from past times about human roles probably concerns gender. In nearly all of Christian history, vocational choices for men and women were radically different. It would be absurd to try to disguise the discrimination against women taken for granted in many of the texts gathered here. A generation of feminist scholarship has made far more women's voices from the past accessible to us, but the record still too often presents a story *of* men, told *by* men. Sometimes we can just generalize what an earlier generation said about men to all of us. Sometimes interesting questions arise about whether such a generalization works. Sometimes we cannot read a passage without reflecting on the pain suffered by generations of women.

Other differences in past texts challenge present assumptions. The very claim that there is something God wants me to do with my life, for instance, threatens many contemporary definitions of freedom. Surely I can do whatever I want with my life, and the choice is mine. Much of the Christian tradition, however, has argued that that vision of life as a sea of infinite choices is more like slavery than freedom. If "freedom" means that every choice is open, and none is the wrong answer, then my choices cease to have any larger meaning. The direction of my life can be shaped by the pervasive siren calls of consumer culture, or by my own quest for immediate satisfaction. Either way, the advent of next year's fashions or the boredom I find in the pleasures of the moment leaves me hungry for something else, a cycle of hunger always unfulfilled.

Maybe, however, "freedom" means something different. What excitement to find that there is some right answer for what to do with my life, some place in the puzzle where my piece fits snugly and exactly! The Book of Common Prayer speaks of that God "whose service is perfect freedom."[9] When we find the match between our joy and the world's need, the place God wants us to be, it does feel more like liberation than imprisonment.

I sense just now, perhaps particularly in the generation of my students, a hunger for such liberation. I have long suspected that most young Christians are more willing to be challenged than their churches are to challenge them.

9. "Collect for Peace," in *Book of Common Prayer, Protestant Episcopal Church in the United States of America* (New York: Oxford University Press, 1952), 17.

We are so concerned to make Christianity seem easy that we fail to notice that maybe young people are not looking for an easy Christianity. Assembling the readings at the beginning of this book, I was worried about including martyrdom stories, or stories of the lives of Christians who gave away everything they had. Might it all seem too extreme? I was reassured not only by the hunger I sensed in my students for a challenge but also by the words of Martin Luther King, Jr., when he was accused of being an extremist: "Was not Jesus an extremist in love? . . . Was not Amos an extremist for justice? . . . Was not Paul an extremist for the gospel of Jesus Christ?"[10] Christian faith is not (not always? not usually?) a call to caution and moderation.

Our hearts are restless, Augustine said so long ago, until they find their rest in God. We accumulate worldly recognition and material goods, but they leave us unsatisfied. The stories of our lives come to seem pointless if they are not part of some larger story. And so it is that we search for what God is calling us to do.

10. Martin Luther King, Jr., "Letter from Birmingham City Jail," in *A Testament of Hope: The Essential Writings of Martin Luther King, Jr.,* ed. James Melvin Washington (San Francisco: Harper and Row, 1986), 297.

Prologue: Some Biblical Texts on Calling

Genesis 12:1-5a

Now the LORD said to Abram, "Go from your country and your kindred and
your father's house to the land that I will show you. I will make of you a
great nation, and I will bless you, and make your name great, so that you will
be a blessing. I will bless those who bless you, and the one who curses you I
will curse; and in you all the families of the earth shall be blessed." So
Abram went, as the LORD had told him; and Lot went with him. Abram was
seventy-five years old when he departed from Haran. Abram took his wife
Sarai and his brother's son Lot, and all the possessions that they had gathered, and the persons whom they had acquired in Haran; and they set forth
to go to the land of Canaan.

Exodus 3:1-15, 4:10-17

Moses was keeping the flock of his father-in-law Jethro, the priest of Midian;
he led his flock beyond the wilderness, and came to Horeb, the mountain of
God. There the angel of the LORD appeared to him in a flame of fire out of a
bush; he looked, and the bush was blazing, yet it was not consumed. Then
Moses said, "I must turn aside and look at this great sight, and see why the
bush is not burned up." When the LORD saw that he had turned aside to see,

God called to him out of the bush, "Moses, Moses!" And he said, "Here I am." Then he said, "Come no closer! Remove the sandals from your feet, for the place on which you are standing is holy ground." He said further, "I am the God of your father, the God of Abraham, the God of Isaac, and the God of Jacob." And Moses hid his face, for he was afraid to look at God. Then the LORD said, "I have observed the misery of my people who are in Egypt; I have heard their cry on account of their taskmasters. Indeed, I know their sufferings, and I have come down to deliver them from the Egyptians, and to bring them up out of that land to a good and broad land, a land flowing with milk and honey, to the country of the Canaanites, the Hittites, the Amorites, the Perizzites, the Hivites, and the Jebusites. The cry of the Israelites has now come to me; I have also seen how the Egyptians oppress them. So come, I will send you to Pharaoh to bring my people, the Israelites, out of Egypt." But Moses said to God, "Who am I that I should go to Pharaoh, and bring the Israelites out of Egypt?" He said, "I will be with you; and this shall be the sign for you that it is I who sent you: when you have brought the people out of Egypt, you shall worship God on this mountain." But Moses said to God, "If I come to the Israelites and say to them, 'The God of your ancestors has sent me to you,' and they ask me, 'What is his name?' what shall I say to them?" God said to Moses, "I AM WHO I AM." He said further, "Thus you shall say to the Israelites, 'I AM has sent me to you.'" God also said to Moses, "Thus you shall say to the Israelites, 'The LORD, the God of your ancestors, the God of Abraham, the God of Isaac, and the God of Jacob, has sent me to you': This is my name forever, and this my title for all generations." . . .

But Moses said to the LORD, "O my Lord, I have never been eloquent, neither in the past nor even now that you have spoken to your servant; but I am slow of speech and slow of tongue." Then the LORD said to him, "Who gives speech to mortals? Who makes them mute or deaf, seeing or blind? Is it not I, the Lord? Now go, and I will be with your mouth and teach you what you are to speak." But he said, "O my Lord, please send someone else." Then the anger of the LORD was kindled against Moses and he said, "What of your brother Aaron the Levite? I know that he can speak fluently; even now he is coming out to meet you, and when he sees you his heart will be glad. You shall speak to him and put the words in his mouth; and I will be with your mouth and with his mouth, and will teach you what you shall do. He indeed shall speak for you to the people; he shall serve as a mouth for you, and you shall serve as God for him. Take in your hand this staff, with which you shall perform the signs."

Judges 4:4-10

At that time Deborah, a prophetess, wife of Lappidoth, was judging Israel. She used to sit under the palm of Deborah between Ramah and Bethel in the hill country of Ephraim; and the Israelites came up to her for judgment. She sent and summoned Barak son of Abinoam from Kedesh in Naphtali, and said to him, "The LORD, the God of Israel, commands you, 'Go, take position at Mount Tabor, bringing ten thousand from the tribe of Naphtali and the tribe of Zebulun. I will draw out Sisera, the general of Jabin's army, to meet you by the Wadi Kishon with his chariots and his troops; and I will give him into your hand.'" Barak said to her, "If you will go with me, I will go; but if you will not go with me, I will not go." And she said, "I will surely go with you; nevertheless, the road on which you are going will not lead to your glory, for the LORD will sell Sisera into the hand of a woman." Then Deborah got up and went with Barak to Kedesh. Barak summoned Zebulun and Naphtali to Kedesh; and ten thousand warriors went up behind him; and Deborah went up with him.

1 Samuel 16:1-13

The LORD said to Samuel, "How long will you grieve over Saul? I have rejected him from being king over Israel. Fill your horn with oil and set out; I will send you to Jesse the Bethlehemite, for I have provided for myself a king among his sons." Samuel said, "How can I go? If Saul hears of it, he will kill me." And the LORD said, "Take a heifer with you, and say, 'I have come to sacrifice to the LORD.' Invite Jesse to the sacrifice, and I will show you what you shall do; and you shall anoint for me the one whom I name to you." Samuel did what the LORD commanded, and came to Bethlehem. The elders of the city came to meet him trembling, and said, "Do you come peaceably?" He said, "Peaceably; I have come to sacrifice to the LORD; sanctify yourselves and come with me to the sacrifice." And he sanctified Jesse and his sons and invited them to the sacrifice. When they came, he looked on Eliab and thought, "Surely the LORD's anointed is now before the LORD." But the LORD said to Samuel, "Do not look on his appearance or on the height of his stature, because I have rejected him; for the LORD does not see as mortals see; they look on the outward appearance, but the LORD looks on the heart." Then Jesse called Abinadab, and made him pass before Samuel. He said, "Neither has the LORD chosen this one." Then Jesse made Shammah pass by. And he said, "Neither has the LORD chosen this one." Jesse made seven of his sons pass before Samuel, and Samuel said to Jesse, "The LORD has not chosen any of these." Samuel said to Jesse, "Are all your sons here?" And he said, "There remains yet the youngest, but he is keeping the sheep." And Samuel said to Jesse, "Send and bring him; for we will not sit down until he comes here." He sent and brought him in. Now he was ruddy, and had beautiful eyes, and was handsome. The LORD said, "Rise and anoint him; for this is the one." Then Samuel took the horn of oil, and anointed him in the presence of his brothers; and the spirit of the LORD came mightily upon David from that day forward. Samuel then set out and went to Ramah.

Isaiah 6:1-8

In the year that King Uzziah died, I saw the Lord sitting on a throne, high and lofty; and the hem of his robe filled the temple. Seraphs were in attendance above him; each had six wings: with two they covered their faces, and with two they covered their feet, and with two they flew. And one called to another and said: "Holy, holy, holy is the LORD of hosts; the whole earth is full of his glory." The pivots on the thresholds shook at the voices of those who called, and the house filled with smoke. And I said: "Woe is me! I am lost, for I am a man of unclean lips, and I live among a people of unclean lips; yet my eyes have seen the King, the LORD of hosts!" Then one of the seraphs flew to me, holding a live coal that had been taken from the altar with a pair of tongs. The seraph touched my mouth with it and said: "Now that this has touched your lips, your guilt has departed and your sin is blotted out." Then I heard the voice of the LORD saying, "Whom shall I send, and who will go for us?" And I said, "Here am I; send me!"

Jeremiah 1:4-10, 20:7-9

Now the word of the LORD came to me saying, "Before I formed you in the womb I knew you, and before you were born I consecrated you; I appointed you a prophet to the nations." Then I said, "Ah, Lord GOD! Truly I do not know how to speak, for I am only a boy." But the LORD said to me, "Do not say, 'I am only a boy'; for you shall go to all to whom I send you, and you shall speak whatever I command you. Do not be afraid of them, for I am with you to deliver you, says the LORD." Then the Lord put out his hand and touched my mouth; and the LORD said to me, "Now I have put my words in your mouth. See, today I appoint you over nations and over kingdoms, to pluck up and to pull down, to destroy and to overthrow, to build and to plant." . . .

O LORD, you have enticed me, and I was enticed; you have overpowered me, and you have prevailed. I have become a laughingstock all day long; everyone mocks me. For whenever I speak, I must cry out, I must shout, "Violence and destruction!" For the word of the LORD has become for me a reproach and derision all day long. If I say, "I will not mention him, or speak any more in his name," then within me there is something like a burning fire shut up in my bones; I am weary with holding it in, and I cannot.

Luke 1:26-56

In the sixth month the angel Gabriel was sent by God to a town in Galilee called Nazareth, to a virgin engaged to a man whose name was Joseph, of the house of David. The virgin's name was Mary. And he came to her and said, "Greetings, favored one! The Lord is with you." But she was much perplexed by his words and pondered what sort of greeting this might be. The angel said to her, "Do not be afraid, Mary, for you have found favor with God. And now, you will conceive in your womb and bear a son, and you will name him Jesus. He will be great, and will be called the Son of the Most High, and the Lord God will give to him the throne of his ancestor David. He will reign over the house of Jacob forever, and of his kingdom there will be no end." Mary said to the angel, "How can this be, since I am a virgin?" The angel said to her, "The Holy Spirit will come upon you, and the power of the Most High will overshadow you; therefore the child to be born will be holy; he will be called Son of God. And now, your relative Elizabeth in her old age has also conceived a son; and this is the sixth month for her who was said to be barren. For nothing will be impossible with God." Then Mary said, "Here am I, the servant of the Lord; let it be with me according to your word." Then the angel departed from her.

In those days Mary set out and went with haste to a Judean town in the hill country, where she entered the house of Zechariah and greeted Elizabeth. When Elizabeth heard Mary's greeting, the child leaped in her womb. And Elizabeth was filled with the Holy Spirit and exclaimed with a loud cry, "Blessed are you among women, and blessed is the fruit of your womb. And why has this happened to me, that the mother of my Lord comes to me? For as soon as I heard the sound of your greeting, the child in my womb leaped for joy. And blessed is she who believed that there would be a fulfillment of what was spoken to her by the Lord." And Mary said, "My soul magnifies the

Lord, and my spirit rejoices in God my Savior, for he has looked with favor on the lowliness of his servant. Surely, from now on all generations will call me blessed; for the Mighty One has done great things for me, and holy is his name. His mercy is for those who fear him from generation to generation. He has shown strength with his arm; he has scattered the proud in the thoughts of their hearts. He has brought down the powerful from their thrones, and lifted up the lowly; he has filled the hungry with good things, and sent the rich away empty. He has helped his servant Israel, in remembrance of his mercy, according to the promise he made to our ancestors, to Abraham and to his descendants forever." And Mary remained with her about three months and then returned to her home.

Matthew 4:18-22

As he walked by the Sea of Galilee, he saw two brothers, Simon, who is called Peter, and Andrew his brother, casting a net into the sea — for they were fishermen. And he said to them, "Follow me, and I will make you fish for people." Immediately they left their nets and followed him. As he went from there, he saw two other brothers, James son of Zebedee and his brother John, in the boat with their father Zebedee, mending their nets, and he called them. Immediately they left the boat and their father, and followed him.

John 3:1-16

Now there was a Pharisee named Nicodemus, a leader of the Jews. He came to Jesus by night and said to him, "Rabbi, we know that you are a teacher who has come from God; for no one can do these signs that you do apart from the presence of God." Jesus answered him, "Very truly, I tell you, no one can see the kingdom of God without being born from above." Nicodemus said to him, "How can anyone be born after having grown old? Can one enter a second time into the mother's womb and be born?" Jesus answered, "Very truly, I tell you, no one can enter the kingdom of God without being born of water and Spirit. What is born of the flesh is flesh, and what is born of the Spirit is spirit. Do not be astonished that I said to you, 'You must be born from above.' The wind blows where it chooses, and you hear the sound of it, but you do not know where it comes from or where it goes. So it is with everyone who is born of the Spirit."

Nicodemus said to him, "How can these things be?" Jesus answered him, "Are you a teacher of Israel, and yet you do not understand these things? Very truly, I tell you, we speak of what we know and testify to what we have seen; yet you do not receive our testimony. If I have told you about earthly things and you do not believe, how can you believe if I tell you about heavenly things? No one has ascended into heaven except the one who descended from heaven, the Son of Man. And just as Moses lifted up the serpent in the wilderness, so must the Son of Man be lifted up, that whoever believes in him may have eternal life. For God so loved the world that he gave his only Son, so that everyone who believes in him may not perish but may have eternal life."

Acts 8:26-38

Then an angel of the Lord said to Philip, "Get up and go toward the south to the road that goes down from Jerusalem to Gaza." (This is a wilderness road.) So he got up and went. Now there was an Ethiopian eunuch, a court official of the Candace, queen of the Ethiopians, in charge of her entire treasury. He had come to Jerusalem to worship and was returning home; seated in his chariot, he was reading the prophet Isaiah. Then the Spirit said to Philip, "Go over to this chariot and join it." So Philip ran up to it and heard him reading the prophet Isaiah. He asked, "Do you understand what you are reading?" He replied, "How can I, unless someone guides me?" And he invited Philip to get in and sit beside him. Now the passage of the scripture that he was reading was this: "Like a sheep he was led to the slaughter, and like a lamb silent before its shearer, so he does not open his mouth. In his humiliation justice was denied him. Who can describe his generation? For his life is taken away from the earth." The eunuch asked Philip, "About whom, may I ask you, does the prophet say this, about himself or about someone else?" Then Philip began to speak, and starting with this scripture, he proclaimed to him the good news about Jesus. As they were going along the road, they came to some water; and the eunuch said, "Look, here is water! What is to prevent me from being baptized?" And Philip said, "If you believe with all your heart, you may." And he replied, "I believe that Jesus Christ is the Son of God." He commanded the chariot to stop, and both of them, Philip and the eunuch, went down into the water, and Philip baptized him.

Acts 9:1-20

Meanwhile Saul, still breathing threats and murder against the disciples of the Lord, went to the high priest and asked him for letters to the synagogues at Damascus, so that if he found any who belonged to the Way, men or women, he might bring them bound to Jerusalem. Now as he was going along and approaching Damascus, suddenly a light from heaven flashed around him. He fell to the ground and heard a voice saying to him, "Saul, Saul, why do you persecute me?" He asked, "Who are you, Lord?" The reply came, "I am Jesus, whom you are persecuting. But get up and enter the city, and you will be told what you are to do." The men who were traveling with him stood speechless because they heard the voice but saw no one. Saul got up from the ground, and though his eyes were open, he could see nothing; so they led him by the hand and brought him into Damascus. For three days he was without sight, and neither ate nor drank. Now there was a disciple in Damascus named Ananias. The Lord said to him in a vision, "Ananias." He answered, "Here I am, Lord." The Lord said to him, "Get up and go to the street called Straight, and at the house of Judas look for a man of Tarsus named Saul. At this moment he is praying, and he has seen in a vision a man named Ananias come in and lay his hands on him so that he might regain his sight." But Ananias answered, "Lord, I have heard from many about this man, how much evil he has done to your saints in Jerusalem; and here he has authority from the chief priests to bind all who invoke your name." But the Lord said to him, "Go, for he is an instrument whom I have chosen to bring my name before Gentiles and kings and before the people of Israel; I myself will show him how much he must suffer for the sake of my name." So Ananias went and entered the house. He laid his hands on Saul and said, "Brother Saul, the Lord Jesus, who appeared to you on your way here, has sent me so that you may regain your sight and be filled with the Holy Spirit." And immediately something like scales fell from his eyes, and his sight was restored. Then he got up and was baptized, and after taking some food, he regained his strength. For several days he was with the disciples in Damascus, and immediately he began to proclaim Jesus in the synagogues, saying, "He is the Son of God."

1

Callings to a Christian Life:
Vocations in the Early Church, 100-500

Introduction

It was not easy to be a Christian during the first several centuries of the church's existence. Christianity began as an obscure cult out on the eastern edge of the Roman Empire, and most of those living in the empire heard of it first in wild rumors: Christians engaged in orgies; they wanted the world to end; when they met together, they ate flesh and drank blood. Most Roman social occasions — almost any time ordinary Romans got together to eat meat or drink wine, for instance — involved participating in a sacrifice to one god or another, so Christians usually felt they could not take part, and naturally got a reputation as unfriendly to their neighbors.[1] Since they would not sacrifice to the divine emperor, they must be traitors. After all, this Jesus they worshipped had been executed by a Roman governor.

Becoming a Christian thus often meant isolation from family and friends. Christians didn't fit in; if they fell victim to persecution they could break their parents' hearts and put their children at risk. Persecution was only occasional, but it carried the risk of torture and death. Yet more and more people kept joining the church. It was as if the blood of the martyrs watered its growth.

Eventually, Christianity became the official religion of the empire, and at that point some Christians promptly started to feel that simply living as a Christian had become too easy, too safe, too socially respectable. They went off to literal or metaphorical deserts to pursue monastic lives of radical self-denial, convinced that only in this way were they truly following Christ.

As noted in the general introduction, in the early church "call" (klēsis in Greek) usually meant the call to become a Christian. Writing to the Christians at Rome, Paul addressed them as those "who are *called* to belong to Jesus Christ" (Rom. 1:6); "God's beloved in Rome, who are *called* to be saints" (Rom. 1:7). Most people in the ancient world had little choice of job or profession anyway; they did what their parents had done before them. What Christians had to decide was not what job to take, but whether "to be con-

---

1. Ramsay MacMullen, *Paganism in the Roman Empire* (New Haven: Yale University Press, 1981), 40.

formed to this world" (Rom. 12:2), or to commit themselves to this new community of "aliens and exiles" (1 Pet. 2:11) that followed Christ.

This chapter includes:

- Two stories of Christian martyrs (Ignatius, Perpetua)
- Two accounts of conversion to Christianity (Justin, Augustine)
- A defense of Christianity in the face of accusations made against it (Tertullian)
- Two discussions of what it meant for prosperous and important people to live as Christians (Clement of Alexandria, Gregory of Nyssa)
- Three texts about the beginnings of monasticism (Athanasius, Palladius, Sayings of the Desert Fathers)

Together, these excerpts give a varied picture of what it meant for early Christians to respond to the call to follow Christ.

Reading these texts, many readers today will be struck by their sheer strangeness. To be sure, there are many parts of the world where it is still dangerous to be a Christian — more people died for their Christian faith in the twentieth century than in any other century, and the risks are not going away in the twenty-first century. Those of us who live today in predominantly or traditionally Christian countries, however, have little fear of martyrdom. Most of us who are Christians were born into Christian families — we have never undergone a conversion from some other set of beliefs. The radical asceticism of the early monks and nuns may well seem just bizarre to us. Do the lives of early Christians connect at all with *our* questions about how God might call *us*?

I think they do. In some respects, the situation of Christians today is more like that of the early church than that of most Christians in between. From roughly the year 500 to just a few generations ago, the vast majority of Christians lived surrounded by other Christians, in societies where Christianity was generally taken for granted. Our situation is more like those first few centuries: many of our neighbors follow another faith or none at all. Many of the values and beliefs common in our culture challenge our faith. Our beliefs may seem quite peculiar to many of our neighbors. Those who enter ministry often do so over the objections of their families, who were hoping that their bright daughter or son would choose a more lucrative and prestigious career.

Why do I believe? How do I answer challenges to my faith? What am I willing to risk, at least in "not fitting in," for my faith? Is my faith just a matter of going along with my family, or is it something I'm willing to let change my life in some radical way? — Such questions, asked long ago, confront Christians once again.

Aliens and Exiles in the Midst of Empire

In its first several centuries Christianity expanded primarily within the boundaries of the Roman Empire, and in most ways the empire was good luck for the church. Roman roads ran everywhere from Spain to Egypt; Roman patrols kept the sea relatively free of pirates; a common Roman currency encouraged trade. It was the best of times for travel all around the Mediterranean basin, and Christianity benefited immensely from the *pax Romana*, the "Roman peace."

The Roman government was usually tolerant of the empire's many religions. As emperors were declared to be gods (first after their deaths and then during their lifetimes), subjects were expected to sacrifice to the deified emperor. Failure to do so was like refusing to pledge allegiance to the flag today — only much worse, grounds for charges of treason and execution. For most of the empire's subjects, this constituted no problem. They performed sacrifices to all sorts of gods; one more made little difference. Jews would have no part in such rituals, but Roman piety always respected faithfulness to the traditions of one's ancestors, so Jewish customs were generally honored. Christians, however, were converting people of every nation to a *new* religion, and that looked suspicious.

The first recorded Roman persecution of Christians occurred under Nero, in 64. On one account, the emperor was suspected of starting a fire during one of his wild parties that eventually burned down much of the city of Rome. To shift the blame away from himself, he accused the Christians, and a number of them (according to tradition including both Peter and Paul) were tortured and killed. Like most Roman persecutions of Christians, this one was brief and local, confined in this case to the city of Rome. For a couple of centuries thereafter, if a local Christian church made enough enemies, the Christians could be accused of refusing to make the proper sacrifices, and at least a few might well be killed. The Emperor Decius in the early third century and Emperors Diocletian and Maximinus Daia at the beginning of the fourth century engaged in systematic but brief persecution of Christians across the empire, but even then only a small percentage of Christians were actually arrested and killed.

From the safe distance of many centuries, we could say that Christianity received just the right amount of persecution to foster its growth. Brave

Christians had the chance to win wide admiration by showing their willing-ness to die for their faith, but persecution never grew extensive enough re-ally to threaten the church's expansion. For Christians at the time, however, persecution must have seemed a terror. It might start up again at any point, stirred up by anyone from local neighbors to a new emperor, and the forms of torture Christians faced were horrible indeed. They could easily enough become "martyrs" — until the second century, the Greek word had just meant a "witness," as in a legal trial, but then Christians began to use it of those who had died for their faith. The martyrs' willingness to suffer and die for their faith, the Christians said, was a "witness" to that faith's power. A call to follow Christ only rarely ended in martyrdom, but the possibility was something any Christian had at least to consider.

Why Then Become a Christian?

Yet the church kept growing. More and more people felt called to be Chris-tians. Perhaps a traveling merchant came around with amazing stories about this man named Jesus. Perhaps a friend issued an invitation to visit the small group of Christians that met in someone's house. Perhaps seeing martyrs die for their beliefs raised questions about how these people could be so sure of their faith.

Whatever the initial impulse, anyone from slaves to officials at the im-perial court came to believe. They believed that there is only one God, who created everything that is, and who, in spite of the fact that all of us are sin-ners, loves us so much that he sent his only Son to save us. Surely we want to avoid eternal punishment; surely we want to show our gratitude to the God who offers us salvation. Both fear and love should thus lead us to "turn around" (our word "convert") and "lead a life worthy of God, who calls you into his own kingdom and glory" (1 Thess. 2:12).

The Christian message had its own persuasive force, but it also suc-ceeded in part because of flaws in the alternatives available to most subjects of the empire in a time of cultural decline. By and large, the worshippers of Greek and Roman gods did not expect love from them. Deities were power-ful; it was important to win their favor or appease their anger. No one even hoped for compassion. Moreover, the behavior of these divine beings, as re-ported in the stories told about them, often seemed scandalous. In the sec-ond century, the Christian writer Clement of Alexandria quoted at length from the Greek poets about Zeus's many rapes of women and boys alike and concluded, "Show him only a woman's girdle, and Zeus is exposed, and

... dishonored. To what a pitch of licentiousness did that Zeus of yours proceed, who spent so many nights in sexual affairs?" This greatest of the gods was not an avenger of wrongs, but rather "the unjust, the violator of right and of law, the impious, the inhuman, the violent, the seducer, the adulterer, the amatory."[2]

Many intellectually sophisticated Greeks and Romans stopped believing in these myths and turned instead to the more abstract consolations of the philosophical schools of the time. Stoicism and Platonism, the most prominent, called for real changes in people's lives, indifference to worldly pleasures, and purification of the soul. Problem was, they often did not work very well. Many of those who followed philosophy led admirable lives, but even at their best, philosophies mostly aimed at the cultural elite, who could follow their arguments and had the luxury of reflecting on the value of turning aside from excessive pleasure. Celsus, the great second-century critic of Christianity, ridiculed the Christians for believing that they could change the moral lives of "the most stupid and uneducated yokels." Exactly right, his Christian opponent Origen replied: such is the power of the gospel that it can transform anyone.[3] Even for the educated, Augustine concluded from his own experience, the best of the philosophers were like people who "from a mountaintop in the forests" see "the land of peace in the distance" but cannot figure out how to get there.[4] They lacked the power to change lives.

Christianity was different, so Christians claimed. Writing around 200, the Christian Aelius Aristides declared that Christians

> do not commit adultery, they do not engage in illicit sex, they do not give false testimony, they do not covet other people's goods, they honor father and mother and love their neighbors, they give just decisions. Whatever they do not want to happen to them, they do not do to another. They appeal to those who treat them unjustly and try to make them their friends. . . . They do not overlook widows, and they save orphans; a Christian with possessions shares generously.[5]

2. Clement of Alexandria, *Exhortation to the Heathen* 2, in *The Ante-Nicene Fathers*, ed. and trans. Alexander Roberts and James Donaldson (Peabody, Mass.: Hendrickson Publishers, 1994), 2:180-81, translation revised.

3. Origen, *Contra Celsum* 6.1, trans. Henry Chadwick (Cambridge: Cambridge University Press, 1953), 316.

4. Augustine, *Confessions* 7.21, trans. Rex Warner (New York: New American Library, 1963), 158.

5. Aelius Aristides, *Apology* 15.3-7, in Wayne A. Meeks, *The Origins of Christian Morality* (New Haven: Yale University Press, 1993), 8-9. Similarly, Justin Martyr: "We who formerly de-

We might expect a Christian to paint too positive a picture, but even their opponents conceded the changes Christians' faith meant to their lives. Their courage in the face of martyrdom was widely acknowledged. Galen, a Roman physician generally rather contemptuous of Christians, admitted that in their sexual morals, in their "self-discipline and self-control in matters of food and drink, and in their keen pursuit of justice," these often lower-class and ill-educated Christians "have attained a pitch not inferior to that of genuine philosophers."[6] The satirist Lucian, holding Christians up to ridicule, noted that these foolish folk think "that they are all brothers of one another.... So if any charlatan and trickster ... comes among them, he quickly acquires sudden wealth by imposing on simple folk."[7] The ridicule itself acknowledges their well-known generosity. Even the forcefully anti-Christian emperor Julian, who tried to restore paganism in the fourth century, had to admit that "the impious Galileans (Christians) support not only their own poor but ours as well."[8]

Corruption and Violence

Christians achieved such moral transformations in an empire that was sick at its heart. Tiberius, who was emperor during most of Jesus' lifetime, starved several of his own relatives to death and departed from Rome to live on the island of Capri in part because his sexual vices had begun to scandalize even the remarkably tolerant Romans. He left the rule of the empire to his notoriously brutal chief of secret police, Sejanus.[9] All the while, the historian Tacitus reports, the most prominent Roman citizens fell over each other, competing in praising their great emperor, so that Tiberius himself used to leave the Senate House muttering, "How ready these men are to be

---

lighted in fornication ... now embrace chastity alone; ... we who valued above all things the acquisition of wealth and possessions, now bring what we have into a common stock, and communicate to every one in need; we who hated and destroyed one another, and on account of their different manners would not live with men of a different tribe, now, since the coming of Christ, live familiarly with them, and pray for our enemies." Justin Martyr, *First Apology* 14, in *The Ante-Nicene Fathers*, 1:167.

6. Richard Walzer, *Galen on Jews and Christians* (London: Oxford University Press, 1949), 15.

7. Lucian, *The Passing of Peregrinus* 13, in *Lucian*, trans. A. M. Harman (Cambridge, Mass.: Harvard University Press, 1936), 5:15.

8. Julian, *Letter* 22, in *The Works of the Emperor Julian*, trans. Wilmer Cave Wright (New York: G. P. Putnam's Sons, 1923), 3:71.

9. Tacitus, *Annals* 4.57, in *Complete Works of Tacitus*, trans. Alfred John Church and William Jordan Brodribb (New York: Modern Library, 1942), 178.

slaves."[10] Tiberius's successor, Caligula, would invite the most prominent senators and their wives to dinner and then take the wives off to have sex with them. He forced sex on important male Romans as well, and seems to have had intercourse with all his own sisters.[11] Sometimes, on a whim, he would condemn people to be branded with hot irons, thrown to wild animals, or sawed in half.

In every way Caligula went too far, but sexual morals allowed all wealthy men considerable freedom. Women who committed adultery faced harsh penalties, but their straying husbands encountered no legal penalty and little moral disapproval. A master owned the bodies of his male and female servants and could do with them as he liked, and some defined the limits of "marital fidelity" by the walls of the house rather than the marriage bed itself.[12]

Brutality too reached far beyond the imperial circle. To take one example, nothing pleased the Roman masses more than "public games," and that meant slaughter of animals, gladiatorial battles to the death, and watching animals attack human beings. Around the year 80 the Emperor Titus sponsored a hundred consecutive days of games, with more than five thousand animals killed in one day.[13] The spectacle won him the love of the Roman people. On other occasions, people were clothed in elaborate costumes soaked with something flammable, and the crowd cheered as they "danced" in their death agony after the clothing was lit.[14]

These were not the entertainments of some sick minority but the dominant public spectacle for every class in the cities of the empire. Augustine talks about his friend Alypius, who detested the violence of the arenas and insisted to his friends, "'You can drag my body there, but don't imagine that you can make me turn my eyes or give my mind to the show.'" So they dragged him off to the amphitheater, and indeed he kept his eyes closed.

> If only he could have blocked up his ears too! For in the course of the
> fight some man fell; there was a great roar from the whole mass of
> spectators which fell upon his ears; he was overcome by curiosity

10. Tacitus, *Annals* 3.65, 137.

11. Anthony A. Barrett, *Caligula: The Corruption of Power* (New Haven: Yale University Press, 1990), 43-44.

12. Peter Brown, *The Body and Society* (New York: Columbia University Press, 1988), 23.

13. Suetonius, *Titus* 7.7, in *The Twelve Caesars*, trans. Robert Graves (Baltimore: Penguin, 1957), 290.

14. Plutarch, "On the Delays of the Divine Vengeance 9," in *Plutarch's Moralia*, trans. Philip H. De Lacy and Benedict Einarson (Cambridge, Mass.: Harvard University Press, 1959), 7:217.

and opened his eyes.... But then ... his own fall was more wretched than that of the gladiator.... He saw the blood and he gulped down savagery. Far from turning away, he fixed his eyes on it. Without knowing what was happening, he drank in madness, he was delighted with the guilty contest, drunk with the lust of blood. He was no longer the man who had come there but was one of the crowd to which he had come, a true companion of those who had brought him.[15]

Even the imperial peace rested on often brutal military victories. The Romans, Augustine said, wanted glory, and to that end, at their best, they were willing to fight and die, to sacrifice their own rewards and pleasures for the success of the empire. And they succeeded! They conquered most of the world they knew. "They were honored in almost all nations; they imposed their laws on many people; and today they enjoy renown in the history and literature of nearly all races. They have no reason to complain of the justice of God."[16] Yet even their greatest successes rested on violence.

Is it reasonable, is it sensible, to boast of the extent and grandeur of empire, when you cannot show that men lived in happiness, as they passed their lives amid the horrors of war, amid the shedding of men's blood — whether the blood of enemies or fellow-citizens — under the shadow of fear and amid the terror of ruthless ambition? The only joy to be attained had the fragile brilliance of glass, a joy outweighed by the fear that it may be shattered in a moment.[17]

An empire based on violence is indeed a fragile thing, and the Roman world, as the third-century Christian bishop Cyprian observed, "is wet with mutual blood; and murder, which in the case of an individual is admitted to be a crime, is called a virtue when it is committed wholesale. Impunity is claimed for the wicked deeds, not on the plea that they are guiltless, but because the cruelty is perpetuated on a grand scale."[18]

Decadence at the top, obscene violence in popular culture, a glory that rested on military victories — in such a culture, Christianity indeed required a radical "turning around." Some Christians feel the same today.

15. Augustine, *Confessions* 6.8, 123-24.

16. Augustine, *The City of God* 5.15, trans. Henry Bettenson (Harmondsworth, Middlesex: Penguin, 1972), 205.

17. Augustine, *City of God* 4.3, 138.

18. Cyprian, *Letter* 1.6, trans. Ernest Wallis, *The Ante-Nicene Fathers*, 5:277.

Most religions in the Roman Empire were not so challenging. Roman religion was primarily a matter of performing the proper sacrifices in hopes of getting appropriate rewards or at least avoiding divine retribution. Taking no chances, a sophisticated Roman might seek initiation in any number of different religious cults, with none of them involving any expectation of ethical transformation. "Chance" or "Luck" was the most popular deity of the time.[19] The very *demandingness* of Christianity constituted part of its appeal.

Athletes of the Desert

Christians found ways to preserve those demands even after the age of persecution. The change, when it came, was dramatic. In the early fourth century, within just a few years of the last great persecution, a new emperor, Constantine, declared himself a Christian, and Christianity was first guaranteed toleration and then gradually became the empire's official religion. People who in their youth had faced death for being Christians came to middle age in a time when it could be socially advantageous to join the church.

Some Christians did not feel altogether happy about all the results of the change. Had it become too easy to be a Christian? Did that put Christian faith in danger? What would it mean to be "strangers and foreigners on the earth" (Heb. 11:13) if the empire itself claimed to be Christian? Few historical events have only one cause, and many factors contributed to the beginnings of Christian monasticism. But it does not seem a coincidence that, just about the time when it grew easier to be an "ordinary" Christian, Christians in large numbers began to go off to the desert to pursue a more rigorous Christian life. They found a more demanding vocation.

In later centuries the "desert" could be metaphorical — the forests of France or an island off Ireland — but in the beginning the term was perfectly literal. Individuals and communities, both men and women, established themselves in the desert regions of Egypt and Syria, withdrawn from ordinary life to a special calling. Sometimes their self-denial took extreme forms. They would get by on one meal a day, or go without food for days at a time. Some slept only two hours a night; few washed at all. One tells of being so horrified that he had swatted a mosquito in anger that he stood many days naked in a swamp, allowing himself to be bitten. Some lived for years atop a high pillar. They were trying to turn away from *everything* else to focus on God.

19. See Pliny the Elder, *Natural History* 2.5, trans. H. Rackam (Cambridge, Mass.: Harvard University Press, 1944), 1:185.

Soon they became the heroes and heroines of ordinary Christians. They were "spiritual athletes," undergoing a training at least as rigorous as that of any modern athlete, but aiming for a religious ideal rather than an Olympic medal. A Christian father whose son was misbehaving would take him on a tour of the local monks, reminding him of what Christianity at its highest could demand and produce. Facing a difficult ethical dilemma in their own lives, Christians would consult some monk famous for ascetic practices — self-denial gave moral authority. Not every Christian went to the desert, but those who did were generally acknowledged as the highest examples of Christian life. They had preserved the spirit of the age of martyrs that was so central to early Christianity.

IGNATIUS OF ANTIOCH

Letter to the Romans

Ignatius (about 35–about 107) was bishop in the city of Antioch in Syria. He knew people who knew Jesus' first apostles. Arrested in a local persecution, he was taken to Rome for trial and eventual execution, guarded by a detachment of ten soldiers he called "ten leopards" — wild beasts to whom he was chained. While on his journey, he wrote a number of letters to Christian communities, including this one on ahead to the Christians in Rome. Apparently by this time the Roman church included members with enough influence that they might have been able to arrange Ignatius's escape; he urges them not to do so. In his appeal, he expresses a powerful sense of union with Christ in suffering and death — this is how Ignatius senses he has been called to follow Jesus. In another of his letters, he strongly rejects the view, held by some early Christians, that Jesus only *appeared* to suffer and die: "If . . . his suffering was a sham . . . why then am I a prisoner? Why do I want to fight with wild beasts? In that case I shall die to no purpose."

Greetings in Jesus Christ, the Son of the Father, from Ignatius, the "God-inspired," to the church that is in charge of affairs in Roman quarters and that the Most High Father and Jesus Christ, his only Son, have magnificently embraced in mercy and love. . . .

Since God has answered my prayer to see you godly people, I have gone on to ask for more. I mean, it is as a prisoner for Christ Jesus that I hope to greet you, if indeed it be (God's) will that I should deserve to meet my end.

Ignatius of Antioch, *Letters,* in *Early Christian Fathers,* ed. and trans. Cyril C. Richardson (New York: Macmillan, 1970), 102-5.

Things are off to a good start. May I have the good fortune to meet my fate without interference! What I fear is your generosity, which may prove detrimental to me. For you can easily do what you want to, whereas it is hard for me to get to God unless you let me alone. I do not want you to please men, but to please God, just as you are doing. For I shall never again have such a chance to get to God, nor can you, if you keep quiet, get credit for a finer deed. For if you quietly let me alone, people will see in me God's Word. But if you are enamored of my mere body, I shall, on the contrary, be a meaningless noise. Grant me no more than to be a sacrifice for God while there is an altar at hand. Then you can form yourselves into a choir and sing praises to the Father in Jesus Christ that God gave the bishop of Syria the privilege of reaching the sun's setting when he summoned him from its rising. It is a grand thing for my life to set on the world, and for me to be on my way to God, so that I may rise in his presence.

You never grudged anyone. You taught others. So I want you to substantiate the lessons that you bid them heed. Just pray that I may have strength of soul and body so that I may not only talk (about martyrdom), but really want it. It is not that I want merely to be called a Christian, but actually to be one. Yes, if I prove to be one, then I can have the name. Then, too, I shall be a convincing Christian only when the world sees me no more. Nothing you can see has real value. Our God Jesus Christ, indeed, has revealed himself more clearly by returning to the Father. The greatness of Christianity lies in its being hated by the world, not in its being convincing to it.

I am corresponding with all the churches and bidding them all realize that I am voluntarily dying for God — if, that is, you do not interfere. I plead with you, do not do me an unseasonable kindness. Let me be fodder for wild beasts — that is how I can get to God. I am God's wheat, and I am being ground by the teeth of wild beasts to make a pure loaf for Christ. I would rather that you fawn on the beasts so that they may be my tomb and no scrap of my body be left. Thus, when I have fallen asleep, I shall be a burden to no one. Then I shall be a real disciple of Jesus Christ when the world sees my body no more. Pray Christ for me that by these means I may become God's sacrifice. I do not give you orders like Peter and Paul. They were apostles: I am a convict. They were at liberty: I am still a slave. But if I suffer, I shall be emancipated by Jesus Christ; and united to him, I shall rise to freedom.

Even now as a prisoner, I am learning to forgo my own wishes. All the way from Syria to Rome I am fighting with wild beasts, by land and sea, night and day, chained as I am to ten leopards (I mean to a detachment of soldiers), who only get worse the better you treat them. But by their injustices I am becoming a better disciple, though not for that reason am I acquitted (1 Cor. 4:4). What a thrill I shall have from the wild beasts that are ready for me! I hope they will make short work of me.

I shall coax them on to eat me up at once and not to hold off, as sometimes happens, through fear. And if they are reluctant, I shall force them to it. Forgive me — I know what is good for me. Now is the moment I am beginning to be a disciple. May nothing seen or unseen begrudge me making my way to Jesus Christ. Come fire, cross, battling with wild beasts, wrenching of bones, mangling of limbs, crushing of my whole body, cruel tortures of the devil — only let me get to Jesus Christ! Not the wide bounds of earth nor the kingdoms of this world will avail me anything. I would rather die and get to Jesus Christ, than reign over the ends of the earth. That is whom I am looking for — the One who died for us. That is whom I want — the One who rose for us. I am going through the pangs of being born. Sympathize with me, my brothers! Do not stand in the way of my coming to life — do not wish death on me. Do not give back to the world one who wants to be God's; do not trick him with material things. Let me get into the clear light and manhood will be mine. Let me imitate the Passion of my God. If anyone has Him in him, let him appreciate what I am longing for, and sympathize with me, realizing what I am going through.

JUSTIN MARTYR

Dialogue with Trypho

Justin (about 100–about 165) grew up in Samaria in Palestine but moved to Rome. He had studied many of the philosophies of the Greco-Roman world and found them all, in various ways, unsatisfactory. His account of his conversion to Christianity gives a sense of what might bring a sophisticated intellectual to Christian faith. It is included in his *Dialogue with*

Justin Martyr, *Dialogue with Trypho*, in *The Ante-Nicene Fathers*, ed. and trans. Alexander Roberts and James Donaldson (Peabody, Mass.: Hendrickson, 1994), 1:195-98. Translation slightly revised.

Trypho, a discussion with a Jew about the nature of Christianity that may be based on real conversations. The conversion story, however, seems at least in part allegorical: Is this mysterious old man, making a personal search for members of his household who have gone away, in fact a symbol for God? Justin later suffered martyrdom, being scourged and beheaded. The various philosophers he mentions at the beginning of this reading represent the prominent philosophical schools of his time; Justin contrasts their teaching with the deeper insights of the biblical prophets.

———————

Philosophy is in fact the greatest possession, and most honorable before God, to whom it leads us and alone commends us; and they are truly holy men who have bestowed attention on philosophy. . . . Being at first desirous of personally conversing with one of these men, I surrendered myself to a certain Stoic; and having spent a considerable time with him, when I had not acquired any further knowledge of God (for he did not know himself, and said such instruction was unnecessary), I left him and betook myself to another, who was called a Peripatetic [a follower of Aristotle] and, as *he* fancied, shrewd. And this man, after having entertained me for the first few days, requested me to settle the fee, in order that our intercourse might not be unprofitable. Him, too, for this reason I abandoned, believing him to be no philosopher at all. But when my soul was eager to hear the peculiar and choice philosophy, I came to a Pythagorean, very celebrated — a man who thought much of his own wisdom. And then, when I had an interview with him, willing to become his hearer and disciple, he said, "What then? Are you acquainted with music, astronomy, and geometry? Do you expect to perceive any of those things which conduce to a happy life, if you have not been first informed on those points which wean the soul from sensible objects, and render it fitted for objects which pertain to the mind, so that it can contemplate that which is honorable in its essence and that which is good in its essence?"

Having commended many of these branches of learning, and telling me that they were necessary, he dismissed me when I confessed to him my ignorance. Accordingly I took it rather impatiently, as was to be expected when I failed in my hope, the more so because I deemed the man had some knowledge; but reflecting again on the space of time during which I would have to linger over those branches of learning, I was not able to endure longer procrastination. In my helpless condition it occurred to me to have a meeting with the Platonists, for their fame was great. I thereupon spent as much of

my time as possible with one who had lately settled in our city — a saga-
cious man, holding a high position among the Platonists — and I progressed, and made the greatest improvements daily. And the perception of
immaterial things quite overpowered me, and the contemplation of ideas
furnished my mind with wings, so that in a little while I supposed that I had
become wise; and such was my stupidity, I expected forthwith to look upon
God, for this is the end of Plato's philosophy.

3. Justin Narrates the Manner of His Conversion

And while I was thus disposed, when I wished at one period to be filled with
great quietness, and to shun the path of men, I used to go into a certain field
not far from the sea. And when I was near that spot one day, which having
reached I sought to be by myself, a certain old man, by no means contemptible in appearance, exhibiting meek and venerable manners, followed me at
a little distance. And when I turned round to him, having halted, I fixed my
eyes rather keenly on him.

And he said, "Do you know me?"

I replied in the negative.

"Why, then," said he to me, "do you so look at me?"

"I am astonished," I said, "because you have chanced to be in my company in this place; for I had not expected to see any man here."

And he said to me, "I am concerned about some of my household.
These are gone away from me; and therefore have I come to make personal
search for them, if, perhaps, they shall make their appearance somewhere." . . .

6. These Things Were Unknown
to Plato and Other Philosophers

(The old man has reviewed the opinions of various philosophers.)

"It makes no matter to me," he said, "whether Plato or Pythagoras, or, in
short, any other man held such opinions. . . . There existed, long before this
time, certain men more ancient than all those who are esteemed philosophers, both righteous and beloved by God, who spoke by the Divine Spirit,
and foretold events which would take place, and which are now taking
place. They are called prophets. These alone both saw and announced the
truth to men, neither reverencing nor fearing any man, not influenced by a

desire for glory, but speaking those things alone which they saw and which they heard, being filled with the Holy Spirit. Their writings are still extant, and he who has read them is very much helped in his knowledge of the beginning and end of things, and of those matters which the philosopher ought to know, provided he has believed them. For they did not use demonstration in their treatises, seeing that they were witnesses to the truth above all demonstration, and worthy of belief; and those events which have happened, and those which are happening, compel you to assent to the utterances made by them, although, indeed, they were entitled to credit on account of the miracles which they performed, since they both glorified the Creator, the God and Father of all things, and proclaimed His Son, the Christ (sent) by Him: which, indeed, the false prophets, who are filled with the lying unclean spirit, neither have done nor do, but venture to work certain wonderful deeds for the purpose of astonishing men, and glorify the spirits and demons of error. But pray that, above all things, the gates of light may be opened to you; for these things cannot be perceived or understood by all, but only by the man to whom God and His Christ have imparted wisdom."

8. Justin by His Conversation Is Kindled with Love to Christ

When he had spoken these and many other things, which there is no time for mentioning at present, he went away, bidding me attend to them; and I have not seen him since. But straightway a flame was kindled in my soul; and a love of the prophets, and of those men who are friends of Christ, possessed me; and while revolving his words in my mind, I found this philosophy alone to be safe and profitable. Thus, and for this reason, I am a philosopher. Moreover, I would wish that all, making a resolution similar to my own, do not keep themselves away from the words of the Savior. For they possess a terrible power in themselves, and are sufficient to inspire those who turn aside from the path of rectitude with awe; while the sweetest rest is afforded those who make a diligent practice of them. If, then, you have any concern for yourself, and if you are eagerly looking for salvation, and if you believe in God, you may — since you are not indifferent to the matter — become acquainted with the Christ of God, and, after being initiated, live a happy life.

The Martyrdom of Perpetua

A North African Christian, Perpetua was martyred in 203 along with several "catechumens" (new converts still studying to become Christians).
The story of her imprisonment, torture, and death was written shortly after
the event (possibly by Tertullian, whose own work appears in a later selection in this chapter) and includes an account of the imprisonment apparently written by Perpetua herself. This account of martyrdom shows that
the Romans were really not eager to kill Christians — even late in the process they would be glad to release Perpetua and her companions if they
were only willing to perform a sacrifice to the emperor. We also see here
how hard families (in this case Perpetua's father) found it when Christians
were ready to die for their faith.

A number of young catechumens were arrested, Revocatus and his fellow
slave Felicitas, Saturninus and Secundulus, and with them Vibia Perpetua, a
newly married woman of good family and upbringing. Her mother and father were still alive and one of her two brothers was a catechumen like herself. She was about twenty-two years old and had an infant son at the breast.
(Now from this point on the entire account of her ordeal is her own, according to her own ideas and in the way that she herself wrote it down.)

While we were still under arrest (she said), my father out of love for me
was trying to persuade me and shake my resolution. "Father," said I, "do you
see this vase here, for example, or waterpot or whatever?" "Yes, I do," said
he. And I told him, "Could it be called by any other name than what it is?"
And he said, "No." "Well, so too I cannot be called anything other than what
I am, a Christian."

At this my father was so angered by the word "Christian" that he moved
towards me as though he would pluck my eyes out. But he left it at that and

---

The Martyrdom of Perpetua, in *The Acts of the Christian Martyrs*, ed. and trans. Herbert Musurillo
(Oxford: Oxford University Press, 1972), 109-15, 117-19, 123-31.

departed, vanquished along with his diabolical arguments. For a few days afterwards I gave thanks to the Lord that I was separated from my father, and I was comforted by his absence. During these few days I was baptized, and I was inspired by the Spirit not to ask for any other favor after the water but simply the perseverance of the flesh. A few days later we were lodged in the prison; and I was terrified, as I had never before been in such a dark hole. What a difficult time it was! With the crowd the heat was stifling; then there was the extortion of the soldiers; and to crown all, I was tortured with worry for my baby there. Then Tertius and Pomponius, those blessed deacons who tried to take care of us, bribed the soldiers to allow us to go to a better part of the prison to refresh ourselves for a few hours.

Everyone then left that dungeon and shifted for himself. I nursed my baby, who was faint from hunger. In my anxiety I spoke to my mother about the child, I tried to comfort my brother, and I gave the child in their charge. I was in pain because I saw them suffering out of pity for me. These were the trials I had to endure for many days. Then I got permission for my baby to stay with me in prison. At once I recovered my health, relieved as I was of my worry and anxiety over the child. My prison had suddenly become a palace, so that I wanted to be there rather than anywhere else. Then my brother said to me: "Dear sister, you are greatly privileged; surely you might ask for a vision to discover whether you are to be condemned or freed." Faithfully I promised that I would, for I knew that I could speak with the Lord, whose great blessings I had come to experience. And so I said: "I shall tell you tomorrow." Then I made my request and this was the vision I had:

> I saw a ladder of tremendous height made of bronze, reaching all the way to the heavens, but it was so narrow that only one person could climb up at a time. To the sides of the ladder were attached all sorts of metal weapons: there were swords, spears, hooks, daggers, and spikes; so that if anyone tried to climb up carelessly or without paying attention, he would be mangled and his flesh would adhere to the weapons.
>
> At the foot of the ladder lay a dragon of enormous size, and it would attack those who tried to climb up and try to terrify them from doing so. And Saturus was the first to go up, he who was later to give himself up of his own accord. He had been the builder of our strength, although he was not present when we were arrested. And he arrived at the top of the staircase and he looked back and said to me: "Perpetua, I am waiting for you. But take care; do not let the dragon bite you."

"He will not harm me," I said, "in the name of Christ Jesus."

Slowly, as though he were afraid of me, the dragon stuck his head out from underneath the ladder. Then, using it as my first step, I trod on his head and went up.

Then I saw an immense garden, and in it a gray-haired man sat in shepherd's garb; tall he was, and milking sheep. And standing around him were many thousands of people clad in white garments. He raised his head, looked at me, and said: "I am glad you have come, my child."

He called me over to him and gave me, as it were, a mouthful of the milk he was drawing; and I took it into my cupped hands and consumed it. And all those who stood around said: "Amen!"

At the sound of this word I came to, with the taste of something sweet still in my mouth. I at once told this to my brother, and we realized that we would have to suffer, and that from now on we would no longer have any hope in this life.

A few days later there was a rumor that we were going to be given a hearing. My father also arrived from the city, worn with worry, and he came to see me with the idea of persuading me.

"Daughter," he said, "have pity on my gray head — have pity on me your father, if I deserve to be called your father, if I have favored you above all your brothers, if I have raised you to reach this prime of your life. Do not abandon me to be the reproach of men. Think of your brothers, think of your mother and your aunt, think of your child, who will not be able to live once you are gone. Give up your pride! You will destroy all of us! None of us will ever be able to speak freely again if anything happens to you."

This was the way my father spoke out of love for me, kissing my hands and throwing himself down before me. With tears in his eyes he no longer addressed me as his daughter but as a woman. I was sorry for my father's sake, because he alone of all my kin would be unhappy to see me suffer.

I tried to comfort him saying: "It will all happen in the prisoner's dock as God wills; for you may be sure that we are not left to ourselves but are all in his power."

And he left me in great sorrow.

One day while we were eating breakfast we were suddenly hurried off for a hearing. We arrived at the forum, and straight away the story went about the neighborhood near the forum and a huge crowd gathered. We walked up to the prisoner's dock. All the others when questioned admitted their guilt. Then, when it came my turn, my father appeared with my son, dragged me from the step, and said: "Perform the sacrifice — have pity on your baby!"

Hilarianus the governor, who had received his judicial powers as the successor of the late proconsul Minucius Timinianus, said to me: "Have pity on your father's gray head; have pity on your infant son. Offer the sacrifice for the welfare of the emperors."

"I will not," I retorted.

"Are you a Christian?" said Hilarianus.

And I said: "Yes, I am."

When my father persisted in trying to dissuade me, Hilarianus ordered him to be thrown to the ground and beaten with a rod. I felt sorry for father, just as if I myself had been beaten. I felt sorry for his pathetic old age.

Then Hilarianus passed sentence on all of us: we were condemned to the beasts, and we returned to prison in high spirits. But my baby had got used to being nursed at the breast and to staying with me in prison. So I sent the deacon Pomponius straight away to my father to ask for the baby. But father refused to give him over. But as God willed, the baby had no further desire for the breast, nor did I suffer any inflammation; and so I was relieved of any anxiety for my child and of any discomfort in my breasts. . . .

Some days later, an adjutant named Pudens, who was in charge of the prison, began to show us great honor, realizing that we possessed some great power within us. And he began to allow many visitors to see us for our mutual comfort.

Now the day of the contest was approaching, and my father came to see me overwhelmed with sorrow. He started tearing the hairs from his beard and threw them on the ground; he then threw himself on the ground and began to curse his old age and to say such words as would move all creation. I felt sorry for his unhappy old age.

The day before we were to fight with the beasts I saw the following vision:

Pomponius the deacon came to the prison gates and began to knock violently. I went out and opened the gate for him. He was dressed in an unbelted white tunic, wearing elaborate sandals. And he said to me: "Perpetua, come; we are waiting for you."

Then he took my hand and we began to walk through rough and broken country. At last we came to the amphitheatre out of breath, and he led me into the center of the arena.

Then he told me: "Do not be afraid. I am here, struggling with you." Then he left.

I looked at the enormous crowd who watched in astonishment. I was surprised that no beasts were let loose on me; for I knew that I was condemned to die by the beasts. Then out came an Egyptian against me, of vicious appearance, together with his seconds, to fight with me. There also came up to me some handsome young men to be my seconds and assistants.

My clothes were stripped off, and suddenly I was a man. My seconds began to rub me down with oil (as they are accustomed to do before a contest). Then I saw the Egyptian on the other side rolling in the dust. Next there came forth a man of marvelous stature, such that he rose above the top of the amphitheatre. He was clad in a beltless purple tunic with two stripes (one on either side) running down the middle of his chest. He wore sandals that were wondrously made of gold and silver, and he carried a wand like an athletic trainer and a green branch on which there were golden apples.

And he asked for silence and said: "If this Egyptian defeats her he will slay her with the sword. But if she defeats him, she will receive this branch." Then he withdrew.

We drew close to one another and began to let our fists fly. My opponent tried to get hold of my feet, but I kept striking him in the face with the heels of my feet. Then I was raised up into the air, and I began to pummel him without as it were touching the ground. Then when I noticed there was a lull, I put my two hands together, linking the fingers of one hand with those of the other, and thus I got hold of his head. He fell flat on his face and I stepped on his head.

The crowd began to shout and my assistants started to sing psalms. Then I walked up to the trainer and took the branch. He kissed me and said to me: "Peace be with you, my daughter!" I began to walk in triumph towards the Gate of Life.

Then I awoke. I realized that it was not with wild animals that I would fight but with the Devil, but I knew that I would win the victory. So much for what I did up until the eve of the contest. About what happened at the contest itself, let him write of it who will. . . .

Such were the remarkable visions of these martyrs, Saturus and Perpetua, written by themselves. As for Secundulus, God called him from this world earlier than the others while he was still in prison, by a special grace that he might not have to face the animals. Yet his flesh, if not his spirit, knew the sword.

As for Felicitas, she too enjoyed the Lord's favor in this respect. She had been pregnant when she was arrested, and was now in her eighth month. As the day of the spectacle drew near she was very distressed that her martyrdom would be postponed because of her pregnancy; for it is against the law for women with child to be executed. Thus she might have to shed her holy, innocent blood afterwards along with others who were common criminals. Her comrades in martyrdom were also saddened; for they were afraid that they would have to leave behind so fine a companion to travel alone on the same road to hope. And so, two days before the contest, they poured forth a prayer to the Lord in one torrent of common grief. And immediately after their prayer the birth pains came upon her. She suffered a good deal in her labor because of the natural difficulty of an eight months' delivery.

Hence one of the assistants of the prison guards said to her: "You suffer so much now — what will you do when you are tossed to the beasts? Little did you think of them when you refused to sacrifice."

"What I am suffering now," she replied, "I suffer by myself. But then another will be inside me who will suffer for me, just as I shall be suffering for him." And she gave birth to a girl; and one of her sisters brought her up as her own daughter.

Therefore, since the Holy Spirit has permitted the story of this contest to be written down and by so permitting has willed it, we shall carry out the command or, indeed, the commission of the most saintly Perpetua, however unworthy I might be to add anything to this glorious story. At the same time I shall add one example of her perseverance and nobility of soul.

The military tribune had treated them with extraordinary severity because on the information of certain very foolish people he became afraid that they would be spirited out of the prison by magical spells.

Perpetua spoke to him directly. "Why can you not even allow us to refresh ourselves properly? For we are the most distinguished of the condemned prisoners, seeing that we belong to the emperor; we are to fight on his very birthday. Would it not be to your credit if we were brought forth on the day in a healthier condition?"

The officer became disturbed and grew red. So it was that he gave the order that they were to be more humanely treated; and he allowed her brothers and other persons to visit, so that the prisoners could dine in their company. By this time the adjutant who was head of the jail was himself a Christian.

On the day before, when they had their last meal, which is called the free banquet, they celebrated not a banquet but rather a love feast. They spoke to the mob with the same steadfastness, warned them of God's judgment, stressing the joy they would have in their suffering, and ridiculing the curiosity of those that came to see them. Saturus said: "Will not tomorrow be enough for you? Why are you so eager to see something that you dislike? Our friends today will be our enemies on the morrow. But take careful note of what we look like so that you will recognize us on the day." Thus everyone would depart from the prison in amazement, and many of them began to believe.

The day of their victory dawned, and they marched from the prison to the amphitheater joyfully as though they were going to heaven, with calm faces, trembling, if at all, with joy rather than fear. Perpetua went along with shining countenance and calm step, as the beloved of God, as a wife of Christ, putting down everyone's stare by her own intense gaze. With them also was Felicitas, glad that she had safely given birth so that now she could fight the beasts, going from one blood bath to another, from the midwife to the gladiator, ready to wash after childbirth in a second baptism.

They were then led up to the gates and the men were forced to put on the robes of priests of Saturn, the women the dress of the priestesses of Ceres. But the noble Perpetua strenuously resisted this to the end.

"We came to this of our own free will, that our freedom should not be violated. We agreed to pledge our lives provided that we would do no such thing. You agreed with us to do this."

Even injustice recognized justice. The military tribune agreed. They were to be brought into the arena just as they were. Perpetua then began to sing a psalm: she was already treading on the head of the Egyptian. Revocatus, Saturninus, and Saturus began to warn the onlooking mob. Then when they came within sight of Hilarianus, they suggested by their motions and gestures, "You have condemned us, but God will condemn you."

At this the crowds became enraged and demanded that they be scourged before a line of gladiators. And they rejoiced at this that they had obtained a share in the Lord's sufferings.

But he who said, "Ask and you shall receive" (Matt. 7:7), answered their prayer by giving each one the death he had asked for. For whenever they would discuss among themselves their desire for martyrdom, Saturninus indeed insisted that he wanted to be exposed to all the different beasts, that his crown might be all the more glorious. And so at the outset of the contest he and Revocatus were matched with a leopard, and then while in the stocks they were attacked by a bear. As for Saturus, he dreaded nothing more than a bear, and he counted on being killed by one bite of a leopard. Then he was matched with a wild boar; but the gladiator who had tied him to the animal was gored by the boar and died a few days after the contest, whereas Saturus was only dragged along. Then when he was bound in the stocks awaiting the bear, the animal refused to come out of the cages, so that Saturus was called back once more unhurt.

For the young women, however, the Devil had prepared a mad heifer.

45

This was an unusual animal, but it was chosen that their sex might be matched with that of the beast. So they were stripped naked, placed in nets and thus brought out into the arena. Even the crowd was horrified when they saw that one was a delicate young girl and the other was a woman fresh from childbirth with the milk still dripping from her breasts. And so they were brought back again and dressed in unbelted tunics.

First the heifer tossed Perpetua and she fell on her back. Then sitting up she pulled down the tunic that was ripped along the side so that it covered her thighs, thinking more of her modesty than of her pain. Next she asked for a pin to fasten her untidy hair: for it was not right that a martyr should die with her hair in disorder, lest she might seem to be mourning in her hour of triumph.

Then she got up. And seeing that Felicitas had been crushed to the ground, she went over to her, gave her hand, and lifted her up. Then the two stood side by side. But the cruelty of the mob was by now appeased, and so they were called back through the Gate of Life.

There Perpetua was held up by a man named Rusticus who was at the time a catechumen and kept close to her. She awoke from a kind of sleep (so absorbed had she been in ecstasy in the Spirit) and she began to look about her. Then to the amazement of all she said: "When are we going to be thrown to that heifer or whatever it is?"

When told that this had already happened, she refused to believe it until she noticed the marks of her rough experience on her person and her dress. Then she called for her brother and spoke to him together with the catechumens and said: "You must all stand fast in the faith and love one another, and do not be weakened by what we have gone through."

At another gate Saturus was earnestly addressing the soldier Pudens. "It is exactly," he said, "as I foretold and predicted. So far not one animal has touched me. So now you may believe me with all your heart: I am going in there and I shall be finished off with one bite of the leopard." And immediately as the contest was coming to a close a leopard was let loose, and after one bite Saturus was so drenched with blood that as he came away the mob roared in witness to his second baptism: "Well washed! Well washed!" For well washed indeed was one who had been bathed in this manner.

Then he said to the soldier Pudens: "Good-bye. Remember me, and remember the faith. These things should not disturb you but rather strengthen you."

And with this he asked Pudens for a ring from his finger, and dipping it into his wound he gave it back to him again as a pledge and as a record of his bloodshed.

Shortly after he was thrown unconscious with the rest in the usual spot to have his throat cut. But the mob asked that their bodies be brought out into the open that their eyes might be the guilty witnesses of the sword that pierced their flesh. And so the martyrs got up and went to the spot of their own accord as the people wanted them to, and kissing one another they sealed their martyrdom with the ritual kiss of peace. The others took the sword in silence and without moving, especially Saturus, who being the first to climb the stairway was the first to die. For once again he was waiting for Perpetua. Perpetua, however, had yet to taste more pain. She screamed as she was struck on the bone; then she took the trembling hand of the young gladiator and guided it to her throat. It was as though so great a woman, feared as she was by the unclean spirit, could not be dispatched unless she herself were willing.

Ah, most valiant and blessed martyrs! Truly are you called and chosen for the glory of Christ Jesus our Lord! And any man who exalts, honors, and worships his glory should read for the consolation of the Church these new deeds of heroism which are no less significant than the tales of old. For these new manifestations of virtue will bear witness to one and the same Spirit who still operates, and to God the Father almighty, to his Son Jesus Christ our Lord, to whom is splendor and immeasurable power for all the ages. Amen.

CLEMENT OF ALEXANDRIA

Who Is the Rich Man That Shall Be Saved?

Clement (about 150–about 215) probably grew up in Athens but spent most of his life in Alexandria in Egypt, one of the greatest cities of early Christianity. All converts to Christianity received basic teaching in the principles of their new faith, but the Alexandrian church had set up a special school for intellectually sophisticated converts, who would presumably of-

---

Clement of Alexandria, *Who Is the Rich Man That Shall Be Saved?* in *The Ante-Nicene Fathers*, ed. Alexander Roberts and James Donaldson and trans. William Wilson (Peabody, Mass.: Hendrickson Publishers, 1994), 2:592-96. Translation slightly revised.

ten have more complex questions than the average new Christian. Clement was appointed head of this school in 190. His new job put him in contact with wealthy, socially important Christians who raised difficult questions about what a call to Christianity meant for people like them, not least about whether they were required to give up all their wealth. He starts with a familiar Gospel text, and gives it a perhaps unexpected interpretation (though interpreting the Bible allegorically rather than literally was characteristic of Alexandrian theologians).

There is nothing like listening again to the very same statements, which till now in the Gospels were distressing you, hearing them as you did without examination, and through childishness misunderstanding them: "And going forth into the way, one approached and kneeled, saying, 'Good Master, what good thing shall I do that I may inherit everlasting life?' And Jesus said, 'Why do you call me good? There is none good but one, that is, God. You know the commandments. Do not commit adultery, Do not kill, Do not steal, Do not bear false witness, Defraud not, Honor your father and your mother.' And he answered him, 'All these have I observed.' And Jesus, looking upon him, loved him, and said, 'One thing you lack. If you would be perfect, sell what you have and give to the poor, and you shall have treasure in heaven: and come, follow me.'

"And he was sad at that saying, and went away grieved: for he was rich, having great possessions. And Jesus looked round about, and said to his disciples, 'How hard it is for those that have riches to enter into the kingdom of God!' And the disciples were astonished at his words. But Jesus answered again, and said to them, 'Children, how hard is it for them that trust in riches to enter into the kingdom of God! More easily shall a camel enter through the eye of a needle than a rich man into the kingdom of God.' And they were astonished out of measure, and said, 'Who then can be saved?' Then he, looking upon them, said, 'What is impossible with men is possible with God. For with God all things are possible.' Peter began to say to him, 'Lord, we have left all and followed you.'

"And Jesus answered and said, 'Truly I say unto you, Whosoever shall leave what is his own, parents, and brethren, and possessions, for my sake and the Gospel's, shall receive a hundredfold now in this world, lands, and possessions, and houses, and fields, with persecutions; and in the world to come is life everlasting. But many that are first shall be last, and the last first'" (Mark 10:17-31).

These things are written in the Gospel according to Mark; and in all the rest (of the Gospels) as well; although it may be that the expressions vary slightly in each, yet all show identical agreement in meaning. But well knowing that the Savior teaches nothing in a merely human way, but teaches all things to His own with divine and mystic wisdom, we must not listen to His utterances carnally; but with due investigation and intelligence must search out and learn the meaning hidden in them. . . .

After ridding himself of the burden of wealth, one may nonetheless have still the lust and desire for money innate and living; and may have abandoned the use of it, but being at once destitute of and desiring what he spent, may doubly grieve both on account of the absence of attendance, and the presence of regret. For it is impossible and inconceivable that those in want of the necessities of life should not be harassed in mind, and hindered from better things in the endeavor to provide them somehow, and from some source. . . .

And how much more beneficial the opposite case, for a man, through possessing a inheritance, both not himself to be in straits about money, and also to give assistance to those to whom it is requisite so to do! For if no one had anything, what room would be left among men for giving? And how can this dogma fail to be found plainly opposed to and conflicting with many other excellent teachings of the Lord? "Make to yourselves friends by means of dishonest wealth, that when ye fail, they may receive you into the everlasting habitations" (Luke 16:9). "Acquire treasures in heaven, where neither moth nor rust destroys, nor thieves break through" (Matt. 6:19). How could one give food to the hungry, and drink to the thirsty, clothe the naked, and shelter the homeless (and for not doing this He threatens with fire and the outer darkness), if each man first divested himself of all these things? Nay, He bids Zacchaeus and Matthew, the rich tax-gatherers, entertain Him hospitably. And He does not bid them part with their property, but, applying the just and removing the unjust judgment, He adds, "Today salvation has come to this house, forasmuch as he also is a son of Abraham" (Luke 19:9). He so praises the use of property as to enjoin, along with this addition, the giving a share of it, to give drink to the thirsty, bread to the hungry, to take the homeless in, and clothe the naked. But if it is not possible to supply those needs without substance, and He bids people abandon their substance, what else would the Lord be doing than exhorting to give and not to give the same things, to feed and not to feed, to take in and to shut out, to share and not to share? This would be the most irrational of all things.

Riches, then, which benefit also our neighbors, are not to be thrown away. For they are possessions, inasmuch as they are possessed, and goods, inasmuch as they are useful and provided by God for the use of men; and they lie to our hand, and are put under our power, as material and instruments which are for good use to those who know the instrument. If you use it skillfully, it is skillful; if you are deficient in skill, it is affected by your want of skill, being itself destitute of blame. Such an instrument is wealth. Are you able to make a right use of it? It is subservient to righteousness. Does one make a wrong use of it? It is, on the other hand, a minister of wrong. For its nature is to be subservient, not to rule. That then which of itself has neither good nor evil, being blameless, ought not to be blamed; but that which has the power of using it well and ill, by reason of its possessing voluntary choice. And this is the mind and judgment of man, which has freedom in itself and self-determination in the treatment of what is assigned to it. So let no man destroy wealth, rather than the passions of the soul, which are incompatible with the better use of wealth. So that, becoming virtuous and good, he may be able to make a good use of these riches. The renunciation, then, and selling of all possessions, is to be understood as spoken of the passions of the soul. . . .

If therefore he who casts away worldly wealth can still be rich in the passions, even though the material (for their gratification) is absent — for the disposition produces its own effects, and strangles the reason, and presses it down and inflames it with its inbred lusts — it is then of no advantage to him to be poor in purse while he is rich in passions. For it is not what ought to be cast away that he has cast away, but what is indifferent; and he has deprived himself of what is serviceable, but set on fire the innate fuel of evil through want of the external means (of gratification). We must therefore renounce those possessions that are injurious, not those that are capable of being serviceable, if one knows the right use of them. And what is managed with wisdom, and sobriety, and piety, is profitable; and what is hurtful must be cast away. But things external hurt not. So then the Lord introduces the use of external things, bidding us put away not the means of subsistence, but what uses them badly. And these are the infirmities and passions of the soul.

The presence of wealth in these is deadly to all, the loss of it salutary. Of which, making the soul pure — that is, poor and bare — we must hear the Savior speaking thus, "Come, follow Me." For to the pure in heart He now becomes the way. But into the impure soul the grace of God finds no entrance. And that (soul) is unclean which is rich in lusts, and is in the throes of many worldly affections. For he who holds possessions, and gold and silver and houses, as the gifts of God; and ministers from them to the God who gives them for the salvation of men; and knows that he possesses them more for the sake of the brethren than his own; and is superior to the possession of them, not the slave of the things he possesses; and does not carry them about in his soul, nor bind and circumscribe his life within them, but is ever laboring at some good and divine work, even should he be necessarily some time or other deprived of them, is able with cheerful mind to bear their removal equally with their abundance. This is he who is blessed by the Lord, and judged poor in spirit, a fitting heir of the kingdom of heaven, not one who could not live rich. So the statement that rich men that shall with difficulty enter into the kingdom is to be apprehended in a scholarly way, not awkwardly, or rustically, or carnally. For if the expression is used thus, salvation does not depend on external things, whether they be many or few, small or great, or illustrious or obscure, or esteemed or disesteemed; but on the virtue of the soul, on faith, and hope, and love, and brotherliness, and knowledge, and meekness, and humility, and truth, the reward of which is salvation.

TERTULLIAN

Apology

Tertullian (about 160–about 225), a North African convert to Christianity, was the first important Christian writer to write in Latin — until his time Greek had been the language of Christian theology. He established many of the key terms for Latin theology; for instance, when Christians talk about the Trinity as three persons *(personae)* in one substance *(substantia),* we are using language put into place by Tertullian. An "apology" was a "speech on behalf of" or "speech in defense of"; Tertullian addressed his *Apology* to the Roman emperor of the time, defending Christians against widespread rumors directed against them. He insists that the chief criti-

---

Tertullian, *Apology*, in *The Ante-Nicene Fathers*, ed. Alexander Roberts and James Donaldson and trans. S. Thelwall (Peabody, Mass.: Hendrickson, 1994), 3:17-18, 20, 26, 31-32, 40-42, 45, 46. Translation slightly revised.

cisms of Christianity are made out of ignorance. His work also, of course, circulated among his fellow Christians. Tertullian thought that too many Christians in his time were losing the rigor of the earlier church, and toward the end of his life he even joined the Montanists, a group of Christians eventually judged heretical who sought to return to the purity of the earliest church. This selection indicates some of the ways in which it was hard to be a Christian even if one was not directly persecuted — abandoned by families, rejected by friends, subject to all sorts of rumors and ridicule.

---

1. Rulers of the Roman Empire . . . what is there more unfair than to hate a thing of which you know nothing, even though it deserves to be hated? Hatred is only merited when it is *known* to be merited. But without that knowledge, how is its justice to be vindicated? For the justice of hatred is to be proved, not from the mere fact that an aversion exists, but from acquaintance with the subject. When men, then, give way to a dislike simply because they are entirely ignorant of the nature of the thing disliked, why may it not be precisely the very sort of thing they should not dislike? So we maintain that they are both ignorant while they hate us, and hate us unrighteously while they continue in ignorance, the one thing being the result of the other way of it.

The proof of their ignorance, at once condemning and excusing their injustice, is this, that those who once hated Christianity because they knew nothing about it, no sooner come to know it than they all lay down at once their enmity. From being its haters they become its disciples. By simply getting acquainted with it, they begin now to hate what they had formerly been, and to profess what they had formerly hated; and their numbers are as great as are laid to our charge. The outcry is that the State is filled with Christians — that they are in the fields, in the citadels, in the islands. Our critics make lamentation, as for some calamity, that both sexes, every age and condition, even high rank, are passing over to the profession of the Christian faith; and yet for all that, their minds are not awakened to the thought of some good they have failed to notice in it. . . .

Yet a thing that is thoroughly evil, not even those whom it carries away venture to defend as good. Nature throws a veil either of fear or shame over all evil. For instance, you find that criminals are eager to conceal themselves, avoid appearing in public, and are in trepidation when they are caught — they deny their guilt when they are accused; even when they are put to the rack, they do not easily or always confess; when there is no doubt about their condemnation, they grieve for what they have done. In their confessions they admit their being impelled by sinful dispositions, but they lay the blame either on fate or on the stars. They are unwilling to acknowledge that the thing is theirs, because they own that it is wicked.

But what is there like this in the Christian's case? The only shame or regret he feels is at not having been a Christian earlier. If he is pointed out, he glories in it; if he is accused, he offers no defense; interrogated, he makes voluntary confession; condemned, he renders thanks. What sort of evil thing is this, which lacks all the ordinary peculiarities of evil — fear, shame, subterfuge, penitence, lamenting? What! Is that a crime in which the criminal rejoices? To be accused of which is his ardent wish, to be punished for which is his joy? You cannot call it madness, you who stand convicted of knowing nothing of the matter. . . .

3. What are we to think of it, that most people so blindly knock their heads against the hatred of the Christian name; that when they bear favorable testimony to anyone, they mingle with it abuse of the name he bears? "A good man," says one, "is Gaius Seius, only that he is a Christian." So another, "I am astonished that a wise man like Lucius should have suddenly become a Christian." Nobody thinks it needful to consider whether Gaius is not good and Lucius wise, by the very reason that he is a Christian; or a Christian, for the reason that he is wise and good. . . .

Others, in the case of persons whom, before they took the name of Christian, they had known as loose, and vile, and wicked, put on them a brand from the very thing which they praise. In the blindness of their hatred, they fall foul of their own approving judgment! "What a woman she was! How wanton! How wild! What a youth he was! How profligate! How lustful! — They have become Christians!" So the hated name is given to a reformation of character. Some even barter away their comforts for that hatred, content to bear injury, if they are kept free at home from the object of their bitter enmity. The husband casts his wife out of his house even though she is now chaste and he has no reason for jealousy. The father, who used to be so patient, now disinherits his son even though he is now obedient. The master, once so mild, commands the servant away from his presence even though he is now faithful. It is a high offence for any one to be reformed by the detested name (of Christian). Goodness is of less value than hatred of Christians. . . .

"You do not worship the gods," you say; "and you do not offer sacrifices for the emperors." Well, we do not offer sacrifice for others, for the same reason that we do not for ourselves — namely, that your gods are not at all the objects of our worship. So we are accused of sacrilege and treason. This is the chief ground of charge against us — nay, it is the sum-total of our offending; and it is worthy then of being inquired into, if neither prejudice nor injustice be the judge, for prejudice has no idea of discovering the truth, and injustice simply and at once rejects it. We do not worship your gods, because we know that there are no such beings. This, therefore, is what you should do: you should call on us to demonstrate their non-existence, and thereby prove that they have no claim to adoration; for only if your gods were truly so, would there be any obligation to render divine homage to them. . . .

17. The object of our worship is the One God, He who by His commanding word, His arranging wisdom, His mighty power, brought forth from nothing this entire mass of our world, with all its array of elements, bodies, and spirits, for the glory of His majesty; whence also the Greeks have bestowed on it the name of "the cosmos." The eye cannot see Him, though He is (spiritually) visible. He is incomprehensible, though in grace He is manifested. He is beyond our utmost thought, though our human faculties conceive of Him. He is therefore equally real and great. That which, in the ordinary sense, can be seen and handled and conceived, is inferior to the eyes by which it is taken in, and the hands by which it is tainted, and the faculties by which it is discovered; but that which is infinite is known only to itself. This it is which gives some notion of God, while yet beyond all our conceptions — our very incapacity of fully grasping Him affords us the idea of what He really is. He is presented to our minds in His transcendent greatness, as at once known and unknown. And this is the crowning guilt of human beings, that they will not recognize One, of whom they cannot possibly be ignorant. Would you have the proof from the works of His hands, so numerous and so great, which both contain you and sustain you, which minister at once to your enjoyment, and strike you with awe; or would you rather have it from the testimony of the soul itself? Though under the oppressive bondage of the body, though led astray by depraving customs, though enervated by lusts and passions, though in slavery to false gods; yet, whenever the soul comes to itself, as out of an eating too much, or a sleep, or a sickness, and attains something of its natural soundness, it speaks of God, using no other word, because this is the peculiar name of the true God. "God is great and good," "Which may God give," are the words on every lip. It bears witness, too, that God is judge, exclaiming, "God sees," and, "I commend myself to God," and, "God will repay me." O noble testimony of the naturally Christian soul! Then, too, in using such words as these, it looks not to the Capitol (site of Zeus' temple), but to the heavens. It knows that there is the throne of the living God, as from Him and from there itself came down. . . .

27. Enough has been said in these remarks to confute the charge of treason against your religion: for we cannot be held to do harm to that which has no existence. When we are called therefore to sacrifice, we resolutely refuse, relying on the knowledge we possess, by which we are well assured of the real objects to whom these services are offered, under profaning of images and the deification of human names. Some, indeed, think it a piece of insanity that, when it is in our power to offer sacrifice at once, and go away unharmed, holding as ever our convictions, we prefer an obstinate persistence in our confession to our safety. You advise us, indeed, to take unjust advantage of you; but we know the source of such suggestions, who is at the bottom of it all, and how every effort is made, now by cunning persuasion, and now by merciless persecution, to overthrow our constancy. No other than that spirit, half devil and half angel, who, hating us because of his own separation from God, and stirred with envy for the favor God has shown us, turns your minds against us by an occult influence, molding and instigating them to all that perversity in judgment, and that unrighteous cruelty, which we have mentioned at the beginning of our work, when entering on this discussion. . . .

29. Let it be made clear, then, first of all, if those to whom sacrifice is offered are really able to protect either emperor or anybody else, and so adjudge us guilty of treason, if angels and demons, spirits of most wicked nature, do any good, if the lost save, if the condemned give liberty, if the dead (I refer to what you know well enough) defend the living. For surely the first thing they would look to would be the protection of their statues, and images, and temples, which rather owe their safety, I think, to the watch kept by Caesar's guards. Nay, I think the very materials of which these are made come from Caesar's mines, and there is not a temple but depends on Caesar's will. Yes, and many gods have felt the displeasure of Caesar. It makes for my argument if they are also partakers of his favor, when he bestows on them some gift or privilege. How shall they who are thus in Caesar's power, who belong entirely to him, have Caesar's protection in their hands, so that you can imagine them able to give to Caesar what they more readily get from him? This, then, is the ground on which we are charged with treason against the imperial majesty, to wit, that we do not put the emperors under their own possessions; that we do not offer a mere mock service on their behalf, as not believing their safety rests in leaden hands. But you are impious in a high degree who look for it where it is not, who seek it from those who have it not to give, passing by Him who has it entirely in His power. Besides this, you persecute those who know where to seek for it, and who, knowing where to seek for it, are able as well to secure it.

30. For we offer prayer for the safety of our princes to the eternal, the true, the living God. . . . To heaven we lift our eyes, with hands outstretched, because free from sin; with head uncovered, for we have nothing whereof to be ashamed; finally, without a monitor, because it is from the heart we supplicate. Without ceasing, for all our emperors we offer prayer. We pray for life prolonged; for security to the empire; for protection to the imperial house; for brave armies, a faithful senate, a virtuous people, the world at rest, whatever, as man or Caesar, an emperor would wish. These things I cannot ask from any but the God from whom I know I shall obtain them, both because He alone bestows them and because I have claims upon Him for their gift, as being a servant of His, rendering homage to Him alone, persecuted for His doctrine, offering to Him, at His own requirement, that costly and noble sacrifice of prayer dispatched from the chaste body, an unstained soul, a sanctified spirit, not the few grains of incense a little money buys — tears of an Arabian tree — not a few drops of wine, not the blood of some worthless ox to which death is a relief, and, in addition to other offensive things, a polluted conscience, so that one wonders, when your victims are examined by these vile priests, why the examination is not rather of the sacrificers than the sacrifices. With our hands thus stretched out and up to God, rend us with your iron claws, hang us up on crosses, wrap us in flames, take our heads from us with the sword, let loose the wild beasts on us — the very attitude of a Christian praying is one of preparation for all punishment. Let this, good rulers, be your work: wring from us the soul, beseeching God on the emperor's behalf. Upon the truth of God, and devotion to His name, put the brand of crime.

31. But we merely, you say, flatter the emperor, and feign these prayers of ours to escape persecution. Thank you for your mistake, for you give us the opportunity of proving our allegations. If you think that we care nothing for the welfare of Caesar, look into God's revelations, examine our sacred books, which we do not keep in hiding, and which many accidents put into the hands of those who are not Christians. Learn from them that a large benevolence is enjoined upon us, even so far as to supplicate God for our enemies, and to beseech blessings on our persecutors. . . .

If we are enjoined, then, to love our enemies, as I have remarked above, whom have we to hate? If injured, we are forbidden to retaliate, lest we become as bad ourselves: who can suffer injury at our hands? In regard to this, recall your own experiences. How often you inflict gross cruelties on Christians, partly because it is your own inclination, and partly in obedience to the laws! How often, too, the hostile mob, paying no regard to you, takes the law into its own hand, and assails us with stones and flames! With the very frenzy of the Bacchanals (drunken revelries in honor of Bacchus, the god of wine, which sometimes descended into wild violence), they do not even spare the Christian dead, but tear them, now sadly changed, no longer entire, from the rest of the tomb, from the asylum we might say of death, cutting them in pieces, rending them asunder. Yet, banded together as we are, ever so ready to sacrifice our lives, what single case of revenge for injury are you able to point to, though, if it were held right among us to repay evil by evil, a single night with a torch or two could achieve an ample vengeance? But away with the idea of a divine sect avenging itself by human fires, or shrinking from the sufferings in which it is tried. If we desired, indeed, to act the part of open enemies, not merely of secret avengers, would there be any lacking in strength, whether of numbers or resources? The Moors, the Marcomanni, the Parthians (nations which at various times fought the Romans) themselves, or any single people, however great, inhabiting a distinct territory, and confined within its own boundaries, surpasses, forsooth, in numbers, one spread over all the world! We are but of yesterday, and we have filled every place among you — cities, islands, fortresses, towns, marketplaces, the very camp, tribes, companies, palace, senate, forum — we have left nothing to you but the temples of your gods. For what wars should we not be fit, not eager, even with unequal forces, we who so willingly yield ourselves to the sword, if in our religion it were not counted better to be slain than to slay? Without arms even, and raising no insurrectionary banner, but simply in enmity to you, we could carry on the contest with you simply by leaving out of ill will. For if such multitudes of men were to break away from you, and betake themselves to some remote corner of the world, why, the very loss of so many citizens, whatever sort they were, would cover the empire with shame; nay, in the very forsaking, vengeance would be inflicted. Why, you would be horror-struck at the solitude in which you would find yourselves, at such an all-prevailing silence, and that stupor as of a dead world. You would have to seek subjects to govern. . . .

39. I shall at once go on, then, to exhibit the peculiarities of the Christian society, that, as I have refuted the evil charged against it, I may point out its positive good. We are a body knit together as such by a common religious profession, by unity of discipline, and by the bond of a common hope. We meet together as an assembly and congregation, that, offering up prayer to God as with united force, we may wrestle with Him in our supplications. This violence God delights in. We pray, too, for the emperors, for their ministers and for all in authority, for the welfare of the world, for the prevalence of peace, for the delay of the final consummation. We assemble to read our sacred writings, if any peculiarity of the times makes either forewarning or

reminiscence needful. However it be in that respect, with the sacred words we nourish our faith, we animate our hope, we make our confidence more steadfast; and no less by inculcations of God's precepts we confirm good habits. In the same place also exhortations are made, rebukes and sacred censures are administered. For with a great gravity is the work of judging carried on among us, as befits those who feel assured that they are in the sight of God; and you have the most notable example of judgment to come when any one has sinned so grievously as to require his separation from us in prayer, in the congregation and in all sacred intercourse.

The tried men of our elders preside over us, obtaining that honor not by purchase, but by established character. There is no buying and selling of any sort in the things of God. Though we have our treasure-chest, it is not made up of purchase-money, as of a religion that has its price. On the monthly day, if he likes, each puts in a small donation; but only if it be his pleasure, and only if he be able: for there is no compulsion; all is voluntary. These gifts are, as it were, piety's deposit fund. For they are not taken from there and spent on feasts, and drinking-bouts, and eating-houses, but to support and bury poor people, to supply the wants of boys and girls destitute of means and parents, and of old persons confined now to the house; such, too, as have suffered shipwreck; and if there happen to be any in the mines, or banished to the islands, or shut up in the prisons, for nothing but their fidelity to the cause of God's Church, they become the nurslings of their confession. But it is mainly the deeds of a love so noble that lead many to put a brand upon us. *See,* they say, *how they love one another,* for themselves are animated by mutual hatred; how they are ready even to die for one another, for they themselves will sooner put to death. And they are angry with us, too, because we call each other brethren; for no other reason, as I think, than because among themselves names of being related are assumed in mere pretence of affection. But we are *your* brothers as well, by the law of our common mother nature, though you are hardly men, because brothers so unkind. At the same time, how much more fittingly they are called and counted brothers who have been led to the knowledge of God as their common Father, who have drunk in one spirit of holiness, who from the same womb of a common ignorance have agonized into the same light of truth!

ATHANASIUS

The Life of Antony

Athanasius (about 296-373) was one of the great theologians of the early church: longtime bishop of Alexandria, defender of the Nicene Creed, explainer of the Trinity. His defense of the Trinity led several emperors who disagreed with his doctrine to drive him into exile, and during one of those exiles, hiding in the Egyptian desert, he met Antony (about 251-356), then a very old man. What follows is a selection from the book Athanasius wrote about Antony's life. It became very influential, and soon many Christians (both men and women) were following Antony into the desert — some, like him, to lead the solitary life of hermits, others to live with fellow ascetics in monasteries and convents.

Antony, you must know, was by descent an Egyptian: his parents were of good family and possessed considerable wealth, and as they were Christians he also was reared in the same faith. In infancy he was brought up with his parents, knowing nothing but them and his home. But when he was grown and arrived at boyhood, and was advancing in years, he could not endure to learn letters, not caring to associate with other boys; but all his desire was, as it is written of Jacob, to live a plain man at home (Gen. 25:27). With his parents he used to attend the Lord's House, and neither as a child was he idle nor when older did he despise them; but was both obedient to his father and mother and attentive to what was read, keeping in his heart what was profitable in what he heard. And though as a child he was brought up in moderate affluence, he did not trouble his parents for varied or luxurious fare, nor was

Athanasius, *The Life of Antony,* in *Nicene and Post-Nicene Fathers,* ed. Alexander Philip Schaff and Henry Wace and trans. H. Ellershaw (Peabody, Mass.: Hendrickson, 1994), 2d ser., 4:195-200. Translation slightly revised.

this a source of pleasure to him. He was content simply with what he found and did not seek anything further.

After the death of his father and mother he was left alone with one little sister: his age was about eighteen or twenty, and on him the care both of home and sister rested. Now it was not six months after the death of his parents, and going as usual into the Lord's House, he reflected as he walked how the Apostles left all and followed the Savior; and how according to Acts the earliest Christians sold their possessions and laid them at the Apostles' feet for distribution to the needy, and what and how great a hope was laid up for them in heaven. Pondering over these things he entered the church, and it happened the Gospel was being read, and he heard the Lord saying to the rich man, "If you would be perfect, go and sell what you have and give it to the poor; and come follow me, and you shall have treasure in heaven" (Matt. 19:21). Antony, as though God had put him in mind of the saints, and the passage had been read on his account, went out immediately from the church, and gave the possessions of his forefathers to the villagers — they were three hundred acres, productive and very fair — that they should no longer be a burden on himself and his sister. And all the rest that was movable he sold, and having got together much money he gave it to the poor, reserving a little however for his sister's sake.

Later as he went into the church, hearing the Lord say in the Gospel, "Be not anxious for the morrow" (Matt. 6:34), he could stay no longer, but went out and gave those things also to the poor. Having committed his sister to known and faithful virgins and put her into a convent to be brought up, he henceforth devoted himself outside his house to discipline, taking heed to himself and training himself with patience. For there were not yet so many monasteries in Egypt then, and no monk at all knew of the distant desert; but all who wished to give heed to themselves practiced the discipline in solitude near their own village. Now there was then in the next village an old man who had lived the life of a hermit from his youth up. Antony, after he had seen this man, imitated him in piety. And at first he began to abide in places outside the village. Then, if he heard of a good man anywhere, like the prudent bee he went forth and sought him, nor turned back to his own place until he had seen him; and he returned, having got from the good man as it were supplies for his journey in the way of virtue. So dwelling there at first, he confirmed his purpose not to return to the house of his fathers nor to the remembrance of his kinsfolk, but to keep all his desire and energy for perfecting his discipline. He worked, however, with his hands, having heard, "He who is idle let him not eat" (2 Thess. 3:10). Part of what he earned he spent on bread and part he gave to the needy. And he was constant in prayer, knowing that a man ought to pray in secret unceasingly. For he had given such heed to what was read that none of the things that were written fell from him to the ground, but he remembered all, and afterwards his memory served him for books.

Thus conducting himself, Antony was beloved by all. He subjected himself in sincerity to the good men whom he visited, and learned thoroughly where each surpassed him in zeal and discipline. He observed the graciousness of one and the unceasing prayer of another. He took knowledge of one's freedom from anger and another's loving-kindness; he gave heed to one as he watched, to another as he studied. One he admired for his endurance, another for his fasting and sleeping on the ground; the meekness of one and the long-suffering of another he watched with care, while he took note of the piety towards Christ and the mutual love which animated all. Thus filled, he returned to his own place of discipline, and henceforth would strive to unite the qualities of each, and was eager to show in himself the virtues of all. With others of the same age he had no rivalry except that he should not be second to them in higher things. And this he did so as to hurt the feelings of nobody, but made them rejoice over him. So all they of that village and the good men in whose intimacy he was, when they saw that he was a man of this sort, used to call him God-beloved. And some welcomed him as a son, others as a brother.

But the devil, who hates and envies what is good, could not endure to see such a resolution in a youth, but endeavored to carry out against him what he had been accustomed to do against others. First of all he tried to lead him away from the discipline, whispering to him the remembrance of his wealth, care for his sister, claims of kindred, love of money, love of glory, the various pleasures of the table and the other relaxations of life, and at last the difficulty of virtue and the labor of it. He suggested also the infirmity of the body and the length of the time. In a word he raised in his mind a great dust of debate, wishing to debar him from his settled purpose. But when the enemy saw himself to be too weak for Antony's determination, and that he rather was conquered by the other's firmness, overthrown by his great faith and falling through his constant prayers, then at length putting his trust in the weapons which are in the navel of his belly and boasting in them — for they are his first snare for the young — he attacked the young man, disturbing him by night and harassing him by day, so that even the onlookers saw the struggle which was going on between them.

The devil would suggest foul thoughts and Antony counter them with prayers; the one fire him with lust, the other, as one who seemed to blush, fortify his body with faith, prayers, and fasting. And the devil, unhappy spirit, one night even took upon him the shape of a woman and imitated all her acts simply to beguile Antony. But he, his mind filled with Christ and the nobility inspired by Him, and considering the spirituality of the soul, quenched the coal of the other's deceit. Again the enemy suggested the ease of pleasure. But he like a man filled with rage and grief turned his thoughts to the threatened fire and the gnawing worm, and setting these in array against his adversary, passed through the temptation unscathed. All this was a source of shame to his foe. For he, deeming himself like God, was now mocked by a young man; and he who boasted himself against flesh and blood was being put to flight by a man in the flesh. For the Lord was working with Antony — the Lord who for our sake took flesh and gave the body victory over the devil, so that all who truly fight can say, "not I but the grace of God which was with me" (1 Cor. 15:10).

But Antony, having learned from the Scriptures that the devices of the devil are many, zealously continued the discipline, reckoning that though the devil had not been able to deceive his heart by bodily pleasure, he would endeavor to ensnare him by other means. For the demon loves sin. Wherefore more and more Antony repressed the body and kept it in subjection, lest it should happen that, conquered on one side, he should be dragged down on the other. He therefore planned to accustom himself to a severer mode of life. And many marveled, but he himself used to bear the labor easily; for the eagerness of soul, through the length of time it was in him, had wrought a good habit in him, so that taking but little initiation from others he showed great zeal in this matter. He kept vigil to such an extent that he often continued the whole night without sleep; and this not once but often, to the marvel of others. He ate once a day, after sunset, sometimes once in two days, and often even in four. His food was bread and salt, his drink, water only. Of flesh and wine it is superfluous even to speak, since no such thing was found with the other earnest men. A rush mat served him to sleep upon, but for the most part he lay upon the bare ground. He would not anoint himself with oil, saying it behooved young men to be earnest in training and not to seek what would enervate the body; but they must accustom it to labor, mindful of the Apostle's words, "When I am weak, then am I strong" (2 Cor. 12:10). "For," said he, "the fiber of the soul is then sound when the pleasures of the body are diminished." And he had come to this truly wonderful conclusion, that progress in virtue, and retirement from the world for the sake of it, ought not to be measured by time, but by desire and fixity of purpose. He at least gave no thought to the past, but day by day, as if he were at the beginning of his discipline, applied greater pains for advancement, often repeating to himself the saying of Paul: "Forgetting the things which are behind and stretching forward to the things which are before" (Phil. 3:13). He was also mindful of the words spoken by the prophet Elijah, "The LORD lives before whose presence I stand today" (1 Kings 17:1). For he observed that in saying "today" the prophet did not compute the time that had gone by: but daily as though ever commencing he eagerly endeavored to make himself fit to appear before God, being pure in heart and ever ready to submit to His counsel, and to Him alone. And he used to say to himself that from the life of the great Elijah the hermit ought to see his own as in a mirror.

Thus tightening his hold upon himself, Antony departed to the tombs, which happened to be at a distance from the village; and having bid one of his acquaintances to bring him bread at intervals of many days, he entered one of the tombs, and the other having shut the door on him, he remained within alone. And when the Enemy could not endure it but was even fearful that in a short time Antony would fill the desert with the discipline, coming one night with a multitude of demons, he so cut him with stripes that he lay on the ground speechless from the excessive pain. For he affirmed that the torture had been so excessive that no blows inflicted by man could ever have caused him such torment. But by the Providence of God — for the Lord never overlooks them that hope in Him — the next day his acquaintance came bringing him the loaves. And having opened the door and seeing him lying on the ground as though dead, he lifted him up and carried him to the church in the village, and laid him upon the ground. And many of his kinsfolk and the villagers sat around Antony as round a corpse. But about midnight he came to himself and arose, and when he saw them all asleep and his comrade alone watching, he motioned with his head for him to approach, and asked him to carry him again to the tombs without waking anybody.

He was carried therefore by the man, and as was his custom, when the door was shut he was within alone. And he could not stand up on account of the blows, but he prayed as he lay. And after he had prayed, he said with a shout, "Here am I, Antony; I flee not from your stripes, for even if you inflict more, nothing shall separate us from the love of Christ." And then he sang, "Though an army be set against me, my heart shall not be afraid." These were the thoughts and words of this ascetic. But the enemy, who hates good, marveling that after the blows he dared to return, called together his hounds and burst forth, "You see," said he, "that neither by the spirit of lust nor by blows did we stop the man, but that he braves us; let us attack him in another fashion." But changes of form for evil are easy for the devil, so in the night they made such a din that the whole of that place seemed to be shaken by an earthquake, and the demons as if breaking the four walls of the dwelling seemed to enter through them, coming in the likeness of beasts and creeping things. And the place was suddenly filled with the forms of lions, bears, leopards, bulls, serpents, asps, scorpions, and wolves, and each of them was moving according to his nature. The lion was roaring, wishing to attack, the bull seeming to toss with its horns, the serpent writhing but unable to approach, and the wolf as it rushed on was restrained. Altogether the noises of the apparitions, with their angry ragings, were dreadful. But Antony, stricken and goaded by them, felt bodily pains severer still. He lay watching, however, with unshaken soul, groaning from bodily anguish; but his mind was clear, and as in mockery he said, "If there had been any power in you, it would have sufficed had one of you come, but, since the Lord hath made you weak, you attempt to terrify me by numbers: and a proof of your weakness is that you take the shapes of brute beasts." And again with boldness he said, "If you are able, and have received power against me, delay not to attack; but if you are unable, why trouble me in vain? For faith in our Lord is a seal and a wall of safety to us." So after many attempts they gnashed their teeth upon him, because they were mocking themselves rather than him.

Nor was the Lord then forgetful of Antony's wrestling, but was at hand to help him. So looking up he saw the roof as it were opened, and a ray of light descending to him. The demons suddenly vanished, the pain of his body straightway ceased, and the building was again whole. But Antony feeling the help, and getting his breath again, and being freed from pain, besought the vision which had appeared to him, saying, "Where were you? Why did you not appear at the beginning to make my pains to cease?" And a voice came to him, "Antony, I was here, but I waited to see your fight, because of which, since you have endured, and have not been defeated, I will ever be a help to you, and will make your name known everywhere." Having heard this, Antony arose and prayed, and received such strength that he perceived that he had more power in his body than formerly. And he was then about thirty-five years old.

And so for nearly twenty years he continued training himself in solitude, never going forth, and but seldom seen by any. After this when many were eager and wishful to imitate his discipline, and his acquaintances came and began to cast down and wrench off the door by force, Antony, as from a shrine, came forth initiated in the mysteries and filled with the Spirit of God. Then for the first time he was seen outside the fort by those who came to see him. And they, when they saw him, wondered at the sight, for he had the same habit of body as before, and was neither fat, like a man without exercise, nor lean from fasting and striving with the demons, but he was just the same as they had known him before his retirement, And again his soul was free from blemish, for it was neither contracted as if by grief, nor relaxed by pleasure, nor possessed by laughter or dejection, for he was not troubled when he beheld the crowd, nor overjoyed at being saluted by so many. But he was altogether even as being guided by reason, and abiding in a natural state. Through him the Lord healed the bodily ailments of many present, and cleansed others from evil spirits. And He gave grace to Antony in speaking, so that he consoled many that were sorrowful, and set those at variance at one, exhorting all to prefer the love of Christ before all that is in the world. And while he exhorted and advised them to remember the good things to come, and the loving-kindness of God towards us, "Who spared not His own Son, but delivered Him up for us all" (Rom. 8:32), he persuaded many to embrace the solitary life. And thus it happened in the end that cells arose even in the mountains, and the desert was colonized by monks, who came forth from their own people, and enrolled themselves for citizenship in the heavens.

GREGORY OF NYSSA

The Life of Macrina

Gregory (about 330–about 395) came from one of the most remarkable families in early Christianity. His older brother Basil wrote the first great treatise on the Holy Spirit and the standard rule for monks in Orthodox churches. Gregory himself was one of the greatest theologians and mystical writers of the early church. Yet as this biography and other works suggest, he saw his sister Macrina as a better Christian than he was, someone with much to teach him about Christian faith and life. By Gregory's time persecution had come to an end, but Christians probably remained a minority in the empire. His *Life of Macrina* provides an image of the sort of life to which the members of a prominent Christian family might feel called.

Gregory of Nyssa, *The Life of Macrina*, trans. W. K. Lowther Clarke (London: SPCK, 1916), 8-14. Translation slightly revised.

. . . such parts of inspired Scripture as you would think were incomprehensible to young children were the subject of the girl's studies; in particular the Wisdom of Solomon, and those parts of it especially which have an ethical bearing. Nor was she ignorant of any part of the Psalter, but at stated times she recited every part of it. When she rose from bed, or engaged in household duties or rested, or partook of food or retired from table, when she went to bed or rose in the night for prayer, the Psalter was her constant companion, like a good fellow traveler that never deserted her.

Her Betrothal

Filling her time with these and similar occupations, and attaining besides a considerable proficiency in woolwork, the growing girl reached her twelfth year, the age when the bloom of adolescence begins to appear. In this connection it is noteworthy that the girl's beauty could not be concealed in spite of efforts to hide it. Nor in all the countryside, so it seems, was there anything so marvelous as her beauty in comparison with that of others. So fair was she that even painters' hands could not do justice to her comeliness; the art that contrives all things and attempts the greatest tasks, so as even to model in imitation the figures of the heavenly bodies, could not accurately reproduce the loveliness of her form. In consequence a great swarm of suitors seeking her in marriage crowded round her parents. But her father — a shrewd man with a reputation for forming right decisions — picked out from the rest a young man related to the family, who was just leaving school, of good birth and remarkable steadiness, and decided to betroth his daughter to him, as soon as she was old enough. Meantime the young man aroused great hopes, and he offered to his future father-in-law his fame in public speaking as one of the bridegroom's gifts; for he displayed the power of his eloquence in forensic contests on behalf of the wronged.

Death of the Young Man

But Envy cut off these bright hopes by snatching away the poor lad from life. Now Macrina was not ignorant of her father's schemes. But when the plan formed for her was shattered by the young man's death, she said her father's intention was equivalent to a marriage, and resolved to remain single henceforward, just as if the intention had become accomplished fact. And indeed her determination was more steadfast than could have been expected from her age. For when her parents brought proposals of marriage to her, as often happened owing to the number of suitors that came attracted by the fame of her beauty, she would say that it was absurd and unlawful not to be faithful to the marriage that had been arranged for her by her father, but to be compelled to consider another; since in the nature of things there was but one marriage, as there is one birth and one death. She persisted that the man who had been linked to her by her parents' arrangement was not dead, but that she considered him who lived to God, thanks to the hope of the resurrection, to be absent only, not dead; it was wrong not to keep faith with the bridegroom who was away.

The Tragic Death of Naucratius

Then there fell on her mother a grievous and tragic affliction, contrived, I think, by the Adversary, which brought trouble and mourning upon all the family. For Macrina's brother Naucratius was snatched suddenly away from life. No previous sickness had prepared them for the blow, nor did any of the usual and well-known misfortunes bring death upon the young man. Having started out on one of the expeditions by which he provided basic needs for the old men under his care, he was brought back home dead, together with Chrysapius who shared his life. His mother was far away, three days distant from the scene of the tragedy. Some one came to her telling the bad news. Perfect though she was in every department of virtue, yet nature dominated her as it does others. For she collapsed, and in a moment lost both breath and speech, since her reason failed her under the disaster, and she was thrown to the ground by the assault of the evil tidings, like some noble athlete hit by an unexpected blow.

Macrina the One Support of Her Mother

And now the virtue of the great Macrina was displayed. Facing the disaster in a rational spirit, she both preserved herself from collapse and, becoming the prop of her mother's weakness, raised her up from the abyss of grief, and by her own steadfastness and imperturbability taught her mother's soul to be brave. In consequence, her mother was not overwhelmed by the affliction, nor did she behave in any ignoble and womanish way, so as to cry out at the calamity, or tear her dress, or lament over the trouble, or strike up funeral chants with mournful melodies. On the contrary, she resisted the impulses of nature, and quieted herself both by such reflections as occurred to her spontaneously, and those that were applied by her daughter to cure the ill. For then was the nobility of Macrina's soul most of all conspicuous; since natural affection was making her suffer as well. For it was a brother, and a favorite brother, who had been snatched away by such a manner of death. Nevertheless, conquering nature, she so sustained her mother by her arguments that she, too, rose superior to her sorrow. Besides which, the moral elevation always maintained by Macrina's life gave her mother the opportunity of rejoicing over the blessings she enjoyed rather than grieving over those that were missing.

Mother and Daughter Make Further Progress in the Ascetic Life

When the cares of bringing up a family and the anxieties of their education and settling in life had come to an end, and the property — a frequent cause of worldliness — had been for the most part divided among the children, then, as I said above, the life of the virgin became her mother's guide and led her on to this philosophic and spiritual manner of life. And weaning her from all accustomed luxuries, Macrina drew her on to adopt her own standard of humility. She induced her to live on a footing of equality with the staff of maids, so as to share with them in the same food, the same kind of bed, and in all the necessaries of life, without any regard to differences of rank. Such was the manner of their life, so great the height of their philosophy, and so holy their conduct day and night, as to make verbal description inadequate. For just as souls freed from the body by death are saved from the cares of this life, so was their life far removed from all earthly follies and ordered with a view of imitating the angelic life. For no anger or jealousy, no hatred or pride, was observed in their midst, nor anything else of this nature, since they had cast away all vain desires for honor and glory, all vanity, arrogance and the like. Continence was their luxury, and obscurity their glory. Poverty, and the casting away of all material superfluities like dust from their bodies, was their wealth. In fact, of all the things after which men eagerly pursue in this life, there were none with which they could not easily dispense. Nothing was left but the care of divine things and the unceasing round of prayer and endless hymnody, coextensive with time itself, practiced by night and day. So that to them this meant work, and work so called was rest. What human words could make you realize such a life as this, a life on the borderline between human and spiritual nature? For that nature should be free from human weaknesses is more than can be expected from humankind. But these women fell short of the angelic and immaterial nature only in so far as they appeared in bodily form, and were contained within a human frame, and were dependent upon the organs of sense. Perhaps some might even dare to say that the difference was not to their disadvantage. Since living in the body and yet after the likeness of the immaterial beings, they were not bowed down by the weight of the body, but their life was exalted to the skies and they walked on high in company with the powers of heaven.

The period covered by this mode of life was no short one, and with the lapse of time their successes increased, as their philosophy continually grew purer with the discovery of new blessings. . . .

Gregory Resolves to Visit His Sister

It was the ninth month or a little longer after this disaster [the death of his brother Basil], and a synod of bishops was gathered at Antioch, in which we also took part. And when we broke up, each to go home before the year was over, then I, Gregory, felt a desire to visit Macrina. For a long time had elapsed during which visits were prevented by the distraction of the troubles which I underwent, being constantly driven out from my own country by the leaders of heresy. And when I came to reckon the intervening time during which the troubles had prevented us meeting face to face, no less than eight years, or very nearly that period, seemed to have elapsed.

Gregory Comes to the Monastery
and Finds Macrina on Her Deathbed

But when I came to the actual place, rumor had already announced my arrival to the brotherhood. Then the whole company of the men came streaming out to meet us from their apartments. For it was their custom to honor friends by meeting them. But the band of virgins on the women's side modestly waited in the church for us to arrive. But when the prayers and the blessing were over, and the women, after reverently inclining their head for the blessing, retired to their own apartments, none of them were left with us. I guessed the explanation, that the abbess was not with them. A man led me to the house in which was my great sister, and opened the door. Then I entered that holy dwelling. I found her already terribly afflicted with weakness. She was lying not on a bed or couch, but on the floor; a sack had been spread on a board, and another board propped up her head, so contrived as to act as a pillow, supporting the sinews of the neck in slanting fashion, and holding up the neck comfortably. Now when she saw me near the door she raised herself on her elbow but could not come to meet me, her strength being already drained by fever. But by putting her hands on the floor and leaning over from the pallet as far as she could, she showed the respect due to my rank. I ran to her and embraced her prostrate form, and raising her, again restored her to her usual position. Then she lifted her hand to God and said, "This favor also You have granted me, O God, and have not deprived me of my desire, because You have stirred up Your servant to visit Your handmaid."

Gregory Returns to Macrina,
Who Recalls the Events of Her Childhood

But when we saw her again, for she did not allow us to spend time by ourselves in idleness, she began to recall her past life, beginning with childhood, and describing it all in order as in a history. She recounted as much as she could remember of the life of our parents, and the events that took place both before and after my birth. But her aim throughout was gratitude towards God, for she described our parents' life not so much from the point of view of the reputation they enjoyed in the eyes of contemporaries on account of their riches, as an example of the divine blessing.

My father's parents had their goods confiscated for confessing Christ. Our maternal grandfather was slain by the imperial wrath, and all his possessions were transferred to other masters. Nevertheless their life abounded so in faith that no one was named above them in those times. And moreover, after their substance had been divided into nine parts according to the number of the children, the share of each was so increased by God's blessing that the income of each of the children exceeded the prosperity of the parents. But when it came to Macrina herself, she kept nothing of the things assigned to her in the equal division between brothers and sisters, but all her share was given into the priest's hands according to the divine command. Moreover, her life became such by God's help that her hands never ceased to work according to the commandment. Never did she even look for help to any human being, nor did human charity give her the opportunity of a comfortable existence. Never were petitioners turned away, yet never did she appeal for help, but God secretly blessed the little seeds of her good works till they grew into a mighty fruit.

As I told my own trouble and all that I had been through, first my exile at the hands of the Emperor Valens on account of the faith, and then the confusion in the Church that summoned me to conflicts and trials, my great sister said, "Will you not cease to be insensible to the divine blessings? Will you not remedy the ingratitude of your soul? Will you not compare your position with that of your parents? And yet, as regards worldly things, we make our boast of being well born and thinking we come of a noble family. Our father was greatly esteemed as a young man for his learning; in fact his fame was established throughout the law courts of the province. Subsequently, though he excelled all others in rhetoric, his reputation did not extend beyond Pontus. But he was satisfied with fame in his own land.

"But you," she said, "are renowned in cities and peoples and nations. Churches summon you as an ally and director, and do you not see the grace of God in it all? Do you fail to recognize the cause of such great blessings, that it is your parents' prayers that are lifting you up on high, you that have little or no equipment within yourself for such success?"

Thus she spoke, and I longed for the length of the day to be further extended, that she might never cease delighting our ears with sweetness. But the voice of the choir was summoning us to the evening service, and, sending me to church, the great one retired once more to God in prayer. And thus she spent the night.

The Events of the Next Day: Macrina's Last Hours

But when day came, it was clear to me from what I saw that the coming day was the utmost limit of her life in the flesh, since the fever had consumed all her innate strength. But she, considering the weakness of our minds, was contriving how to divert us from our sorrowful anticipations, and once more with those beautiful words of hers poured out what was left of her suffering soul with short and difficult breathing. Many, indeed, and varied, were the emotions of my heart at what I saw. For nature herself was afflicting me and making me sad, as was only to be expected, since I could no longer hope ever to hear such a voice again. Nor as yet was I reconciled to the thought of losing the common glory of our family, but my mind, as it were inspired by the spectacle, supposed that she would actually rise superior to the common lot. For that she did not even in her last breath find anything strange in the hope of the Resurrection, nor even shrink at the departure from this life, but with lofty mind continued to discuss up to her last breath the convictions she had formed from the beginning about this life — all this seemed to me more than human. Rather did it seem as if some angel had taken human form with a sort of incarnation, to whom it was nothing strange that the mind should remain undisturbed, since he had no kinship or likeness with this life of flesh, and so the flesh did not draw the mind to think on its afflictions. Therefore I think she revealed to the bystanders that divine and pure love of the invisible bridegroom, which she kept hidden and nourished in the secret places of the soul, and she published abroad the secret disposition of her heart — her hurrying towards Him Whom she desired, that she might speedily be with Him, loosed from the chains of the body. For in very truth her course was directed towards virtue, and nothing else could divert her attention.

Macrina's Dying Prayer

Most of the day had now passed, and the sun was declining towards the west. Her eagerness did not diminish, but as she approached her end, as if she discerned the beauty of the Bridegroom more clearly, she hastened towards the Beloved with greater eagerness. Such thoughts as these did she utter, no longer to us who were present, but to Him in person on Whom she gazed fixedly. Her couch had been turned towards the east; and, ceasing to converse with us, she spoke henceforward to God in prayer, making supplication with her hands and whispering with a low voice, so that we could just hear what was said. Such was the prayer; we need not doubt that it reached God and that she, too, was hearing His voice.

"You, O Lord, have freed us from the fear of death. You have made the end of this life the beginning to us of true life. You for a season rest our bodies in sleep and awake them again at the last trumpet. You give our earth, which You have fashioned with Your hands, to the earth to keep in safety. One day You will take again what You have given, transfiguring with immortality and grace our mortal and unsightly remains. You have saved us from the curse and from sin, having become both for our sakes. You have broken the heads of the dragon who had seized us with his jaws, in the yawning gulf of disobedience. You have shown us the way of resurrection, having broken the gates of hell, and brought to nothing him who had the power of death — the devil. You have given a sign to those that fear You in the symbol of the Holy Cross, to destroy the adversary and save our life. O God eternal, to Whom I have been attached from my mother's womb, Whom my soul has loved with all its strength, to Whom I have dedicated both my flesh and my soul from my youth up until now — give me an angel of light to conduct me to the place of refreshment, where is the water of rest, in the bosom of the holy Fathers. You who broke the flaming sword and restored to Paradise the man that was crucified with You and implored Your mercies, remember me, too, in Your kingdom; because I, too, was crucified with You, having nailed my flesh to the cross for fear of You, and of Your judgments have I been afraid. Let not the terrible chasm separate me from Your elect. Nor let the slanderer stand against me in the way; nor let my sin be found before Your eyes, if in anything I have sinned in word or deed or thought, led astray by the weakness of our nature. O You Who have power on earth to forgive sins, forgive me, that I may be refreshed and may be found before You when I put off my body, without defilement on my soul. But may my soul be received into Your hands spotless and undefiled, as an offering before You."

As she said these words she sealed her eyes and mouth and heart with the cross. And gradually her tongue dried up with the fever, she could articulate her words no longer, and her voice died away, and only by the trembling of her lips and the motion of her hands did we recognize that she was praying.

Meanwhile evening had come and a lamp was brought in. All at once she opened the orb of her eyes and looked towards the light, clearly wanting to repeat the thanksgiving sung at the Lighting of the Lamps. But her voice failed, and she fulfilled her intention in the heart and by moving her hands, while her lips stirred in sympathy with her inward desire. But when she had finished the thanksgiving, and her hand brought to her face to make the sign that signified the end of the prayer, she drew a great deep breath and closed her life and her prayer together.

PALLADIUS

The Lausiac History

Palladius (about 365-425) lived most of his life in Asia Minor (present-day Turkey), where he was for a time an important bishop. In his twenties,

Palladius, *The Lausiac History*, trans. Robert T. Meyer (Westminster, Md.: Newman, 1965), 31-33, 40-41, 49-51, 58-59, 96-98.

however, he had spent several years visiting the monks now dwelling in substantial numbers in the Egyptian desert. His *Lausiac History* was dedicated to and therefore named after Lausus, a high official in the court of the emperor (who was now a Christian). It provides a firsthand account of early monastic life.

Isidore

When I first came to Alexandria during the second consulate of Theodosius, the great emperor who now dwells with the angels because of his wonderful faith in Christ, I met a wonderful man in the city. This was the thoroughly accomplished person, Isidore the elder, guest-master of the church of Alexandria, who was reported to have fought the first battles of youth in the desert. I have even seen his cell in the mountain of Nitria. I met him when he was an old man of seventy years, and he lived still another fifteen years before his peaceful death.

Up to the very end of his life he wore no fine linen except for a headband. He neither bathed nor ate meat. He kept his poor body so well disciplined by grace that all who did not know of his way of life imagined that he lived in luxury. Time would fail me were I to attempt a detailed description of his virtues. He was so tender-hearted and peaceful that even his enemies, unbelievers that they were, revered his very shadow because of his great goodness. . . .

He was acquainted with the entire Roman senate and all the wives of the great men when he came first with Athanasius, later with Bishop Demetrius. Very rich and exceedingly generous, he made no will when on the point of death, and he left neither money nor property to his own virgin sisters, but rather entrusted them to Christ, saying: "He who created you will regulate your life as He has ordered mine." There was a band of seventy virgins with his sisters.

When I was a young man and visited him, begging to be instructed in the solitary life, I was in my full prime, needing not so much precept as hard bodily toil. He, like a good colt-breaker, led me out of the city to the so-called Solitudes, some five miles out.

Dorotheus

He handed me over to Dorotheus, a Theban ascetic, who had lived sixty years in a cave, and he commanded me to stay three full years with him in subduing my passions. He commanded me to return to him for spiritual training, for he knew the old man passed his life in unremitting discipline. As I fell ill, I could not stay the full time, so I left before the end of three years — his way of life was squalid and harsh.

He used to collect stones in the desert all day long in the burning heat along the sea and to build cells for those who could not build their own, finishing one each year. When I asked him: "What are you doing, Father, killing your body in such heat?" he answered: "It kills me, I will kill it." He would eat six ounces of bread, a bunch of small vegetables, and a proportionate amount of water. God is my witness, I never knew him to stretch out his feet or to sleep on a mat or on a couch, but all night long he would sit up weaving rope of date-palm leaves to earn his food.

Having a suspicion that he did this because of me, I inquired about him among his disciples who lived solitary lives, and I found that such had been his way of life from early youth. He had never gone to sleep on purpose, but closed his eyes only when overcome with sleep while at work or eating, so that often a morsel of food would fall from his mouth while he was eating, so drowsy had he become. Once when I was urging him to rest a little while on a rush mat, he said, saddened at heart: "If you persuade the angels to rest, then you can perhaps persuade the eager man." . . .

The Monks of Nitria

Now I spent three years in the monasteries in the neighborhood of Alexandria with their some two thousand most noble and zealous inhabitants. Then I left and crossed over to Mount Nitria. Between this mountain and Alexandria there lies a lake called Marea, seventy miles long. I was a day and a half crossing this to the mountain on its southern shore.

Beyond the mountain stretches the Great Desert, reaching as far as Ethiopia, Mazicae, and Mauritania. On the mountain live close to five thousand men following different ways of life, each as he can or will. Thus some live alone, others in pairs, and some in groups. There are seven bakeries on this mountain serving these men as well as the hermits in the Great Desert, six hundred in all.

I tarried then for a year on the mountain and was greatly helped by the blessed fathers Arsisius the Great, Poutoubastes, Asius, Cronius, and Sarapion; and as I was spurred on by their many stories about the fathers, I went into the depths of the desert. On this mountain of Nitria there is a great church in which stand three date palms, each with a whip hanging on it. Now one is for backsliding monks, another for any robbers that attack, the third for any robbers that happen by. All transgressors who are sentenced to a lashing are made fast to a date palm, and are freed when they have received the requisite number of lashes on the back.

The guesthouse is close to the church. Here the arriving guest is received until such time as he leaves voluntarily. He stays here all the time, even if for a period of two or three years. They allow a guest to remain at leisure for one week; from then on he must help in the garden, bakery, or kitchen. Should he be a noteworthy person, they give him a book, not allowing him to converse with anyone before the sixth hour. On this mountain there are doctors living, and also pastry cooks. They use wine, too, and wine is sold.

All these work with their hands at making linen, so that none of them is in want. And indeed, along about the ninth hour one can stand and hear the divine psalmody is sung forth from each cell and imagine one is high above in paradise. They occupy the church on Saturdays and Sundays only. Eight priests have charge of the church; while the senior priest lives, none of the others celebrates or gives the sermon, but they simply sit quietly by him.

This Arsisius and many other old men whom we saw with him were contemporaries of Saint Antony. Some among them said they had also known Amoun of Nitria, whose soul Antony saw received and taken up by the angels. Arsisius said that he also knew Pachomius of Tabennisi, who was prophet and archimandrite of three thousand men; of him I will speak later.

Paesius and Isaias

Also there were Paesius and Isaias, sons of a Spanish merchant. When their father died, they divided the estate they held, namely five thousand coins, clothes, and slaves. They deliberated and planned together: "Brother, what kind of life shall we lead? If we become merchants, such as our father was, we will still be entrusting our work to others. Then we would risk harm at the hands of pirates on the high seas. Come, let us take up the monastic life so that we may profit by our father's goods and still not lose our souls."

The prospect of monastic life pleased them, but they found themselves in disagreement. For when they had divided the property, they each had in mind to please God, but by taking different ways of life. Now the one shared everything among the monasteries, churches, and prisons; he learned a trade so that he might provide bread for himself, and he spent his time at ascetic practices and prayer. The other, however, made no distribution of his share, but built a monastery for himself and took in a few brethren. Then he took in every stranger, every invalid, every old man, and every poor one as well, setting up three or four tables every Saturday and Sunday. In this way he spent his money.

After they both were dead, various pronouncements were made about them as though they had both been perfect. Some preferred one, some the other. Then rivalry developed among the brethren in regard to the eulogies. They went to the blessed Pambo and entrusted the judgment to him, thinking to learn from him which was the better way of life. He told them: "Both were perfect. One showed the work of Abraham; the other, that of Elijah."

One faction said: "By your feet, we implore you, how can they be equal?" And this group considered the ascetic the greater, and insisted that he did what the Gospel commended, selling all and giving to the poor, and every hour both day and night carried the cross and followed the Savior even in his prayers. But the others argued heatedly, saying that Isaias had shared everything with the needy and even used to sit on the highways and gather together the oppressed. Not only did he relieve his own soul, but many others as well by tending the sick and helping them.

Pambo told them: "Again I say to you, they are both equal. I firmly insist to each of you that the one, if he had not lived so ascetically, would not be worthy to be compared with the goodness of the other. As for the other, he refreshed strangers, and thereby himself as well, and even if he appeared to carry the load of toil, he had also its relief thereafter. Wait until I have a revelation from God, and then come back and learn it." They returned some days later, and he told them: "I saw both of them standing in paradise in the presence of God."

Macarius of Alexandria

I met the other Macarius, however, the one from Alexandria, a priest of so-called Cellia, where I stayed for nine years, and he was actually alive during three of those years. Some of the things I saw, others I heard about, and some I had by hearsay from others. Such was his practice that whenever he heard of any asceticism, he surpassed it to perfection. He heard from some that the Tabennesiote monks eat their food uncooked throughout the

Lenten period, so he made up his mind to eat no food that had come in contact with fire. For seven years he partook of nothing but raw vegetables, if these could be found, with a little moistened vegetable porridge.

He brought this virtue to perfection, and then heard about some other monk who ate but a pound of bread a day. He broke up his ration-biscuit into small bits, and put it into a measuring jar, and determined to eat only as much as his hand brought up. And he used to say jokingly: "I would take hold of quite a few morsels, but could not take them all out because of the narrow neck; for just like a toll-collector, it would not let me pass." He kept this up for three years, eating about four or five ounces and drinking about the equivalent amount of water, and a pint of olive oil lasted him a year.

Here is another example of his asceticism: He decided to be above the need for sleep, and he claimed that he did not go under a roof for twenty days in order to conquer sleep. He was burned by the heat of the sun and was drawn up with the cold at night. And he also said: "If I had not gone into the house and obtained the advantage of some sleep, my brain would have shriveled up for good. I conquered to the extent I was able, but I gave in to the extent my nature required sleep."

Early one morning when he was sitting in his cell a gnat stung him on the foot. Feeling the pain, he killed it with his hands, and it was gorged with his blood. He accused himself of acting out of revenge, and he condemned himself to sit naked in the marsh of Scete out in the great desert for a period of six months. Here the mosquitoes lacerate even the hides of the wild swine just as wasps do. Soon he was bitten all over his body, and he became so swollen that some thought he had elephantiasis. When he returned to his cell after six months, he was recognized as Macarius only by his voice. . . .

The Nun Who Feigned Madness

In this monastery there was another maiden who feigned madness and demon-possession. The others felt such contempt for her that they never ate with her, which pleased her entirely. Taking herself to the kitchen, she used to perform every menial service, and she was, as the saying goes, "the sponge of the monastery," really fulfilling the Scriptures: "If any one among you seem to be wise in this world, let him become a fool that he may be wise" (1 Cor. 3:18). She wore a rag around her head — all the others had their hair closely cropped and wore cowls. In this way she used to serve.

Not one of the four hundred ever saw her chewing all the years of her life. She never sat down at table or partook of a particle of bread, but she wiped up with a sponge the crumbs from the tables and was satisfied with scouring pots. She was never angry at anyone, nor did she grumble or talk, either little or much, although she was maltreated, insulted, cursed, and loathed.

Now an angel appeared to Saint Piteroum, the famous anchorite dwelling at Porphyrites, and said to him: "Why do you think so much of yourself for being pious and residing in a place such as this? Do you want to see someone more pious than yourself, a woman? Go to the women's monastery at Tabennisi and there you will find one with a band on her head. She is better than you are. While being cuffed about by such a crowd, she has never taken her heart off God. But you dwell here and wander about cities in your mind." And he, who had never gone away, left that monastery and asked the prefects to allow him to enter into the monastery of women. They admitted him, since he was well on in years and, moreover, had a great reputation.

So he went in and insisted upon seeing all of them. She did not appear. Finally he said to them: "Bring them all to me, for she is missing."

They told him: "We have one inside in the kitchen who is touched" (which is what they call the afflicted ones).

He told them: "Bring her to me. Let me see her."

They went to call her; but she did not answer, either because she knew of the incident or because it was revealed to her. They seized her forcibly and told her: "The holy Piteroum wishes to see you" — for he was renowned.

When she came he saw the rag on her head and, falling down at her feet, he said: "Bless me!"

In similar manner she too fell down at his feet and said: "Bless me, lord."

All the women were amazed at this and said: "Father, take no insults. She is touched."

Piteroum then addressed all the women: "You are the ones who are touched! This woman is spiritual mother" — so they called them spiritually — "to both you and me, and I pray that I may be deemed as worthy as she on the Day of Judgment."

Hearing this, they fell at his feet, confessing various things — one how she had poured the leavings of her plate over her; another had beaten her with her fists; another had blistered her nose. So they confessed various and sundry outrages. After praying for them, he left. And after a few days she was unable to bear the praise and honor of the sisters, and all their apologizing was so burdensome to her that she left the monastery.

Sayings of the Desert Fathers

The *Sayings of the Fathers*, collected in the fourth and fifth centuries, gathered a wide range of anecdotes about the early Egyptian monks, organized alphabetically by the name of the monk who is the principal figure in the story. Some are no doubt more historically accurate than others, but, all in all, they at least provide a sense of the general picture Christians had of the monastic life.

Abba Anthony said, "A time is coming when men will go mad, and when they see someone who is not mad, they will attack him saying, 'You are mad, you are not like us.'" . . .

Abba Agathon said, "If I could meet a leper, give him my body and take his, I should be very happy." That indeed is perfect charity.

It was also said of him that, coming to the town one day to sell his wares, he encountered a sick traveler lying in the public place without anyone to look after him. The old man rented a cell and lived with him there, working with his hands to pay the rent and spending the rest of his money on the sick man's needs. He stayed there four months till the sick man was restored to health. Then he returned in peace to his cell. . . .

One day Saint Epiphanius sent someone to Abba Hilarion with this request, "Come, and let us see one another before we depart from the body." When he came, they rejoiced in each other's company. During their meal, they were brought a fowl; Epiphanius took it and gave it to Hilarion. Then the old man said to him, "Forgive me, but since I received the habit I have not eaten meat that has been killed." Then the bishop answered, "Since I took the habit, I have not allowed anyone to go to sleep with a complaint against me and I have not gone to rest with a complaint against anyone." The old man replied, "Forgive me, your way of life is better than mine." . . .

The Desert Christian: Sayings of the Desert Fathers, trans. Benedicta Ward (New York: Macmillan, 1980), 3, 6, 24, 36, 57, 74, 85, 89, 103, 120, 160, 235.

A brother lived in the Cells, and in his solitude he was troubled. He went to tell Abba Theodore of Pherme about it. The old man said to him, "Go, be more humble in your aspirations, place yourself under obedience and live with others." Later, he came back to the old man and said, "I do not find any peace with others." The old man said to him, "If you are not at peace either alone or with others, why have you become a monk? Is it not to suffer trials? Tell me how many years you have worn the habit?" He replied, "For eight years." Then the old man said to him, "I have worn the habit seventy years and on no day have I found peace. Do you expect to obtain peace in eight years?" At these words the brother went away strengthened. . . .

It was said of Abba John the Dwarf that he withdrew and lived in the desert at Scetis with an old man of Thebes. His abba, taking a piece of dry wood, planted it and said to him, "Water it every day with a bottle of water, until it bears fruit." Now the water was so far away that he had to leave in the evening and return the following morning. At the end of three years the wood came to life and bore fruit. Then the old man took some of the fruit and carried it to the church, saying to the brethren, "Take and eat the fruit of obedience." . . .

There was an old man at Scetis, very austere of body, but not very clear in his thoughts. He went to see Abba John to ask him about forgetfulness. Having received a word from him, he returned to his cell and forgot what Abba John had said to him. He went off again to ask him and, having heard the same word from him, he returned with it. As he got near his cell, he forgot it again. This he did many times; he went there, but while he was returning he was overcome by forgetfulness. Later, meeting the old man he said to him, "Do you know, abba, that I have forgotten again what you said to me? But I did not want to overburden you, so I did not come back." Abba John said to him, "Go and light a lamp." He lit it. He said to him, "Bring some more lamps, and light them from the first." He did so. Then Abba John said to the old man, "Has that lamp suffered any loss from the fact that other lamps have been lit from it?" He said, "No." The old man continued, "So it is with John; even if the whole of Scetis came to see me, they would not separate me from the love of Christ. Consequently, whenever you want to, come to me without hesitation." So, thanks to the endurance of these two men, God took forgetfulness away from the old man. Such was the work of the monks of Scetis; they inspire fervor in those who are in the conflict and do violence to themselves to win others to do good. . . .

Abba Lot went to see Abba Joseph and said to him, "Abba, as far as I can I say my little office, I fast a little, I pray and meditate, I live in peace and, as far as I can, I purify my thoughts. What else can I do?" Then the old man stood up and stretched his hands towards heaven. His fingers became like ten lamps of fire, and he said to him, "If you will, you can become all flame." . . .

Some of the monks who are called Euchites went to Enaton to see Abba Lucius. The old man asked them, "What is your manual work?" They said, "We do not touch manual work but, as the Apostle says, we pray without ceasing." The old man asked them if they did not eat, and they replied they did. So he said to them, "When you are eating, who prays for you then?" Again he asked them if they did not sleep, and they replied they did. And he said to them, "When you are asleep, who prays for you then?" They could not find any answer to give him. He said to them, "Forgive me, but you do not act as you speak. I will show you how, while doing my manual work, I pray without interruption. I sit down with God, soaking my reeds and plaiting my ropes, and I say, 'God, have mercy on me; according to your great goodness and according to the multitude of your mercies, save me from my sins.'" So he asked them if this were not prayer, and they replied it was. Then he said to them, "So when I have spent the whole day working and praying, making thirteen pieces of money more or less, I put two pieces of money outside the door and I pay for my food with the rest of the money. He who takes the two pieces of money prays for me when I am eating and when I am sleeping; so, by the grace of God, I fulfill the precept to pray without ceasing."

Abba Olympius of the Cells was tempted to fornication. His thoughts said to him, "Go, and take a wife." He got up, found some mud, made a woman and said to himself, "Here is your wife, now you must work hard in order to feed her." So he worked, giving himself a great deal of trouble. The next day, making some mud again, he formed it into a girl and said to his thoughts, "Your wife has had a child, you must work harder so as to be able to feed her and clothe your child." So, he wore himself out doing this, and said to his thoughts, "I cannot bear this weariness any longer." They answered, "If you cannot bear such weariness, stop wanting a wife." God, seeing his efforts, took away the conflict from him and he was at peace.

AUGUSTINE

Confessions

Augustine (354-430) grew up in North Africa, the son of a Christian mother and a pagan father. At least as he encountered it in his small North African town, Christianity did not seem intellectually sophisticated enough to satisfy him. He was for a while intrigued by Platonic philosophy and for several years followed Manicheanism, a religion founded in Babylon in the third century by the prophet Mani. The pure "elect" among the Manicheans lived austere lives and were supported by second-class Manicheans, "hearers" like Augustine. One Manichean belief was that, by eating certain foods, the "elect" could free spirits trapped in those foods. Augustine came to see intellectual problems in Manicheanism, and he was also frustrated that, while both it and various philosophies in theory urged people to purify themselves, in practice none of them could help him overcome his sexual passions.

Augustine had been trained for one of the important professions in the later Roman Empire. He was a teacher of rhetoric, who could prepare people for successful careers in anything from law to politics. He traveled first to Rome and then to the current imperial capital, Milan, partly to advance his career and partly to get away from his mother, a sometimes overpowering figure, much as he loved her. He was moving forward in his career and enjoying the attentions of his mistress (like many young men on the rise in his time, he was waiting until he had climbed higher up the social ladder before taking a wife), but he felt himself unsatisfied, searching for something that would truly change his life.

His *Confessions*, written around 400, are a middle-aged bishop's recollections of his own youth, composed in the form of a prayer to God. The title implies that Augustine is confessing — both his sin and his faith.

The Confessions of St. Augustine, trans. Rex Warner (New York: Mentor-Omega, 1963), 69-71, 73-75, 99-102, 107-8, 119-21, 160-64, 167-74, 181-83, 184-86.

Book IV

So for the space of nine years (from my nineteenth to my twenty-eighth year) I lived a life in which I was seduced and seducing, deceived and deceiving, the prey of various desires. My public life was that of a teacher of what are called "the liberal arts." In private I went under cover of a false kind of religion. I was arrogant in the one sphere, superstitious in the other, and vain and empty from all points of view. On the one hand I and my friends would be hunting after the empty show of popularity — theatrical applause from the audience, verse competitions, contests for crowns of straw, the vanity of the stage, immoderate lusts — and on the other hand we would be trying to get clean of all this filth by carrying food to those people who were called "the elect" and "the holy ones," so that in the factory of their own stomachs they could turn this food into angels and gods, by whose aid we should be liberated. This was my way of life, and these were the things I did, I and my friends, who were deceived through me and with me. Let proud-hearted men laugh at me, and those who have not yet, for their own health, been struck down and crushed by you, my God. I shall still confess to you the story of my shame, since it is to your glory. Allow me this, I beg, and grant me the power to survey in my memory now all those wanderings of my error in the past and to offer unto You the sacrifice of rejoicing. For without you what am I to myself except a guide to my own downfall? Or what am I, even at the best, except an infant sucking the milk you give and feeding upon you, the food that is imperishable? And what sort of man is any man one can name, seeing that he is only a man? So let the strong and the powerful laugh at us; but let us, weak and needy as we are, make our confession to you.

In those years I taught the art of rhetoric. Overcome myself by a desire for gain, I took money for instructing my pupils how to overcome other people by speechmaking. Nevertheless, Lord, as you know, I preferred to have honest pupils (as honesty is reckoned nowadays); without deceit I taught them the arts of deception, to be used not against the life of any innocent man, though sometimes to save the life of the guilty. And, God, from afar you saw me stumbling in that slippery way and in all that smoke showing just a spark of honor; for in my teaching I did act honorably toward those who loved vanity and sought after a lie, being indeed their companion. In those years I lived with a woman who was not bound to me by lawful marriage; she was one who had come my way because of my wandering desires and my lack of considered judgment; nevertheless, I had only this one woman and I was faithful to her. And with her I learned by my own experience how great a difference there is between the self-restraint of the marriage covenant which is entered into for the sake of having children, and the mere pact made between two people whose love is lustful and who do not want to have children — even though, if children are born, they compel us to love them. . . .

In the time when I first began to teach rhetoric in the town where I was born, I had found a very dear friend who was following the same studies. We were both of the same age, now at the beginning of manhood; he had grown up with me as a child, and we had gone to school together and played together. But he was not in those early days, nor even in this later time, a friend in the true meaning of friendship, because there can be no true friendship unless those who cling to each other are welded together by you in that love which is spread throughout our hearts by the Holy Spirit which is given to us. But still this friendship was something very sweet to us and had ripened in the enthusiasm of the studies which we had pursued together. For I had turned him away from the true faith (in which, being so young, he was not soundly or thoroughly grounded) and had led him into that deadly superstitious folly of my own, which had so saddened my mother. His mind was wandering astray with mine, and my soul could not be without him. But you were there, you who are always close upon the heels of those who run away from you, you who are at the same time the God of vengeance and the fountain of mercy and who turn us to yourself in ways that are wonderful. You were there, and you took him away from this life, when he had scarcely had a year of this friendship with me, a friendship that was sweeter to me than all sweetnesses that in this life I had ever known.

Who can recount your praises? Who can recount the praises due for what he personally has experienced in himself? What was it, my God, that you did then? And how unsearchable is the abyss of your judgments! For a long time my friend suffered from a high fever and lay unconscious in a sweat that looked like death. When they despaired of his recovery, he was baptized. He knew nothing of this himself, and I paid little attention to the fact of his baptism. I assumed that his soul would retain what it had learned from me and would not be affected by something done to his body while he was unconscious. But it turned out very differently. For he got better and came back to life again, and, as soon as I could speak to him — which was as soon as he could speak to me, since I never left his side and indeed we depended too much on each other — I began to make jokes with him, assuming that he would join in, about the baptism which he had received when he could neither feel nor know what was being done, and yet had now been told that he had received it. But he shrunk back from me as though I were an enemy. With a sudden confident authority which took me aback he told me that, if I wanted to be a friend of his, I must give up talking to him in this way. I was astonished and amazed, and I put off telling him what was in my mind until he should get well again and should be strong enough in health for me to be able to discuss things with him as I wished. But he was taken away beyond the reach of my folly, so that with you he might be kept safe for my comfort. A few days later, when I was not there, his fever returned and he died.

My heart was darkened over with sorrow, and whatever I looked at was death. My own country was a torment to me, my own home was a strange unhappiness. All those things which we had done and said together became, now that he was gone, sheer torture to me. My eyes looked for him everywhere and could not find him. And as to the places where we used to meet, I hated all of them for not containing him; nor were they able to say to me now, "Look, he will soon come," as they used to say when he was alive and away from me. I had become a great riddle to myself, and I used to ask my soul why it was sad and why it disquieted me so sorely. And my soul did not know what to answer. If I said, "Trust in God," she very rightly did not obey me, because the man whom she had lost, my dearest friend, was more real and better than the fantastic god in whom she was asked to trust. Only tears were sweet to me, and tears had taken the place of my friend in my heart's love. . . .

Book V

You acted upon me in such a way that I was persuaded to set out for Rome to teach there the same subjects as I had been teaching in Carthage. How it was that I came to be persuaded to do this must not be passed over in my confession to you; here too I must ponder over and openly declare the deep secrecy of your ways and your mercy, which is always so close to us. I wanted to go to Rome not only because of the higher earnings and the greater reputation which my friends, who persuaded me to go, thought I would get there, though these reasons did have some weight with me at that time; in fact, however, my main and almost my only reason for going was that I heard that in Rome the young men followed their studies in a more orderly manner and were controlled by a stricter discipline. They were not allowed, for instance, insolently and at their own pleasure to come rushing into the school of a man who was not their own teacher; in fact they were not allowed to enter the school at all without the master's permission.

At Carthage, on the other hand, the students are disgracefully out of control. They come breaking into a class in the most unmannerly way and, behaving almost like madmen, disturb the order which the master has established for the good of his pupils. They commit a number of disorderly acts which show an incredible stupidity and which ought to be punished by law. However, custom protects them, and this is a fact which makes their state even more wretched, because the things they do appear to them permissible, though by your eternal law such things can never be permitted, and they imagine that they are getting away scot-free with what they do, whereas the very blindness with which they act is their punishment, and the harm which they do to themselves is incomparably worse than what they do to others. When I was a student myself, I refused to become one of those who behaved in this way, though when I became a teacher I had to put up with this behavior from other people. And so the reason why I wanted to go to Rome was that all who knew about it told me that there these things were not done. But you, my hope and my portion in the land of the living, were urging me to change countries for the salvation of my soul. In Carthage you prepared goads for me, so that I should be driven from the place, and at Rome you provided attractions which would draw me there, and in both cases you made use of men who were in love with this deathly life; on the one side were people acting like lunatics, and on the other people who promised me mere vanities. So, to reform my ways, you secretly made use both of their perversity and of my own. For those who were disturbing my peace were blinded by a disgraceful frenzy, and those who urged me to go elsewhere savored of earth. And I, hating my real misery in Carthage, looked for a false happiness in Rome.

But you, God, knew why it was that I was going from the one place to the other, and you did not reveal the reason either to me or to my mother, who was most bitterly distressed at my going away and who followed me right down to the seacoast. She clung to me with all her force, begging me either to return or to take her with me, but I deceived her and pretended that I had a friend whom I did not want to leave until the wind was right for him to set sail. So I told a lie to her, my mother, and such a mother, and I got away from her. And this too you have mercifully forgiven me. You saved me, full as I was with the most execrable uncleanness, from the waters of the sea and brought me to the water of your grace, so that, when I was washed in this water, the rivers that flowed from my mother's eyes, tears daily shed for me that watered the ground below her downcast looks, should be dried up. Still she refused to go home without me, and I had much difficulty in persuading her to stay that night in a place near the ship where there was an oratory in memory of St. Cyprian. That night I stole away, leaving her behind; she stayed there weeping and praying. And the whole purport, my God, of the prayers which she addressed to you with so many tears was that you would not allow me to sail. But your counsels are deep; you granted what was the key point of her prayer and did not do what she was asking for at that moment so that you might make me what she always wanted me to be. The wind blew and filled our sails; we lost sight of the land where, that morning, my mother was frantic with grief and filled your ears with her lamentations and complaints, and you seemed not to hear her, yet all the time you were dragging me away by the force of my own desires in order that these desires might be brought to an end, and you were justly punishing her with the whip of sorrow for an affection that was too much of the flesh. For she loved having me with her, as all mothers do, only she much more than most, and she did not know what great joys you were preparing for her by my going away. This she did not know, and so she wept and cried aloud and by all this agony she showed in herself the heritage of Eve, seeking in sorrow what in sorrow she had brought forth. Nevertheless, after accusing me of treachery and cruelty, she turned once more to her prayers to you for me. She went home and I went on my way to Rome. . . .

I started at once to do what I had come to do, namely to teach rhetoric at Rome. First of all I collected a few pupils at my house and by means of them I began to become known. I soon found out that things went on in Rome which I had not had to put up with in Africa. True enough I discovered that in Rome there was none of that subversive behavior which I knew on the part of the worst types of young men; but, so I was told, "in order to avoid paying their fees to the professor, a number of young men form a conspiracy and suddenly go off to study under another professor, thus breaking their pledged words and showing that to them justice is cheap compared with the love of money." I hated them too in my heart, though the hatred I felt was not a perfect hatred. I think that I hated them more because of what I was likely to suffer from them personally than because of the wrong they did to everyone concerned. Such people, however, are certainly vile characters; they fornicate against you in loving the fleeting mockeries of time and the filthy lucre which soils the hand that holds it and in embracing this fleeting world and in despising you who abide and who call them back to you and who give pardon to the adulterous soul of man when it returns to you. I still hate wicked and depraved people of this sort, though I love the thought of their being corrected and taught to love learning more than money and to love you, God, the truth and fullness of certain good, and the purest peace, more than learning. But at that time I was more anxious not to have to put up with their evil ways for my own sake than that they should learn good for your sake. . . .

So when the prefect of the city in Rome received a message from Milan, asking him to provide them with a professor of rhetoric and promising to pay the expenses of his journey out of public funds, I applied for the post myself. My application was supported by those very people who were intoxicated with the vanities of Manichaeism, and it was just to be rid of these people that I was going — though neither they nor I realized the fact. So I had the opportunity to make a speech on a set subject; Symmachus, who was then prefect, approved of it, and I was sent to Milan. And at Milan I came to Bishop Ambrose, who had a worldwide reputation, was a devout servant of yours and a man whose eloquence in those days gave abundantly to *Thy people the fatness of Thy wheat, the gladness of Thy oil and the sober intoxication of Thy wine* (Pss. 4:7 and 104:15). Though I did not realize it, I was led to him by you so that, with full realization, I might be led to you by him. That man of God welcomed me as a father and, in his capacity of bishop, was kind enough to approve of my coming there. I began to love him at first not as a teacher of the truth (for I had quite despaired of finding it in your Church) but simply as a man who was kind and generous to me. I used to listen eagerly when he preached to the people, but my intention was not what it should have been; I was, as it were, putting his eloquence on trial to see whether it came up to his reputation, or whether its flow was greater or less than I had been told. So I hung intently on his words, but I was not interested in what he was really saying and stood aside from this in contempt. I was much pleased by the charm of his style, which, although it was more learned, was still, so far as the manner of delivery was concerned, not so warm and winning as the style of Faustus. [Faustus was a Manichean teacher Augustine had known earlier.] With regard to the actual matter there was, of course, no comparison. Faustus was merely roving around among Manichaean fallacies, while Ambrose was healthily teaching salvation. But salvation is far from sinners of the kind that I was then. Yet, though I did not realize it, I was drawing gradually nearer. . . .

Book VI

I panted for honors, for money, for marriage, and you were laughing at me. I found bitterness and difficulty in following these desires, and your graciousness to me was shown in the way you would not allow me to find anything sweet which was not you. Look into my heart, Lord; for it was you who willed me to remember all this and to confess it to you. And let my soul cling to you now that you have freed it from that gripping birdlime of death! How unhappy it was then! And you pricked its wound on the quick, so that it might leave everything else and turn to you, who are above all things and without whom all things would be nothing — so that it might turn to you and be cured. I was unhappy indeed, and you made me really see my unhappiness. It was on a day when I was preparing a speech to be delivered in praise of the emperor; there would be a lot of lies in the speech, and they would be applauded by those who knew that they were lies. My heart was all wrought up with the worry of it all and was boiling in a kind of fever of melting thoughts. I was going along one of the streets of Milan when I noticed a poor beggar; he was fairly drunk, I suppose, and was laughing and enjoying himself. It was a sight which depressed me, and I spoke to the friends who were with me about all the sorrows which come to us because of our own madness. I thought of how I was toiling away, spurred on by my desires and dragging after me the load of my unhappiness and making it all the heavier by dragging it, and it seemed to me that the goal of this and all such endeavors was simply to reach a state of happiness that was free from care; the beggar had reached this state before us, and we, perhaps, might never reach it at all. With the few pennies that he had managed to beg he had actually obtained what I, by so many painful turns and such devious ways, was struggling to reach — namely, the joy of a temporary happiness.

No doubt the beggar's joy was not true joy; but it was a great deal truer than the joy which I, with my ambition, was seeking. And undoubtedly he was happy while I was worried; he was carefree while I was full of fears. And if I were asked which I would prefer, to be merry or to be frightened, I should reply "to be merry." But if I were asked next whether I would prefer to be a man like the beggar or a man like I then was myself, I should choose to be myself, worn out as I was with my cares and my fears. Was not this absurd? Was there any good reason for making such a choice? For I had no right to put myself in front of the beggar on the grounds that I was more learned than he, since I got no joy out of my learning. Instead I used it to give pleasure to men — not to teach them, only to please them. And therefore you were breaking my bones with the rod of your discipline.

So I will not allow my soul to listen to those who say to her: "The difference is in the source of a man's happiness. That beggar found his joy in being drunk, you were looking for your joy in winning glory." What glory, Lord? A glory that was not in you. For just as the beggar's joy was not true joy, so my glory was not true glory. Moreover, it had a worse effect on my mind. The beggar would sleep off his drunkenness that very night; but I had gone to bed with mine and woken up with it day after day after day, and I should go on doing so. Certainly it makes a difference what is the source of a man's happiness. I know it does. And the joy of a faithful hope is incomparably beyond all such vanity. Yes, and so was the beggar then beyond me; without any doubt he was the happier, not only because he was drenched in merriment while I eaten up with anxieties, but also because he by wishing people good luck had got some wine for himself while I by lying was seeking for an empty bubble of praise.

I said much along these lines to my intimate friends at the time, and I often noticed that it was the same with them as it was with me, and I found that things were not at all well with me, and I worried about it and by worrying made matters twice as bad, and if fortune seemed to smile on me at all, I felt too tired to grasp my opportunity, for it fled away almost before I could take hold of it. . . .

Book VIII

My God, let me remember with thanks and let me confess to you your mercies done to me. Let my bones be penetrated with your love and let them say: *Who is like unto Thee, O Lord?* (Ps. 35:10). *Thou hast broken my bonds in sunder, I will offer unto Thee the sacrifice of thanksgiving* (Ps. 116:16-17). I will tell how it was that you broke my bonds, and all your worshipers who hear this will say: "Blessed be the Lord in heaven and in earth, great and wonderful is His name."

Your words had stuck in my heart, and *I was hedged around about on all sides by Thee* (Job 1:10). Of your eternal life I was now certain, although I had seen it in an enigma and as through a glass. But I had ceased to have any doubt that there was an incorruptible substance from which came every substance. I no longer desired to be more certain of you, only to stand more firmly in you.

In my own temporal life everything was unsettled and *my heart had to be purged from the old leaven* (1 Cor. 5:7). The way — the Savior Himself — pleased me; but I was still reluctant to enter its narrowness. It was you who put the idea into my mind (and the idea seemed good to me) to go to Simplicianus. He seemed to me a good servant of you, and your grace shone in him. I had heard too that from his youth he had lived a life devoted to you. He had now grown old, and it seemed to me that he must have experienced much and learned much as a result of having lived so long in so earnestly following your way, and so indeed he had. So, after telling him of my troubles, I wanted him to make use of his experience and learning in order to show me the best means by which someone feeling as I did could set his foot on your way.

For I saw the Church full, and one went this way, and another that way. But I was displeased with the worldly life which I was leading. It was a great burden to me, and to help me bear such a heavy form of slavery I no longer had the impulse and encouragement of my old hopes and desires for position and wealth. Compared with your sweetness and the beauty of your house, which I loved, these things no longer pleased me. But I was still closely bound by my need of woman. Not that the apostle forbade me to marry, although he might recommend something better, his great wish being that all men should be as he was. But I lacked the strength and was inclined to choose the softer place, and because of this one thing everything else with me was in confusion; I was tired out and wasted away with gnawing anxieties, because I was compelled to put up with all sorts of things which I did not want simply because they were inseparable from that state of living with a wife to which I was utterly and entirely bound. I had heard from the mouth of Truth that *there were some eunuchs, which had made themselves eunuchs for the Kingdom of heaven's sake; but, he says, let him who can receive it, receive it* (Matt. 19:12). *Surely vain are all men who are ignorant of God, and could not out of the good things which are seen, find out Him who is good* (Wisd. of Sol. 43:1). But I was no longer in that kind of vanity; I had gone beyond it, and, by the common witness of all creation, I had found you, our Creator, and your Word, God with you, and one God together with you, by whom you created all things. But there is also another kind of impiety, that of those *who knowing God, glorified Him not as God, neither were thankful* (Rom. 1:21). I had fallen into this wickedness too, but your right hand upheld me, took me out of it, and placed me where I might recover. For you have said to man, *Behold, the fear of the Lord is wisdom* (Job 28:28), and *Desire not to seem wise* (Prov. 3:7); because they *who affirmed themselves to be wise, became fools* (Rom. 1:22). And I had now found that pearl of great price, and I ought to have sold all that I had and bought it. But I hesitated.

So I went to Simplicianus who, in the matter of receiving grace, had been the father of Ambrose, now bishop, and indeed Ambrose loved him as a father. I described to him the winding paths of my error. But when I told him that I had read some books of the Platonists which had been translated into Latin by Victorinus — once professor of rhetoric at Rome, who, so I had heard, had died a Christian — he congratulated me for not having fallen upon the writings of other philosophers full of *fallacies and deceits, after the rudiments of this world* (Col. 2:8), whereas in the Platonists God is everywhere implied. Then, in order to lead me toward the humility of Christ (*hidden from the wise, and revealed to little ones* [Matt. 11:25]), he went on to speak of Victorinus himself, with whom he had been on very friendly terms when he was in Rome. I shall make no secret of what he told me about him, for it is a story which ought to be confessed to you, containing, as it does, great praise of your grace. For Victorinus was an extremely learned old man, an expert scholar in all the liberal sciences, one who had read and weighed very many of the works of the philosophers, one who had been the teacher of numbers of distinguished senators and who, because of the exceptional brilliance of his teaching, had earned and accepted the honor of having his statue set up in the Roman forum, a thing which the citizens of this world regard as something quite remarkable, and up to old age he worshiped idols and took part in those sacrilegious ceremonies which were the craze with nearly all the Roman nobility, who had inspired the people with their enthusiasm for Osiris and the dog Anubis and that monstrous brood of deities which once took arms and fought in arms against Minerva, Neptune, Venus — gods which Rome had conquered and to which she now prayed, and for all these years old Victorinus, with his thundering eloquence, had been the champion of these gods; yet he did not blush to become the child of your Christ, an infant at your font, bending his neck to the yoke of humility and submitting his forehead to the ignominy of the Cross.

O Lord, Lord, *Which has bowed the heavens and come down, touched the mountains and they did smoke* (Ps. 144:5), by what means did you find your way into that man's heart? According to Simplicianus, he read the Holy Scripture and examined all Christian literature with the most thorough and exact attention. He then said to Simplicianus — not in public, but in a private friendly conversation — "I should like you to know that I am now a Christian." Simplicianus replied: "That I will not believe, and I shall not count you as a Christian until I see you in the Church of Christ." Victorinus smiled and said: "Is it the walls, then, that make Christians?" And he often repeated that he was a Christian, and Simplicianus often made the same reply, which was again countered by the joke about the walls. For Victorinus was afraid of offending his friends, who were important people and worshipers of these devils; he feared a great torrent of ill will falling upon him from the height of their Babylonian dignity, as from tree tops of the cedars of Lebanon which the Lord had not yet brought down. But from his reading and deep meditation he drew strength. He feared that, if he was afraid to confess Christ before men, Christ might deny him in front of the holy angels, and it seemed to him that he was guilty of a great crime in being ashamed of the sacraments of the humility of your Word, while not being ashamed of the sacrilegious rites of those proud demons, in which he, imitating their pride, had taken part. So he turned his pride against what was vain, and kept his humility for the truth. Quite suddenly and unexpectedly he said to Simplicianus, as Simplicianus himself told me, "Let us go to the Church. I want to be made a Christian." And Simplicianus, who could not contain himself for joy, went along with him. Soon after he had received instruction in the first mysteries, he gave in his name as one who wished to be regenerated by baptism. Rome wondered and the Church rejoiced. The proud *saw and were wroth; they gnashed with their teeth and melted away* (Ps. 112:10). But the Lord God was the hope of your servant, and he regarded not vanities and lying madness.

Finally the time came for him to make his profession of faith. At Rome this was usually done by those who were about to enter into your grace, and there was a fixed form of words which was learned by heart and spoken from a platform in the sight of the faithful. In the case of Victorinus, however, so Simplicianus told me, the priests gave him the opportunity to make his profession in a less public manner — as was often allowed to those who seemed likely to be frightened or embarrassed by the ceremony. But Victorinus preferred to declare openly his salvation in front of the holy congregation. In the past he had taught rhetoric, and there had been no salvation in that; yet he had publicly professed it. He had shown no nervousness when using his own words in front of crowds of people who could scarcely be described as sane; why, then, in front of your meek flock, should he fear to pronounce your Word? So, when he mounted the platform to make his profession, all those who knew him (and who was there who did not?) began to whisper his name one to another in glad murmurs. From the lips of the whole rejoicing people came the soft sound: "Victorinus, Victorinus." Quickly the sound had arisen because of the exultation they felt when they saw him, and now quickly they became silent again so as to hear him speak. With a fine confidence he declared openly the true faith, and they all wished that they could draw him into their very hearts. And in their love and their rejoicing (for these were the hands they used) they did take him into their hearts. . . .

When this man of yours, Simplicianus, told me all this about Victorinus, I was on fire to be like him, and this, of course, was why he had told me the story. He told me this too — that in the time of the Emperor Julian, when a law was passed forbidding Christians to teach literature and rhetoric, Victorinus had obeyed the law, preferring to give up his talking shop rather than your Word, by which you make even the tongues of infants eloquent. In this I thought that he was not only brave but lucky, because he had got the chance of giving all his time to you. This was just what I longed for myself, but I was held back, and I was held back not by fetters put on me by someone else, but by the iron bondage of my own will. The enemy held my will and made a chain of it and bound me with it. From a perverse will came lust, and slavery to lust became a habit, and the habit, being constantly yielded to, became a necessity. These were like links hanging each to each (which is why I called it a chain), and they held me fast in a hard slavery. And the new will which I was beginning to have and which urged me to worship you in freedom and to enjoy you, God, the only certain joy, was not yet strong enough to overpower the old will which by its oldness had grown hard in me. So my two wills, one old, one new, one carnal, one spiritual, were in conflict, and they wasted my soul by their discord.

In this way my personal experience enabled me to understand what I had read — that *the flesh lusteth against the spirit, and the spirit against the flesh* (Gal. 5:17). I, no doubt, was on both sides, but I was more myself when I was on the side which I approved of for myself than when I was on the side of which I disapproved. For it was no longer really I myself who was on this second side, since there to a great extent I was rather suffering things against my will than doing them voluntarily. Yet it was my own fault that habit fought back so strongly against me; for I had come willingly where I now did not will to be. And who has any right to complain when just punishment overtakes the sinner? Nor did I have any longer the excuse which I used to think I had when I said that the reason why I had not yet forsaken the world and given myself up to your service was because I could not see the truth clearly. Now I could see it perfectly clearly. But I was still tied down to earth and refused to take my place in your army. And I was just as frightened of being freed from all my hampering baggage as I ought to have been frightened of being hampered. The pack of this world was a kind of pleasant weight upon me, as happens in sleep, and the thoughts in which I meditated on you were like the efforts of someone who tries to get up but is so overcome with drowsiness that he sinks back again into sleep. Of course no one wants to sleep forever, and everyone in his senses would agree that it is better to be awake; yet all the same, when we feel a sort of lethargy in our limbs, we often put off the moment of shaking off sleep, and, even though it is time to get up, we gladly take a little longer in bed, conscious though we may be that we should not be doing so. In just the same way I was quite certain that it was better to give myself up to your charity rather than to give in to my own desires; but, though the former course was a conviction to which I gave my assent, the latter was a pleasure to which I gave my consent. For I had no answer to make to you when you called me: *Awake, thou that sleepest, and arise from the dead, and Christ shall give thee light* (Eph. 5:14). And, while you showed me wherever I looked that what you said was true, I, convinced by the truth, could still find nothing at all to say except lazy words spoken half asleep: "A minute," "just a minute," "just a little time longer." But there was no limit to the minutes, and the little time longer went a long way. It was in vain that *I delighted in Thy law according to the inner man, when another law in my members rebelled against the law of my mind, and led me captive under the law of sin which was in my members* (Rom. 7:22-23). For the law of sin is the strong force of habit, which drags the mind along and controls it even against its will — though deservedly, since the habit was voluntarily adopted. *Who then should deliver me thus wretched from the body of this death, but Thy grace only, through Jesus Christ our Lord?* (Rom. 7:24-25).

Now, Lord, my helper and my redeemer, I shall tell and confess to your name how it was that you freed me from the bondage of my desire for sex, in which I was so closely fettered, and from my slavery to the affairs of this world. I was leading my usual life; my anxiety was growing greater and greater, and every day I sighed to you. I went often to your Church, whenever I had time to spare from all that business, under the weight of which I was groaning. Alypius was with me. He was free from his official legal work after a third term as assessor and was now waiting to sell his legal advice to anyone who came along, just as I was selling the ability to make speeches — if such an ability can be imparted by teaching. Nebridius, as an act of friendship to us, had consented to teach under Verecundus, a great friend of us all, a citizen and elementary schoolmaster of Milan. He had been very eager to have Nebridius on his staff and indeed had claimed it as something due from our friendship that one of us should come and give him the help and support which he badly needed. Nebridius was not influenced by any desire for profit; he could have done better for himself by teaching literature, if he had wanted. But he was the kindest and best of friends, and, being always ready to help others, would not turn down our request. He conducted himself very carefully in his work, being unwilling to become known in what are regarded by the world as "distinguished circles," and avoiding everything which could disturb his peace of mind; for he wanted to have his mind free and at leisure for as many hours as possible so as to pursue wisdom, to read about it, or to hear about it.

One day, when Alypius and I were at home (Nebridius, for some reason which I cannot remember, was away), we were visited by a man called Ponticianus, coming from Africa, who was a fellow countryman of ours and who held an important appointment at the emperor's court. He had something or other which he wanted to ask us, and we sat down to talk. In front of us was a table for playing games on, and he happened to notice a book lying on the table. He took it, opened it, and found that it was the apostle Paul. He was quite surprised at this, since he had imagined it would be one of the books over which I wearied myself out in the course of my profession. Next he began to smile and, looking closely at me, told me that he was not only surprised but pleased at his unexpected discovery that I had this book and only this book at my side. For he was a Christian, and baptized. He often knelt before you, our God, in Church, praying long and frequently to you. I told him that I gave the greatest attention to these works of Scripture, and then, on his initiative, a conversation began about the Egyptian monk Antony, whose name was very well known among your servants, although Alypius and I up to this time had never heard of him. When Ponticianus discovered this, he talked all the more about him, since he wanted us in our ignorance, at which he was much surprised, to learn more about such a great man. And we were amazed as we heard of these wonderful works of yours, which had been witnessed by so many people, had been done in the true faith and the Catholic Church, and all so recently — indeed practically in our own times. All of us were full of wonder, Alypius and I at the importance of what we were hearing, Ponticianus at the fact that we had never heard the story before.

He went on to speak of the communities living in monasteries, of their way of life which was full of the sweet fragrance of you, and of the fruitful deserts in the wilderness, about which we knew nothing. There was actually a monastery in Milan outside the walls of the city. It was full of good brothers and was under the care of Ambrose, but we had not even heard of this. So Ponticianus went on speaking and we sat quietly, listening to him eagerly. In the course of his talk he told us how once, when the emperor was at Treves and busy with holding the chariot races in the Circus, he himself with three friends had gone for a walk in the afternoon through the gardens near the city walls. It happened that they walked in two groups, one of the three going one way with him, and the others going another way by themselves. These other two, as they strolled along, happened to come to a small house which was inhabited by some of your servants, *poor in spirit, of whom is the kingdom of heaven* (Matt. 5:3), and there they found a book in which was written an account of the life of Antony. One of the two friends began to read it. He became full of wonder and excitement, and, as he read, he began to think of how he himself could lead a life like this and, abandoning his profession in this world, give his service to you. For these two men were both officials in the emperor's civil service. Suddenly, then, he was filled with a holy love; he felt a sober shame, and, angry with himself, he looked toward his friend and said: "Tell me now; in all this hard work which we do, what are we aiming at? What is it that we want? Why is it that we are state officials? Can we have any higher hope at court than to become friends of the emperor? And is not that a position difficult to hold and full of danger? Indeed, does one not have to go through danger after danger simply to reach a place that is more dangerous still? And how long will it take to get there? But, if I want, I can be the friend of God now, this moment." After saying this, he turned back to the book, troubled and perplexed by the new life to which he was giving birth. So he read on, and his heart, where you saw it, was changed, and, as soon appeared, his mind shook off the burden of the world. While he was reading and the waves in his heart rose and fell, there were times when he cried out against himself, and then he distinguished the better course and chose it for his own. Now he was yours, and he said to his friend: "I have now broken away from all our hopes and ambitions and have decided to serve God, and I am entering on this service now, this moment, in this place. You may not like to imitate me in this, but you must not oppose me."

The other replied that he would stay with him and be his comrade in so great a service and for so great a reward. Both of them were now yours; they were building their own fortress at the right cost — namely, the forsaking of all that they had and the following of you.

At this point Ponticianus and his companion, who had been walking in a different part of the garden, looking for their friends, came and found them in this place. When they found them, they suggested that they should go back, as it was now nearly sunset. The others, however, told them of the decision which they had reached and what they proposed to do; they described how the whole thing had started and how their resolution was now fixed, and they begged their friends, if they would not join them, not to interfere with their purpose. Ponticianus and his friend, while not changing from their former ways, did (as Ponticianus told us) weep for themselves and, devoutly and sincerely congratulating the others, asked them to remember them in their prayers; then, with their own hearts still down on the earth, they went off to the palace. But the other two, with their hearts fixed on heaven, remained there in the cottage. Each of these two was engaged to be married, and when the girls to whom they were engaged heard what had happened, they also dedicated their virginity to you.

This was what Ponticianus told us. But you, Lord, while he was speaking, were turning me around so that I could see myself; you took me from behind my own back, which was where I had put myself during the time when I did not want to be observed by myself, and you set me in front of my own face so that I could see how foul a sight I was — crooked, filthy, spotted, and ulcerous. I saw and I was horrified, and I had nowhere to go to escape from myself. If I tried to look away from myself, Ponticianus still went on with his story, and again you were setting me in front of myself, forcing me to look into my own face, so that I might see my sin and hate it. I did know it, but I pretended that I did not. I had been pushing the whole idea away from me and forgetting it.

But now the more ardent was the love I felt for those two men of whom I was hearing and of how healthfully they had been moved to give themselves up entirely to you to be cured, the more bitter was the hatred I felt for myself when I compared myself with them. Many years (at least twelve) of my life had gone by since the time when I was nineteen and was reading Cicero's *Hortensius* and had been fired with an enthusiasm for wisdom. Yet I was still putting off the moment when, despising this world's happiness, I should give all my time to the search for that of which not only the finding but merely the seeking must be preferred to the discovered treasures and kingdoms of men or to all the pleasures of the body easily and abundantly available. But I, wretched young man that I was — even more wretched than at the beginning of my youth — had begged you for chastity and had said: "Make me chaste and continent, but not yet." I was afraid that you might hear me too soon and cure me too soon from the disease of a lust which I preferred to be satisfied rather than extinguished. And I had gone along evil ways, following a sacrilegious superstition — not because I was convinced by it, but simply preferring it to the other doctrines into which I never inquired in a religious spirit, but merely attacked them in a spirit of spite.

I had thought that the reason why I was putting off from day to day the time when I should despise all worldly hopes and follow you alone was because I could see no certainty toward which I could direct my course. But now the day had come when in my own eyes I was stripped naked and my conscience cried out against me: "Can you not hear me? Was it not this that you used to say, that you would not throw off the burden of vanity for a truth that was uncertain? Well, look. Now the truth is certain, and you are still weighed down by your burden. Yet these others, who have not been so worn out in the search and not been meditating the matter for ten years or more, have had the weight taken from their backs and have been given wings to fly."

So I was being gnawed at inside, and as Ponticianus went on with his story I was lost and overwhelmed in a terrible kind of shame. When the story was over and the business about which he had come had been settled, he went away, and I retired into myself. Nor did I leave anything unsaid against myself. With every scourge of condemnation I lashed my soul on to follow me now that I was trying to follow you. And my soul hung back; it refused to follow, and it could give no excuse for its refusal. All the arguments had been used already and had been shown to be false. There remained a mute shrinking; for it feared like death to be restrained from the flux of a habit by which it was melting away into death. . . .

And now from my hidden depths my searching thought had dragged up and set before the sight of my heart the whole mass of my misery. Then a huge storm rose up within me bringing with it a huge downpour of tears. So that I might pour out all these tears and speak the words that came with them I rose up from Alypius (solitude seemed better for the business of weeping) and went further away so that I might not be embarrassed even by his presence. This was how I felt, and he realized it. No doubt I had said something or other, and he could feel the weight of my tears in the sound of my voice. And so I rose to my feet, and he, in a state of utter amazement, remained in the place where we had been sitting. I flung myself down on the ground somehow under a fig tree and gave free rein to my tears; they streamed and flooded from my eyes, an *acceptable sacrifice to Thee* (1 Pet. 2:5). And I kept saying to you, not perhaps in these words, but with this sense: *"And Thou, O Lord, how long? How long, Lord; wilt Thou be angry forever? Remember not our former iniquities"* (Ps. 6:3). For I felt that it was these which were holding me fast. And in my misery I would exclaim: "How long, how long this 'tomorrow and tomorrow'? Why not now? Why not finish this very hour with my uncleanness?"

So I spoke, weeping in the bitter contrition of my heart. Suddenly a voice reaches my ears from a nearby house. It is the voice of a boy or a girl (I don't know which), and in a kind of singsong the words are constantly repeated: "Take it and read it. Take it and read it." At once my face changed, and I began to think carefully of whether the singing of words like these came into any kind of game which children play, and I could not remember that I had ever heard anything like it before. I checked the force of my tears and rose to my feet, being quite certain that I must interpret this as a divine command to me to open the book and read the first passage which I should come upon. For I had heard this about Antony: he had happened to come in when the Gospel was being read, and as though the words read were spoken directly to himself, had received the admonition: *Go, sell all that thou hast, and give to the poor, and thou shalt have treasure in heaven, and come and follow me* (Matt. 19:21). And by such an oracle he had been immediately converted to you.

So I went eagerly back to the place where Alypius was sitting, since it was there that I had left the book of the Apostle when I rose to my feet. I snatched up the book, opened it, and read in silence the passage upon which my eyes first fell: *Not in reveling and drunkenness, not in debauchery and licentiousness, not in quarreling and jealousy. Instead, put on the Lord Jesus Christ, and make no provision for the flesh, to gratify its desires* (Rom. 13:13-14). I had no wish to read further; there was no need to. For immediately I had reached the end of this sentence it was as though my heart was filled with a light of confidence and all the shadows of my doubt were swept away.

Before shutting the book I put my finger or some other marker in the place and told Alypius what had happened. By now my face was perfectly calm. And Alypius in his turn told me what had been going on in himself, and which I knew nothing about. He asked to see the passage which I had read. I showed him, and he went on further than the part I had read, nor did I know the words which followed. They were these: *Him that is weak in the faith, receive* (Rom. 14:1). He applied this to himself and told me so. He was strengthened by the admonition; calmly and unhesitatingly he joined me in a purpose and a resolution so good, and so right for his character, which had always been very much better than mine.

The next thing we do is to go inside and tell my mother. How happy she is! We describe to her how it all took place, and there is no limit to her joy and triumph. Now she was praising you, *Who art able to do above that which we ask or think* (Eph. 3:20); for she saw that with regard to me you had given her so much more than she used to ask for when she wept so pitifully before you. For you converted me to you in such a way that I no longer sought a wife nor any other worldly hope. I was now standing on that rule of faith, just as you had shown me to her in a vision so many years before. And so you had changed her mourning into joy, a joy much richer than she had desired and much dearer and purer than that which she looked for by having grandchildren of my flesh.

Book IX

O Lord, I am Thy servant; I am Thy servant and the son of Thy handmaid: Thou hast broken my bonds in sunder. I will offer to Thee the sacrifice of praise (Ps. 116:16-17). Let my heart and my tongue praise you, and let *all my bones say, O Lord, who is like unto Thee?* (Ps. 35:10). Let them speak, and then, Lord, answer me and *say unto my soul, I am thy salvation* (Ps. 35:10). . . .

Now my mind was free of those gnawing cares that came from ambition and the desire for gain and wallowing in filth and scratching the itching scab of lust. And now I was talking to you easily and simply, my brightness and my riches and my health, my Lord God.

And I decided in your sight that, without making any violent gesture, I would gently withdraw from a position where I was making use of my tongue in the talking-shop; no longer should my young students (who were not so much interested in your law and your peace as in absurd deceptions and legal battles) buy from my mouth material for arming their own madness. And luckily it happened that there were only a few days more before the Vintage Vacation, and I decided to endure them so that I might retire from the profession in a regular way. I had been bought by you and was not going to return again to put myself up for sale. So our plan was known to you, but not known to men — except to our own friends. We had agreed among ourselves not to let the news out at all, although, as we were making our way up from *the valley of tears* (Ps. 84:6) and singing that *song of degrees,* you had given us *sharp arrows* and *destroying coals* (Ps. 120:3-4) against the subtle tongues of people who, under a show of care for us, would try to thwart us and by loving us would eat us up, as men do with their food.

You had shot through our hearts with your charity, and we carried about with us your words like arrows fixed deep in our flesh; stored up in the recesses of our thought were the examples of your servants whose darkness you had turned to light and whose death to life, and so that heavy sluggishness of ours that might have dragged us down again to the depths was utterly burned up and consumed. So much on fire were we that all the blasts of the subtle tongue of contradiction, so far from extinguishing the fire, only made it burn more fiercely. However, because of your name, which you have sanctified throughout the earth, there would no doubt also be people who would praise the resolution and vows which we had taken, and I thought it would look like ostentation if, instead of waiting for the vacation which was now so close, I should resign from a public position which every one knew about. All eyes would be upon me and upon what I had done; it would be noticed that I had not wished to wait for the day of the Vintage, although it was so close, and there would be much talk of me to the effect that I wanted to make myself seem important. And what good would it do me to have people thinking and talking about my state of mind and to have *our good to be evil spoken of* (Rom. 14:16)?

There was also the fact that that summer my lungs had begun to give way as the result of overwork in teaching. I found it difficult to breathe deeply; pains in the chest were evidence of the injury and made it impossible for me to speak loudly or for long at a time. At first this had distressed me, since I was being almost forced and compelled to give up this burden of teaching — or, at any rate, if I were able to be cured and made well again, to give it up for the time being. But now my will in its entirety had arisen and was set on having leisure and on seeing *how that Thou art the Lord* (Ps. 46:10), and from this moment I began actually to be pleased that in this illness also I had quite a genuine excuse to soften the injured feelings of those parents who, so that their children might be free to learn, wanted me never to be free at all. And so, filled with such joy as this, I put up with the interval of time — I think it was about twenty days — which still had to pass. But I needed some resolution to do this. What had helped me in the past to bear my hard labor had been the desire to make money. The desire had now gone, and, if its place had not been taken by patience, I should have been quite overwhelmed by staying on at my work. Some of your servants, my brothers, may say that I sinned in this, because, with my heart fully set on your service, I continued to hold even for one hour my professorship of lies. It may be so. But I know that you, most merciful Lord, have pardoned and remitted this sin too along with any other terrible and deadly sins in the holy water of Baptism.

2

Called to a Religious Life:
Vocations in the Middle Ages, 500-1500

Introduction

Some European towns still preserve their medieval shape. Coming across the plains of central France to Chartres, or along the river meadows to Salisbury in England, one sees the massive cathedral towering over everything else. It is a good symbol of the pattern of medieval vocations. In most modern cities, the largest buildings belong to major banks, hospitals, office towers for lawyers and businesspeople, government agencies, perhaps a university. Churches mostly sit in the shadow of something else. Perhaps our skyline mirrors the prominence of vocational options. But in Europe for more than a thousand years, churches dominated — both physically and vocationally. The central vocational questions for most medieval Christians was whether to choose a celibate life in service of the church.

Somewhere around the year 400 the western part of the Roman Empire collapsed; masses of Germanic peoples moved through the former empire more or less at will. In the seventh and eighth centuries, Muslim armies conquered North Africa, home to most of the writers included in the previous chapter but after about 700 no longer a part of the Christian world. With the collapse of empire, trade became difficult, and therefore cities and specialized crafts diminished. The standard medieval social division was among those who pray (priests, nuns, and monks), those who fight (the nobles), and those who work (mostly peasants in the fields). Except for church officials, for several centuries in the early Middle Ages almost no one could read and write. Charlemagne, the greatest ruler of the era and a man deeply committed to education and culture, could read but never really learned to write. (We still speak of church officials as "clerics" and people whose work involves writing as "clerks," preserving the medieval identification of churchfolk and the literate.)

The Monastic World

Things were different in monasteries. Even in the north of England in the dark years around 700, the monk Bede wrote books on everything from astronomy to the Bible, quoting a range of classical authors and church fathers in both Latin and Greek. Monastic libraries preserved the only surviving copies of many Roman and Greek works; monastic schools provided virtually the only places to study.

Western monasticism drew initial inspiration from the deserts of Egypt. Around 400, John Cassian moved from Egypt to southern France, and by his personal example and his writings did much to introduce monasticism to western Europe. About the same time, Martin of Tours offered another characteristic example of the transition from the Roman to the early medieval world — a Roman soldier who became a monk and then a bishop, providing leadership from a monastery to guide the church through difficult times. But monks were generally different in the West than they had been in Egypt: much more likely to live as part of a community, less inclined to extremes of self-denial. Benedict of Nursia, who lived in southern Italy around 500, had originally withdrawn into a cave to live as a hermit, but followers gathered around him, and he founded several monasteries and wrote a "rule" to guide them. In the 800s, it became the standard rule for life in virtually all the monasteries of western Europe. By most modern standards, Benedict's rule demands a very tough life, but what struck many of his contemporaries was its moderation and common sense.

In *The City of God* Augustine, another great influence on Western monasticism, sketched the story of the two "cities" whose history runs through every era. One, founded by Cain, the son of Adam and Eve who murdered his brother, is the "city of man," focused on self-love and worldly glory, and destined at best for the temporary peace of this-worldly truces. In contrast, the "city of God," founded by Cain's brother Abel, focuses on love of God and is destined for the eternal peace of the heavenly kingdom.

Augustine remained carefully ambiguous about just who belonged to which city, but in the early Middle Ages most people would have agreed that it was generally those who lived in monasteries and convents who were citizens of the City of God. They were "religious"; they had "vocations." One image for the heavenly realm was the *city* of God, but perhaps an even more popular one was the *garden* of paradise, and the monastery or convent, with its fields and walls and peaceful cycle of daily prayer, was the earthly manifestation of the heavenly garden. In their daily round of chanted psalms and prayers, the nuns and monks approximated the heavenly court where God's praises are sung eternally, and thus they were already halfway to that other world.

Theme and Variations

Monastic reality, of course, often failed to live up to that ideal, and monasticism was in regular need of reform. In the 900s the French monastery at Cluny led a reform effort that focused on a return to the original ideals of Benedict. Where each Benedictine community had traditionally been independent, however, the Cluniacs founded daughter houses under the supervision of the abbot of Cluny. Tighter control meant, at least in theory, higher standards.

In the 1100s another French abbey, Cîteaux, became the center of another reform movement, soon energized by a young French monk named Bernard, trained at Cîteaux and then abbot of a nearby "Cistercian" (the adjective for Cîteaux) monastery at Clairvaux and, as preacher, writer, theologian, and mystic, one of the most influential people in the Europe of his time. Cluniac monasteries were aesthetically grand; the Cistercians favored a far more austere design. Bernard claimed that he had never noticed how many windows there were in the church where he had prayed for many years — he did not care about such worldly matters.[1] Writing in a biblical commentary on the word "Jerusalem," he explained, "Jerusalem means those who, in this world, lead the religious life." In a letter he was more specific: "And if you must know, I am speaking of Clairvaux (his own monastery). There one can find a Jerusalem associated with the heavenly one through the heart's complete devotion."[2]

Though many were pledged by their parents to the monastic life when they were small children, callings still came to adults. Monks wrote their friends and relatives, inviting them to join in the wonderful new life they had found. Sometimes, like college recruiters today, monks made a pitch for their own monastery in contrast to others — Cluny and Cîteaux were particularly competitive, and occasionally even had to struggle with mutual tensions when a young man ran away from one to join the other. Yet all these orders followed basically the same Benedictine pattern of withdrawal to a communal life of prayer and liturgy.

In the 1200s a different kind of order appeared — Dominicans and Franciscans, "friars" rather than monks. Francis of Assisi, son of an Italian mer-

---

1. But his prose is beautiful. "These Cistercians have renounced everything save the art of good writing." Etienne Gilson, *The Mystical Theology of Saint Bernard* (London: Sheed & Ward, 1940), 63.

2. Bernard, *On the Song of Songs* 55.2, *Patrologia Latina* 183:1045; Letter 64, *Patrologia Latina* 182:169, quoted in Jean LeClercq, *The Love of Learning and the Desire for God*, trans. Catharine Misrahi (New York: Fordham University Press, 1961), 60.

chant, found himself called to a life of radical poverty — at first, he even gave away all his clothes. He and his followers resisted owning property and worked to care for lepers and other despised outsiders of their society. Benedictine monks, to be sure, prayed for the whole world, but their primary vocation was to work out their own salvation. Franciscans, after the model of their founder, also actively cared for others. At about the same time as Francis, a Spaniard named Dominic similarly gave away all his possessions to help the poor. But Dominic sensed a different calling. Heretics like the Cathars in southern France had turned away from the faith of the church; church leaders were organizing crusades to kill them off. Dominic wanted, if possible, to *persuade* them back into the fold; he thought the church needed more effective and better-educated preachers. The Order of Preachers or Dominicans he founded soon came to be among the educational leaders of the church.

Like Benedictine monks, Franciscans and Dominicans (who both soon had orders of women as well as men) formed groups with special rules and lives dedicated to God. But their vocations were also directed more toward their neighbors: as examples — poor folks who had given up everything for Christ, begging on the roadside or in the town — or as teachers and preachers. It was a life very different from that in a distinguished monastery. When he was growing up amid the nobility of southern Italy in the early 1200s, Thomas Aquinas's family had him earmarked to join the local Benedictine monastery and, given his own abilities and the family's connections, eventually become its abbot, a powerful official in the whole region. Instead, Thomas ran away and joined the Dominicans; his family was so horrified that they had him kidnapped and imprisoned for most of a year before yielding to his own sense of vocation. Called to the "religious" life, but also to activities like teaching and writing, Aquinas, the greatest theologian of the Middle Ages, struggled to sort out the relations of the active and contemplative lives and the importance of the "religious" life with its vows of poverty, chastity, and obedience.

The Franciscans and Dominicans were much more engaged in ordinary life than Benedictines, but they remained orders separated out and committed to rules of poverty, chastity, and obedience. Beginning in the twelfth century, a few Christians in the Netherlands began to explore a sort of compromise position between lay and "religious" life. Beguines (the women) and Beghards (the men) lived in communities and devoted themselves particularly to prayer and charity. But they held regular jobs, kept some private property, took no permanent vows, and could leave the community and get married if they wished. This exploration of an alternative to monasticism alarmed many church authorities, and Beguines and Beghards regularly faced persecution.

A couple of centuries later, the Netherlands saw the beginning of a similar movement. About 1375 a Dutch merchant named Geert Grote gave away his wealth and lived for a while in a monastery. He found the monastic life unsatisfactory, however, and got himself ordained a deacon and granted a special license to preach. His preaching, often highly critical of local priests, won many supporters, who began to meet in private homes after the model of the first apostles. These members of the "New Devout" (*Devotio Moderna*) supported themselves by copying books and making textiles and lace. They took no vows and attended their local parishes rather than forming separate religious communities. In the language of the time, they were "devout" without being "religious."[3] Grote's influence also contributed to the founding of the Windesheim Congregation, which much more nearly fit the pattern of a traditional monastery but preserved many of the themes and attitudes characteristic of the New Devout. These circles produced one of the most famous devotional works in the history of Christianity, *The Imitation of Christ*, probably written by Thomas à Kempis, a remarkable effort to think through how an ordinary Christian can in some sense lead a "religious" life.

What about Everybody Else?

I have been focusing on monks, and that leaves too many other people out of the story. First, nearly everything said about monks and monasteries can also be said about nuns and convents. In the Middle Ages they were just as numerous and as important. Indeed, these communities of women were in some ways more remarkable, for, in a patriarchal society, they allowed women to advance to positions of significant leadership. Other than the occasional queen born into the job, the abbesses of great convents were the most powerful women in medieval Europe, and nuns were the most important women writers. One author included in this chapter, Mechthild von Magdeburg, illustrates that common pattern. Another, however, radically broke it. In the late fourteenth century, Christine de Pisan, finding herself a widow at 25, figured out a way to support herself as a professional writer, an almost unheard of accomplishment in the Middle Ages. She reminds us that generalizations about the role of women in medieval society, like most generalizations, always admit of exceptions.

Of course family connections and social influence always counted, but,

3. See John van Engen, "Introduction," in *Devotio Moderna: Basic Writings* (New York: Paulist, 1988), 13-14.

for both men and women, the church offered more social mobility than any other part of society. For most medieval people, as the historian Jacques Le Goff puts it, one's duty "was to remain where God had placed him. Rising in society was a sign of pride; demotion was a shameful sin."[4] Few opportunities arose for the child of a peasant to become a knight or a noble lady. But — although even in the church noble birth usually helped one's career — a poor boy could end up a bishop, a peasant's daughter could become an abbess.

Medieval people rarely talked about other kinds of "callings." To have a *vocatio* meant to be on the way to becoming a monk, nun, friar, or priest. Even parish priests (often ill-educated) were generally thought to have failed to go all the way to the heights of the monastic life. Some biographies of monarchs, nobles, and knights pictured them as serving God in their roles in ordinary life, but the most admirable start to sound like monks, so dominant was the monastic ideal. Moreover, in the basic divisions of medieval society, monarchs and nobles were classified as "those who *fought*." Medieval writers could recognize the need for good fighters and even praise their courage and skill, but war and Christian calling always remained in some tension. It is not always sinful to wage war, Thomas Aquinas admitted, but it is wrong for clerics to participate, since "warlike pursuits are full of unrest, so that they hinder the mind very much from the contemplation of Divine things, the praise of God, and prayers for the people, which belong to the duties of a cleric."[5] Waging a just war is meritorious, but incompatible with the duties of a cleric, which are "more meritorious still."[6] Still, a king like Louis IX of France could manifest all the Christian virtues as a ruler and warrior. And Joan of Arc could lead French troops to battle inspired by the most direct kind of "calling" — the voices of saints that spoke to her.

Trade and commerce ranked even lower than fighting on the medieval scale. The medieval church consistently condemned usury (loaning money at interest) as a sin, and Aquinas worried at length over whether it is intrinsically dishonest to sell something for more than the price for which you bought it. In such cases one was somehow making money without producing any product, and that looked fishy. In Aquinas's words, "Hence trading, considered in itself, has a certain debasement attaching thereto, in so far as, by its very nature, it does not imply a virtuous or necessary end."[7] Could

---

4. Jacques Le Goff, "Introduction," in *Medieval Callings*, ed. Jacques Le Goff, trans. Lydia G. Cochrane (Chicago: University of Chicago Press, 1990), 34.

5. Thomas Aquinas, *Summa Theologica* 2a2ae.40.2, trans. Fathers of the English Dominican Province (Westminster, Md.: Christian Classics, 1981), 1355.

6. *ST* 2a2ae.40.2 ad 4, 1356.

7. *ST* 2a2ae.77.4, 1511.

one claim a calling from God to such a rather degraded role? Many medieval writers were inclined to doubt it.

If medieval laypeople thought of themselves as having a calling at all, that calling probably had to do with family rather than job. In our age of worries about overpopulation, we can forget that for most pre-modern societies the challenge was to produce enough children to keep the population from declining. Given the high rate of infant mortality, a typical medieval woman needed to have nine children in order to keep the adult population at stable levels. Work was not about finding fulfillment or even directly contributing to the glory of God; it was mostly about supporting one's family.

Medieval to Modern

Monastic orders still attract some Catholic men and women, and there are even a few Protestant monastic communities. But we seem unlikely ever to return to the days when the possibility of a call to the monastic life was *the* central vocational question for most Christians. What then can we learn from medieval reflections on vocation?

First, we learn something about the rhythms of life. Bernard of Clairvaux talked about the importance of *otium,* leisure, in the monastic life, though he admitted it could be a *negotiosissimum* otium, a "very busy leisure." Getting up at two every morning for early prayers may not be our idea of leisure, but the round of prayer, study, and work in the monastic day remained relatively free of interruptions and distractions. Unlike most of us, medieval monks and nuns chose a life that left plenty of time for disciplined thinking about God. We twenty-first-century folk are so focused on doing that we can forget about being.

Second, from Benedictine moderation to Franciscan radical poverty, medievals who chose the "religious" life cultivated simplicity. "Fastings, vigils, meditation on the Scriptures, self-denial, and the giving up of all possessions," John Cassian wrote, "are not perfection, but aids to perfection."[8] But, most medieval theologians thought, they were important aids. Self-denial took away distractions and also freed one to devote oneself to God without feeling the guilt of taking advantage of others. Whether you lived off monastic land or begged, you were at any rate not taking more than what would fulfill your very basic needs.

8. John Cassian, *Conferences,* First Conference of Abbot Moses 7, in *Nicene and Post-Nicene Fathers,* 2d ser., trans. Edgar C. S. Gibson, 11:298.

Third, in terms of this world, there is a wonderful impracticality to medieval monasticism. Monks did not feed the hungry or improve social conditions; their work as teachers and preservers of culture was secondary to their true calling. They prayed and prepared themselves for death. Most modern folk are so eager to justify religious activities in terms of the social goods they serve that we are embarrassed to celebrate them as ends in themselves.

When the first Christian missionaries came to the kingdom of Northumbria in northern England in the early seventh century, one of the king's counselors advised adopting this new faith:

> When we compare the present life of man on earth with that time of which we have no knowledge, it seems to me like the swift flight of a single sparrow through the banqueting-hall . . . on a winter's day. . . . In the midst there is a comforting fire to warm the hall; outside the storms of winter rain or snow are raging. This sparrow flies swiftly in through one door of the hall and out through another. . . . Even so, man appears on earth for a little while; but of what went before this life or of what follows, we know nothing. Therefore, if this new teaching has brought any more certain knowledge, it seems only right that we should follow it.[9]

We are likely to live much longer than most medieval folk, but life remains but a short flight between what can seem from our perspective one darkness and another. The ways in which some medieval people thought of their vocations remind Christians today that, pilgrims and travelers that we are in this world, we ought to direct our lives toward thinking about the light that lies in the dark mystery beyond death.

---

9. Bede, *A History of the English Church and People* 2.13, trans. Leo Sherley-Price (Harmondsworth, Middlesex: Penguin, 1968), 127.

JOHN CASSIAN

Institutes

John Cassian (about 360-435) spent his youth among the monks of Egypt
but then moved west, founding two monasteries near Marseilles in southern France. He was a key figure in introducing monasticism to western Europe, where this calling would become so influential throughout the Middle Ages. In these selections, Cassian talks about the rigorous rules for
entering a monastery and the importance of absolute poverty for a monk.
He then discusses the sin of *accidie*, variously translated as "sloth" or "depression," the restlessness in which a monk cannot either work or pray.

Book 4

3. *Of the ordeal by which one who is to be received in the monastery is tested.*

One, then, who seeks to be admitted to the discipline of the monastery
is never received before he gives, by lying outside the doors for ten days or
even longer, an evidence of his perseverance and desire, as well as of humility and patience. And when, prostrate at the feet of all the brethren that pass
by, and deliberately repelled and scorned by all of them, as if he was wanting
to enter the monastery not for the sake of religion but because he was
obliged; and when, too, covered with many insults and affronts, he has
given a practical proof of his steadfastness, and has shown what he will be
like in temptations by the way he has borne the disgrace; and when, with the
ardor of his soul thus ascertained, he is admitted, then they enquire with the
utmost care whether he is contaminated by a single coin from his former

John Cassian, *Institutes*, in *Nicene and Post-Nicene Fathers*, trans. Edgar C. S. Gibson (Peabody,
Mass.: Hendrickson, 1994), 2d ser., 11:219-20, 222, 231, 239-42, 266-68.

possessions clinging to him. For they know that he cannot stay for long under the discipline of the monastery, nor ever learn the virtue of humility and obedience, nor be content with the poverty and difficult life of the monastery, if he knows that ever so small a sum of money has been kept hid; but, as soon as ever a disturbance arises on some occasion or other, he will at once dart off from the monastery like a stone from a sling, impelled to this by trusting in that sum of money.

4. The reason why those who are received in the monastery are not allowed to bring anything in with them.

And for these reasons they do not agree to take from him money to be used even for the good of the monastery: First, in case he may be puffed up with arrogance, owing to this offering, and so not agree to put himself on a level with the poorer brethren; and next, lest he fail through this pride of his to stoop to the humility of Christ, and so, when he cannot hold out under the discipline of the monastery, leave it, and afterwards, when he has cooled down, want in a bad spirit to receive and get back — not without loss to the monastery — what he had contributed in the early days of his renunciation, when he was aglow with spiritual fervor. And that this rule should always be kept they have been frequently taught by many instances. For in some monasteries where they are not so careful some who have been received unreservedly have afterwards tried most sacrilegiously to demand a return of that which they had contributed and which had been spent on God's work.

5. The reason why those who give up the world, when they are received in the monasteries, must lay aside their own clothes and be clothed in others by the Abbot.

Wherefore each one on his admission is stripped of all his former possessions, so that he is not allowed any longer to keep even the clothes which he has on his back: but in the council of the brethren he is brought forward into the midst and stripped of his own clothes, and clad by the Abbot's hands in the dress of the monastery, so that by this he may know not only that he has been despoiled of all his old things, but also that he has laid aside all worldly pride, and come down to the want and poverty of Christ, and that he is now to be supported not by wealth sought for by the world's arts, nor by anything reserved from his former state of unbelief, but that he is to receive out of the holy and sacred funds of the monastery his rations for his service; and that, as he knows that he is thence to be clothed and fed and that he has nothing of his own, he may learn, nevertheless, not to be anxious about the morrow, according to the saying of the Gospel, and may not be ashamed to be on a level with the poor, that is, with the body of the brethren, with whom Christ was not ashamed to be numbered, and to call himself their brother, but that rather he may glory that he has been made to share the lot of his own servants. . . .

13. How wrong it is considered for anyone to say that anything, however trifling, is his own.

Among their other practices I fancy that it is unnecessary even to mention this virtue, namely, that no one is allowed to possess a box or basket as his special property, nor any such thing which he could keep as his own and secure with his own seal, as we are well aware that they are in all respects stripped so bare that they have nothing whatever except their shirt, cloak, shoes, sheepskin, and rush mat; for in other monasteries as well, where some indulgence and relaxation is granted, we see that this rule is still most strictly kept, so that no one ventures to say even in word that anything is his own; and it is a great offence if there drops from the mouth of a monk such an expression as "my book," "my tablets," "my pen," "my coat," or "my shoes"; and for this he would have to make satisfaction by a proper penance, if by accident some such expression escaped his lips through thoughtlessness or ignorance. . . .

36. How our renunciation of the world is of no use if we are again entangled in those things which we have renounced.

Beware therefore lest at any time you take again any of those things which you renounced and forsook, and, contrary to the Lord's command, return from the field of evangelical work, and be found to have clothed yourself again in your coat which you had stripped off; neither sink back to the low and earthly lusts and desires of this world, and in defiance of Christ's word come down from the roof of perfection and dare to take up again any of those things which you have renounced and forsaken. Beware that you remember nothing of your kinsfolk or of your former affections, and that you are not called back to the cares and anxieties of this world, and (as our Lord says) putting your hand to the plough and looking back be found unfit for the kingdom of heaven (Luke 9:62). Beware lest at any time, when you have begun to dip into the knowledge of the Psalms and of this life, you be little by little puffed up and think of reviving that pride which now at your beginning you have trampled under foot in the ardor of faith and in fullest humility; and thus (as the Apostle says) building again those things which you had destroyed, you make yourself a backslider (Gal. 2:18). But rather take heed to continue even to the end in that state of nakedness of which you made profession in the sight of God and of his angels. In this humility too and patience, with which you persevered for ten days before the doors and entreated with many tears to be admitted into the monastery, you should not only continue but also increase and go forward. For it is too bad that when you ought to be carried on from the rudiments and beginnings, and go forward to perfection, you should begin to fall back from these to worse things. For not he who begins these things, but he who endures in them to the end, shall be saved. . . .

39. *Of the way in which we shall mount towards perfection, whereby we may afterwards ascend from the fear of God up to love.*

"The beginning" of our salvation and the safeguard of it is, as I said, "the fear of the Lord" (Prov. 1:7). For through this those who are trained in the way of perfection can gain a start in conversion as well as purification from vices and security in virtue. And when this has gained an entrance into a man's heart it produces contempt of all things, and begets a forgetfulness of kinsfolk and a horror of the world itself. But by the contempt for the loss of all possessions humility is gained. And humility is attested by these signs: First of all, if a man has all his desires mortified; secondly, if he conceals none of his actions or even of his thoughts from his superior; thirdly, if he puts no trust in his own opinion, but all in the judgment of his superior, and listens eagerly and willingly to his directions; fourthly, if he maintains in everything obedience and gentleness and constant patience; fifthly, if he not only hurts nobody else, but also is not annoyed or vexed at wrongs done to himself; sixthly, if he does nothing and ventures on nothing to which he is not urged by the Common Rule or by the example of our elders; seventhly, if he is contented with the lowest possible position, and considers himself a bad workman and unworthy in the case of everything enjoined to him; eighthly, if he does not only outwardly profess with his lips that he is inferior to all, but really believes it in the inmost thoughts of his heart; ninthly, if he governs his tongue, and is not over talkative; tenthly, if he is not easily moved or too ready to laugh. For by such signs and the like is true humility recognized. And when this has once been genuinely secured, then at once it leads you on by a still higher step to love which knows no fear; and through this you begin, without any effort and as it were naturally, to keep up everything that you formerly observed not without fear of punishment; no longer now from regard of punishment or fear of it but from love of goodness itself, and delight in virtue. . . .

Book 5

15. *How a monk must always be eager to preserve his purity of heart.*

It is like the case when one endeavors to strike some mighty prize of virtue on high pointed out by some very small mark; with the keenest eyesight he points the aim of his dart, knowing that large rewards of glory and prizes depend on his hitting it; and he turns away his gaze from every other consideration, and must direct it there, where he sees that the reward and prize is placed, because he would be sure to lose the prize of his skill and the reward of his prowess if the keenness of his gaze should be diverted ever so little. . . .

19. *That the athlete of Christ, so long as he is in the body, is never without a battle.*

The athlete of Christ, as long as he is in the body, is never in want of a victory to be gained in contests: but in proportion as he grows by triumphant successes, so does a severer kind of struggle confront him. For when the flesh is subdued and conquered, what swarms of foes, what hosts of enemies are incited by his triumphs and rise up against the victorious soldier of Christ! for fear lest in the ease of peace the soldier of Christ might relax his efforts and begin to forget the glorious struggles of his contests, and be rendered slack through the idleness which is caused by immunity from danger, and be cheated of the reward of his prizes and the recompense of his triumphs.

And so if we want to rise with ever-growing virtue to these stages of triumph, we ought also in the same way to enter the lists of battle and begin by saying with the Apostle: "I so fight, not as one that beats the air, but I chastise my body and bring it into subjection" (1 Cor. 9:26-27), that when this conflict is ended we may once more be able to say with him: "we wrestle not against flesh and blood, but against principalities, against powers, against world-rulers of this darkness, against spiritual wickedness in heavenly places" (Eph. 6:12). For otherwise we cannot possibly join battle with them nor deserve to make trial of spiritual combats if we are baffled in a physical contest, and knocked down in a struggle with the belly: and deservedly will it be said of us by the Apostle in the language of blame: "Temptation does not overtake you, except what is common to man" (1 Cor. 10:13).

20. *How a monk should not overstep the proper hours for taking food, if he wants to proceed to the struggle of interior conflicts.*

A monk therefore who wants to proceed to the struggle of interior conflicts should lay down this as a precaution for himself to begin with, that he will not in any case allow himself to be overcome by any delicacies, or take anything to eat or drink before the fast is over and the proper hour for refreshment has come, outside meal times; nor, when the meal is over, will he allow himself to take a morsel however small; and likewise that he will observe the canonical time and measure of sleep. For that self-indulgence must be cut off in the same way that the sin of unchastity has to be rooted out. For if a man is unable to check the unnecessary desires of the appetite, how will he be able to extinguish the fire of bodily lust? And if a man is not able to control passions, which are openly manifest and are but small, how will he be able with temperate discretion to fight against those which are secret, and excite him, when none are there to see? And therefore strength of mind is tested in separate impulses and in any sort of passion, and if it is overcome in the case of very small and manifest desires, how it will endure in those that are really great and powerful and hidden, each man's conscience must witness for himself.

21. Of the inward peace of a monk, and of spiritual abstinence.

For it is not an external enemy whom we have to dread. Our foe is shut up within ourselves, an internal warfare is daily waged by us, and if we are victorious in this, all external things will be made weak, and everything will be made peaceful and subdued for the soldier of Christ. We shall have no external enemy to fear, if what is within is overcome and subdued to the spirit. And let us not believe that that external fast from visible food alone can possibly be sufficient for perfection of heart and purity of body unless with it there has also been united a fast of the soul. For the soul also has its foods which are harmful, fattened on which, even without superfluity of meats, it is involved in a downfall of wantonness. Slander is its food, and indeed one that is very dear to it. A burst of anger also is its food, even if it be a very slight one; yet supplying it with miserable food for an hour, and destroying it as well with its deadly savor. Envy is a food of the mind, corrupting it with its poisonous juices and never ceasing to make it wretched and miserable at the prosperity and success of another. Vainglory is its food, which gratifies it with a delicious meal for a time; but afterwards strips it clear and bare of all virtue, and dismisses it barren and void of all spiritual fruit, so that it makes it not only lose the rewards of huge labors, but also makes it incur heavier punishments. All lust and shifty wanderings of heart are a sort of food for the soul, nourishing it on harmful meats, but leaving it afterwards without share of the heavenly bread and of really solid food. If then, with all the powers we have, we abstain from these in a most holy fast, our observance of the bodily fast will be both useful and profitable. For labor of the flesh, when joined with contrition of the spirit, will produce a sacrifice that is most acceptable to God, and a worthy shrine of holiness in the pure and undefiled inmost chambers of the heart. But if, while fasting as far as the body is concerned, we are entangled in the most dangerous vices of the soul, our humiliation of the flesh will do us no good whatever, while the most precious part of us is defiled: since we go wrong through that substance by virtue of which we are made a shrine of the Holy Ghost. For it is not so much the corruptible flesh as the clean heart which is made a shrine for God, and a temple of the Holy Ghost. We ought therefore, whenever the outward man fasts, to restrain the inner man as well from food which is bad for him: that inner man, namely, which the blessed Apostle above all urges us to present pure before God, that it may be found worthy to receive Christ as a guest within, saying "that in the inner man Christ may dwell in your hearts through faith" (Eph. 3:16-17). . . .

Book 10

1. How our sixth combat is against the spirit of *accidie*, and what its character is.

Our sixth combat is with what the Greeks call *accidie*, which we may term "weariness" or "distress of heart." This is akin to dejection, and is especially trying to solitaries, and a dangerous and frequent foe to dwellers in the desert; and especially disturbing to a monk about the sixth hour, like some fever which seizes him at stated times, bringing the burning heat of its attacks on the sick man at usual and regular hours. Lastly, there are some of the elders who declare that this is the "midday demon" spoken of in the ninetieth Psalm.

2. A description of *accidie*, and the way in which it creeps over the heart of a monk, and the injury it inflicts on the soul.

And when this has taken possession of some unhappy soul, it produces dislike of the place, disgust with the cell, and disdain and contempt of the brethren who dwell with him or at a little distance, as if they were careless or unspiritual. It also makes the man lazy and sluggish about all manner of work which has to be done within the enclosure of his dormitory. It does not suffer him to stay in his cell, or to take any pains about reading, and he often groans because he can do no good while he stays there, and complains and sighs because he can bear no spiritual fruit so long as he is joined to that society; and he complains that he is cut off from spiritual gain, and is of no use in the place, as if he were one who, though he could govern others and be useful to a great number of people, yet was edifying none, nor profiting any one by his teaching and doctrine. He praises distant monasteries and those which are a long way off, and describes such places as more profitable and better suited for salvation; and besides this he paints the intercourse with the brethren there as sweet and full of spiritual life. On the other hand, he says that everything about him is rough, and not only that there is nothing edifying among the brethren who are stopping there, but also that even food for the body cannot be procured without great difficulty. Lastly he fancies that he will never be well while he stays in that place, unless he leaves his cell (in which he is sure to die if he stays in it any longer) and takes himself off from there as quickly as possible. Then the fifth or sixth hour brings him such bodily weariness and longing for food that he seems to himself worn out and wearied as if with a long journey, or some very heavy work, or as if he had put off taking food during a fast of two or three days. Then besides this he looks about anxiously this way and that, and sighs that none of the brethren come to see him, and often goes in and out of his cell, and frequently gazes up at the sun, as if it was too slow in setting, and so a kind of unreasonable confusion of mind takes possession of him like some foul darkness, and makes him idle and useless for every spiritual work, so that he imagines that no cure for so terrible an attack can be found in anything except visiting some one of the brethren, or in the solace of sleep alone.

Then the disease suggests that he ought to show courteous and friendly hospitalities to the brethren, and pay visits to the sick, whether near at hand or far off. He talks too about some dutiful and religious offices; that those kinsfolk ought to be inquired after, and that he ought to go and see them oftener; that it would be a real work of piety to go more frequently to visit that religious woman, devoted to the service of God, who is deprived of all support of kindred; and that it would be a most excellent thing to get what is needful for her who is neglected and despised by her own kinsfolk; and that he ought piously to devote his time to these things instead of staying uselessly and with no profit in his cell.

3. Of the different ways in which accidie overcomes a monk.

And so the wretched soul, embarrassed by such contrivances of the enemy, is disturbed, until, worn out by the spirit of *accidie*, as by some strong battering ram, it either learns to sink into slumber, or, driven out from the confinement of its cell, accustoms itself to seek for consolation under these attacks in visiting some brother, only to be afterwards weakened even more by this remedy which it seeks for the present. For more frequently and more severely will the enemy attack one who, when the battle is joined, will, as he well knows, immediately turn his back, and whom he sees to look for safety neither in victory nor in fighting but in flight: until little by little he is drawn away from his cell, and begins to forget the object of his profession, which is nothing but meditation and contemplation of that divine purity which excels all things, and which can only be gained by silence and continually remaining in the cell, and by meditation, and so the soldier of Christ becomes a runaway from His service, and a deserter, and "entangles himself in secular business," without at all pleasing Him to whom he engaged himself.

4. How accidie hinders the mind from all contemplation of the virtues.

All the inconveniences of this disease are admirably expressed by David in a single verse, where he says, "My soul slept from weariness" (Ps. 109:28, LXX), that is, from *accidie*. Quite rightly does he say, not that his body, but that his soul slept. For in truth the soul which is wounded by the shaft of this passion does sleep, as regards all contemplation of the virtues and insight of the spiritual senses.

SULPICIUS SEVERUS

Life of St. Martin

Sulpicius Severus (about 360–about 420), a lawyer in the last years of the Roman Empire, was converted to Christianity by Martin of Tours (born either 316 or 335, died 397) and later wrote this account of Martin's life. Martin represents themes characteristic of early medieval saints — he leaves his secular career as a soldier, becomes a monk, works miracles, and ends up an influential bishop. This biography became widely influential. (Early in the story Martin is a "catechumen," someone learning about Christianity in preparation for baptism.)

Sulpicius Severus, *Life of St. Martin*, in *Nicene and Post-Nicene Fathers*, trans. Alexander Roberts (Peabody, Mass.: Hendrickson, 1994), 2d ser., 11:5-7. Translation slightly revised.

2. Military Service of St. Martin

Martin, then, was born at Sabaria in Pannonia [roughly southern Hungary today], but was brought up at Ticinum, which is situated in Italy. His parents were, according to the judgment of the world, of no mean rank, but were heathens. His father was at first simply a soldier, but afterwards a military tribune. He himself in his youth followed military pursuits and was enrolled in the imperial guard, first under King Constantine, and then under Julian Caesar. This, however, was not done of his own free will, for, almost from his earliest years, this remarkable boy aspired rather to the service of God. For, when he was of the age of ten years, he betook himself, against the wish of his parents, to the Church, and begged that he might become a catechumen. Soon afterwards, becoming in a wonderful manner completely devoted to the service of God, when he was twelve years old, he desired to enter on the life of a hermit; and he would have followed up that desire with the necessary vows, had not his as yet too youthful age prevented it. His mind, however, being always engaged on matters pertaining to the monasteries or the Church, already meditated in his boyish years what he afterwards, as a professed servant of Christ, fulfilled.

But when an edict was issued by the ruling powers in the state, that the sons of veterans should be enrolled for military service, and he, on the information furnished by his father (who looked with an evil eye on his blessed actions), having been seized and put in chains, when he was fifteen years old, was compelled to take the military oath, then showed himself content with only one servant as his attendant. And even to him, changing places as it were, he often acted as though, while really master, he had been inferior; to such a degree that, for the most part, he drew off his (servant's) boots and cleaned them with his own hand; while they took their meals together, the real master, however, generally acting the part of servant. During nearly three years before his baptism, he was engaged in the profession of arms, but he kept completely free from those vices in which that class of men become too frequently involved. He showed exceeding kindness towards his fellow-soldiers, and held them in wonderful affection; while his patience and humility surpassed what seemed possible to human nature. There is no need to praise the self-denial which he displayed: it was so great that, even at that date, he was regarded not so much as being a soldier as a monk.

By all these qualities he had so endeared himself to the whole body of his comrades that they esteemed him while they marvelously loved him. Although not yet made a new creature in Christ, he, by his good works, acted the part of a candidate for baptism. This he did, for instance, by aiding those

who were in trouble, by furnishing assistance to the wretched, by supporting the needy, by clothing the naked, while he reserved nothing for himself
from his military pay except what was necessary for his daily sustenance.
Even then, far from being a senseless hearer of the Gospel, he so far com-
plied with its precepts as to take no thought about the morrow.

3. Christ Appears to St. Martin

Accordingly, at a certain period, when he had nothing except his arms and
his simple military dress, in the middle of winter, a winter which had shown
itself more severe than ordinary, so that the extreme cold was proving fatal
to many, he happened to meet at the gate of the city of Amiens a poor man
destitute of clothing. He was entreating those that passed by to have compassion upon him, but all passed the wretched man without notice, when
Martin, that man full of God, recognized that a being to whom others
showed no pity was, in that respect, left to him. Yet, what should he do? He
had nothing except the cloak in which he was clad, for he had already parted
with the rest of his garments for similar purposes. Taking, therefore, his
sword, he divided his cloak into two equal parts, and gave one part to the
poor man, while he again clothed himself with the remainder. Upon this,
some of the bystanders laughed, because he was now an unsightly object,
and stood out as but partly dressed. Many, however, who were of sounder
understanding, groaned deeply because they themselves had done nothing
similar. They especially felt this because, being possessed of more than Martin, they could have clothed the poor man without reducing themselves to
nakedness.

In the following night, when Martin had resigned himself to sleep, he
had a vision of Christ arrayed in that part of his cloak with which he had
clothed the poor man. He contemplated the Lord with the greatest attention, and was told to own as his the robe which he had given. Before long, he
heard Jesus saying with a clear voice to the multitude of angels standing
round — "Martin, who is still but a catechumen, clothed me with this robe."
The Lord, truly mindful of his own words (who had said when on earth, "Inasmuch as you have done these things to one of the least of these, you have
done them unto me" [Matt. 25:40]), declared that he himself had been
clothed in that poor man; and to confirm the testimony he bore to so good a
deed, he condescended to show him himself in that very dress which the
poor man had received. After this vision the sainted man was not puffed up
with human glory, but, acknowledging the goodness of God in what had

been done, and being now of the age of twenty years, he hastened to receive baptism. He did not, however, all at once, retire from military service, yielding to the entreaties of his tribune, whom he admitted to be his familiar tent-companion. For the tribune promised that, after the period of his office had expired, he too would retire from the world. Martin, kept back by the expectation of this event, continued, although but in name, to act the part of a soldier, for nearly two years after he had received baptism.

4. Martin Retires from Military Service

In the meantime, as the barbarians were rushing within the two divisions of Gaul, Julian Caesar, bringing an army together at the city of the Vaugiones, began to distribute a bonus to the soldiers. As was the custom in such a case, they were called forward, one by one, until it came to the turn of Martin. Then, indeed, judging it a suitable opportunity for seeking his discharge — for he did not think it would be proper for him, if he were not to continue in the service, to receive a bonus — he said to Caesar, "Until now I have served you as a soldier: allow me now to become a soldier to God: let the man who is to serve you receive your bonus. I am the soldier of Christ; it is not lawful for me to fight." Then truly the tyrant stormed on hearing such words, declaring that, from fear of the battle, which was to take place on the morrow, and not from any religious feeling, Martin withdrew from the service. But Martin, full of courage, indeed all the more resolute from the danger that had been set before him, exclaimed, "If this conduct of mine is ascribed to cowardice, and not to faith, I will take my stand unarmed before the line of battle tomorrow, and in the name of the Lord Jesus, protected by the sign of the cross, and not by shield or helmet, I will safely penetrate the ranks of the enemy." He was ordered, therefore, to be thrust back into prison, determined on proving his words true by exposing himself unarmed to the barbarians.

But, on the following day, the enemy sent ambassadors to treat about peace and surrendered both themselves and all their possessions. In these circumstances who can doubt that this victory was due to the saintly man? It was granted him that he should not be sent unarmed to the fight. And although the good Lord could have preserved his own soldier, even amid the swords and darts of the enemy, yet that his blessed eyes might not be pained by witnessing the death of others, he removed all necessity for fighting. For Christ did not require to secure any other victory in behalf of his own soldier, than that, the enemy being subdued without bloodshed, no one should suffer death.

5. Martin Converts a Robber to the Faith

From that time quitting military service, Martin earnestly sought after the society of Hilarius, bishop of the city Pictava [in western France], whose faith in the things of God was then regarded as of high renown, and in universal esteem. For some time Martin made his abode with him. Now, this same Hilarius, having instituted him in the office of the diaconate, endeavored still more closely to attach him to himself, and to bind him by leading him to take part in Divine service. But when he constantly refused, crying out that he was unworthy, Hilarius, as being a man of deep penetration, perceived that he could only be constrained in this way, if he should lay that sort of office upon him, in discharging which there should seem to be a kind of injury done him. He therefore appointed him to be an exorcist. Martin did not refuse this appointment, from the fear that he might seem to have looked down upon it as somewhat humble. Not long after this, he was warned in a dream that he should visit his native land, and more particularly his parents, who were still involved in heathenism, with a regard for their religious interests. He set forth in accordance with the expressed wish of the holy Hilarius, after being made by him to promise with many prayers and tears that he would in due time return. According to report Martin entered on that journey in a melancholy frame of mind, after calling the brethren to witness that many sufferings lay before him. The result fully justified this prediction. For, first of all, having followed some devious paths among the Alps, he fell into the hands of robbers. And when one of them lifted up his axe and poised it above Martin's head, another of them met with his right hand the blow as it fell; nevertheless, having had his hands bound behind his back, he was handed over to one of them to be guarded and stripped. The robber, having led him to a private place apart from the rest, began to enquire of him who he was. Upon this, Martin replied that he was a Christian. The robber next asked him whether he was afraid. Then indeed Martin most courageously replied that he never before had felt so safe, because he knew that the mercy of the Lord would be especially present with him in the midst of trials. He added that he grieved rather for the man in whose hands he was, because, by living a life of robbery, he was showing himself unworthy of the mercy of Christ. And then entering on a discourse concerning Evangelical truth, he preached the word of God to the robber. Why should I delay stating the result? The robber believed; and, after expressing his respect for Martin, he restored him to the way, entreating him to pray the Lord for him. That same robber was afterwards seen leading a religious life; so that, in fact, the narrative I have given above is based upon an account furnished by himself.

BENEDICT OF NURSIA

The Rule of St. Benedict

Benedict of Nursia (about 480–about 550) moved into a cave near the Italian town of Subiaco when he was about twenty, intending to live as a solitary hermit, but a community of other monks soon gathered around him. Some years later, he established another monastery at Monte Cassino and wrote this "rule" to guide his monks. A document intended to regulate only the local community gradually spread in its use and by the 800s became the rule for monks throughout western Europe, shaping the lives of Benedictines and other orders of monks and nuns that have emerged from their tradition into a pattern of prayer, work, and study.

Listen, my son, and with your heart hear the principles of your Master. Readily accept and faithfully follow the advice of a loving Father, so that through the labor of obedience you may return to Him from whom you have withdrawn because of the laziness of disobedience. My words are meant for you, whoever you are, who laying aside your own will, take up the all-powerful and righteous arms of obedience to fight under the true King, the Lord Jesus Christ.

First, with fervent prayer, beg of Him to finish the good work begun, so that He who has so generously considered us among His true children, may never be saddened by our evil deeds. We must serve Him always with our God-given talents so that He may not disinherit His children like an angered father, nor enraged by our sins, give us up to eternal punishment like a dreaded Lord whose worthless servants refuse to follow Him to glory.

Therefore, let us arise without delay, the Scriptures stirring us: "It is now the hour for us to awake from sleep" (Rom. 13:11). Let us open our eyes to the

The Rule of St. Benedict, trans. Anthony C. Meisel and M. L. del Mastro (New York: Image Books, 1975), 43-45, 54-55, 76-78, 86-87.

Divine light and attentively hear the Divine voice, calling and exhorting us daily: "Today if you shall hear his voice, harden not your hearts" (Ps. 95:7-8); and again, "He who has ears, let him hear what the Spirit says to the churches" (Rev. 2:7). And what does He say? "Come, you children, and listen to Me: I will teach you the fear of the Lord" (Ps. 34:11). "Run where you have the light, lest the shadows of death come upon you" (John 12:35).

The Lord looks for His workman among the masses of men. He calls to him: "Who is the man that will have life, and desires to see good days?" (Ps. 34:12). And if, hearing this, you answer, "I am he," God says to you, "If you desire true and everlasting life, keep your tongue from evil and make sure your lips speak without guile; renounce evil and do good; seek peace and pursue it" (Ps. 34:13-14). "If you do this, My eyes will see you, and My ears will hear your prayers" (Ps. 34:17). "And before you can call out to Me, I will say to you: 'Behold, I am here'" (Isa. 58:9). What can be more pleasing, dear brothers, than the voice of the Lord's invitation? See how He shows us the way of life in his benevolence.

We are about to open a school for God's service, in which we hope nothing harsh or oppressive will be directed. For preserving charity or correcting faults, it may be necessary at times, by reason of justice, to be slightly more severe. Do not fear this and retreat, for the path to salvation is long and the entrance is narrow.

As our lives and faith progress, the heart expands and with the sweetness of love we move down the paths of God's commandments. Never departing from His guidance, remaining in the monastery until death, we patiently share in Christ's passion, so we may eventually enter into the Kingdom of God. . . .

Obedience

The first degree of humility is prompt obedience. This is necessary for all who think of Christ above all else. These souls, because of the holy servitude to which they have sworn themselves, whether through fear of Hell or expectation of eternity, hasten to obey any command of a superior as if it were a command of God. As the Lord says: "At the hearing of the ear he has obeyed me" (Ps. 17:44). And He says to the teacher: "He who hears you, hears me" (Luke 10:16).

These disciples must obediently step lively to the commanding voice — giving up their possessions and their own will, and even leaving their chores unfinished. Thus the order of the master and the finished work of the disciple are fused, with the swiftness of the fear of God — by those who deeply desire to walk in the path of the Lord. They walk the narrow path, as the Lord says: "Narrow is the way which leads to life" (Matt. 7:14). They do not live as they please, nor as their desires and will dictate, but they rather live under the direction and judgment of an abbot in a monastery. Undoubtedly, they find their inspiration in the Lord's saying: "I come not to do my own will, but the will of Him Who sent me" (John 6:38).

But this very obedience will be deemed acceptable to God and pleasant to men only when the commands are carried out without fear, laziness, hesitance or protest. The obedience shown to superiors is, through them, shown to God, who said: "He who hears you, hears Me" (Luke 10:16). Orders should be carried out cheerfully, for "God loves a cheerful giver" (2 Cor. 9:7). God will not be pleased by the monk who obeys grudgingly, not only murmuring in words but even in his heart. For even if he should fulfill the command, his performance would not be pleasing to God who listens to his complainings. Work done in such a dispirited manner will go without reward; in fact, unless he makes amends, he will suffer the punishment meted out to gripers.

Private Ownership by Monks

The vice of private ownership must be uprooted from the monastery. No one, without the abbot's permission, shall dare give, receive or keep anything — not book, tablet or pen — nothing at all. Monks have neither free will nor free body, but must receive all they need from the abbot. However, they may keep nothing unless permitted or given them by the abbot.

All things are to be common to everyone for, "Neither did any one say or think that anything whatever was his own" (Acts 4:32). If anyone is found with a predilection to this terrible vice, he is to be scolded twice. If he does not reform, then he is to be punished.

Weekly Kitchen Service

The brothers should wait on one another. No one is to be excused from kitchen duty unless he is ill or he is engaged in a task of greater import, for he can thus obtain greater charity and commendation. Depending on the size of the monastery and the convenient arrangement of the kitchens, let the weaker brothers have help to keep them from sorrow. The cellarer may be exempted from kitchen service in a large monastery, as may those engaged in more vital jobs, as we have said. Let the remainder serve each other in charity.

After completing his weekly kitchen chores, the monk should clean on Saturday. He must wash the towels the brothers use for drying hands and feet. Everyone's feet are to be washed by the monk finishing his week's service and the one starting his. The monk ending service should return the utensils he has used clean and in good order to the cellarer, who will then give them to the new kitchen staff. This is done so the cellarer may keep track of his inventory.

One hour before the meal each server may have a portion of drink and bread over his daily allowance, so he may serve his brothers without complaint or fatigue. The servers should wait until after Mass on feast days, however.

Right after Sunday Lauds [the morning prayer] both incoming and outgoing servers shall fall on their knees and ask for the prayers of all. When one finishes his week's service, he should say, "Blessed are You, O Lord God, who did help me and console me" (Ps. 86:17). When he has repeated this three times, he shall receive a blessing. After this, let the one entering his week of service say, "O God, come to my assistance; O Lord, make haste to help me" (Ps. 70:1). When this has been repeated three times by all, and the blessing received, these brothers may enter their week of service.

Daily Manual Labor

Idleness is an enemy of the soul. Therefore, the brothers should be occupied according to schedule in either manual labor or holy reading. These may be arranged as follows: from Easter to October, the brothers shall work at manual labor from Prime [6 a.m.] until the fourth hour [10 a.m.]. From then until the sixth hour [noon] they should read. After dinner they should rest (in bed) in silence. However, should anyone desire to read, he should do so without disturbing his brothers.

None [afternoon prayer] should be chanted at about the middle of the eighth hour [2:30 p.m.]. Then everyone shall work as they must until Vespers [prayer at sunset]. If conditions dictate that they labor in the fields [harvesting], they should not be grieved, for they are truly monks when they must live by manual labor, as did our fathers and the apostles. Everything should be in moderation, though, for the sake of the timorous.

From October first until Lent, the brothers should read until the end of the second hour [7 a.m.]. Tierce will then be said, after which they will work at their appointed tasks until None. At the first signal for None all work shall come to an end. Thus all may be ready as the second signal sounds. After eating they shall read or study the psalms.

During Lent the brothers shall devote themselves to reading until the end of the third hour. Then they will work at their assigned tasks until the end of the tenth hour. Also, during this time, each monk shall receive a book from the library, which he should read carefully cover to cover. These books should be handed out at the beginning of Lent.

It is important that one or two seniors be chosen to oversee the reading periods. They will check that no one is slothful, lazy or gossiping, profiting little himself and disturbing others. If such a brother is discovered, he is to be corrected once or twice. If he does not change his ways, he shall be punished by the Rule (to set an example for others). Nor should brothers meet at odd and unsuitable hours.

All shall read on Saturdays except those with specific tasks. If anyone is so slothful that he will not or cannot read or study, he will be assigned work so as not to be idle.

Sick and frail brothers should be given work that will keep them from idleness but not so oppressive that they will feel compelled to leave the monastery. Their frailty is to be considered by the abbot.

BERNARD OF CLAIRVAUX

Letters

Bernard of Clairvaux (1090-1153) joined the Cistercian order (a strict re-form movement in monasticism) in 1112 and was later sent out as abbot of a new Cistercian monastery at Clairvaux, in central France. He lived a life of severest austerity but became one of the most influential church-

Some Letters of Saint Bernard, Abbot of Clairvaux, trans. Samuel J. Eales (London: John Hodges, 1904). Translation altered.

men in Europe. His eloquence, vivid in his many letters, as well as his example inspired many young men to join the Cistercians; his biographer writes, "Mothers hid their sons, women shut up their husbands, friends sent away friends, because the Holy Spirit gave his voice such a ring of virtue."

The first of these letters addresses a young man, Walter of Chaumont, who feels some obligation to stay home and care for his mother rather than entering the monastery at Clairvaux. Bernard sees no dilemma: if his mother's needs keep Walter at home, she will ultimately suffer before God's judgment as much as he will. The second letter deals with a worse case: a young man named Fulk had joined the monastery but then had been persuaded by his uncle to return to the secular life. So he has broken a vow as well as given up the best form of Christian life.

Letter 48, To Walter de Chaumont

My Dear Walter,

It often grieves my heart whenever the most pleasant remembrance of you comes back to me, seeing how you consume in vain occupations the flower of your youth, the sharpness of your intellect, the store of your learning and skill, and also, what is more excellent in a Christian than all of these gifts, the pure and innocent character which distinguishes you. You use such great endowments to serve not Christ their giver, but transitory things. What if (which God forbid!) a sudden death should seize and shatter at a stroke all those gifts of yours, as it were with the rush of a burning and raging wind, just as the winds whirl dry grass or as the leaves of trees quickly fall? What, then, will you carry with you of all the labor you have done on the earth? What return will you render to the Lord for all the benefits he has done for you? What gain will you bring to your creditor for those many talents committed to you, if he shall find your hand empty, who, though a liberal bestower of his gifts, exacts a strict account of their use? For he that shall come will come and will not delay, and will require that which is his own with interest (Matt. 25:27). For he claims all as his own, which seems to ennoble you in your land, with favors full at once of dignity and of danger. Noble parentage, sound health, elegance of person, quick apprehension, useful knowledge, uprightness of life are glorious things indeed, but they are his from whom they are. If you use them for yourself, there is one who seeks and judges.

But be it so; suppose that you may for a while call these things yours, and boast in the praise they bring you, and have men call you Rabbi and make for yourself a great name, though only upon the earth; what shall be left to you after death of all these things? Scarcely a remembrance — and that, too, only upon earth. For it is written, "They have slept their sleep, and all the men whose hands were mighty have found nothing" (Ps. 76:5). If this be the end of all your labors — allow me to say so — what have you been more than a beast of burden? Indeed, it will be said even of your horse when he is dead that he was good. Look to it, then, how you must answer before that terrible judgment throne if you have received your soul in vain (and such a soul!), if you are found to have done nothing more with your immortal and reasonable soul than some beast with his. For the soul of a brute lives no longer than the body which it animates, and at one and the same moment it both ceases to give life and to live. Of what will you deem yourself worthy, who, being made in the image of your Creator, do not guard the dignity of so great a majesty? And being a human being, but not understanding your honor, you are compared to the foolish beasts and made like them, seeing that indeed you labor at nothing of a spiritual or eternal nature, but, like the spirit of a beast which as soon as it is loosed from the body is dissolved with the body, have been content to think of nothing but material and temporal goods, turning a deaf ear to the Gospel precept: "Labor not for the food that perishes, but for that food which endures to everlasting life" (John 6:27). But you know well that it is written that only he ascends the hill of the Lord who has not lifted up his mind to vanity (Ps. 24:3). And not even he ascends unless he has clean hands and a pure heart. I leave you to decide if you dare to claim this of your deeds and thoughts at the present. But if you are not able to do so, judge what is the reward of iniquity, if mere unfruitfulness is enough for damnation. And, indeed, the thorn or thistle will not be safe when the axe shall be seen laid to the root of the fruit tree, nor will he spare the thorn which stings, who threatens even the barren plant. Woe, then; yes, double woe to him of whom it shall be said, I "looked that he should bring forth grapes, and he has brought forth wild grapes" (Isa. 5:4).

I know how freely and fully you can nourish these thoughts, though I be silent, but yet I know that, constrained by love of your mother, you are not as yet able to abandon what you have long known how to despise. What answer shall I make to you in this matter? That you should leave your mother? That seems inhuman. That you should remain with her? But what a misery for her to be a cause of ruin to her son! That you should fight at once for the world and for Christ? But no man can serve two masters. Your mother's wish, being contrary to your salvation, is equally so to her own. Choose, therefore, of these two alternatives which you will; either, that is, to secure the wish of one or the salvation of both. But if you love her so much, have the courage to leave her for her sake, lest if you leave Christ to remain with her she also perish on your account. Else you have ill-served her who bore you if she perish on your account. For how will she escape destruction if she has ruined him to whom she gave birth? I have spoken this in order in some way to stoop to assist your somewhat worldly affection. Moreover, it is a faithful saying and worthy of all acceptance, that although it is impious to despise a mother, yet to despise her for Christ's sake is most pious. For he who said, "Honor your father and mother" (Matt. 15:4) also said, "He who loves father or mother more than me is not worthy of me" (Matt. 10:37).

Letter 45, To a Youth Named Fulk, Who Afterwards Was Archdeacon of Langres

To the honorable young man Fulk, Brother Bernard, a sinner, wishes such joy in youth as in old age he will not regret.

I do not wonder at your surprise; I should wonder if you were not surprised that I should write to you — a countryman to a townsman, a monk to a student, there being no apparent or pressing reason for so doing. But if you recall what is written — "I am debtor both to the wise and to the unwise" (Rom. 1:14), and that "Charity seeks not her own" (1 Cor. 13:5) — perhaps you will understand that what it orders is not mere presumption. For it is Charity which compels me to reprove you; to offer you condolences, though you do not grieve; to pity you though you do not think yourself pitiable. Nor shall it be unserviceable to you to hear patiently why you are viewed with compassion. In feeling your pain you may get rid of its cause, and knowing your misery you may begin to cease to be miserable. O Charity, good mother who nourishes the weak, employs the vigorous, and blames the restless, using various expedients with various people, as loving all her sons! She blames with gentleness, and with simplicity praises. It is she who is the mother of men and angels, and makes the peace not only of earth but of heaven. It is she who, rendering God favorable to humanity, has reconciled humanity to God. She, my Fulk, makes those brothers with whom you once shared pleasant bread to dwell in one manner of life in a house (Ps. 68:6). Such and so honorable a parent complains of being injured, of being wounded by you.

But in what way have I injured, you reply, or wounded her? In this, without doubt, that you whom she had taken in her maternal bosom and nourished with her milk, have in untimely fashion withdrawn yourself, and having known the sweetness of the milk which can train you up for salvation, have rejected and disdained it so quickly and carelessly. O most foolish boy! boy more in understanding than in age! who has led you to depart so quickly from a course so well begun? My uncle, you will say. So Adam once threw the blame of sin upon his wife, and his wife upon the serpent, to excuse themselves; yet each received the well-deserved sentence of their own fault. I am unwilling to accuse your uncle; I am unwilling that you should excuse yourself by this means, for you are inexcusable. His fault does not excuse yours. What did he do? Did he use violence? Did he take you by force? No, he begged, not insisted; attracted you by flatteries, not dragged you by violence. Who forced you to yield to his flatteries? He had not yet given up what was his own. What wonder that he should reclaim you, who was his! If he demands a lamb from the flock, a calf from the herd, and no one disputes his right, who can wonder that having lost you, who are of more value in his sight than many lambs or calves, he should reclaim you? Probably he does not aim at that degree of perfection of which it is said, "If any one has taken away thy goods, seek them not again" (Luke 6:30). But you, who had already rejected the world, what had you to do with following a man of the world? The timid sheep flies when the wolf approaches; the gentle dove when she sees the hawk; the mouse, though hungry, dares not leave his hole when the cat is prowling around; and yet you, "when you saw a thief you consented with him" (Ps. 50:18). For what else than a thief shall I call him who has not hesitated to steal that most precious pearl of Christ, your soul?

I should wish, if it were possible, to pass over his fault, lest the truth should obtain for me only hatred and no result. But I am not able, I confess, to pass a man untouched, who up to this very day is found to have resisted the Holy Spirit with all his power. For he who does not hinder evil when he can, even although the evil purpose may be frustrated, is not clear of that purpose. Assuredly he tried to dampen my fervor when it was new, but, thanks to God, he did not succeed. Another nephew of his, Guarike, your kinsman, he much opposed, but what harm did he do? On the contrary, he was of service. For the old man at length unwillingly desisted from persecution, and as the youth, his nephew, remained unsubdued, he was the more meritorious for his temptation. But, alas! how was he able to overcome you, who was not able to overcome him? Was he stronger or more prudent than you? Assuredly those who knew both before preferred Fulk to Guarike. But the event of the combat showed that men's judgment had erred.

But what shall I say concerning the malice of an uncle who withdraws his own nephews from the Christian warfare to drag them with himself to perdition? Is it thus he is accustomed to benefit his friends? Those whom Christ calls to abide with him forever this uncle calls back to burn with him for evermore. I wonder if Christ is not reproving him when he says, "How often would I have gathered [thy nephews] as a hen gathers her chickens under her wings, and you would not? Behold your house is left to you desolate" (Matt. 23:37). Christ says, "Suffer the little children to come to me, for of such is the kingdom of heaven" (Matt. 19:14). This uncle says, "Suffer my nephews to burn with me." Christ says, "They are mine; they ought to serve me." But their uncle says, "They ought to perish with me." Christ says, "They are mine, I have redeemed them." "But I," says the uncle, "have brought them up." "You, indeed," says Christ, "have fed them, but with my bread, not yours; while I have redeemed them not with your blood, but my own." Thus the uncle according to the flesh struggles against the Father of spirits for his nephews, whom he disinherits of heavenly possessions while he desires to load them with earthly ones. Yet Christ, not considering it robbery to draw to himself those whom he has made and redeemed with his own blood, has done when they came to him what he had earlier promised: "Him who comes to me, I will in no way cast out" (John 6:37). He opened gladly to Fulk, the first who knocked, and made him glad also. What more? He put off the old man and put on the new, and showed forth in his character and life the canonical function which had existed in name alone. The report of it flies abroad, to Christ, a sweet savor; and the novelty of the thing diffused on all sides brought it to the ears of his uncle.

What then did the carnal guardian do, who lost the carnal solace of the flesh which he had brought up and loved after a carnal fashion? . . . Adopting then this counsel of the flesh, forgetful of reason and law, as it were a lion prepared for prey; and as a lioness robbed of her whelp, raging and roaring, not respecting holy things, he burst into the dwelling of the saints, in which Christ had hidden his young soldier from the strife of tongues, who was one day to be joined to the company of angels. He demands that his nephew be restored to him; he loudly complains that he had been wrongly deserted by him; while Christ resists, saying, "Unhappy man, what are you doing? Why do you rob? Why persecute me? Is it not enough that you have taken away your own soul from me, and the souls of many others by your example, but you must tear him also from my hand with impious daring? Do you not fear the coming judgment, or do you despise my terrors? Upon whom do you wage war? Upon the terrible One, who takes away the spirit of princes (Ps. 76:12). Madman, return to yourself. Remember your final end and do not sin, call to mind with salutary fear what you are." "And you, O youth," He says, "if you assent and agree to his wishes, you shall die. Remember that Lot's wife was, indeed, delivered from Sodom because she believed God, but was transformed along the way because she looked back (Gen. 19:26). Learn in the Gospel that he who has once put his hand to the plough is not permitted to look back (Luke 9:62). Your uncle, who has already lost his own soul, seeks yours. The words of his mouth are iniquity and guile. Do not learn, my son, to do evil (Ps. 36:4). Do not turn aside to vanities and falsehoods (Ps. 40:4). Behold, in the way in which you walk he hides snares — he has stretched nets. His discourses are smooth as butter, and yet they are sharp spears (Ps. 55:21). See, my son, that you are not taken with lying lips and a deceitful tongue. Let divine fear transfix your flesh, that the desire of the flesh may not deceive you. It flatters, but under its tongue is suffering and sorrow; it weeps, but betrays; it betrays to catch the poor one when it has attracted him (Ps. 10:9). Beware, I say, my son, that you do not confer with flesh and blood (Gal. 1:16), for 'My sword shall devour flesh' (Deut. 32:42). Despise entreaties and promises. He promises great things, but I greater; he offers more, but I most of all. Will you throw away heavenly things for earthly, eternal for temporal? Otherwise it behooves you to dissolve the vows which your lips have pronounced. He is rightly required to dissolve who was not forced to vow, for, although I did not repulse you when you knocked, I did not oblige you to enter. You cannot, therefore, put aside what you promised of your own accord. Behold, each of you I warn, and to each give salutary counsel. Do not you," He says to the uncle, "draw back a monastic to the world, for in so doing you make him to apostatize. Do not you, a monastic, follow the secular life, for in so doing you persecute me.". . .

In the house of your uncle you are not able to drink deep of the fullness of the house of God. Why, you say? Because it is a house of carnal delights. Now, as fire and water cannot be together, so the delights of the spirit and those of the flesh are incompatible. Christ will not deign to pour His wine, which is more sweet than honey and the honeycomb, into the soul of him whom he finds among his cups breathing forth the fumes of wine. Where there is delicate variety of food, where the richness and splendor of the service of the table delights equally the eyes and the stomach, the food of heaven is wanting to the soul. Rejoice, O young man, in your youth! but then, when temporal joy departs in time to come, everlasting sorrow will possess you! May God preserve you, his child, from this: May he rather destroy the deceiving and perfidious lips of those who give you such advice, who say to you every day, "Good, good!" and who seek your soul! They are those with whom you are dwelling, and who corrupt the good manners of a young man by their evil communications. . . .

12. What do you do in the town at all, O cowardly soldier? Your fellow soldiers whom you have deserted by flight are fighting and overcoming; they knock and they enter in, they seize heaven and reign while you scour the streets and squares, sitting upon your ambling horse, and clad in purple and fine linen. These are the ornaments of peace, not the weapons of war. Or do you say, "Peace, and there is no peace" (Ezek. 13:10)? The purple tunic does not put to flight lust and pride and avarice, nor does it protect against other fiery darts of the enemy. Lastly, it does not ward off from you the fever which you more fear, nor secure you from death. Where are your warlike weapons, the shield of faith, the helmet of salvation, the breastplate of patience? Why do you tremble? There are more with us than with our enemies. Take your arms, recover your strength while yet the combat lasts. Angels are spectators and helpers, the Lord himself is your aid and your support, who will teach your hands to war and your fingers to fight (Ps. 144:1). Let us come to the help of our brothers, lest if they fight without us they vanquish without us, and without us enter into heaven; lest, last of all, when the door has been shut it be replied from within to us knocking too late, "Verily I say unto you, I know you not" (Matt. 25:12). Make yourself known then and seen beforehand, lest you be unknown for glory and known only for punishment. If Christ recognizes you in the strife, He will recognize you in heaven, and as He has promised, will manifest Himself to you (John 14:21). If only you by repenting and returning will show yourself such as to be able to say with confidence, "Then shall I know even as also I am known" (1 Cor. 13:12). In the meantime I have by these admonitions knocked sufficiently at the heart of a young man modest and docile; and nothing remains for me now except to knock by my prayers also for him at the door of the Divine Mercy, that the Lord may finish my work if my remonstrances have found his heart ever so little softened, so that I may speedily rejoice over him with great joy.

JOHN DE JOINVILLE

Chronicle of the Crusade of St. Louis

The monastic ideal did not affect just monks and nuns. Louis IX (1214-1270), king of France, lived virtually a monastic life in terms of self-denial. He led two crusades and settled disputes among the French nobles more or less by sheer moral force. As this partial biography, written by one of his nobles, suggests, he became the model of a Christian king; shortly after his death, he was recognized as a saint.

In the midst of attending to the affairs of his realm King Louis so arranged his day that he had time to hear the Hours sung by a full choir and a Requiem mass without music. In addition, if it was convenient, he would hear low mass for the day, or high mass on Saints' days. Every day after dinner he rested on his bed, and when he had slept and was refreshed, he and one of his chaplains would say the Office for the Dead privately in his room. Later in the day he attended vespers, and compline at night.

A Franciscan friar once came to see him at the castle of Hyères, where we had disembarked on our return to France. In his sermon, intended for the king's instruction, he said that in his reading of the Bible and other books that speak of non-Christian princes he had never found, in the history of either heathen or Christian peoples, that a kingdom had been lost or had changed its ruler, except where justice had been ignored. "Therefore," said he, "let the king who is now returning to France take good care to see that he administers justice well and promptly to his people, so that our Lord may allow him to rule his kingdom in peace to the end of his days." . . .

"The Life of St. Louis," in *Joinville and Villehardouin: Chronicles of the Crusades*, ed. and trans. M. R. B. Shaw (New York: Penguin, 1963), 176, 331, 334-35, 336-37.

After the king's return from overseas he lived with such a disregard for worldly vanities that he never wore ermine or squirrel fur, nor scarlet cloth, nor were his stirrups or his spurs gilded. His clothes were made of camlet or grey woolen cloth; the fur on these and on the coverings of his bed was either deerskin, hare-skin, or lambskin. He had such sober tastes in food that he never ordered any special dish for himself but took what his cook prepared, and ate whatever was put before him. He had water mixed with his wine and drank it from a glass goblet, with more or less water according to the strength of the wine; he would hold the goblet in his hand while his servants were preparing the wine behind his table. He always took care to see that his poor were fed and, after they had eaten, sent money to be distributed among them.

When minstrels in some nobleman's service arrived with their viols to entertain him after dinner, the king would always wait till they had finished singing before he would let grace be said. Then he would rise, and the priests would stand before him to say grace. On occasions when we paid him an informal visit, he would sit at the foot of his bed. If some predicant friar or Franciscan in the company happened to speak of a book he might like to hear read, the king would say: "Don't read it to me. There's no book so good after meals as free and friendly conversation, when everybody says just what it pleases him to say." Whenever strangers of some importance came to dine with the king, they always found him the best of company. . . .

No man in the world worked more assiduously than our king to maintain peace among his subjects, especially among great nobles who were neighbors, and the princes of the realm; as he did, for instance, in the case of the Comte de Chalon — the Lord of Joinville's uncle — and his son the Comte de Bourgogne, who were making violent war on each other when we came back from overseas. To make peace between them the king sent certain members of his council to Burgundy at his own expense; and thanks to his untiring efforts peace was established between father and son.

The saintly king used to say: "I would willingly allow myself to be branded with a hot iron on condition that all wicked oaths were banished from my realm." I spent over twenty-two years in his company without ever hearing him swear by God, or our Lord's mother, or His saints. When he wished to emphasize any statement he would say: "Indeed it was so," or "Indeed it is so."

I never heard him name the Devil, unless the name appeared in some book where it was right to mention it, as for instance when the lives of saints were part of the subject matter. It is a great shame to the realm of France and to the king who now allows it, that today scarcely anyone can speak without saying: "Devil take it!" It is, moreover, a sinful misuse of speech to consign to the Devil men and women who were given to God from the time they were baptized. In my castle of Joinville anyone who says such things has his ears boxed or is slapped for it, and bad language is almost non-existent here.

The king asked me once if I washed the feet of the poor on Maundy Thursday. I replied that I did no such thing, for I thought it unbecoming. He told me I should not disdain to perform such an act, seeing that our Lord had done so. "I suppose," said he, "you would be very unwilling to follow the example of the King of England, who washes the feet of lepers, and kisses them."

Before he went to bed the king used to send for his children and tell them of the deeds of good kings and emperors, at the same time pointing out that they should take such men as an example. He would also tell them of the deeds of wicked princes, who by their dissolute lives, their rapacity, and their avarice had brought ruin on their kingdoms. "I'm drawing your attention to such things," he would say, "so that you may avoid them, and not make God angry with you." He made them learn the Hours of our Lady, and repeat to him the Hours of each day, so as to accustom them to hear these regularly when they came to rule over their own lands.

The king was so generous in giving alms that wherever he went in his kingdom he would distribute money to poorly endowed churches, to leper-houses, to alms-houses and hospitals, and also to men and women of gentle birth in distress. Every day he gave food to a great number of poor people, besides those who ate in his hall. I have often seen him cutting bread for these himself; and handing them their drink.

‒‒‒‒‒‒

BONAVENTURE

The Life of St. Francis

Francis of Assisi (1181 or 1182-1226), the son of an Italian merchant, found himself called to a life of radical poverty and service. When others sought to follow him, he obtained the permission of Pope Innocent III to found a new order, eventually called the Franciscans. Bonaventure (about 1217-1274) joined the Franciscan order less than twenty years after Francis's death and became one of the great theologians of his time and eventually Minister General of the Franciscans. His biography of Francis came to be the official account of the saint's life.

‒‒‒‒‒‒

God implanted in the heart of the youthful Francis a certain openhanded compassion for the poor. Growing from his infancy (Job 31:18), this compassion had so filled his heart with generosity that even at that time he determined not to be deaf to the Gospel but to give to everyone who begged (Luke 6:30), especially if he asked "for the love of God." On one occasion when Francis was distracted by the press of business, contrary to his custom, he sent away empty-handed a certain poor man who had begged alms for the love of God. As soon as he came to his senses, he ran after the man and gave him a generous alms, promising God that from that moment onward, while he had the means, he would never refuse those who begged from him for the love of God. He kept this promise with untiring fidelity until his death and merited an abundant increase of grace and love for God. Afterwards, when he had perfectly put on Christ (Gal. 3:27), he used to say that even while he was in secular attire, he could scarcely ever hear any mention of the love of God without being deeply moved in his heart.

His gentleness, his refined manners, his patience, his superhuman affa-

Bonaventure, *The Life of St. Francis,* trans. Ewert Cousins (Mahwah, N.J.: Paulist, 1978), 186-88, 191-95, 200-201, 203-6.

bility, his generosity beyond his means, marked him as a young man of flourishing natural disposition. This seemed to be a prelude to the even greater abundance of God's blessings that would be showered on him in the future. Indeed, a certain man of Assisi, an exceptionally simple fellow who, it is believed, was inspired by God, whenever he chanced to meet Francis going through the town, used to take off his cloak and spread it under his feet saying that Francis deserved every sign of respect since he was destined to do great things in the near future and would be magnificently honored by the entire body of the faithful.

2. Up to this time, however, Francis was ignorant of God's plan for him. He was distracted by the external affairs of his father's business and drawn down toward earthly things by the corruption of human nature. As a result, he had not yet learned how to contemplate the things of heaven nor had he acquired a taste for the things of God. Since affliction can enlighten our spiritual awareness (Isa. 28:19), the hand of the Lord came upon him (Ezek. 1:3), and the right hand of God effected a change in him (Ps. 76:11), God afflicted his body with a prolonged illness in order to prepare his soul for the anointing of the Holy Spirit. After his strength was restored, when he had dressed as usual in his fine clothes, he met a certain knight who was of noble birth, but poor and badly clothed. Moved to compassion for his poverty, Francis took off his own garments and clothed the man on the spot. At one and the same time he fulfilled the two-fold duty of covering over the embarrassment of a noble knight and relieving the poverty of a poor man.

3. The following night, when he had fallen asleep, God in his goodness showed him a large and splendid palace full of military weapons emblazoned with the insignia of Christ's cross. Thus God vividly indicated that the compassion he had exhibited toward the poor knight for love of the supreme King would be repaid with an incomparable reward. And so when Francis asked to whom these belonged, he received an answer from heaven that all these things were for him and his knights. When he awoke in the morning, he judged the strange vision to be an indication that he would have great prosperity; for he had no experience in interpreting divine mysteries nor did he know how to pass through visible images to grasp the invisible truth beyond. Therefore, still ignorant of God's plan, he decided to join a certain count in Apulia, hoping in his service to obtain the glory of knighthood, as his vision seemed to foretell.

He set out on his journey shortly afterwards; but when he had gone as far as the next town, he heard during the night the Lord address him in a familiar way, saying: "Francis, who can do more for you, a lord or a servant, a rich man or a poor man?" When Francis replied that a lord and a rich man could do more, he was at once asked: "Why, then, are you abandoning the Lord for a servant and the rich God for a poor man?" And Francis replied: "Lord, what will you have me do?" (Acts 9:6). And the Lord answered him: "Return to your own land (Gen. 32:9), because the vision which you have seen foretells a spiritual outcome which will be accomplished in you not by human but by divine planning." In the morning (John 21:4), then, he returned in haste to Assisi, joyous and free of care; already a model of obedience, he awaited the Lord's will.

4. From that time on he withdrew from the bustle of public business and devoutly begged God in his goodness to show him what he should do. The flame of heavenly desire was fanned in him by his frequent prayer, and his desire for his heavenly home led him to despise as nothing (Song of Sol. 8:7) all earthly things. He realized that he had found a hidden treasure, and like the wise merchant he planned to sell all he had and to buy the pearl he had found (Matt. 13:44-46). Nevertheless, how he should do this, he did not yet know; but it was being suggested to him inwardly that to be a spiritual merchant one must begin with contempt for the world, and to be a knight of Christ one must begin with victory over one's self. . . .

One day when Francis went out to meditate in the fields (Gen. 24:63), he walked beside the church of San Damiano, which was threatening to collapse because of extreme age. Inspired by the Spirit, he went inside to pray. Prostrate before an image of the Crucified, he was filled with no little consolation as he prayed. While his tear-filled eyes were gazing at the Lord's cross, he heard with his bodily ears a voice coming from the cross, telling him three times: "Francis, go and repair my house which, as you see, is falling completely into ruin."

Trembling with fear, Francis was amazed at the sound of this astonishing voice, since he was alone in the church; and as he received in his heart the power of the divine words, he fell into a state of ecstasy. Returning finally to his senses, he prepared to obey, gathering himself together to carry out the command of repairing the church materially, although the principal intention of the words referred to that Church which Christ purchased with his own blood (Acts 20:28), as the Holy Spirit taught him and as he himself later disclosed to the friars.

He rose then, made the sign of the cross, and taking some cloth to sell, hurried off to the town called Foligno. There he sold all he had brought with him, and, lucky merchant that he was, even sold the horse he was riding. Returning to Assisi, he reverently entered the church which he had been commanded to repair. When he found the poor priest there, he greeted him with fitting reverence, offered him money for the repairs on the church and for the poor, and humbly requested that the priest allow him to stay with him for a time. The priest agreed to his staying there but would not accept the money out of fear of his parents. True despiser of money that he was, Francis threw it on a window sill, valuing it no more than if it were dust.

2. When his father learned that the servant of God was staying with this priest, he was greatly disturbed and ran to the place. But Francis, upon hearing about the threats of those who were pursuing him and having a premonition that they were approaching, wished to give place to wrath (Rom. 12:19), and hid himself — being still untrained as an athlete of Christ — in a secret pit. There he remained in hiding for some days, imploring the Lord incessantly with a flood of tears to deliver him from the hands of those who were persecuting his soul (Ps. 30:16; 108:31; 141:7), and in his kindness to bring to realization the pious desires he had inspired. He was then filled with excessive joy and began to accuse himself of cowardice. He cast aside his fear, left the pit and took the road to the town of Assisi. When the townspeople saw his unkempt face and his changed mentality, they thought that he had gone out of his senses. They threw filth from the streets and stones at him, shouting insults at him, as if he were insane and out of his mind. But the Lord's servant passed through it as if he were deaf to it all, unbroken and unchanged by any of these insults. When his father heard the shouting, he ran to him at once, not to save him but to destroy him. Casting aside all compassion, he dragged him home, tormenting him first with words, then with blows and chains. But this made Francis all the more eager and stronger to carry out what he had begun, as he recalled the words of the Gospel: "Blessed are they who suffer persecution for justice' sake, for theirs is the kingdom of heaven" (Matt. 5:10).

3. After a little while, when his father went out of the country, his mother, who did not approve what her husband had done and had no hope of being able to soften her son's inflexible constancy, released him from his chains and permitted him to go away. He gave thanks to Almighty God and went back to the place where he had been before. Returning and not finding him at home, his father violently reproached his wife and in rage ran to that place. If he could not bring Francis back home, he would at least drive him out of the district. But strengthened by God, Francis went out on his own accord to meet his furious father, calling out in a clear voice that he cared nothing for his chains and blows. Besides, he stated that he would gladly undergo any evil for the name of Christ. When his father, therefore, saw that he could not bring him around, he turned his attention to getting his money back. When he finally found it thrown on the window sill, his rage was mitigated a little, and the thirst of his avarice was somewhat alleviated by the draught of money.

4. Thereupon his carnally minded father led this child of grace, now stripped of his money, before the bishop of the town. He wanted to have Francis renounce into his hands his family possessions and return everything he had. A true lover of poverty, Francis showed himself eager to comply; he went before the bishop without delaying or hesitating. He did not wait for any words nor did he speak any, but immediately took off his clothes and gave them back to his father. Then it was discovered that the man of God had a hairshirt next to his skin under his fine clothes. Moreover, drunk with remarkable fervor, he even took off his underwear, stripping himself completely naked before all. He said to his father: "Until now I have called you father here on earth, but now I can say without reservation, *Our Father who art in heaven* (Matt. 6:9), since I have placed all my treasure and all my hope in him." When the bishop saw this, he was amazed at such intense fervor in the man of God. He immediately stood up and in tears drew Francis into his arms, covering him with the mantle he was wearing, like the pious and good man that he was. He bade his servants give Francis something to cover his body. They brought him a poor, cheap cloak of a farmer who worked for the bishop. Francis accepted it gratefully and with his own hand marked a cross on it with a piece of chalk, thus designating it as the covering of a crucified man and a half-naked beggar.

Thus the servant of the Most High King was left naked so that he might follow his naked crucified Lord, whom he loved. Thus the cross strengthened him to entrust his soul to the wood of salvation that would save him from the shipwreck of the world.

5. Released now from the chains of all earthly desires, this despiser of the world left the town and in a carefree mood sought out a hidden place of solitude where alone and in silence he could hear the secrets God would convey to him. While Francis, the man of God, was making his way through a certain forest, merrily singing praises to the Lord in the French language, robbers suddenly rushed upon him from an ambush. When they asked in a brutal way who he was, the man of God, filled with confidence, replied with these prophetic words: "I am the herald of the great King." But they struck him and hurled him into a ditch filled with snow, saying: "Lie there, you hick herald of God!" When they went away, he jumped out of the ditch, and brimming over with joy, in a loud voice began to make the forest resound with the praises of the Creator of all. . . .

3. When the truth of his simple teaching and his way of life became widely known, certain men began to be inspired to live a life of penance. Leaving everything, they joined him in his way of life and dress. The first among

these was Bernard, a venerable man, who was made a sharer in a divine vocation (Heb. 3:1) and merited to be the firstborn son of our blessed father, both in priority of time and in the gift of holiness. When he discovered for himself the holiness of Christ's servant and decided to despise the world completely after his example, he sought his advice on how to carry this out. On hearing this, God's servant was filled with the consolation of the Holy Spirit over the conception of his first child. "We must ask God's advice about this," he said. In the morning they went to the church of Saint Nicholas, where they said some preliminary prayers; then Francis, who was devoted to the Trinity, opened the book of the Gospel three times, asking God to confirm Bernard's plan with a threefold testimony. The book opened the first time to the text: "If you will be perfect, go, sell all that you have, and give to the poor" (Matt. 19:21). The second time to the text: "Take nothing on your journey" (Luke 9:3). And the third time to: "If anyone wishes to come after me, let him deny himself and take up his cross and follow me" (Matt. 16:24). "This is our life and our rule," the holy man said, "and the life and the rule of all who wish to join our company. Go, then, if you wish to be perfect (Matt. 19:21) and carry out what you have heard."

4. Not long afterwards five other men were called by the same Spirit, and the number of Francis's sons reached six. . . .

8. Seeing that the number of friars was gradually increasing, Christ's servant wrote in simple words a rule of life for himself and his friars. He based it on the unshakable foundation of the observance of the Gospel and added a few other things that seemed necessary for their way of life in common. He very much wanted to have what he had written approved by the Supreme Pontiff; so he decided to go with his band of simple men before the presence of the Apostolic See, placing his trust solely in God's guidance.

9. When he arrived in Rome, he was led into the presence of the Supreme Pontiff. The Vicar of Christ was in the Lateran Palace, walking in a place called the Hall of the Mirror, occupied in deep meditation. Knowing nothing of Christ's servant, he sent him away indignantly. Francis left humbly, and the next night God showed the Supreme Pontiff the following vision. He saw a palm tree sprout between his feet and grow gradually until it became a beautiful tree. As he wondered what this vision might mean, the divine light impressed upon the mind of the Vicar of Christ that this palm tree symbolized the poor man whom he had sent away the previous day. The next morning he commanded his servants to search the city for the poor man. When they found him near the Lateran at St. Anthony's hospice, he ordered him brought to his presence without delay.

When he was led before the Supreme Pontiff, Francis explained his plan, humbly and urgently imploring him to approve the rule of life mentioned above. Now the Vicar of Christ, Innocent III, was a man famous for his wisdom; and when he saw in the man of God such remarkable purity and simplicity of heart, such firmness of purpose and such fiery ardor of will, he was inclined to give his assent to the request. Yet he hesitated to do what Christ's little poor man asked because it seemed to some of the cardinals to be something novel and difficult beyond human powers. There was among the cardinals a most venerable man, John of St. Paul, bishop of Sabina, a lover of holiness and helper of Christ's poor. Inspired by the Holy Spirit, he said to the Supreme Pontiff and his brother cardinals: "If we refuse the request of this poor man as novel or too difficult, when all he asks is to be allowed to lead the Gospel life, we must be on our guard lest we commit an offense against Christ's Gospel. For if anyone says that there is something novel or irrational or impossible to observe in this man's desire to live according to the perfection of the Gospel, he is guilty of blasphemy against Christ, the author of the Gospel." At this observation, the successor of the Apostle Peter turned to the poor man of Christ and said: "My son, pray to Christ that he may show us his will through you. When we know this with more certainty, we can give our approval to your pious desires with more assurance."

10. The servant of Almighty God totally gave himself to prayer, and through his devout supplications obtained for him self-knowledge of what he should say outwardly and for the pope what he should think inwardly. Francis told the pope a parable, which he had learned from God, about a rich king who voluntarily married a poor but beautiful woman. She bore him children who resembled the king and for this reason could be brought up at his table. Then Francis added by way of interpretation: "The sons and heirs of the eternal King should not fear that they will die of hunger. They have been born of a poor mother by the power of the Holy Spirit in the image of Christ the King, and they will be begotten by the spirit of poverty in our poor little Order. For if the King of heaven promises his followers an eternal kingdom (2 Pet. 1:11; cf. Matt. 19:28ff.), he will certainly supply them with those things that he gives to the good and the bad alike" (Matt. 5:45). When the Vicar of Christ had listened to this parable and its interpretation, he was quite amazed and recognized without the slightest doubt that here Christ had spoken through man. And he affirmed that a vision which he had recently received from heaven through the inspiration of the divine Spirit would be fulfilled in this man. He had seen in a dream, as he recounted, that a little poor man, insignificant and despised, was holding up on his back the

Lateran basilica which was about to collapse. "This is certainly the man," he said, "who by his work and teaching will hold up the Church of Christ."

MECHTHILD OF MAGDEBURG

The Flowing Light of the Godhead

Mechthild (about 1210–about 1280) is one of the great medieval German mystics. She grew up in a noble family but then committed herself to an austere life by joining a Beguine community, one of those controversial groups that lived more or less monastic lives without taking permanent vows. Her confessor, a Dominican priest, urged her to write down an account of her visions and her reflections on them, and she produced this book, completed about 1269. This excerpt shows her characteristically gentle (but systematic!) approach, her admiration of St. Dominic and the "Order of Preachers" (Dominicans) he founded, and her ideal of leaders who would be truly the servants of those they led.

Book 3

6. If You Would Follow God Rightly, You Should Have Seven Things

Whoever wants to follow God in faithful toil should not stand quietly. He should often rouse himself. He should consider what he was in sin, how he is now in virtue, and what can yet become of him if he falls. He should lament and praise and pray day and night. When the faithful bride awakens, she thinks of her lover. If she cannot possess him, then she begins to weep. Alas, how often this happens spiritually to God's brides!

Mechthild of Magdeburg, *The Flowing Light of the Godhead*, trans. Frank Tobin (New York: Paulist, 1998), 112-13, 164-65, 223-28.

7. Concerning Seven Obvious Enemies of Our Happiness That Cause Seven Kinds of Harm

Aimless activity is a very harmful trait for us. Bad habits harm us everywhere. Earthly desires blot out in us the holy word of God. Base strife because of self-will brings about in us many a harmful murder. Enmity in our heart drives out the Holy Spirit. An angry temperament robs us of God's intimacy. False holiness can never win out. Pure love of God can never perish. If we are not willing to leave these enemies, they will take from us more than heaven; for if we live holy lives here, it is a pre-heavenly existence. But if we allow these enemies their deceits and their power over us, they rob us of the seven gifts of the Holy Spirit, and they extinguish for us the true light of the genuine love of God. They also blind our eyes to holy understanding and lead us thus blinded into the seven capital sins. Where else does that path lead but to the eternal abyss? . . .

20. The Six Virtues of St. Dominic

On the feast of St. Dominic I prayed to our Lord for the whole Order of Preachers. Our dear Lord deigned to come to me himself, and he brought along St. Dominic whom, if I dare say it, I love above all the saints. Our Lord said: "My son Dominic had four things about him while on earth that all priors should have about them. He loved his fellow Dominicans so much that he could never bear to trouble them with things arising from some whim of his own. The second is that he often improved the food to help and show affection for his brethren, so that the young brothers might not think back on the world and so that the older ones might not succumb on the way. The third is that in holy wisdom he provided for them the model for being moderate, for the sake of God, in their whole being, in all their customs, and in all their wants. The fourth is that he was so merciful that he never wanted to burden his dear brethren with any kind of penance that the order did not require for wrongdoing."

And our Lord continued: "I shall mention two more things. Whenever Dominic laughed, he did so with true delight of the Holy Spirit. But when he wept, he wept with such sincerity that first and foremost among his desires he always put his brethren before my eyes and, in addition, with all his strength, Holy Christianity." Before this I did not know that any laughing could be free of frivolity and not wrong. . . .

Book 6

1. How a Prior or a Prioress or Other Religious Superiors Should Conduct Themselves toward Those under Them

Great fear is bound up with power. When one says, "You are now our superior or our prior or our prioress," God knows, my dear friend, you are in dire straits. You should then perform your *venia* [prayer for forgiveness] with great humility, turn immediately to prayer, and let God console you. You should so transform your heart in God's holy love that you love in a special way each and every brother or sister entrusted to you in all his needs. In all their difficulties you should show your subordinates and brothers loving cheerfulness or kind concern and compassion. With friendly words you should bid them go forth and preach boldly and hear confessions competently, for this is why God has sent them into this world — that they should be redeemers and helpers for poor sinners in the same way Christ was the Redeemer of the whole world, coming down from the lofty palace of the Holy Trinity into this stench-oozing world.

Thus shall you speak to each of your brothers in the deep humility of your pure heart: "Alas, my dear fellow, I, though unworthy of anything good, am your servant in all the ways I can be and not your master. Unfortunately, however, I have authority over you and send you forth with the heartfelt love of God. The difficulty of your task moves me deeply, and yet I make the decisions. I rejoice in the sublime honor the heavenly Father has prepared for you.

"I hereby send you forth in the same name, just as Jesus went forth from his Father, when he went searching for the one lost sheep for such a long time that he died of love. May God's true love go with you on holy paths and in productive efforts. I shall send along with you the longings of my soul, the prayers of my heart, and the tears of my sinful eyes, that as a favor to me God might send you back here holy and full of love. Amen."

Thus shall you encourage all your brothers as they go forth. You should also raise their spirits when they return. You should go in advance to the guest quarters and with God's liberality make all arrangements for the basic comfort of God's disciples as far as is in your power. Indeed, dear fellow, you should even wash their feet yourself. You still remain their master or mistress. And be subject to them in humility. You should not spend a long time with guests. You should keep good order in the religious community. The guests should not stay up late; this is a holy matter. You should visit the infirmary every day and comfort the sick with the consoling words of God and refresh them generously with earthly things, for God is rich beyond all accounting. You should clean for the sick and in God cheerfully laugh with them. You should yourself carry away their personal waste, lovingly ask them in confidence what their private infirmity is, and truly stand by them. Then God's sweetness shall flow into you in marvelous ways.

You should also go into the kitchen and see to it that the needs of the brethren of the community are well taken care of, that your own stinginess and the laziness of the cook do not steal from our Lord's sweet song in the choir. For a starving cleric does not sing well. Also, a hungry man cannot study with concentration. And so God often loses the best through the worst.

At chapter meetings you should be just but with a gentle spirit, basing your judgments completely on the amount of guilt. You should be very careful not to use your authority contrary to the will of the brethren or the community, for that is the source of much dissension.

You should always bless yourself when prideful thoughts come to you. Unfortunately, these do come into the heart under the semblance of good and say, "Well, after all, you are prior (or prioress) in all matters. You can certainly do what you think is best." No, dear fellow, in so doing you disturb God's holy peace. With a submissive spirit and endearing cheerfulness you should say: "Dear brother (or sister), how does this suit you?" and then take action according to their best-intentioned wishes.

Whenever the brothers (or sisters) in your community offer you honor, you should be inwardly afraid with a sharp watch on your heart, and outwardly you should show moderate embarrassment. You should receive all complaints with sympathy and you should offer all advice with sincerity. . . .

Indeed, dear fellow, you should readily offer our dear Lord God a free hour, day or night, during which you can pray lovingly and undisturbed. For heaven's gift with which God greets and instructs his chosen dear ones is in its nature so noble and so refined and flows so sweetly that when God eternal, gravely wounded by love for her, wants to visit the love-hungry soul in the cozy bridal bed, he would renounce for more than thirty years everything that he found pleasant if he might kiss her again and again and embrace her with his bare arms. If you were to think about this, how could you act so crudely as not to give him an hour a day in return for those thirty years?

When I, the most wretched of persons, go to my prayer, I deck myself out according to my worthlessness. I dress myself in the foul puddle that I myself am. Then I put on the shoes of precious time that I wasted day after day. Then I gird myself with the suffering I have caused. Then I put on a cloak of wickedness of which I am full. Then I put on my head a crown of secret shameful acts that I have committed against God. After this I take in my hand the mirror of true knowledge. Then I look at myself in it and see who I really am. . . .

If we want to overcome our shame with great honors, we must clothe ourselves with ourselves. So adorned, I seek Jesus, my sweet Lord, and I find him so quickly by no other means as by those things that are repugnant and burdensome. One should very eagerly step forward with intense desire, ashamed of one's guilt, and with flowing love and humble fear. Then the filth of sin disappears from the divine sight of our Lord. And then lovingly he begins to cast his radiance toward the soul and she begins to dissolve out of deeply felt love. . . .

Now, dear fellow, there are still two more things that you must guard against with holy zeal, for they have never borne fruit. The first is that a man or woman wants to accomplish much in pursuing good deeds and fine conduct in order to achieve a high church office. Such an attitude vexes my soul. When such people have then achieved power, their baseness becomes so many-faceted that no one who voted for them with great enthusiasm is happy with them. They then become misguided by honors and their false virtues turn into vices.

The second is when a person is chosen rightfully with no meddling on his part and he then changes so completely that he never feels the urge to leave this office. This is a sign of many failings. For even if he is irreproachable in it, he should still be fearful and humble.

A sincere woman and a good man who after my death would have liked to talk with me but cannot should read this little book.

THOMAS AQUINAS

Summa Theologiae

Thomas Aquinas (1225-1274) was born into the Italian nobility. His family had intended him for a prominent position in the Benedictines and were horrified when he joined the new Dominican order. He studied the works

---

Thomas Aquinas, *Summa Theologica* Part 2 of Part 2, trans. Fathers of the English Dominican Province (New York: Christian Classics, 1981), 1923, 1926-27, 1931-34, 1941-42, 1954-55.

of Aristotle, many of them newly translated into Latin, and taught, among other places, at the University of Paris. Thomas's theology constructed a synthesis between Aristotle's philosophy and biblical revelation, developed in greatest detail in his masterpiece, the *Summa Theologiae.* (He always refers to Aristotle simply as "the Philosopher.")

In a closely reasoned style common to his times, Aquinas divides his argument into questions, subdivided into articles. In each article, he first presents arguments against his own position ("objections"), then cites an authority or basic principle in support of his position ("on the contrary"), and then gives his own argument for his view ("I answer that") before concluding by answering the objections. In these excerpts he discusses the relation of the active and contemplative lives, the centrality of charity to Christian life, and the importance of the monastic virtues of poverty, chastity, and obedience. In addition to quoting Scripture and a wide range of other authorities, Aquinas often cites "glosses," the then standard notes or short commentaries on biblical passages.

Q. 182, a.1: Whether the active life is more excellent than the contemplative?

Objection 1

It would seem that the active life is more excellent than the contemplative. For "that which belongs to better men would seem to be worthier and better," as the Philosopher says. Now the active life belongs to persons of higher rank, namely prelates, who are placed in a position of honor and power; wherefore Augustine says that "in our actions we must not love honor or power in this life." Therefore it would seem that the active life is more excellent than the contemplative.

Objection 2

Further, in all habits and acts, direction belongs to the more important; thus the military art, being the more important, directs the art of the bridle-maker. Now it belongs to the active life to direct and command the contemplative, as appears from the words addressed to Moses (Exod. 19:21), "Go down and charge the people, lest they should have a mind to pass the" fixed "limits to see the Lord." Therefore the active life is more excellent than the contemplative.

Objection 3

Further, no man should be taken away from a greater thing in order to be occupied with lesser things: for the Apostle says (1 Cor. 12:31): "Be zealous for the better gifts." Now some are taken away from the state of the contemplative life to the occupations of the active life, as in the case of those who are transferred to the state of prelacy. Therefore it would seem that the active life is more excellent than the contemplative.

On the contrary,

Our Lord said (Luke 10:42): "Mary hath chosen the best part, which shall not be taken away from her." Now Mary figures the contemplative life. Therefore the contemplative life is more excellent than the active.

I answer that,

Nothing prevents certain things being more excellent in themselves, whereas they are surpassed by another in some respect. Accordingly we must reply that the contemplative life is simply more excellent than the active: and the Philosopher proves this by eight reasons. The first is, because the contemplative life becomes man according to that which is best in him, namely the intellect, and according to its proper objects, namely things intelligible; whereas the active life is occupied with externals. Hence Rachel, by whom the contemplative life is signified, is interpreted "the vision of the principle," whereas as Gregory [Pope Gregory I, about 540-604] says the active life is signified by Leah who was blear-eyed (Gen. 29:17). The second reason is because the contemplative life can be more continuous, although not as regards the highest degree of contemplation, as stated above, wherefore Mary, by whom the contemplative life is signified, is described as "sitting" all the time "at the Lord's feet." Thirdly, because the contemplative life is more delightful than the active; wherefore Augustine says that "Martha was troubled, but Mary feasted." Fourthly, because in the contemplative life man is more self-sufficient, since he needs fewer things for that purpose; wherefore it was said (Luke 10:41): "Martha, Martha, thou art careful and art troubled about many things." Fifthly, because the contemplative life is loved more for its own sake, while the active life is directed to something else. Hence it is written (Ps. 27:4): "One thing I have asked of the Lord, this will I seek after, that I may dwell in the house of the Lord all the days of my life, that I may see the delight of the Lord." Sixthly, because the contemplative life consists in leisure and rest, according to Psalm 46:10, "Be still and see that I am God." Seventhly, because the contemplative life is according to Divine things, whereas active life is according to human things; wherefore Augustine says: "'In the beginning was the Word': to Him was Mary hearkening: 'The Word was made flesh': Him was Martha serving." Eighthly, because the contemplative life is according to that which is most proper to man, namely his intellect; whereas in the works of the active life the lower powers also, which are common to us and brutes, have their part; wherefore (Ps. 36:6) after the words, "Men and beasts Thou wilt preserve, O Lord," that which is special to man is added (Ps. 36:9): "In Thy light we shall see light."

Our Lord adds a ninth reason (Luke 10:42) when He says: "Mary hath chosen the best part, which shall not be taken away from her," which words Augustine expounds thus: "Not — Thou hast chosen badly but — she has chosen better. Why better? Listen — because it shall not be taken away from her. But the burden of necessity shall at length be taken from thee: whereas the sweetness of truth is eternal."

Yet in a restricted sense and in a particular case one should prefer the active life on account of the needs of the present life. Thus too the Philosopher says: "It is better to be wise than to be rich, yet for one who is in need, it is better to be rich. . . ."

Reply to Objection 1

Not only the active life concerns prelates, they should also excel in the contemplative life; hence Gregory says: "A prelate should be foremost in action, more uplifted than others in contemplation."

Reply to Objection 2

The contemplative life consists in a certain liberty of mind. For Gregory says that "the contemplative life obtains a certain freedom of mind, for it thinks not of temporal but of eternal things." And Boethius [philosopher and theologian, about 480–about 524] says, "The soul of man must needs be more free while it continues to gaze on the Divine mind, and less so when it stoops to bodily things." Wherefore it is evident that the active life does not directly command the contemplative life, but prescribes certain works of the active life as dispositions to the contemplative life; which it accordingly serves rather than commands. Gregory refers to this when he says that "the active life is bondage, whereas the contemplative life is freedom."

Reply to Objection 3

Sometimes a man is called away from the contemplative life to the works of the active life, on account of some necessity of the present life, yet not so as to be compelled to forsake contemplation altogether. Hence Augustine says: "The love of truth seeks a holy leisure, the demands of charity undertake an honest toil," the work namely of the active life. "If no one imposes this burden upon us we must devote ourselves to the research and contemplation of truth, but if it be imposed on us, we must bear it because charity demands it of us. Yet even then we must not altogether forsake the delights of truth, lest we deprive ourselves of its sweetness, and this burden overwhelm us." Hence it is clear that when a person is called from the contemplative life to the active life, this is done by way not of subtraction but of addition.

Q. 182, a.2: Whether the contemplative life is hindered by the active life?

Objection 1

It would seem that the contemplative life is hindered by the active life. For the contemplative life requires a certain stillness of mind, according to Ps. 46:10, "Be still, and see that I am God"; whereas the active life involves restlessness, according to Luke 10:41, "Martha, Martha, thou art careful and troubled about many things." Therefore the active life hinders the contemplative.

Objection 2

Further, clearness of vision is a requisite for the contemplative life. Now active life is a hindrance to clear vision; for Gregory says that it "is blear-eyed and fruitful, because the active life, being occupied with work, sees less." Therefore the active life hinders the contemplative.

Objection 3

Further, one contrary hinders the other. Now the active and the contemplative life are apparently contrary to one another, since the active life is busy about many things, while the contemplative life attends to the contemplation of one; wherefore they differ in opposition to one another. Therefore it would seem that the contemplative life is hindered by the active.

On the contrary,

Gregory says: "Those who wish to hold the fortress of contemplation, must first of all train in the camp of action."

I answer that,

The active life may be considered from two points of view. First, as regards the attention to and practice of external works: and thus it is evident that the active life hinders the contemplative, in so far as it is impossible for one to be busy with external action, and at the same time give oneself to Divine contemplation. Secondly, active life may be considered as quieting and directing the internal passions of the soul; and from this point of view the active life is a help to the contemplative, since the latter is hindered by the inordinateness of the internal passions. Hence Gregory says: "Those who wish to hold the fortress of contemplation must first of all train in the camp of action. Thus after careful study they will learn whether they no longer wrong their neighbor, whether they bear with equanimity the wrongs their neighbors do to them, whether their soul is neither overcome with joy in the presence of temporal goods, nor cast down with too great a sorrow when those goods are withdrawn. In this way they will know when they withdraw within themselves, in order to explore spiritual things, whether they no longer carry with them the shadows of the things corporeal, or, if these follow them, whether they prudently drive them away." Hence the work of the active life conduces to the contemplative, by quelling the interior passions which give rise to the phantasms whereby contemplation is hindered.

This suffices for the Replies to the Objections; for these arguments consider the occupation itself of external actions, and not the effect which is the quelling of the passions. . . .

Q. 184, a.1: Whether the perfection of the Christian life consists chiefly in charity?

Objection 1

It would seem that the perfection of the Christian life does not consist chiefly in charity. For the Apostle says (1 Cor. 14:20): "In malice be children, but in sense be perfect." But charity regards not the senses but the affections. Therefore it would seem that the perfection of the Christian life does not chiefly consist in charity.

Objection 2

Further, it is written (Eph. 6:13): "Take unto you the armor of God, that you may be able to resist in the evil day, and to stand in all things perfect"; and the text continues (Eph. 6:14, 16), speaking of the armor of God: "Stand therefore having your loins girt about with truth, and having on the breastplate of justice . . . in all things taking the shield of faith." Therefore the perfection of the Christian life consists not only in charity, but also in other virtues.

Objection 3

Further, virtues, like other habits, are specified by their acts. Now it is written (James 1:4) that "patience hath a perfect work." Therefore seemingly the state of perfection consists more specially in patience.

On the contrary,

It is written (Col. 3:14): "Above all things have charity, which is the bond of perfection," because it binds, as it were, all the other virtues together in perfect unity.

I answer that,

A thing is said to be perfect in so far as it attains its proper end, which is the ultimate perfection thereof. Now it is charity that unites us to God, Who is the last end of the human mind, since "he that abideth in charity abideth in God, and God in him" (1 John 4:16). Therefore the perfection of the Christian life consists radically in charity.

Reply to Objection 1

The perfection of the human senses would seem to consist chiefly in their concurring together in the unity of truth, according to 1 Cor. 1:10, "That you be perfect in the same mind (*sensu*), and in the same judgment." Now this is effected by charity which operates consent in us men. Wherefore even the perfection of the senses consists radically in the perfection of charity.

Reply to Objection 2

A man may be said to be perfect in two ways. First, simply: and this perfection regards that which belongs to a thing's nature; for instance, an animal may be said to be perfect when it lacks nothing in the disposition of its members and in such things as are necessary for an animal's life. Secondly, a thing is said to be perfect relatively: and this perfection regards something connected with the thing externally, such as whiteness or blackness or something of the kind. Now the Christian life consists chiefly in charity whereby the soul is united to God; wherefore it is written (1 John 3:14): "He that loveth not abideth in death." Hence the perfection of the Christian life consists simply in charity, but in the other virtues relatively. And since that which is simply, is paramount and greatest in comparison with other things, it follows that the perfection of charity is paramount in relation to the perfection that regards the other virtues.

Reply to Objection 3

Patience is stated to have a perfect work in relation to charity, in so far as it is an effect of the abundance of charity that a man bears hardships patiently, according to Rom. 8:35, "Who . . . shall separate us from the love of Christ? Shall tribulation? Or distress?" etc. . . .

Q. 186, a.3: Whether poverty is required for religious perfection?

Objection 1

It would seem that poverty is not required for religious perfection. For that which it is unlawful to do does not apparently belong to the state of perfection. But it would seem to be unlawful for a man to give up all he possesses; since the Apostle (2 Cor. 8:12) lays down the way in which the faithful are to give alms saying: "If the will be forward, it is accepted according to that which a man hath," i.e., "you should keep back what you need," and afterwards he adds (2 Cor. 8:13): "For I mean not that others should be eased, and you burdened," i.e., "with poverty," according to a gloss. Moreover, a gloss on 1 Tim. 6:8, "Having food, and wherewith to be covered," says: "Though we brought nothing, and will carry nothing away, we must not give up these temporal things altogether." Therefore it seems that voluntary poverty is not requisite for religious perfection.

Objection 2

Further, whosoever exposes himself to danger sins. But he who renounces all he has and embraces voluntary poverty exposes himself to danger — not only spiritual, according to Prov. 30:9, "Lest perhaps . . . being compelled by poverty, I should steal and forswear the name of my God," and Ecclesiasticus 27:1, "Through poverty many have sinned" — but also corporal, for it is written (Eccles. 7:13): "As wisdom is a defense, so money is a defense," and the Philosopher says that "the waste of property appears to be a sort of ruining of one's self, since thereby man lives." Therefore it would seem that voluntary poverty is not requisite for the perfection of religious life.

Objection 3

Further, "Virtue observes the mean," as stated in Aristotle's *Ethics* 2.6. But he who renounces all by voluntary poverty seems to go to the extreme rather than to observe the mean. Therefore he does not act virtuously: and so this does not pertain to the perfection of life.

Objection 4

Further, the ultimate perfection of man consists in happiness. Now riches conduce to happiness; for it is written (Ecclesiasticus 31:8): "Blessed is the rich man that is found without blemish," and the Philosopher says that "riches contribute instrumentally to happiness." Therefore voluntary poverty is not requisite for religious perfection.

Objection 5

Further, the episcopal state is more perfect than the religious state. But bishops may have property, as stated above. Therefore religious may also.

Objection 6

Further, almsgiving is a work most acceptable to God, and as Chrysostom [John Chrysostom, about 347-407, preacher, theologian, and patriarch of Constantinople] says, "is a most effective remedy in repentance." Now poverty excludes almsgiving. Therefore it would seem that poverty does not pertain to religious perfection.

On the contrary,

Gregory says: "There are some of the righteous who, bracing themselves up to lay hold of the very height of perfection, while they aim at higher objects within, abandon all things without." Now, as stated above, it belongs properly to religious to brace themselves up in order to lay hold of the very height of perfection. Therefore it belongs to them to abandon all outward things by voluntary poverty.

I answer that,

As stated above, the religious state is an exercise and a school for attaining to the perfection of charity. For this it is necessary that a man wholly withdraw his affections from worldly things; since Augustine says, speaking to God: "Too little doth he love Thee, who loves anything with Thee, which he loveth not for Thee." Wherefore he says that "greater charity means less cupidity [either greed or carnal desire], perfect charity means no cupidity." Now the possession of worldly things draws a man's mind to the love of them: hence Augustine says that "we are more firmly attached to earthly things when we have them than when we desire them: since why did that young man go away sad, save because he had great wealth? For it is one thing not to wish to lay hold of what one has not, and another to renounce what one already has; the former are rejected as foreign to us, the latter are cut off as a limb." And Chrysostom says that "the possession of wealth kindles a greater flame and the desire for it becomes stronger."

Hence it is that in the attainment of the perfection of charity the first foundation is voluntary poverty, whereby a man lives without property of his own, according to the saying of our Lord (Matt. 19:21), "If thou wilt be perfect, go, sell all thou hast, and give to the poor . . . and come, follow Me."

Reply to Objection 1

As the gloss adds, "when the Apostle said this (namely 'not that you should be burdened,' i.e., with poverty)," he did not mean that "it were better not to give: but he feared for the weak, whom he admonished so to give as not to suffer privation." Hence in like manner the other gloss means not that it is unlawful to renounce all one's temporal goods, but that this is not required of necessity. Wherefore Ambrose [about 339-397, theologian and bishop of Milan] says: "Our Lord does not wish," namely does not command us "to pour out our wealth all at once, but to dispense it; or perhaps to do as did Elisha, who slew his oxen and fed the poor with that which was his own, so that no household care might hold him back."

Reply to Objection 2

He who renounces all his possessions for Christ's sake exposes himself to no danger, neither spiritual nor corporal. For spiritual danger ensues from poverty when the latter is not voluntary; because those who are unwillingly poor, through the desire of money-getting, fall into many sins, according to 1 Tim. 6:9, "They that will become rich, fall into temptation and into the snare of the devil." This attachment is put away by those who embrace voluntary poverty, but it gathers strength in those who have wealth, as stated above. Again bodily danger does not threaten those who, intent on following Christ, renounce all their possessions and entrust themselves to divine providence. Hence Augustine says: "Those who seek first the kingdom of God and His justice are not weighed down by anxiety lest they lack what is necessary."

Reply to Objection 3

According to the Philosopher, the mean of virtue is taken according to right reason, not according to the quantity of a thing. Consequently whatever may be done in accordance with right reason is not rendered sinful by the greatness of the quantity, but all the more virtuous. It would, however, be against right reason to throw away all one's possessions through intemperance, or without any useful purpose; whereas it is in accordance with right reason to renounce wealth in order to devote oneself to the contemplation of wisdom. Even certain philosophers are said to have done this; for Jerome [about 342-420, theologian and biblical translator] says: "The famous Theban, Crates, once a very wealthy man, when he was going to Athens to study philosophy, cast away a large amount of gold; for he considered that he could not possess both gold and virtue at the same time." Much more therefore is it according to right reason for a man to renounce all he has, in order perfectly to follow Christ. Wherefore Jerome says: "Poor thyself, follow Christ poor."

Reply to Objection 4

Happiness or felicity is twofold. One is perfect, to which we look forward in the life to come; the other is imperfect, in respect of which some are said to be happy in this life. The happiness of this life is twofold: one is according to the active life, the other according to the contemplative life, as the Philosopher asserts. Now wealth conduces instrumentally to the happiness of the active life which consists in external actions, because, as the Philosopher says, "we do many things by friends, by riches, by political influence, as it were by instruments." On the other hand, it does not conduce to the happiness of the contemplative life; rather is it an obstacle thereto, inasmuch as the anxiety it involves disturbs the quiet of the soul, which is most necessary to one who contemplates. Hence it is that the Philosopher asserts that "for actions many things are needed, but the contemplative man needs no such things," namely external goods, "for his operation; in fact they are obstacles to his contemplation."

Man is directed to future happiness by charity; and since voluntary poverty is an efficient exercise for the attaining of perfect charity, it follows that it is of great avail in acquiring the happiness of heaven. Wherefore our Lord said (Matt. 19:21): "Go, sell all thou hast, and give to the poor, and thou shalt have treasure in heaven." Now riches once they are possessed are in themselves of a nature to hinder the perfection of charity, especially by enticing and distracting the mind. Hence it is written (Matt. 13:22) that "the care of this world and the deceitfulness of riches choketh up the word" of God, for, as Gregory says, by "preventing the good desire from entering into the heart, they destroy life at its very outset." Consequently it is difficult to safeguard charity amidst riches: wherefore our Lord said (Matt. 19:23) that "a rich man shall hardly enter into the kingdom of heaven," which we must understand as referring to one who actually has wealth, since He says that this is impossible for him who places his affection in riches, according to the explanation of Chrysostom, for He adds (Matt. 19:24): "It is easier for a camel to pass through the eye of a needle, than for a rich man to enter into the kingdom of heaven." Hence it is not said simply that the "rich man" is blessed, but "the rich man that is found without blemish, and that hath not gone after gold," and this because he has done a difficult thing, wherefore the text continues: "Who is he? and we will praise him; for he hath done wonderful things in his life," namely by not loving riches though placed in the midst of them.

Reply to Objection 5

The episcopal state is not directed to the attainment of perfection, but rather to the effect that, in virtue of the perfection which he already has, a man may govern others, by administering not only spiritual but also temporal things. This belongs to the active life, wherein many things occur that may be done by means of wealth as an instrument, as stated. Wherefore it is not required of bishops, who make profession of governing Christ's flock, that they have nothing of their own, whereas it is required of religious who make profession of learning to obtain perfection.

Reply to Objection 6

The renouncement of one's own wealth is compared to almsgiving as the universal to the particular, and as the holocaust to the sacrifice. Hence Gregory says that those who assist "the needy with the things they possess, by their good deeds offer sacrifice, since they offer up something to God and keep back something for themselves; whereas those who keep nothing for themselves offer a burnt offering which is greater than a sacrifice." Wherefore Jerome also says: "When you declare that those do better who retain the use of their possessions, and dole out the fruits of their possessions to the poor, it is not I but the Lord Who answers you; If thou wilt be perfect," etc., and afterwards he goes on to say: "This man whom you praise belongs to the second and third degree, and we too commend him: provided we acknowledge the first as to be preferred to the second and third." For this reason in order to exclude the error of Vigilantius [opponent of Jerome, active around 400, whom Jerome accused of rejecting the cult of the saints and the discipline of the ascetic life] it is said: "It is a good thing to give away one's goods by dispensing them to the poor: it is better to give them away once for all with the intention of following the Lord, and, free of solicitude, to be poor with Christ."

Q. 186, a.4: Whether perpetual continence is required for religious perfection?

Objection 1

It would seem that perpetual continence is not required for religious perfection. For all perfection of the Christian life began with Christ's apostles. Now the apostles do not appear to have observed continence, as evidenced by Peter, of whose mother-in-law we read in Matt. 8:14. Therefore it would seem that perpetual continence is not requisite for religious perfection.

Objection 2

Further, the first example of perfection is shown to us in the person of Abraham, to whom the Lord said (Gen. 17:1): "Walk before Me, and be perfect." Now the copy should not surpass the example. Therefore perpetual continence is not requisite for religious perfection.

Objection 3

Further, that which is required for religious perfection is to be found in every religious order. Now there are some religious who lead a married life. Therefore religious perfection does not require perpetual continence.

On the contrary,

The Apostle says (2 Cor. 7:1): "Let us cleanse ourselves from all defilement of the flesh and of the spirit, perfecting sanctification in the fear of God." Now cleanness of flesh and spirit is safeguarded by continence, for it is said (1 Cor. 7:34): "The unmarried woman and the virgin thinketh on the things of the Lord, that she may be holy both in spirit and in body." Therefore religious perfection requires continence.

I answer that,

The religious state requires the removal of whatever hinders man from devoting himself entirely to God's service. Now the use of sexual union hinders the mind from giving itself wholly to the service of God, and this for two reasons. First, on account of the strong feeling of pleasure it induces, which by frequent repetition increases sexual desire, as also the Philosopher observes: and hence it is that the sexual activity withdraws the mind from that perfect intentness on tending to God. Augustine expresses this when he says: "I consider that nothing so casts down the manly mind from its height as the fondling of women, and those bodily contacts which belong to the married state." Secondly, because it involves man in solicitude for the control of his wife, his children, and his temporalities which serve for their upkeep. Hence the Apostle says (1 Cor. 7:32, 33): "He that is without a wife is solicitous for the things that belong to the Lord, how he may please God: but he that is with a wife is solicitous for the things of the world, how he may please his wife."

Therefore perpetual continence, as well as voluntary poverty, is requisite for religious perfection. Wherefore just as Vigilantius was condemned for equaling riches to poverty, so was Jovinian [another of Jerome's opponents; he argued that marriage was just as good as the celibate life] condemned for equaling marriage to virginity.

Reply to Objection 1

The perfection not only of poverty but also of continence was introduced by Christ Who said (Matt. 19:12): "There are eunuchs who have made themselves eunuchs for the kingdom of heaven," and then added: "He that can take, let him take it." And lest anyone should be deprived of the hope of attaining perfection, he admitted to the state of perfection those even who were married. Now the husbands could not without committing an injustice forsake their wives, whereas men could without injustice renounce riches. Wherefore Peter, whom He found married, He severed not from his wife, while "He withheld from marriage John, who wished to marry."

Reply to Objection 2

As Augustine says, "The chastity of celibacy is better than the chastity of marriage, one of which Abraham had in use, both of them in habit. For he lived chastely, and he might have been chaste without marrying, but it was not requisite then." Nevertheless if the patriarchs of old had perfection of mind together with wealth and marriage, which is a mark of the greatness of their virtue, this is no reason why any weaker person should presume to have such great virtue that he can attain to perfection though rich and married; as neither does a man unarmed presume to attack his enemy, because Samson slew many foes with the jaw-bone of an ass. For those fathers, had it been seasonable to observe continence and poverty, would have been most careful to observe them.

Reply to Objection 3

Such ways of living as admit of the use of marriage are not the religious life simply and absolutely speaking, but in a restricted sense, in so far as they have a certain share in those things that belong to the religious state.

Q. 186, a.5: Whether obedience belongs to religious perfection?

Objection 1

It would seem that obedience does not belong to religious perfection. For those things seemingly belong to religious perfection, which are works of supererogation and are not binding upon all. But all are bound to obey their superiors, according to the saying of the Apostle (Heb. 13:17), "Obey your prelates, and be subject to them." Therefore it would seem that obedience does not belong to religious perfection.

Objection 2

Further, obedience would seem to belong properly to those who have to be guided by the sense of others, and such persons are lacking in discernment. Now the Apostle says (Heb. 5:14) that "strong meat is for the perfect, for them who by custom have their senses exercised to the discerning of good and evil." Therefore it would seem that obedience does not belong to the state of the perfect.

Objection 3

Further, if obedience were requisite for religious perfection, it would follow that it is befitting to all religious. But it is not becoming to all; since some religious lead a solitary life, and have no superior whom they obey. Again religious superiors apparently are not bound to obedience. Therefore obedience would seem not to pertain to religious perfection.

Objection 4

Further, if the vow of obedience were requisite for religion, it would follow that religious are bound to obey their superiors in all things, just as they are bound to abstain from all sexual intercourse by their vow of continence. But they are not bound to obey them in all things, as stated above, when we were treating of the virtue of obedience. Therefore the vow of obedience is not requisite for religion.

Objection 5

Further, those services are most acceptable to God which are done freely
·and not of necessity, according to 2 Corinthians 9:7, "Not with sadness or of
necessity." Now that which is done out of obedience is done of necessity of
precept. Therefore those good works are more deserving of praise which are
done of one's own accord. Therefore the vow of obedience is unbecoming to
religion whereby men seek to attain to that which is better.

On the contrary,

Religious perfection consists chiefly in the imitation of Christ, according to
Matthew 19:21, "If thou wilt be perfect, go, sell all thou hast, and give to the
poor, and follow Me." Now in Christ obedience is commended above all according to Philippians 2:8, "He became obedient unto death." Therefore
seemingly obedience belongs to religious perfection.

I answer that,

As stated above the religious state is a school and exercise for tending to perfection. Now those who are being instructed or exercised in order to attain a
certain end must needs follow the direction of someone under whose control they are instructed or exercised so as to attain that end as disciples under a master. Hence religious need to be placed under the instruction and
command of someone as regards things pertaining to the religious life;
wherefore it is said: "The monastic life denotes subjection and discipleship."
Now one man is subjected to another's command and instruction by obedience; and consequently obedience is requisite for religious perfection.

Reply to Objection 1

To obey one's superiors in matters that are essential to virtue is not a work
of supererogation, but is common to all: whereas to obey in matters pertaining to the practice of perfection belongs properly to religious. This latter
obedience is compared to the former as the universal to the particular. For
those who live in the world keep something for themselves, and offer something to God; and in the latter respect they are under obedience to their su-

periors: whereas those who live in religion give themselves wholly and their possessions to God, as stated above. Hence their obedience is universal.

Reply to Objection 2

As the Philosopher says, by performing actions we contract certain habits, and when we have acquired the habit we are best able to perform the actions. Accordingly those who have not attained to perfection, acquire perfection by obeying, while those who have already acquired perfection are most ready to obey, not as though they need to be directed to the acquisition of perfection, but as maintaining themselves by this means in that which belongs to perfection.

Reply to Objection 3

The subjection of religious is chiefly in reference to bishops, who are compared to them as perfecters to perfected, as Dionysius [great mystic theologian, now thought to have lived in Syria around 500 but believed in the Middle Ages to have been the convert of St. Paul mentioned in Acts 17:34] states, where he also says that the "monastic order is subjected to the perfecting virtues of the bishops, and is taught by their godlike enlightenment." Hence neither hermits nor religious superiors are exempt from obedience to bishops; and if they be wholly or partly exempt from obedience to the bishop of the diocese, they are nevertheless bound to obey the Sovereign Pontiff, not only in matters affecting all in common, but also in those which pertain specially to religious discipline.

Reply to Objection 4

The vow of obedience taken by religious extends to the disposition of a man's whole life, and in this way it has a certain universality, although it does not extend to all individual acts. For some of these do not belong to religion, through not being of those things that concern the love of God and of our neighbor, such as rubbing one's beard, lifting a stick from the ground and so forth, which do not come under a vow nor under obedience; and some are contrary to religion. Nor is there any comparison with continence whereby acts are excluded which are altogether contrary to religion.

Reply to Objection 5

The necessity of coercion makes an act involuntary and consequently deprives it of the character of praise or merit; whereas the necessity which is consequent upon obedience is a necessity not of coercion but of a free will, inasmuch as a man is willing to obey, although perhaps he would not be willing to do the thing commanded considered in itself. Wherefore since by the vow of obedience a man lays himself under the necessity of doing for God's sake certain things that are not pleasing in themselves, for this very reason that which he does is the more acceptable to God, though it be of less account, because man can give nothing greater to God, than by subjecting his will to another man's for God's sake. Hence in the Conferences of the Fathers it is stated that "the Sarabaitae [monks who lived in informal communities without anyone in charge] are the worst class of monks, because through providing for their own needs without being subject to superiors, they are free to do as they will; and yet day and night they are more busily occupied in work than those who live in monasteries."

Q. 187, a.2: Whether it is lawful for religious to occupy themselves with secular business?

Objection 1

It would seem unlawful for religious to occupy themselves with secular business. For in the decree quoted above of Pope Boniface it is said that the "Blessed Benedict bade them to be altogether free from secular business; and this is most explicitly prescribed by the apostolic doctrine and the teaching of all the Fathers, not only to religious, but also to all the canonical clergy," according to 2 Tim. 2:4, "No man, being a soldier to God, entangleth himself with secular business." Now it is the duty of all religious to be soldiers of God. Therefore it is unlawful for them to occupy themselves with secular business.

Objection 2

Further, the Apostle says (1 Thess. 4:11): "That you use your endeavor to be quiet, and that you do your own business," which a gloss explains thus — "by refraining from other people's affairs, so as to be the better able to attend to the amendment of your own life." Now religious devote themselves in a special way to the amendment of their life. Therefore they should not occupy themselves with secular business.

Objection 3

Further, Jerome, commenting on Matt. 11:8, "Behold, they that are clothed in soft garments are in the houses of kings," says: "Hence we gather that an austere life and severe preaching should avoid the palaces of kings and the mansions of the voluptuous." But the needs of secular business induce men to frequent the palaces of kings. Therefore it is unlawful for religious to occupy themselves with secular business.

On the contrary,

The Apostle says (Rom. 16:1): "I commend to you Phoebe our Sister," and further on (Rom. 16:2), "that you assist her in whatsoever business she shall have need of you."

I answer that,

As stated above, the religious state is directed to the attainment of the perfection of charity, consisting principally in the love of God and secondarily in the love of our neighbor. Consequently that which religious intend chiefly and for its own sake is to give themselves to God. Yet if their neighbor be in need, they should attend to his affairs out of charity, according to Gal. 6:2, "Bear ye one another's burdens: and so you shall fulfill the law of Christ," since through serving their neighbor for God's sake, they are obedient to the divine love. Hence it is written (James 1:27): "Religion clean and undefiled before God and the Father is this: to visit the fatherless and widows in their tribulation," which means, according to a gloss, to assist the helpless in their time of need.

We must conclude therefore that it is unlawful for either monks or clerics to carry on secular business from motives of avarice; but from motives of charity, and with their superior's permission, they may occupy themselves with due moderation in the administration and direction of secular business. Wherefore it is said in the Decretals [papal letters setting forth church law]: "The holy synod decrees that henceforth no cleric shall buy property or occupy himself with secular business, save with a view to the care of the fatherless, orphans, or widows, or when the bishop of the city commands him to take charge of the business connected with the Church." And the same applies to religious as to clerics, because they are both debarred from secular business on the same grounds, as stated above.

Reply to Objection 1

Monks are forbidden to occupy themselves with secular business from motives of avarice, but not from motives of charity.

Reply to Objection 2

To occupy oneself with secular business on account of another's need is not officiousness but charity.

Reply to Objection 3

To haunt the palaces of kings from motives of pleasure, glory, or avarice is not becoming to religious, but there is nothing unseemly in their visiting them from motives of piety. Hence it is written (2 Kings 4:13): "Hast thou any business, and wilt thou that I speak to the king or to the general of the army?" Likewise it becomes religious to go to the palaces of kings to rebuke and guide them, even as John the Baptist rebuked Herod, as related in Matthew 14:4.

CHRISTINE DE PISAN

The Treasure of the City of Ladies

Christine de Pisan (1365-about 1430) grew up in Italy. Her father, a physician and astrologer, was a great success at the court of the King of France, Charles V, and Christine married a promising young nobleman. When both her husband and her father died, Christine found herself, at the age of twenty-five, a widow with three children, a mother, and a niece to support. She turned to writing poems and essays dedicated to noble patrons and became one of the few "professional authors" in the Middle Ages.

One scholar has described *The Treasure of the City of Ladies*, written in 1405, as "part etiquette book, part survival manual . . . written for women who had to live from day to day in the world as it was." In other works, Christine protested the mistreatment of women in her society; here she is more concerned with how women are to cope with the situations in which they find themselves, however unfair those may be. She faces the question of how the wealthy and powerful can be good Christians but also has advice for those further down the social scale.

2. How Temptations Can Come to a High-Born Princess

When the princess or high-born lady wakes up in the morning, she sees herself lying luxuriously in her bed between soft sheets, surrounded by rich accoutrements and everything for bodily comfort, and ladies-in-waiting around her focusing all their attention on her and seeing that she lacks for nothing, ready to run to her if she gives the least sigh or if she breathes a word, their knees flexed to administer any service to her and to obey all her commands. And so it often happens that temptation will assail her, singing

Christine de Pisan, *The Treasure of the City of Ladies*, trans. Sarah Lawson (New York: Penguin Classics, 1986), 35-38, 39-41, 43-50, 167-71.

sweetly: "By Almighty God, is there in this world a greater lady than you or one with more authority? To whom should you defer, for don't you take precedence over everyone else? This or that woman, even if she is married to a great prince, cannot be compared to you. You are richer, or have a better lineage, or are more respected because of your children, more feared, and more renowned and wield more authority because of your husband's power. Therefore who would dare to displease you in any way? Would you not well and truly avenge yourself with such power and such other advantages?

"Therefore there is no one so great that you do not have power over him. Any time such and such a man or woman is arrogant towards you and presumptuously intends to harm you and does such and such a thing to cause your displeasure, you can avenge yourself later when you see your chance, and you will be able to do it very well with the power you have."

But what good does it do you to do that?

"No one accomplishes anything, however skilled he may be, nor is anyone feared if he has no money or considerable financial resources. If you can manage to amass treasure so that you can look after your own needs, it is the surest course and the best friend you can have. Who would dare to disobey you, seeing that you have great resources to dispense? If you pay only low wages, your servants will still serve you gladly in the hope of eventually getting more money, for your wealth will be well known. You will have no trouble with this, and if there is any talk about it, such gossip cannot hurt you. What should you care? All you have to worry about is pleasing yourself. You have only your leisurely life in this world — what else can you need? You cannot lack for wines and foods; you can have them whenever you like, and every other pleasure. In brief, you need not bother about anything else except having all the delight and all the amusement that you can in this world. No one has a good time if he does not provide it for himself. You must have a carefree heart to make you happy and to give you a merry life. You must have such gowns, such ornaments, such jewels and such clothing made in a particular way and of a particular cut. It's no more than you deserve."

3. How the Good Princess Who Loves and Fears Our Lord Can Resist Temptations by Means of Divine Inspiration

All the above-mentioned things or similar ones are the dishes that Temptation sets before everyone who lives a life of ease and pleasure. But what will the good princess do when she feels herself tempted in this way? Then she will need the unshakeable love and fear of Our Lord God Jesus Christ, who will teach her some home truths, speaking like this: "O foolish and ill-advised simpleton, what can you be thinking of? Have you forgotten what you really are? Don't you realize that you are a poor and miserable creature, frail, weak, and subject to all infirmities, passions, diseases and other pains that a mortal body can suffer? What advantage do you have over anyone else? What advantage would a pile of earth covered by finery have over one that was under a poor rag? O pitiful creature given to sin and every vice, do you want then, in that case, to ignore your true essence and forget how this wretched vessel empty of any virtue, that desires honors and comforts so much, will break and die shortly? It will be food for the worms and will rot in the earth as much as the poorest woman there is, and the unhappy soul will take with it nothing except the good or evil that the wretched body has done on earth. What will honors be worth to you then, or possessions or your family, which you boast of so much in this world? Will they help you in the torments you will endure if you have lived wickedly in this world? Certainly not, but rather everything that you have abused will lead you to ruin. Alas, pitiful woman, it would have been better for you to have lived a troubled life as a poor woman than to be elevated to such great rank, which will be (if you are not on your guard against it) the cause of your damnation. For it is difficult to be among the flames without getting burned.

"Don't you know what God says in the Gospel, that the poor are blessed and that theirs is the kingdom of heaven? And elsewhere He says that a rich man can no more enter paradise than a laden camel can go through the eye of a needle.

"O pitiful woman, you are so blinded that you do not perceive your great peril. The cause of it is great pride, which, because of the vain honors that surround you, overrides all reason in you, so that you do not imagine yourself to be only a princess or a great lady, but like a veritable goddess in this world. Oh, this false pride! How can you tolerate it in yourself? You know very well, from the report of the Scriptures, that God hates it so much that He cannot endure it, for because of this He exiled Lucifer, the prince of devils, from Heaven into Hell, and He will undoubtedly do the same to you if you are not careful." . . .

Know for certain, and do not doubt it, that you will never use with much joy the wealth you have acquired and amassed unfairly, for just when you have assembled it with the intention of using it in some way at your pleasure, God will send you so much adversity or affliction or other burdens that this damnable treasure will turn out to be disagreeable and painful to use, quite contrary to what you intend. What will you do then with this treasure? Will you take it with you when you die? Certainly not, but only the burden of what you have wickedly acquired and used. But look again where this cursed pride puts you. Because it makes you believe that you surpass everyone else in grandeur and authority, it makes your heart quite sad and fearful that someone else may be able to overtake you and reach your high estate. Because it makes you always wish to be greater, if it happens that you see or learn about someone with as much or more authority or honor than you, no pain could be greater than the sorrow that your heart carries. This pain makes you spiteful, wrathful and malicious.

A second little flame from Hell makes you proud. You say to yourself, "It's not your duty, place or trade to labor or to work at anything. You have nothing to do but to see to your own comforts, to sleep late in the morning, and then after dinner to rest, inspect your chests of jewels and ornaments — this is your rightful employment." And so, unhappy witless creature that you are, does it seem to you that God, who has given time to each person to put to good use, has given you, more than another, the authority to spend it in lazy idleness? O wretched creature, you have heard it preached before that St. Bernard says of the Canticles that Idleness is the mother of all error and the wicked stepmother of the virtues. Idleness makes even a strong and constant man stumble into sin, which destroys all the virtues, nourishes Pride and builds the road to Hell. But what else comes of this Pride? This Pride, which thus makes you love your comforts, and those comforts, which nourish that Pride so much, make you desire voluptuous pleasures in eating and drinking, and by no means common things nor customary food, for you are quite tired of them. The cooks, to please you and to earn their wages, have to devise seasonings, garnishes and new sauces to make the meat more pleasant to your taste. Likewise, you demand the finest wines.

O sorrowful woman, is it necessary thus to fill up this belly which is, after all, only food for worms and the vessel of all wickedness? But what happens to it when it is thus filled? What does it ask, just like the mouth, but the nourishment of passion, luxury, and voluptuousness, and excess of wines and of meats and the nourishment of carnality? This is what inflames Pride and predisposes the will to desire in all ways everything that can delight the body. Flesh thus nourished resembles the horse which, when its master tries hard to spur it on, is so strong and skittish that when he thinks to ride it he cannot control it. It bolts with him in spite of the roads being hazardous, and finally through its resistance and wrongheadedness it breaks the rider's neck. In exactly this way the body too much overfed and excited by voluptuous foods kills the soul and the virtues, but Pride, which flourishes on this rich food, makes you so much desire extravagant clothing, jewels and finery that you hardly think of anything else, neither what they must have cost nor where they must have come from, nor how you may have acquired them. Besides leading you to other unseemly, disreputable and boundless vices, Pride makes you so disdainful and aloof to serve that one can hardly find jewels, clothing or ornaments that are good enough for you. In addition to all these things, you are so impertinent and presumptuous that it seems to you that neither God Himself nor anything else can impose upon you.

O miserable, wretched and blind creature! How can this outrageous pride have so much power over you that it makes you forget the punishments of God, even though He allows you to stay immersed for so long in so many faults without paying you your just deserts? Do you not know that a holy doctor of the Church says that the slower the vengeance of God is in coming, the more perilous it is when it does come? Likewise, the more the bow is bent, the more piercing is the arrow when it comes. Have you forgotten how Our Lord punished for his pride Nebuchadnezzar, who was king of Babylon and so great a prince that he feared no one? Similarly the great king of Persia, Antiochus, was punished, and also the Emperor Xerxes and a great number of others who were so great and powerful that there was nothing in Heaven or earth that they feared. And always by the vengeance and will of God they were so humbled and reduced to such confusion for their punishment that there was no man born in the world who was more miserable or more unfortunate than they became.

Do you not remember in connection with this that it is written in the Book of Ecclesiasticus in the tenth chapter, as you have heard your confessor relate, that God has cast down the thrones of proud princes and has set up the meek in their stead, and has plucked up the roots of the proud nations and has planted the lowly in their place? This means nothing else than that He destroys the proud and exalts the humble. So you are doing the right thing if you want to be destroyed!

By Almighty God, you who are a simple little woman who has no strength, power or authority unless it is conferred on you by some one else, do you imagine that you are surrounded by luxury and honor so that you can dominate and outdo the whole world at your will? . . .

5. Of the Two Holy Lives, Namely the Active Life and the Contemplative Life

Now, therefore, here is what you have to do if you wish to be saved. Scripture mentions two paths that lead to Heaven, and without following one or the other of these paths it is impossible to enter it. One is called the contemplative life, and the other the active life. But what exactly are the contemplative life and the active life?

The contemplative life is a manner and condition of serving God in which a person so ardently desires Our Lord that she entirely forgets everyone else — father, mother, children, and even herself — for a very great and passionate concentration on her Creator. She constantly thinks of Him and Him alone. All other things are nothing to her, nor does she experience poverty, tribulation or other torment with which any other creature might be afflicted. These afflictions could be an obstacle to the upright contemplative heart, but it pays no attention to them. Her approach to life is to scorn utterly everything that is of the world and its pleasures. Her object is to keep herself solitary and withdrawn from human society, on bended knee, her hands joined together, her eyes looking to Heaven, her heart exalted by high thoughts. She goes before God to contemplate and consider by holy inspiration the blessed Trinity, the heavenly host and the joys of Heaven. In this condition the perfect contemplative is often so ecstatic that she does not seem to be herself. The consolation, peacefulness and joy that she then feels cannot be described, neither can any other joy be compared to that one, for she is tasting the glories and joys of Paradise — that is, she sees God in spirit through contemplation. She burns in her love and has perfect contentment in this world, for she neither wishes nor desires anything else, and God comforts her, for she is His servant. He sets before her fragrant dishes from His holy Paradise; they are pure and holy thoughts which come from Heaven and give confident hope of joining that happy company. There is truly no joy like it. Those who know it have tried to describe it. I regret that I can only talk about it in this indirect way, as a blind person might discourse upon colors. That this life is more agreeable to God than any other has often been made clear to the world. It has been demonstrated and written by various men and women contemplative saints who have been seen in their contemplation raised above the earth by a miracle of God, as though the body wished to follow the thoughts that had mounted to Heaven. Of this holy and most exalted life I am not worthy to speak nor to describe it as it deserves, but there are many sacred writings that describe this fully, and so my attempt would be unnecessary anyway.

The active life is another way of serving God. The active life means that the person who wishes to follow it will be so charitable that, if she could, she would render service to everyone for the love of God. She goes around to the hospitals, visits the sick and the poor, according to her ability, helps them at her own expense and physical effort for the love of God. She has such great pity for people she sees in sin or misery that she weeps for them as though their distress were her own. She loves her neighbor's welfare as much as her own, is always striving to do good, is never idle; her heart burns ceaselessly with desire to do works of mercy, to which she devotes herself with all her might. Such a woman bears all injuries and tribulations patiently for the love of God. As you can see, this active life has more use in the world than the other one. These are both of great excellence, but Our Lord Jesus Christ himself judged the greater excellence of the two, when Mary Magdalene [Christine is reflecting on the story of Mary and Martha in Luke 10; like many Medievals she identifies this Mary with Mary Magdalene, though most modern scholars would disagree], who represents the contemplative life, was seated at the feet of Our Lord as one who had no thought for anything else and who utterly burned with her holy love. And Martha, her sister, by whom is understood the active life, was the hostess of Our Lord. She worked in the house in the service of Jesus and his Apostles and complained that Mary her sister did not help her. But Our Lord excused her, saying, "Martha, you are very diligent, and your work is good and necessary, but Mary has chosen the better part." By this "part" that she had chosen it can be understood that, although the active life is of great excellence and necessary for the help and succor of many, contemplation, which is to give up the world and all its cares to think only of Him, is the greatest and worthiest perfection. For this reason holy men have in the past established religious orders. In God's eyes life in a religious community is the highest level of life there is. Anyone who founds a religious order so that those who wish to live in contemplation can be separated there from the world in the service of God without any other cares pleases not only those people, but also God, who would be pleased indeed that each one said his offices there.

6. The Life That the Good Princess Decides to Lead

The good princess who has been inspired by God says to herself, "You must decide which of these paths you wish to take. It is commonly said, and it is true, that Discretion is the mother of the virtues. And why is she the mother? Because she guides and sustains the others, and anyone who fails to do any undertaking through her will find that all the work comes to nothing and is of no effect, because it is necessary to work by Discretion. This is what I must consider before I undertake anything at all.

"First I ought to think of the strength or weakness of my poor body and the frailty to which I am inclined, and also of what level of submission it is appropriate for me to assume, according to the estate where God has called me and which He has entrusted to me in this world. If I consider these things honestly, I will find that although I have some good intentions, I am too weak to suffer great abstinence and great pain, and my spirit is weak through frailty and inconstancy. And since I feel myself to be like that, I should not imagine that I am more virtuous than I am, even though God says, 'You must forsake father and mother for my name.' I'm afraid that I would not be at all able to fulfill my pledge and leave husband, children, everyday life, and all worldly concerns with the hope of serving only God, as women of the greatest perfection have done. Therefore I should not attempt something I wouldn't be able to persevere with. What shall I do then? Choose the active life? Alas, happy are those who succeed in the work they have been commanded to perform. O God, as You have established me in the world as a mere woman, I can at least serve You perfectly in ministering and doing service to Your 'members,' that is, the poor, for love of You. Alas, how would I ever manage to abandon all worldly position? Although I know very well that there is nothing else I love and desire except only You, and that all pleasure is nothing, I do not have the strength in myself to be able to abandon every worldly thing. I am very frightened about what to do, for You say that it is impossible for the rich to be saved."

At this juncture Holy Inspiration comes to the good princess and speaks to her in this manner:

"Now here is what you must do. God does not command anyone to leave everything to follow Him; that is only for those who wish to pursue the very most ideal life. Each person can be saved in his own station in life, and when God says it is impossible for a rich person to be saved, that means a person who has riches without virtues and who does not distribute his riches in alms and good deeds, a person whose whole happiness is in possessing great wealth. There is no doubt that God hates such people and that they will never enter the Kingdom of Heaven unless they change their ways. And as for the poor, who He says are blessed, those are the poor in spirit. Even a very rich and wealthy man could be poor in spirit if he does not prize the riches of the world, and if he has any of them, he distributes them in good works and in the service of God, and if he neither prides himself on his honor nor thinks himself greater because of his wealth. Such a person, even though he is wealthy in worldly goods, is poor of spirit and will possess the Kingdom of Heaven, and you can see the evidence of it. Have there not been a great host of kings and princes who are saints in Paradise, like St. Louis, King of France, and several others who did not retire from the world but reigned and possessed their lordships at the pleasure of God? They lived justly, but not because they did not appreciate glory or rejected the honors that they were given. They considered that honor belonged not to their own persons, but to the status of their power and wealth, of which they were vicars of God on earth. Similarly there are a great many queens and princesses who are saints in Paradise, like the wife of King Clovis of France and St. Badour and St. Elizabeth, Queen of Hungary, and many others. There is no doubt at all that God wishes to be served by people of all conditions. At every level of society anyone who wants to can be saved, for the rank does not cause damnation, but rather not knowing how to use it wisely."

Therefore in conclusion, the princess says to herself, "I see very well that, as I do not feel myself to be the sort of person who can wholeheartedly choose and follow one of these two lives, I will try hard at least to strike a happy medium, as St. Paul counsels, and take as much as I can from both lives according to my ability."

7. How the Good Princess Will Wish to Cultivate All Virtues

The good princess will have these or similar ideas by divine inspiration, and in order to put them into effect, she will see that she needs to be well informed by good and wise people about what is right and what is wrong, so that she can choose the one and avoid the other. Although every mortal person is by nature given to sin, to the best of her ability she will avoid mortal sin especially, and will try to follow the example of a good physician who cures a disease by its opposite. She will follow the words of Chrysostom on the Gospel of St Matthew, who says, "Whoever wishes to have riches in Heaven should cultivate earthly humility, for in the eyes of God the one who is most grand and elevated in honors here below is not the greatest, but the one who is most just on earth is the greatest in Heaven." And because the good princess will know that honors usually increase pride, her heart will be altogether inclined towards humility. She will think that although it is appropriate to the rank of her husband and of her class that she should receive honors, she will control her heart and it will not be wounded with arrogance nor puffed up with pride, but she will render thanks to God and attribute all honor to Him. She will always recognize in her heart that she is a poor mortal creature, frail and sinful, and that the rank that she receives is only an office for which she will soon have to account to God, for her life in comparison to the life everlasting is only a short time. This noble princess, therefore, although the dignity of her rank requires that she receive great reverence from people, will not take any personal delight in it when it is paid her. At the very least, she should preserve the honor of her position. She will behave respectably and speak softly; her conduct will be kindly and her expression gentle and pleasant, greeting everyone with lowered eyes. She will greet people in words so humane and so sweet that they may be agreeable both to God and to the world.

Besides this virtue of humility, the noble lady will wish to be so patient that although the world delivers a good deal of adversity to great lords and ladies as well as to humble persons, she will not be impatient, regardless of what comes to her. She will take all adversity willingly for the love of Our Lord and will give thanks to Him for it with a good heart. Indeed, she will be so much disposed towards this virtue of patience, that if it should happen that she receives some wrong or sorrow from some person or group of people (as often happens to many ladies without cause), she will not seek, nor wish, nor try to obtain their punishment. If it happens that they are punished by law and by justice, she will have pity on them, remembering that God commanded us to love our enemies and that St. Paul says that charity does not seek even what is its own; she will pray to God for them that He may have mercy on them and give them patience.

This noble lady, so disposed by great steadfastness and strength of courage, will not take much notice of the darts of the envious. That is, if she finds out that some words have been said against her, as happens every day to the best of ladies, she will nevertheless not be perturbed about it nor will she regard it as a great crime, but will pardon it easily. Nor will she ever for her high rank bear a grudge against anyone who has done her a great injury, being mindful of the great injuries that Our Lord suffered for us, and yet He prayed for those who tormented Him. The excellent lady will suspect that in some way she may have deserved it, and so virtue will provide her with the teaching of Seneca, who says, speaking of princes and princesses or powerful persons, that it is a very great merit In God's eyes, praiseworthy to the world, and a sign of noble virtue to dismiss easily the wrong that one might easily avenge, and it sets a good example to the common people. St. Gregory asserts this same thing in the twenty-second book of *Morals* [Pope Gregory I's *Moralia*], where he says that no one is perfect if he has not patience in the face of the evils that his neighbors do him. For whoever does not bear patiently the wrongdoing of another is impatient and proves that he is far from the fullness of virtues. In praising patience St. Gregory says that just as the rose flowers sweetly and is beautiful among the sharp thorns, the patient person is also victoriously resplendent among those who strive to harm him.

This princess who would strive to amass virtue upon virtue will remember that St. Paul says that if someone has all other virtues and continually worships, goes on pilgrimages, makes great fasts and great abstinences and does all the good that he can and yet does not have charity in himself, all this will profit him nothing. And for this reason she, ever mindful of this teaching, will wish to have this excellent virtue so that she will be so compassionate towards all people that the wrongdoing of another will pain her like her own. Her charity will make her not only feel sorrow when she sees people in affliction, but oblige her to roll up her sleeves and help them as much as she can. And as a wise doctor of the Church says, charity exists in many modes and is not to be understood as helping another person only with money from your purse, but also with help and comfort by your speech and advice wherever the need arises and with all the good that you can do. . . .

8. Of the Wives of Artisans and How They Ought to Conduct Themselves

Now it is time for us to speak of the station in life of women married to artisans who live in cities and fine towns, like Paris, and elsewhere. They can use all the good things that have been said before, but yet some tradesmen like goldsmiths, embroiderers, armorers, tapestry makers and many others are more respectable than are masons, shoemakers and such like. All wives of artisans should be very painstaking and diligent if they wish to have the necessities of life. They should encourage their husbands or their workmen to get to work early in the morning and work until late, for mark our words, there is no trade so good that if you neglect your work you will not have difficulty putting bread on the table. And besides encouraging the others, the wife herself should be involved in the work to the extent that she knows all about it, so that she may know how to oversee his workers if her husband is absent, and to reprove them if they do not do well. She ought to oversee them to keep them from idleness, for through careless workers the master is sometimes ruined. And when customers come to her husband and try to drive a hard bargain, she ought to warn him solicitously to take care that he does not make a bad deal. She should advise him to be chary of giving too much credit if he does not know precisely where and to whom it is going, for in this way many come to poverty, although sometimes the greed to earn more or to accept a tempting proposition makes them do it.

In addition, she ought to keep her husband's love as much as she can, to this end: that he will stay at home more willingly and that he may not have any reason to join the foolish crowds of other young men in taverns and indulge in unnecessary and extravagant expense, as many tradesmen do, especially in Paris. By treating him kindly she should protect him as well as she can from this. It is said that three things drive a man from his home: a quarrelsome wife, a smoking fireplace and a leaking roof. She too ought to stay at home gladly and not go every day traipsing hither and yon gossiping with the neighbors and visiting her chums to find out what everyone is doing. That is done by slovenly housewives roaming about the town in groups. Nor should she go off on these pilgrimages got up for no good reason and involving a lot of needless expense. Furthermore, she ought to remind her husband that they should live so frugally that their expenditure does not exceed their income, so that at the end of the year they do not find themselves in debt.

If she has children, she should have them instructed and taught first at school by educated people so that they may know how better to serve God. Afterwards they may be put to some trade by which they may earn a living, for whoever gives a trade or business training to her child gives a great possession. The children should be kept from wantonness and from voluptuousness above all else, for truly it is something that most shames the children of good towns and is a great sin of mothers and fathers, who ought to be the cause of the virtue and good behavior of their children, but they are sometimes the reason (because of bringing them up to be finicky and indulging them too much) for their wickedness and ruin.

9. Of Servant-Women and Chambermaids

So that everyone may benefit from our advice on living well, we will speak even to servant-women and chambermaids of Paris and elsewhere. As in many places the necessity of earning their living causes many of them to be put quite young to serve, the occupation of secular service has perhaps prevented them from knowing as thoroughly as other people things that concern the salvation of their souls. They may not know as much about serving God by hearing Masses and sermons and saying Our Fathers and other prayers, which some good women would like to do, but their serving duties do not allow them.

It seems a good idea to say a little about the manner in deed, work and thought that is advantageous for them to have for their salvation, and also something about what they ought to avoid. Any servant-woman ought to know that she can be excused, even by God, for not doing things for which her mistress or another lady of leisure would not be excused. For example, if she is in service because of the necessity of earning a living and in order to perform her service better, she must work very hard, rise early and go to bed late, dine and sup after everyone else and with scarcely the time for it, but go about eating here and there all the time in the midst of her duties — and perhaps she will not get very much to eat, but a rather scanty amount and catch as catch can — if such a woman does not fast on all the days ordained by the Church, God will excuse her. Indeed, she may feel that she cannot do it without harming her health, which might perhaps be damaged so that she could not earn her living. But she should not break her fast out of gluttony and foolish presumption, saying, "I am a servant. I don't have to fast." Discretion and a good conscience ought to determine the right thing to do and be the judges of the matter, for there are chambermaids with more leisure in all respects than many housewives who fast for the love of God; what we say does not apply to those women. Likewise we advise going into the church and praying.

But what should the good servant-woman do to deserve salvation? Certainly she ought to understand that God, who knows and sees everything, asks only that she have a good heart towards Him, for then she cannot go wrong. The one who has a good heart will be saved and thereby will protect herself from all odious and wicked sins. She will be loyal in deed and in word to master and mistress and will serve them with care, and even while doing her duties she will be able to say her Our Fathers and her devotions. If she is prevented from getting to church, she can be there in spirit, although it is scarcely to be believed that anyone is so busy that if she wanted to take the trouble to get up early she could not easily find the time on most days to hear a Mass and recommend herself to God, and then come back to do her chores. If she adopts such a course, together with the other good deeds that a good serving-woman can do, these things will inevitably lead her to salvation.

But to behave as some debauched and wicked women do is the road to damnation! In order to reprimand them for their follies and wicked ways let us say this: there are some dishonest chambermaids who are given great responsibility because they know how to insinuate themselves into the great houses of the middle classes and of rich people by cleverly acting the part of good household managers. They get their position of buying the food and going to the butcher's, where they only too well "hit the fruit basket," which is a common expression meaning to claim that the thing costs more than it really does and then keep the change. So they pretend that a piece of mutton costs them four *sous* that they got for ten *blancs* or less, and so on with other things, and in this way they can do great harm over a period of a year. For they put to one side a little tidbit, have a pie made and baked, charging it up to their master, and then when their master is at court or in town, and their mistress at church hearing high Mass, a delightful little banquet is spread in the kitchen, and not without plenty to drink, and only the best wine! The other housemaids in the street who are part of the crowd of cronies turn up, and God knows how they plunder the place! Someone takes the pie to the room she has in the town and her paramour comes over, and they have a merry time together.

There may be women who frequent the house and help to do the laundry or scour the pots who are in cahoots with the housemaid, and so they do the work of the household while she loafs, so that the master and the mistress find everything in order when they come home, but God knows how cheated they are of wine and food! Or sometimes, when the laundry is done at home, the mistress, preoccupied with something else, will think that her maid is at the river to wash her laundry, but instead she is at the baths in peace and ease, and has her friends doing her work for her. She does not pay them or her relatives and her pals who sometimes come asking for her at the house and wanting to see her, but God knows that the relatives and the many cronies she has in the town cost the house many bottles of wine!

If such a woman serves in some place where there is a young, newly married mistress who is a bit silly, she is on to a good thing. She will know how to flatter the master and speak to him as an equal and fawn on him so that he has confidence in her about his wife and about everything else. But she will always pull the wool over his eyes! On the other hand she will also flatter the girl, so that in this way she will have them both believing that she is practically the Messiah! And then wine and food, candles, bread, salted pork, salt and every other staple of the house will be very well taken care of indeed, and if the master sometimes says that the provisions run out too quickly, she will have her answer ready, saying that it is because they give too many big dinner parties and invite so many people to drink. But if some gallant promises to give, or does give, her a cloak or a gown for taking a message to her mistress, if she does not do it discreetly, the mistress could be burnt! Such greedy housemaids can pose a very great danger in a house, for because of the excellent service that they know how to give, and their flatteries, and by preparing meals well, keeping the house neat and clean, and speaking well and answering questions politely, they blind people so much that no one is on the look-out for their wicked deeds. The better to cover up everything, they pretend to be pious and go to church for all the prayers, and therein lies the danger.

So you ladies who have servants, watch out for these tricks so that you are not deceived. And to you who serve, we say this so that you may regard doing such things as an abomination, for inevitably those who do them damn themselves and deserve death of both body and soul, for because of people like this, many are burnt or buried alive who do not deserve it.

<hr/>

The Mission of Joan of Arc

Joan of Arc (1412-1431), daughter of a peasant, began to hear her voices when she was only thirteen. It was the middle of the Hundred Years' War, and England had conquered much of France. The voices told Joan to go to the Dauphin, the prince not yet officially crowned King of France, and seek to lead the French forces against the English. With Joan, sixteen years old, in a suit of white armor at its head, the French army defeated the English at Orleans, and the Dauphin, with Joan beside him, was crowned king. Later, in a less successful campaign, Joan was captured and became a prisoner of the English, who had her tried for witchcraft and heresy. Throughout her trial, she refused to answer some questions, insisting that the voices told her to keep these things secret. In particular, she said that she had given the king a secret sign which convinced him of her authenticity, but it was up to him to reveal it. He never did. These excerpts come from the official record of the trial. She was found guilty and burned at the stake.

(From Trial Testimony of Thursday, February 22)

She then said that, since the age of thirteen, she had been having revelations from Our Lord through a voice that taught her how to behave. And that the

The Mission of Joan of Arc, ed. and trans. Nadia Margolis, in *Medieval Hagiography, An Anthology*, ed. Thomas Head (New York: Routledge, 2001), 814-17, 819-20.

first time she was very afraid. And she said that the said voice came at noon, in summertime, when she was in her father's garden during a fast day, and that the said voice came from the right, toward the church. And she said that the said voice is rarely without light, which always comes from the same direction as the said voice [Latin record adds here: And when Joan herself came to France she heard that voice often. Asked how she could see the light of which she spoke, since it came from the side, she answered nothing to this, but went on to other things. She said that if she were in a forest, she could clearly hear voices coming to her. She said in fact that it seemed to her a worthy voice and she believed that this voice was sent from God].

She went on to say that after hearing the said voice three times, she knew it was the voice of an angel. She also said that this voice had always taken good care of her. Asked what advice this voice had given her for the salvation of her soul, she answered that it taught her how to conduct herself and that she should go to church often. And then the voice told her it was necessary that she go into France . . . and told her two or three times a week that she must leave to go into France. And that her father knew nothing of her departure.

With this, it said to her that she must hasten to go and that she should lift the siege at Orleans; and that she should go to Robert de Baudricourt, captain of Vaucouleurs, and that he would provide her with men to accompany her.

To which she responded that she was nothing but a poor girl who knew neither how to ride a horse nor how to lead an army.

And after her words with this voice, she went off to the house of an uncle, where she remained for a week. And that afterward her uncle led her to the said Robert de Baudricourt, whom she recognized even though she had never met him before. And this she knew because the voice had told her who he was.

She went on to say that the said Baudricourt refused her twice. Then on the third occasion, he welcomed her and gave her men to escort her into France, just as the voice had told her. . . .

She then said that when she left Vaucouleurs, she assumed male clothing, and also a sword Baudricourt had given her, but no other armor or weapons. And she said she was accompanied by a knight and four other men; and that on that day they took lodging in the town of Saint-Urbain, where she slept in the abbey.

She also said that on the way to Chinon, she passed through Auxerre where she heard Mass in the great church; and that she often had her voices with her. . . .

She said she never asked anything of the voice except at the end, for the salvation of her soul.

(From Trial Testimony of Saturday, February 24)

Questioned as to when she last heard her voice, she answered that she had heard it yesterday and today.

Asked at what time she had heard it, she said that she had heard it three times: once in the morning, once at the hour of Vespers, and another at the hour of the Hail Mary; and sometimes more often than this.

Asked what she was doing yesterday when she heard this voice, she answered that she was sleeping and that the said voice woke her.

Asked whether the said voice woke her by its sound or by touching her on the arm or elsewhere, she answered that the voice woke her without touching her.

Asked whether the voice were still in her room, she responded that to her knowledge, no; but that it was in the castle.

Asked what the voice told her, once awake, she replied that it told her to seek advice from Our Lord.

Asked if it said any more to her than what she asked of it, she answered . . . "You say that you are my judge; take care what you do with me; for in truth I have been sent by God and you are putting yourself in grave danger." . . .

Questioned as to whether the voice told her in her youth to hate the Burgundians, she responded that ever since she heard that the voices were for the king of France, she has not liked the Burgundians.

(From Trial Testimony of Tuesday, February 27)

Questioned as to whether she fasted every day of this Lenten season, she answered, "Does this pertain to your trial?"

To which Beaupère (the interrogator) said, "Yes, it really is relevant to the trial."

She responded, "Yes, truly, I have been fasting every day."

Asked if, since Saturday (February 24) she had heard her voice, she replied, "Yes, in fact quite often."

Asked if she had heard it in this chamber since Saturday, she replied, "This has nothing to do with your trial." And afterward said yes.

Questioned as to what the voice said to her on Saturday, she said, "I could not hear it very well; and could not understand anything I could recall for you, until I returned to my room."

Asked what it said to her when she had returned to her room, she responded, "May you answer boldly." And she said she asked it for advice on things asked of her.

Questioned as to whether it was the voice of an angel that spoke to her, or of a male or female saint, or directly from God, she answered, "The voice is from Sts. Catherine or Margaret. And their heads are crowned with beautiful crowns most lavishly and preciously. And I have Our Lord's permission to tell you that. If you doubt me, then send to Poitiers or other places where I was interrogated."

Asked how she knew they were those two saints and if she could tell one from the other, she answered that she certainly knew who they were and one from the other.

Asked how she knew one from the other, she responded that she recognized them by the greeting they gave her. She said that it was seven years ago that they first taught her how to behave. She said she also knew them by the way in which they named themselves to her.

Asked if they were dressed in the same cloth, she answered, "Now I shall tell you nothing else." And that she was not permitted to reveal more. "And if you do not believe me, go to Poitiers."

She said, "There are revelations that belong to the king of France and not to those interrogating me."

Asked if they were the same age, she answered, "I am not allowed to tell you."

Asked if they spoke together or one after the other, she answered, "I am not allowed to tell you; and in any case I am always receiving advice from both of them. . . ."

Questioned as to which came first, she answered that it was St. Michael.

Asked if it were long ago, she answered, "I don't know that I identified St. Michael's voice in itself, but rather I could tell by the great comfort it brought me."

Asked who was the first voice coming to her when she was thirteen years old, she responded that it was St. Michael whom she saw before her eyes; and that he was not alone, but with angels from heaven. And she added that she would not have come to France were it not under orders from God.

Asked whether she saw St. Michael and the others bodily and in real form, she answered, "I see them with the eyes of my body, just as I see you." And when they left her, she wept and wanted them to carry her away with them.

Asked in what form St. Michael appeared, "I have not yet answered such questions of you and do not yet have any permission to do so."

Questioned as to what St. Michael said to her that first time, she answered, "You will have no other answer."

(From Trial Testimony of Thursday, March 1)

Asked if he were naked, "Do you think that Our Lord cannot afford to clothe his angels?" . . .

Joan Meets with the Dauphin

(From Trial Testimony of Thursday, February 22)

She said she found her king at Chinon where she arrived at around noon; and stayed in an inn. After dinner she went before the king, who was in the castle.

She said she went right into the room where the king was, and that she recognized him from the others because of the voice's guidance.

She said she told the king that she wanted to make war against the English. Asked whether, when the voice pointed out the king, there was a ray of light over him, she answered, "Next question."

Asked whether she saw an angel over the king, she answered, "Spare me, next question."

She said that, before the king put her to work, she had had several apparitions and beautiful revelations.

Asked which revelations, she answered, "I cannot tell you yet, but go to the king and he'll tell you about them."

She said that the voice promised her that, soon after her arrival, the king would welcome her.

She said that those of her entourage knew well that the voice was from God, and that they saw and knew the voice, and that she knew it well.

She said the king and several others of his council heard and saw the voices coming to her, and among them was Charles, duke of Bourbon.

(From Trial Testimony of Thursday, March 1)

Asked what sign she gave her king to show him that she had been sent by God, she answered, "I have always answered you that you will never pull it out of me. Go ask the king."

Asked to whom she had promised [not to reveal the secret between her and the king], she replied that it was either to St. Catherine or St. Margaret; and this was demonstrated to the king. . . .

Joan Is Allowed to Embark upon Her Mission

(Summary of Conclusions of the Examination at Poitiers [March-April 1429])

This is the opinion of the doctors summoned by the king in the matter of the Maiden sent by God.

The king, given his needs and those of his realm, and in consideration of the continuous prayers by his poor people to God and all others who cherish peace and justice, must neither rebuff nor reject the Maiden, who claims herself sent by God to help him, even though these promises be only human efforts. Nor must he believe her too readily and without reflection. But in following the Holy Scriptures, we might test her in two ways: by human prudence, in inquiring about her life, her habits and intentions — as St. Paul the apostle has said, *Probate spiritus si ex Deo sint* ["Test the spirits to see if they are of God," 1 John 4:1]; and by devout prayer, requesting a sign of some divine work or expectation, by which we might judge whether she has truly come via God's will. God also commanded Ahaz to ask him for a sign, when God promised him victory by saying to him: *Pete signum a Domino* ["Ask a sign of the Lord," Isa. 7:11]; likewise did Gideon, who asked for a sign (Judg. 6:17), and several others, etc.

The king, since the arrival of the aforementioned Maiden, has observed the two conditions cited above: that is, by examination using human prudence and also by prayer, requesting a sign from God. Concerning the first, by human prudence, he has probed details of her life, her habits and intentions, and has had her stay with him for a period of six weeks, in order to demonstrate her worth to all — be they clerks, men of the Church, devout practitioners, men at arms, women, widows and others. She has conversed with all manner of people, both publicly and secretly. In her they have found no evil; only goodness, humility, virginity, devotion, honesty, simplicity. Of her birth and life many marvels have been spoken of as true.

As for the second means of examining her, the king asked her for a sign, to which she responded that she would demonstrate it at the city of Orleans and nowhere else, for that is what God commanded of her.

The king — given the examination performed on the said Maiden, inasmuch as it was possible for him, having found no evil in her, considering her response promising to give a divine sign at Orleans, in light of her consistent and unwavering words, and her insistence on going to Orleans in order to give the sign of divine aid — should in no way prevent her from going to Orleans with her men at arms, but rather should have her escorted there honestly and hoping in God. For to doubt or abandon her without any evidence of evil would be to reject the Holy Spirit, and to abase God's help, as Gamaliel said during a council of Jews regarding the Apostles (Acts 5:39).

THOMAS À KEMPIS

The Imitation of Christ

Thomas à Kempis (about 1380-1471), who lived in Germany and Holland, was educated in one of the schools of the Brethren of the Common Life before entering a monastery related to that movement (though most of the Brethren did not become monastics). He was thus shaped by the *Devotio Moderna* or "New Devout," with its emphasis on simple piety and suspicion of complex theology. He is now generally credited with writing *The Imitation of Christ*, though scholars long debated its authorship. It became one of the most admired of Christian spiritual texts.

Thomas à Kempis, *The Imitation of Christ*, trans. Richard Whitford (New York: Doubleday/Image, 1955), 31-34, 51-53, 198-200.

1. Of the Imitation or Following of Christ and the Despising of All Vanities of the World

He who follows Me, says Christ our Savior, walks not in darkness, for he will have the light of life. These are the words of our Lord Jesus Christ, and by them we are admonished to follow His teachings and His manner of living, if we would truly be enlightened and delivered from all blindness of heart.

Let all the study of our heart be from now on to have our meditation fixed wholly on the life of Christ, for His holy teachings are of more virtue and strength than the words of all the angels and saints. And he who through grace has the inner eye of his soul opened to the true beholding of the Gospels of Christ will find in them hidden manna.

It is often seen that those who hear the Gospels find little sweetness in them; the reason is that they do not have the spirit of Christ. So, if we desire to have a true understanding of His Gospels, we must study to conform our life as nearly as we can to His.

What avail is it to a man to reason about the high, secret mysteries of the Trinity if he lack humility and so displeases the Holy Trinity? Truly, it avails nothing. Deeply inquisitive reasoning does not make a man holy or righteous, but a good life makes him beloved by God.

I would rather feel compunction of heart for my sins than merely know the definition of compunction. If you know all the books of the Bible merely by rote and all the sayings of the philosophers by heart, what will it profit you without grace and charity? All that is in the world is vanity except to love God and to serve Him only. This is the most noble and the most excellent wisdom that can be in any creature: by despising the world to draw daily nearer and nearer to the kingdom of heaven.

It is therefore a great vanity to labor inordinately for worldly riches that will shortly perish or to covet honor or any other inordinate pleasures or fleshly delights in this life, for which a man after this life will be sorely and grievously punished. How great a vanity it also is to desire a long life and to care little for a good life; to heed things of the present and not to provide for things that are to come; to love things that will shortly pass away and not to haste to where joy is everlasting. Have this common proverb often in your mind: The eye is not satisfied or pleased with seeing any material thing, nor the ear with hearing. Study, therefore, to withdraw the love of your soul from all things that are visible, and to turn it to things that are invisible. Those who follow their own sensuality hurt their own cause and lose the grace of God.

2. Against Vain, Secular Learning, and of a Humble Knowledge of Ourselves

Every man by nature desires to know, but of what avail is knowledge without the fear of God? A humble farm laborer who serves God is more acceptable to Him than an inquisitive philosopher who, considering the constellations of heaven, willfully forgets himself. He who knows himself well is mean and abject in his own sight and takes no delight in the vain praise of men. If I knew all things in this world, but knew without charity, what would it avail me before God, who judges every man according to his deeds? Let us, therefore, cease from the desire of such vain knowledge, for often great distraction and the deceit of the enemy are found in it, and so the soul is much hindered and blocked from the perfect and true love of God.

Those who have great learning desire generally to seem to be accounted wise in the world. But there are many things whose knowledge brings but little profit and little fruit to the soul; he is most unwise who gives heed to any other thing except what will profit him to the health of his soul. Words do not feed the soul, but a good life refreshes the mind, and a clean conscience brings a man to a firm and stable trust in God. The more knowledge you have, the more grievously will you be judged for its misuse, if you do not live according to it. Therefore, do not lift yourself up into pride, because of any skill or knowledge that is given you, but have the more fear and dread in your heart — for it is certain that, hereafter, you must yield a stricter accounting. If you think that you know many things and have great learning, then know for certain that there are many more things you do not know. So with true wisdom you may not think yourself learned, but ought rather to confess your ignorance and folly. Why will you prefer yourself in knowledge before another, since there are many others more excellent and more wise than you and better learned in the Law? If you would learn anything and know it profitably to the health of your soul, learn to be unknown and be glad to be considered despicable and as nothing.

The highest and most profitable learning is this: that a man have a truthful knowledge and a full despising of himself. More, not to presume of himself, but always to judge and think well and blessedly of another, is a sign and token of great wisdom and of great perfection and of singular grace. If you see any person sin or commit any great crime openly before you, do not judge yourself to be better than he, for you know not how long you shall persevere in goodness. We are all frail, but you shall judge no man more frail than yourself.

18. Of the Example of the Holy Fathers

Behold the lively example of the holy fathers and blessed saints in whom flourished and shone all true perfection of life and all perfect religion, and you will see how little, almost nothing, we do nowadays in comparison with them.

Oh, what is our life when it is compared to theirs? They served our Lord in hunger and in thirst, in heat, in cold, in nakedness, in labor and in weariness, in vigils and fastings, in prayer and in holy meditations, in persecutions and in many reproofs.

Oh, how many and how grievous tribulations the apostles, martyrs, confessors, virgins, and other holy saints suffered who were willing to follow the steps of Christ. They refused honors and all bodily pleasures here in this life that they might have everlasting life. Oh, how strict and how abject a life the holy fathers in the wilderness led. How grievous the temptations they suffered, and how fiercely they were assailed by their spiritual enemies. How fervent the prayer they daily offered to God, what rigorous abstinence they kept. What great zeal and fervor they had for spiritual profit, how strong a battle they waged against all sin, and how pure and entire their purpose toward God in all their deeds.

In the day they labored and in the night they prayed, and though they labored bodily in the day, they prayed in mind, and so they always spent their time fruitfully. They felt every hour short for the service of God, and because of the great sweetness they had in heavenly contemplation they often forgot their bodily nourishment. All riches, honor, dignity, kinsmen, and friends they renounced for the love of God. They desired to have nothing in the world, and scarcely would they take what was necessary for their bodily sustenance.

They were poor in worldly goods, but they were rich in grace and virtue; they were needy outwardly, but inwardly in their souls they were replenished with grace and spiritual comfort. To the world they were aliens and strangers, but to God they were dear and familiar friends. In the sight of the world and in their own sight they were vile and mean, but in the sight of God and of His saints they were precious and singularly elect. In them shone forth all perfection of virtue — true meekness, simple obedience, charity, and patience, with other similar virtues and gracious gifts of God; and so, they profited daily in spirit and obtained great grace from God. They are left as an example to all religious persons, and their lives should stir us to devotion, and to advance more and more in virtue and grace, than should the example of dissolute and idle persons hinder us in any way.

Oh, what fervor was in religious persons at the beginning of their religious lives, what devotion in prayer, what zeal for virtue, what love for spiritual discipline; and what reverence and humble obedience flourished in them under the rule of their superior. Truly, their deeds still bear witness that they, who so mightily subdued the world and thrust it under foot, were holy and perfect.

Nowadays he is accounted virtuous who is not an offender, and who may with patience keep some little spark of that virtue and of that fervor he had at first — but alas, for sorrow, it is through our own sloth and negligence, and through wasting our time, that we have so soon fallen from our first fervor into such a spiritual weakness and dullness that it is boring, as it were, to be alive. Would to God that the desire to profit in virtue were not so utterly asleep in us, who have so often seen the example of the blessed saints.

59. That All Our Hope and Trust Is to Be Put in God Alone

O Lord, what is the trust that I can have in this life, or what is my greatest solace among all things under heaven? Is it not You, my Lord God, whose mercy is without measure? Where have things been well with me without You, and when have things not been well with me if You were present? I would rather be poor with You than rich without You. I would rather be with You a pilgrim in this world, than without You to be in heaven. Where You are is heaven, and where You are not is both death and hell. You are to me all that I desire, and therefore it behooves me to cry to You and heartily to pray to You. I have nothing save You to trust in that can help me in my necessity, for You are my hope, You are my trust, You are my comfort, and You are my most faithful helper in every need.

Man seeks what is his, but You seek my salvation and profit and turn all things to the best for me. If You send temptations and other adversities, You order all to my profit, for You are accustomed to test Your chosen people in a thousand ways. And in such testing You are no less to be glorified and praised than if You had filled your people with heavenly comfort. In You, therefore, Lord, I put my trust, and in You I bear patiently all my adversities, for without You I find nothing but instability and folly. I see well that a multitude of worldly friends is no profit to me, that strong helpers can avail nothing, nor wise counselors give profitable counsel, nor skillful teachers give consolation, nor riches deliver in time of need, nor secret place in any way defend, if You, Lord, do not assist, help, comfort, counsel, instruct, and defend. Everything that seems to be ordained for man's solace in this world is worth nothing if You are absent; nor may all these things bring any man to true happiness, for You, Lord, are the end of all good things. You are the sublimity of life, the profound wisdom of every thing that is in heaven and on earth, and so, to trust in You above all things is the greatest comfort to all Your servants. To You, therefore, the Father of mercy, I lift up my eyes; in You alone, my Lord, my God, do I put my trust. May my soul bless and hallow You with Your own heavenly blessings, so that it may be Your dwelling place and the seat of Your eternal glory, so that nothing may be found in me at any time that may offend the eye of Your majesty. Behold me, Lord, according to the greatness of Your goodness and Your manifold mercies, and graciously hear my prayer, the prayer of your poorest servant, outlawed and exiled far away in the country of the shadow of death. Defend and keep me among the manifold perils and dangers of this corruptible life, and direct me through Your grace by the ways of peace into the country of everlasting clarity without end.

3

Every Work a Calling:
Vocations after the Reformation, 1500-1800

Introduction

Martin Luther was a good monk. Looking back years later, the man who began the Protestant Reformation wrote, "When I was a monk, I made a great effort to live according to the requirements of the monastic rule. I made a practice of confessing and reciting all my sins, but always with proper contrition; I went to confession frequently, and I performed the assigned penances faithfully."[1] Yet he found that following this monastic vocation left him deeply unsure of his salvation. The late medieval theology in which Luther had been trained (Aquinas would not have said this) taught that God will forgive our sins if we repent and do our best. But how, he wondered, can I be *sure* that I have done my best? He made himself a considerable nuisance to his confessor by always thinking of one more sin he should confess, and his uncertainty about salvation was driving him crazy.

Reading Paul, he then concluded that our salvation does not depend on what *we* do at all. "To trust in works . . . is equivalent to giving oneself the honor and taking it from God."[2] Rather, we are saved purely by the grace of God, a God who "loves sinners, evil persons, fools and weaklings."[3] Whatever we do in gratitude to the God who loves us, it contributes nothing to our salvation. Thanks to God, our salvation is secure. Thus we can serve our neighbors simply to serve our neighbors, without worrying how much we are helping toward our own salvation.

Therefore, he argued, no one should feel compelled to enter a monastery or convent and become some sort of super-Christian in order to contribute to one's salvation through works. Rather, we should stick to where God has put us and serve God there. Luther offered biblical examples. The shepherds, having heard the angels and visited the Christ child, did not go off to enter a monastery. They went back to their fields to take care of their

---

1. Martin Luther, *Lectures on Galatians* (1535) (on Gal. 5:3), trans. Jaroslav Pelikan, *Luther's Works*, vol. 27 (St. Louis: Concordia, 1964), 13.

2. Martin Luther, "Heidelberg Disputation," trans. Harold J. Grimm, *Luther's Works*, vol. 31 (Philadelphia: Muhlenberg, 1957), 46.

3. Luther, "Heidelberg Disputation," 57.

sheep.[4] Luke tells of the prophetess Anna, a widow of eighty-four who "never went away from the temple" (Luke 2:37). This was her calling. On the other hand, if she had been a married woman with a family to care for, Luther remarked, then "never leaving the church and neglecting to manage her household in a God-pleasing manner" would have been wrong. "To leave one's own calling and to attach oneself to alien undertakings, surely amounts to walking on one's ears, to veiling one's feet, to putting a shoe on one's head, and to turning everything upside down."[5] After all, if you are a shoemaker, you can glorify God perfectly well by making shoes. Similarly, spouses and parents can find a "vocation" in those tasks. If a father washes diapers, his smart-aleck friends may ridicule him "as an effeminate fool," but "God, with all his angels and creatures, is smiling."[6]

Reformation ideas about vocation made a quick difference in the Protestant parts of Europe. When Luther began the Reformation, about 1520, between six and ten percent of the whole population of Germany were priests, monks, and nuns. They had their own courts, did not pay taxes, and did not marry. Only a generation later, in Protestant territories, their number had dropped by two-thirds; monasteries and convents were almost entirely closed, and the vast majority of the clergy had married.[7] Social changes are rarely more dramatic. Henceforth, at least among Protestants, one could no longer limit the term "vocation" to *some* Christians. *Every* Christian had at least two vocations: the call to become part of the people of God (Luther called it "spiritual calling," the Puritans later called it "general calling") and the call to a particular line of work (for Luther, "external calling," for the Puritans "particular calling"). Luther, indeed, had so emphasized that there was nothing that special about the calling of pastors that in one of the sermons here excerpted he had to backtrack a bit and urge his followers to keep their children in school so that at least some of them could become ordained.

4. Martin Luther, "Gospel for the Early Christmas Service, Luke 2:15-20," trans. John G. Kunstmann, *Luther's Works*, vol. 52 (Philadelphia: Fortress, 1974), 37.

5. Martin Luther, "Gospel for the Sunday after Christmas, Luke 2:33-40," *Luther's Works*, 52:123-24.

6. Martin Luther, "The Estate of Marriage," trans. Walther I. Brandt, *Luther's Works*, vol. 45 (Philadelphia: Muhlenberg, 1962), 40.

7. Steven Ozment, *Protestants: The Birth of a Revolution* (New York: Doubleday, 1992), 25-27.

Options after the Reformation

On the one hand, the idea that any station in life (and by *"Stand"* or station, Luther meant family role as parent, grandparent, child, and so on, as well as job) could be equally a place from which to serve God constituted a great breakthrough toward equality. No longer was "vocation" a category that fit only those who entered the priesthood, the monastery, or the convent. On the other hand, Luther's conviction that each person has a calling and should stick to it was an enemy of social mobility. The simple shepherd who wanted to work his way up to be a merchant found no support in Luther's theology. (While Luther praised the father who washed diapers, moreover, he had strong convictions about the separate roles of mothers and fathers.) Thus when the leaders of the Peasants' Revolt in Germany in 1525 or, in the 1640s, the radical English Protestant group known as the "Levellers," insisted that they could have a call from God to abandon their ordinary occupations and organize a revolution,[8] they were turning completely away from Luther's position.

On this issue John Calvin, the founder of the Reformed tradition of Protestants, occupied a middle position. God recognized, he said, "with what great restlessness human nature flames," and therefore, "lest through our stupidity and rashness everything be turned topsy-turvy, he has appointed duties for every man in his particular way of life."[9] We should not be constantly looking over the vocational fence at someone else's apparently greener grass, and should therefore, most of the time, accept the calling in which we find ourselves. "From this will arise also a singular consolation: that no task will be so sordid and base, provided you obey your calling in it, that it will not shine and be reckoned very precious in God's sight."[10] Yet Calvin allowed for some social motion from one job to another and thought that some government officials had a calling to stand up for the rights of the people against the wishes of tyrants[11] — a conviction that would have political implications in Scotland, England, and America.

Both Luther and Calvin, as well as most of their followers, wanted to change their whole societies in accordance with their new values. They accepted the fact that Christians in different territories would have different

8. John Wildman, "The Case of the Army," in *The Leveller Tracts*, ed. William Haller and Godfrey Davies (New York: Columbia University Press, 1944), 86.

9. John Calvin, *Institutes of the Christian Religion* 3.11.6, trans. Ford Lewis Battles (Philadelphia: Westminster, 1960), 724.

10. Calvin, *Institutes* 3.11.6, 725.

11. Calvin, *Institutes* 4.20.31, 1519.

beliefs, but they wanted to bring the whole population, as well as the prince or city council, of the territory where they lived to their view of things. They were willing to make compromises or put up with delays in order to win over a majority.

Other Christians — sometimes called the "radical Reformation" — were more impatient. They thought Christians ought to live up to their ideals, and, if most of their neighbors were not willing to go along, better to withdraw into an isolated but pure community and offer everyone else an example of the ideal in practice rather than sell out to compromise. Groups like the Mennonites in Holland and North Germany or the Hutterites in Switzerland and Moravia lived simple lives, often sharing what they had, regarding government with suspicion, and opposing warfare on principle. One way of marking the separation of their members from the, to their mind, lukewarm Christians around them was by baptizing only adults ready to make a commitment to the community and rebaptizing those who had been baptized as infants. The "Anabaptist" ("re-baptist") ideal obviously shaped a strong and very particular sense of vocation.

For Catholics, the Reformation period required finding new ways to defend old principles. Most Catholics still thought of vocation in terms of priesthood or the monastic life, but now they could not take those values for granted and had to find ways to defend them. Ignatius Loyola, founder of the Jesuits, developed one of the most forceful defenses. In Spain, Teresa of Ávila showed how much passion could still be brought to the monastic life. In far-off Mexico, Sor Juana Inés de la Cruz showed how the life of a nun could still provide escape from social demands and the context for a writer's life.

Civil War in England

The Reformation began in the 1520s and spread over much of Europe. A more localized religious revolution took place in England in the 1640s. In the 1630s King Charles I tried to rule England without ever calling Parliament. Supporters of Parliament, who also tended to belong to the "Puritan" party that wanted to purify the Church of England by simplifying its worship and raising its moral standards, organized to oppose the king. One of their generals, Oliver Cromwell, proved to be a military strategist of genius. In the Civil War that followed, King Charles was defeated, arrested, and eventually beheaded. Cromwell became "Lord Protector," in effect the ruler of England.

The parliamentary armies gathered together many men of the lower and middle classes, united in challenging the king. They began to debate all sorts of political and religious issues, and all sorts of religious points of view came to have their advocates. Puritans simply wanted to reform the Church of England. Presbyterians wanted to replace bishops with elected regional assemblies they called "presbyteries." Independents or Congregationalists wanted to give autonomy to each local congregation. Baptists concluded that Christianity could be purified only if the church included only those who had committed themselves to their faith by being baptized as adults. Quakers found guidance in the inner light of the Holy Spirit. Levellers sought to level out all social classes. All in all, England in the 1640s had more religious diversity than any predominantly Christian country had ever known.

When Cromwell died in 1658, no strong leader replaced him, and Charles II, the son of Charles I, had a relatively easy time reclaiming the throne when he returned from France in 1660. But the English kings had not learned their lesson. Charles II, and even more his brother James II, who succeeded him in 1685 (and whose Catholicism particularly worried the Protestant majority in England), still sought to rule without consulting Parliament. In 1688 the parliamentary leaders invited a Dutch prince, William of Orange, and his wife Mary (who had a distant claim on the English throne) to replace James II as king, and the transition took place without bloodshed.

During the restored monarchy, the Church of England reestablished itself as the nation's official religion. Those who opposed it suffered persecution, or went underground, or moved to the American colonies. But many of the new ideas that had emerged during the English Civil War continued to generate interest, and indeed the Church of England itself shifted among different positions. All this created a greater need for clear articulation of positions of theological topics, including that of vocation. Among the essays that follow, William Perkins takes a classic Puritan position. John Bunyan fought in the Civil War on the parliamentary side and became a Baptist; George Fox, feeling direct inspiration, developed the radical ideas of the Society of Friends or Quakers; Gerrard Winstanley pushed social revolution farther than anyone else. Richard Baxter, George Herbert, and William Law represent moderate voices who in different ways sought compromise.

The Experience of Being Called

Puritanism encouraged its adherents to look inward. John Calvin always insisted that, if I want to be sure of my salvation, I should not look at myself but look to Christ. Most Puritans thought of themselves as standing in the Reformed tradition Calvin had founded, but they took a more individualistic approach to salvation. After the Reformation, both Protestants and Catholics faced a religiously divided world, and so they wanted to be able to *prove* that they were right. In the empiricist philosophy common in the seventeenth century, the best way to prove something was to appeal to direct experience. Thus Puritans and others — especially the Pietists in Germany — wanted to analyze their own religious experience in detail, and that included their experience of calling. That emphasis on the experiential continued, and the last section of this chapter includes excerpts from two of the greatest theologians of religious experience, Jonathan Edwards and John Wesley.

Careful analysis, however, even of experience, can come to be the very opposite of liberating. Protestants who believed in free grace in principle sometimes sought in practice for particular kinds of experience as the evidence of proper vocation, and in the process looked as if they were turning the right kind of faith into a work. Some even saw success in the jobs to which they had been called as evidence of salvation. Moreover, "vocation" increasingly meant exclusively "job," and "job" was increasingly defined by the economic rules of an ever more complex society. The Reformers and their followers argued that any job could be a vocation, but in more recent centuries, as we will see in the next chapter, many Christians have hoped that their job does not have to define the whole meaning of their life.

MARTIN LUTHER

An Open Letter to the Christian Nobility
of the German Nation Concerning the Reform
of the Christian Estate

Martin Luther (1483-1546), as noted in the introduction to this chapter, began the Reformation and in the process redefined how Protestants would
understand "vocation" or "calling." In this "open letter," published in
1520, Luther appealed to the German princes to support the movement he
had just begun. But his appeal faced several objections, one of which was
the church's general insistence that laypeople had no authority in religious
matters. Luther responded that priests and monks had particular jobs or
"offices" in the church, but they were not a special, superior caste, set
apart from all others. He thereby opened the door for a different kind of
thinking about the "calling" of all Christians.

It is pure invention that pope, bishops, priests and monks are to be called
the "spiritual estate"; princes, lords, artisans, and farmers the "temporal estate." That is indeed a fine bit of lying and hypocrisy. Yet no one should be
frightened by it; and for this reason — namely, that all Christians are truly
of the "spiritual estate," and there is among them no difference at all but that
of office, as Paul says in 1 Corinthians 12:12: We are all one body, yet every
member has its own work, whereby it serves every other, all because we
have one baptism, one Gospel, one faith, and are all alike Christians; for
baptism, Gospel and faith alone make us "spiritual" and a Christian people.

Martin Luther, *To the Christian Nobility of the German Nation*, in *Three Treatises*, trans. C. M. Jacobs
(Philadelphia: Muhlenberg, 1943, 1960), 13-16.

But that a pope or a bishop anoints, confers tonsures, ordains, consecrates, or prescribes dress unlike that of the laity, this may make hypocrites and graven images, but it never makes a Christian or "spiritual" man. Through baptism all of us are consecrated to the priesthood, as St. Peter says in 1 Peter 2:9, "Ye are a royal priesthood, a priestly kingdom," and the book of Revelation says, "Thou hast made us by Thy blood to be priests and kings" (5:10). For if we had no higher consecration than pope or bishop gives, the consecration by pope or bishop would never make a priest, nor might anyone either say mass or preach a sermon or give absolution. Therefore when the bishop consecrates it is the same thing as if he, in the place and stead of the whole congregation, all of whom have like power, were to take one out of their number and charge him to use this power for the others; just as though ten brothers, all king's sons and equal heirs, were to choose one of themselves to rule the inheritance for them all — they would all be kings and equal in power, though one of them would be charged with the duty of ruling.

To make it still clearer: if a little group of pious Christian laymen were taken captive and set down in a wilderness, and had among them no priest consecrated by a bishop, and if there in the wilderness they were to agree in choosing one of themselves, married or unmarried, and were to charge him with the office of baptizing, saying mass, absolving and preaching, such a man would be as truly a priest as though all bishops and popes had consecrated him. That is why in cases of necessity anyone can baptize and give absolution, which would be impossible unless we were all priests. This great grace and power of baptism and of the Christian Estate they have well-nigh destroyed and caused us to forget through the canon law. It was in the manner just described that Christians in olden days chose from their number bishops and priests, who were afterwards confirmed by other bishops, without all the show which now obtains. It was thus that Sts. Augustine, Ambrose and Cyprian became bishops.

Since, then, the temporal authorities are baptized with the same baptism and have the same faith and Gospel as we, we must grant that they are priests and bishops, and count their office one which has a proper and a useful place in the Christian community. For whoever comes out the water of baptism can boast that he is already consecrated priest, bishop and pope, though it is not seemly that everyone should exercise the office. Nay, just because we are all in like manner priests, no one must put himself forward and undertake, without our consent and election, to do what is in the power of all of us. For what is common to all, no one dare take upon himself without the will and the command of the community; and should it happen that one chosen for such an office were deposed for malfeasance, he would then be just what he was before he held office. Therefore a priest in Christendom is nothing else than an officeholder. While he is in office, he has precedence; when deposed, he is a peasant or a townsman like the rest. Beyond all doubt, then, a priest is no longer a priest when he is deposed. But now they have invented *characteres indelebilis* [indelible character], and prate that a deposed priest is nevertheless something different from a mere layman. They even dream that a priest can never become a layman, or be anything else than a priest. All this is mere talk and man-made law.

From all this it follows that there is really no difference between laymen and priests, princes and bishops, "spirituals" and "temporals," as they call them, except that of office and work, but not of "estate"; for they are all of the same estate — true priests, bishops and popes — though they are not all engaged in the same work, just as all priests and monks have not the same work. This is the teaching of St. Paul in Romans 12:4 and 1 Corinthians 12:12, and of St. Peter in 1 Peter 2:9, as I have said above, namely, that we are all one body of Christ, the Head, all members one of another. Christ has not two different bodies, one "temporal," the other "spiritual." He is one Head, and He has One body.

MARTIN LUTHER

The Gospel for the Early Christmas Service

This excerpt comes from a collection of sermons Luther wrote in 1521-22, while hiding out in the Wartburg castle. The text for this sermon is Luke 2:15-20, in which the shepherds visit the baby Jesus and then return to their sheep.

Martin Luther, *The Gospel for the Early Christmas Service*, trans. John G. Kunstmann, *Luther's Works*, vol. 52 (Philadelphia: Fortress, 1974), 36-38.

... all works are the same to a Christian, no matter what they are. For these shepherds do not run away into the desert, they do not don monk's garb, they do not shave their heads, neither do they change their clothing, schedule, food, drink, nor any external work. They return to their place in the fields to serve God there! For being a Christian does not consist in external conduct, neither does it change anyone according to his external position; rather it changes him according to the inner disposition, that is to say, it provides a different heart, a different disposition, will, and mind which do the works which another person does without such a disposition and will. For a Christian knows that it all depends upon faith; for this reason he walks, stands, eats, drinks, dresses, works, and lives as any ordinary person in his calling, so that one does not become aware of his Christianity, as Christ says in Luke 17[vv. 20-21]: "The kingdom of God does not come in an external manner and one cannot say, 'Lo, here and there,' but the kingdom of God is within you." Against this liberty the pope and the spiritual estate fight with their laws and their choice of clothing, food, prayers, localities, and persons. They catch themselves and everybody else with such foul snares, with which they have filled the world, just as St. Antony saw in a vision. For they are of the opinion that salvation depends on their person and work. They call other people worldly, whereas they themselves in all likelihood are worldly seven times over, inasmuch as their doings are entirely human works concerning which God has commanded nothing.

... For we are unable to give to God anything, in return for his goodness and grace, except praise and thanksgiving, which, moreover, proceed from the heart and have no great need of organ music, bells, and rote recitation. Faith teaches such praise and thanksgiving; as it is written concerning the shepherds that they returned to their flocks with praise and thanksgiving and were well satisfied, even though they did not become wealthier, were not awarded higher honors, did not eat and drink better, were not obliged to carry on a better trade. See, in this Gospel you have a picture of true Christian life, especially as pertains to its external aspects: on the outside, it shines forth not at all or at most a little bit in the sight of the people so that, indeed, most people see it as error and foolishness; but on the inside it is sheer light, joy, and bliss. Thus we see what the apostle has in mind when he enumerates the fruits of the spirit in Galatians 5[v. 22]: "The fruits of the spirit [that is, the works of faith] are love, joy, peace, kindness, being able to get along, patience, confidence, mercy, chastity."

MARTIN LUTHER

Trade and Usury

If one assigns greater value to business as a vocation, then it becomes more important to think about Christian business ethics. Medieval theology generally condemned "usury" (loaning money at interest without sharing in the risk of the project for which the loan was used), and Luther agreed. But in this essay, written in 1524, he addressed a range of more particular ethical issues that arise in business — how to pursue such callings as a Christian.

It is our purpose here to speak about the abuses and sins of trade, insofar as they concern the conscience. The matter of their detrimental effect on the purse we leave to the princes and lords, that they may do their duty in this regard.

First, among themselves the merchants have a common rule which is their chief maxim and the basis of all their sharp practices, where they say: "I may sell my goods as dear as I can." They think this is their right. Thus occasion is given for avarice, and every window and door to hell is opened. What else does it mean but this: I care nothing about my neighbor; so long as I have my profit and satisfy my greed, of what concern is it to me if it injures my neighbor in ten ways at once? There you see how shamelessly this maxim flies squarely in the face not only of Christian love but also of natural law. How can there be anything good then in trade? How can it be without sin when such injustice is the chief maxim and rule of the whole business? On such a basis trade can be nothing but robbing and stealing the property of others.

When once the rogue's eye and greedy belly of a merchant find that people must have his wares, or that the buyer is poor and needs them, he

---

Martin Luther, *Trade and Usury*, trans. Charles M. Jacobs, *Luther's Works*, vol. 45 (Philadelphia: Muhlenberg, 1962), 247-51.

takes advantage of him and raises the price. He considers not the value of the goods, or what his own efforts and risk have deserved, but only the other man's want and need. He notes it not that he may relieve it but that he may use it to his own advantage by raising the price of his goods, which he would not have raised if it had not been for his neighbor's needs. Because of his avarice, therefore, the goods must be priced as much higher as the greater need of the other fellow will allow, so that the neighbor's need becomes as it were the measure of the goods' worth and value. Tell me, isn't that an un-Christian and inhuman thing to do? . . . Observe that this and like abominations are the inevitable consequence when the rule is that I may sell my goods as dear as I can.

The rule ought to be, not, "I may sell my wares as dear I can or will," but, "I may sell my wares as dear as I ought, or, as is right and fair." For your selling ought not to be an act that is entirely within your own power and discretion, without law or limit, as though you were a god and beholden to no one. Because your selling is an act performed toward your neighbor, it should rather be so governed by law and conscience that you do it without harm and injury to him, your concern being directed more toward doing him no injury than toward gaining profit for yourself. But where are there such merchants? How few merchants there would be, and how trade would decline, if they were to amend this evil rule and put things on a fair and Christian basis!

You ask, then, "How dear may I sell? How am I to arrive at what is fair and right so I do not take increase from [my] neighbor or overcharge him?" . . . In order not to leave the question entirely unanswered, the best and safest way would be to have the temporal authorities appoint in this matter wise and honest men to compute the costs of all sorts of wares and accordingly set prices which would enable the merchant to get along and provide for him an adequate living, as is being done at certain places with respect to wine, fish, bread, and the like. But we Germans have too many other things to do; we are too busy drinking and dancing to provide for rules and regulations of this sort. Since this kind of ordinance therefore is not to be expected, the next best thing is to let goods be valued at the price for which they are bought and sold in the common market, or in the land generally. In this matter we can accept the proverb, "Follow the crowd and you won't get lost." Any profit made in this way I consider honest and proper, because here there is always the risk involved of having to suffer loss in wares and outlay, and excessive profits are scarcely possible. . . .

I would not have anyone's conscience be so overly scrupulous or so closely bound in this matter that he feels he must strike exactly the right measure of profit to the very penny. It is impossible for you to arrive at the exact amount that you have earned with your trouble and labor. It is enough that with a good conscience you make the effort to arrive at what is right, though the very nature of trade makes it impossible to determine this exactly. . . .

In determining how much profit you ought to take on your business and your labor, there is no better way to reckon it than by computing the amount of time and labor you have put into it, and comparing that with the effort of a day laborer who works at some other occupation and seeing how much he earns in a day. On that basis figure how many days you have spent in getting your wares and bringing them to your place of business, and how much labor and risk was involved; for a great amount of labor and time ought to have a correspondingly greater return. That is the most accurate, the best, and the most definite advice and direction that can be given in this matter. Let him who dislikes it, better it himself. I base my case (as I have said) on the gospel that the laborer deserves his wages (Luke 10:7). . . .

MARTIN LUTHER

Whether Soldiers, Too, Can Be Saved

The Reformation Luther had begun raised all sorts of questions about basic Christian beliefs. Anabaptists (the ancestors of today's Mennonites), for instance, proposed that going back to the New Testament as Luther proposed would lead to the conclusion that Christians ought to be pacifists. Assa von Kram, a professional soldier and advisor to one of the noblemen supporting Luther, found his conscience deeply troubled over such matters and obtained from Luther this analysis of the issues, published in 1526. The case of soldiers raises questions about the limits of what a Christian's vocation can be.

Martin Luther, *Whether Soldiers, Too, Can Be Saved,* trans. Charles M. Jacobs, *Luther's Works,* vol. 46 (Philadelphia: Fortress, 1967), 94-98.

In the first place, we must distinguish between an occupation and the man who holds it, between a work and the man who does it. An occupation or a work can be good and right in itself and yet be bad and wrong if the man who does the work is evil or wrong or does not do his work properly. The occupation of a judge is a valuable divine office. This is true both of the office of the trial judge who declares the verdict and the executioner who carries out the sentence. But when the office is assumed by one to whom it has not been committed or when one who holds it rightly uses it to gain riches or popularity, then it is no longer right or good. The married state is also precious and godly, but there are many rascals and scoundrels in it. It is the same way with the profession or work of the soldier; in itself it is right and godly, but we must see to it that the persons who are in this profession and who do the work are the right kind of persons, that is, godly and upright, as we shall hear.

In the second place, I want you to understand that here I am not speaking about the righteousness that makes men good in the sight of God. Only faith in Jesus Christ can do that; and it is granted and given us by the grace of God alone, without any works or merits of our own, as I have written and taught so often and so much in other places. Rather, I am speaking here about external righteousness which is to be sought in offices and works. In other words, to put it plainly, I am dealing here with such questions as these: whether the Christian faith, by which we are accounted righteous before God, is compatible with being a soldier, going to war, stabbing and killing, robbing and burning, as military law requires us to do to our enemies in wartime. Is this work sinful or unjust? Should it give us a bad conscience before God? Must a Christian only do good and love, and kill no one, nor do anyone any harm? I say that this office or work, even though it is godly and right, can nevertheless become evil and unjust if the person engaged in it is evil and unjust. . . .

Now slaying and robbing do not seem to be works of love. A simple man therefore does not think it is a Christian thing to do. In truth, however, even this is a work of love. For example, a good doctor sometimes finds so serious and terrible a sickness that he must amputate or destroy a hand, foot, ear, eye, to save the body. Looking at it from the point of view of the organ that he amputates, he appears to be a cruel and merciless man; but looking at it from the point of view of the body, which the doctor wants to save, he is a fine and true man and does a good and Christian work, as far as the work itself is concerned. In the same way, when I think of a soldier fulfilling his office by punishing the wicked, killing the wicked, and creating so much misery, it seems an un-Christian work completely contrary to Christian love. But when I think of how it protects the good and keeps and preserves wife and child, house and farm, property, and honor and peace, then I see how precious and godly this work is; and I observe that it amputates a leg or a hand, so that the whole body may not perish. For if the sword were not on guard to preserve peace, everything in the world would be ruined because of lack of peace. Therefore, such a war is only a very brief lack of peace that prevents an everlasting and immeasurable lack of peace, a small misfortune that prevents a great misfortune.

What men write about war, saying that it is a great plague, is all true. But they should also consider how great the plague is that war prevents. If people were good and wanted to keep peace, war would be the greatest plague on earth. But what are you going to do about the fact that people will not keep the peace, but rob, steal, kill, outrage women and children, and take away property and honor? The small lack of peace called war or the sword must set a limit to this universal, worldwide lack of peace which would destroy everyone.

This is why God honors the sword so highly that he says that he himself has instituted it (Rom. 13:1) and does not want men to say or think that they have invented it or instituted it. For the hand that wields this sword and kills with it is not man's hand, but God's; and it is not man, but God, who hangs, tortures, beheads, kills, and fights. All these are God's works and judgments.

To sum it up, we must, in thinking about a soldier's office, not concentrate on the killing, burning, striking, hitting, seizing, etc. This is what children with their limited and restricted vision see when they regard a doctor as a sawbones who amputates, but do not see that he does this only to save the whole body. So, too, we must look at the office of the soldier, or the sword, with the eyes of an adult and see why this office slays and acts so cruelly. Then it will prove itself to be an office which, in itself, is godly and as needful and useful to the world as eating and drinking or any other work.

There are some who abuse this office, and strike and kill people needlessly simply because they want to. But that is the fault of the persons, not of the office, for where is there an office or a work or anything else so good that self-willed, wicked people do not abuse it? They are like mad physicians who would needlessly amputate a healthy hand just because they wanted to. Indeed, they themselves are a part of that universal lack of peace which must be prevented by just wars and the sword and be forced into peace. It always happens and always has happened that those who begin war unnecessarily are beaten. Ultimately, they cannot escape God's judgment and sword. In the end God's justice finds them and strikes, as happened to the peasants in the revolt. [Luther had encouraged the violent suppression of the revolt of German peasants in 1525.]

As proof, I quote John the Baptist, who, except for Christ, was the greatest teacher and preacher of all. When soldiers came to him and asked what they should do, he did not condemn their office or advise them to stop doing their work; rather, according to Luke 3 [v. 14], he approved it by saying, "Rob no one by violence or by false accusation, and be content with your wages." Thus he praised the military profession, but at the same time he forbade its abuse. Now the abuse does not affect the office. When Christ stood before Pilate he admitted that war was not wrong when he said, "If my kingship were of this world, then my servants would fight that I might not be handed over to the Jews" (John 18:36). Here, too, belong all the stories of war in the Old Testament, the stories of Abraham, Moses, Joshua, the Judges, Samuel, David, and all the kings of Israel. If the waging of war and the military profession were in themselves wrong and displeasing to God, we should have to condemn Abraham, Moses, Joshua, David, and all the rest of the holy fathers, kings, and princes, who served God as soldiers and are highly praised in Scripture because of this service, as all of us who have read even a little in Holy Scripture know well, and there is no need to offer further proof of it here.

MARTIN LUTHER

A Sermon on Keeping Children in School

Before the Reformation, as seen in the previous chapter, church positions generally ranked as the highest of all callings. When Luther and others began to say that a Christian could serve God equally in any line of work, many parents saw little reason to keep their children in school to prepare them for ministry when they could be starting work in business or a trade and contribute to the family income right away. In this pamphlet, published in 1530, Luther insisted that the ministry was still a particularly important calling, and children needed to be educated for it.

Martin Luther, *A Sermon on Keeping Children in School*, trans. Charles M. Jacobs, *Luther's Works*, vol. 46 (Philadelphia: Fortress, 1967), 217-24, 225-28, 229.

From Martin Luther to all my dear friends, pastors, and preachers who truly love Christ: Grace and peace in Christ Jesus, our Lord.

My dear sirs and friends, you see with your own eyes how that wretch of a Satan is now attacking us on all sides with force and guile. He is afflicting us in every way he can to destroy the holy gospel and the kingdom of God, or, if he cannot destroy them, at least to hinder them at every turn and prevent them from moving ahead and gaining the upper hand. Among his wiles, one of the very greatest, if not the greatest of all, is this — he deludes and deceives the common people so that they are not willing to keep their children in school or expose them to instruction. He puts into their minds the dastardly notion that because monkery, nunning, and priestcraft no longer hold out the hope they once did, there is therefore no more need for study and for learned men, that instead we need to give thought only to how to make a living and get rich.

This seems to me to be a real masterpiece of the devil's art. He sees that in our time he cannot do what he would like to do; therefore, he intends to have his own way with our offspring. Before our very eyes he is preparing them so that they will learn nothing and know nothing. Then when we are dead, he will have before him a naked, bare, defenseless people with whom he can do as he pleases. . . . Then they will be willing to give a hundred gulden for half a scholar, where today they will not give ten gulden for two whole scholars.

And it will serve them right. Because they are not now willing to support and keep the honest, upright, virtuous schoolmasters and teachers offered them by God to raise their children in the fear of God, and in virtue, knowledge, learning, and honor by dint of hard work, diligence, and industry, and at small cost and expense, they will get in their place incompetent substitutes, ignorant louts such as they have had before, who at great cost and expense will teach the children nothing but how to be utter asses, and beyond that will dishonor men's wives and daughters and maidservants, taking over their homes and property, as has happened before. This will be the reward of the great and shameful ingratitude into which the devil is so craftily leading them. . . .

I know very well that many of you, without any exhortation on my part, are acting in this matter and would do so anyway better than I can advise. Moreover, I have already published a message to the councilmen in the cities. Nevertheless, because some may have forgotten this, or would be more persistent as a result of my example, I have sent you this sermon of mine, which I have preached more than once to our people. From it you can observe that I am working faithfully with you in this matter, and that we are doing our best everywhere and are guiltless before God in the conduct of our office. The case is truly in our hands because we see that even the clergy, who are called spiritual, appear to take the view that they would let all schools, discipline, and teaching go by the board, or themselves even help to destroy them, simply because they cannot have their own way with them as they once did. This too is the devil's doing, through them. God help us. Amen.

A Sermon on Keeping Children in School

Dear friends, the common people appear to be quite indifferent to the matter of maintaining the schools. I see them withdrawing their children from instruction and turning them to the making of a living and to caring for their bellies. Besides, they either will not or cannot think what a horrible and un-Christian business this is and what great and murderous harm they are doing everywhere in so serving the devil. For this reason I have undertaken to give you this exhortation, on the chance that there may be some who still have at least a modicum of belief that there is a God in heaven and a hell prepared for unbelievers, and that by this exhortation they might be led to change their minds. (Actually, almost everybody is acting as if there were neither a God in heaven nor a devil in hell.) I propose, therefore, to take up the question of what is at stake in this matter in the way of gains and losses, first those that are spiritual or eternal, and then those that are temporal or worldly.

I hope, indeed, that believers, those who want to be called Christians, know very well that the spiritual estate has been established and instituted by God, not with gold or silver but with the precious blood and bitter death of his only Son, our Lord Jesus Christ (1 Pet. 1:18-19). From his wounds indeed flow the sacraments (they used to depict this on broadsides). He paid clearly that men might everywhere have this office of preaching, baptizing, loosing, binding, giving the sacrament, comforting, warning, and exhorting with God's word, and whatever else belongs to the pastoral office. For this office not only helps to further and sustain this temporal life and all the worldly estates, but it also gives eternal life and delivers from sin and death, which is its proper and chief work. Indeed, it is only because of the spiritual estate that the world stands and abides at all; if it were not for this estate, the world would long since have gone down to destruction. I am not thinking, however, of the spiritual estate as we know it today in the monastic houses and the foundations with their celibate way of life, for it has long since fallen from its glorious beginning and is now nothing more than an estate founded by worldly wisdom for the sake of getting money and revenues. There is nothing spiritual about it except that the clergy are not married (they do not need marriage, for they have something else in its place); except for this, everything about it is merely external, temporal, perishable pomp. They give no heed to God's word and the office of preaching — and where the word is not in use the clergy must be bad.

The estate I am thinking of is rather one which has the office of preaching and the service of the word and sacraments and which imparts the Spirit and salvation, blessings that cannot be attained by any amount of pomp and pageantry. It includes the work of pastors, teachers, preachers, lectors, priests (whom men call chaplains), sacristans, schoolmasters, and whatever other work belongs to these offices and persons. This estate the Scriptures highly exalt and praise. St. Paul calls them God's stewards and servants (1 Cor. 4:1); bishops (Acts 20:28); doctors, prophets (1 Cor. 12:28); also God's ambassadors to reconcile the world to God (2 Cor. 5:20). Joel calls them saviors. In Psalm 68 David calls them kings and princes. Haggai (1:13) calls them angels, and Malachi (2:7) says, "The lips of the priest keep the law, for he is an angel of the Lord of hosts." Christ himself gives them the same name, not only in Matthew 11(:10) where he calls John the Baptist an angel, but also throughout the entire book of the Revelation to John. . . .

Now if it is true and certain that God himself has established and instituted the spiritual estate with his own blood and death, we may conclude that he will have it highly honored. He will not allow it to be destroyed or to die out, but will have it maintained until the Last Day. For the gospel and the church must abide until the Last Day, as Christ says in the last chapter of Matthew (28:20), "Lo, I am with you always, to the close of the age." But by whom then shall it be maintained? Oxen and horses, dogs and swine will not do it; neither will wood and stone. We men shall have to do it, for this office is not committed to oxen and horses, but to us men. But where shall we get men for it except from those who have children? If you will not raise your child for this office, and the next man will not, and so on, and no fathers or mothers will give their children to our God for this work, what will become of the spiritual office and estate? The old men now in the office will not live forever. They are dying off every day and there are no others to take their place. What will God say to this at last? Do you think he will be pleased that we shamefully despise his office, divinely instituted to his honor and glory and for our salvation and won at such a price — so despise it that we ungratefully let it fade away and die?

He has not given you your children and the means to support them simply so that you may do with them as you please, or train them just to get ahead in the world. You have been earnestly commanded to raise them for God's service, or be completely rooted out — you, your children, and everything else, in which case everything you have done for them is condemned, as the second commandment says, "I visit the iniquities of the fathers upon the children to the third and fourth generation of those who hate me" (Exod. 20:5). But how will you raise them for God's service if the office of preaching and the spiritual estate have fallen into oblivion?

And it is your fault. You could have done something about it. You could have helped to maintain them if you had allowed your child to study. And where it is possible for you to do this but you fail to do so, where your child has the ability and the desire to learn but you stand in the way, then you — and mark this well! — you are guilty of the harm that is done when the spiritual estate disappears and neither God nor God's word remains in the world. To the extent that you are able you are bringing about its demise. You refuse to give one child — and would do the same if all the children in the world were yours. So far as you are concerned, the serving of God can just die out altogether. It does not help your case to say, "My neighbor keeps his son in school, so I don't need to." For your neighbor can say the same thing, and so can all the neighbors. Meanwhile, where is God to get people for his spiritual office? You have someone you could give, but you refuse — as does your neighbor. The office simply goes down to destruction so far as you are concerned. But because you allow the office instituted and established by your God and so clearly won to go to ruin, because you are so horribly ungrateful as to let it be destroyed, you yourself will be accursed. You will have nothing but shame and misery both for yourself and for your children, or be so tormented in other ways that both you and they will be damned, not only here on earth but eternally in hell. This will happen so that you may learn that your children are not so wholly yours that you need give nothing of them to God. He too will have what is rightfully his — and they are more his than yours!

And lest you think I am being too severe with you in this matter, I shall lay before you a partial statement of the gains and losses you are effecting — for who can recount them all? — such that you will have to admit yourself that you indeed belong to the devil and rightly deserve to be damned eternally in hell if you acquiesce in this fault and do not amend your ways. On the other hand, you may rejoice and be glad from the heart if you find that you have been chosen by God to devote your means and labor to raising a son who will be a good Christian pastor, preacher, or schoolmaster, and thereby to raise for God a special servant, yes (as was said above), an angel of

God, a true bishop before God, a savior of many people, a king and prince in the kingdom of Christ, a teacher of God's people, a light of the world — indeed, who can recount all the distinction and honor that a good and faithful pastor has in the eyes of God? There is no dearer treasure, no nobler thing on earth or in this life than a good and faithful pastor and preacher.

Just think, whatever good is accomplished by the preaching office and the care of souls is assuredly accomplished by your own son as he faithfully performs this office. For example, each day through him many souls are taught, converted, baptized, and brought to Christ and saved, and redeemed from sin, death, hell, and the devil. Through him they come to everlasting righteousness, to everlasting life and heaven, so that Daniel (12:3) says well that "those who teach others shall shine like the brightness of the firmament; and those who turn many to righteousness shall be like the stars for ever and ever." . . .

Ought you not leap for joy that with your money you are privileged to accomplish something so great in the sight of God? For what are all the foundations and monastic houses of our day with their self-appointed works in comparison with one such pastor, preacher, or schoolmaster? To be sure, they were originally founded long ago by pious kings and lords precisely for this precious work of training such preachers and pastors. But now, sad to say, the devil has brought them to such a wretched state that they have become death traps, the very ramparts of hell, to the hurt and detriment of the church.

Now just look at what your son does — not just one of these works but many, indeed, all of them! And he does them every day. Best of all, he does them in the sight of God who, as we have said, looks upon them so highly and regards them as precious, even though men may not recognize or esteem them. Indeed, if all the world should call your son a heretic, deceiver, liar, and rebel, so much the better. That is a good sign that he is an upright man, like his Lord Christ. For Christ too had to be a rebel, a murderer, and a deceiver, and be condemned and crucified with the murderers. What would it matter to me as a preacher if the world were to call me a devil, so long as I knew that God calls me his angel? Let the world call me a deceiver as much as it pleases, so long as God calls me his faithful servant and steward, the angels call me their comrade, the saints call me their brother, believers call me their father, souls in anguish call me their savior, the ignorant call me their light, and God adds, "Yes, it is so," and the angels and all creatures join in. Ah! How prettily the world, with the devil, has deceived me with its slanders and scoffing! How the dear world has hurt me and gained at my expense!

I have spoken so far about the works and miracles which your son does for individual souls, helping them against sin, death, and the devil. Beyond that, however, he does great and mighty works for the world. He informs and instructs the various estates on how they are to conduct themselves outwardly in their several offices and estates, so that they may do what is right in the sight of God. Every day he can comfort and advise those who are troubled, resolve difficulties, relieve troubled consciences, help maintain peace and settle and remove differences, and countless other works of this kind. For a preacher confirms, strengthens, and helps to sustain authority of every kind, and temporal peace generally. He checks the rebellious; teaches obedience, morals, discipline, and honor; instructs fathers, mothers, children, and servants in their duties; in a word, he gives direction to all the temporal estates and offices. Of all the good things a pastor does these are, to be sure, the least. Yet they are so high and noble that the wisest of all the heathen have never known or understood them, much less been able to do them. Indeed, even to the present day no jurist, university, foundation, or monastery knows these works, and they are not taught either in canon law or secular law. For there is no one who regards these offices as God's great gifts, his gracious ordinances. It is only the word of God and the preachers that praise and honor them so highly.

Therefore, to tell the truth, peace, the greatest of earthly goods, in which all other temporal goods are comprised, is really a fruit of true preaching. For where the preaching is right, there war and discord and bloodshed do not come; but where the preaching is not right, it is no wonder that there is war, or at least constant unrest and the desire to fight and to shed blood....

A true pastor thus contributes to the well-being of men in body and soul, in property and honor. But beyond that see how he also serves God and what glorious worship and sacrifice he renders. For by his work and word there are maintained in this world the kingdom of God, the name and honor and glory of God, the true knowledge of God, the right faith and understanding of Christ, the fruits of the suffering and blood and death of Christ, the gifts and works and power of the Holy Spirit, the true and saving use of baptism and the sacrament, the right and pure teaching of the gospel, the right way of disciplining and crucifying the body, and much more. Who could ever adequately praise any one of these things? And what more can still be said? How much he accomplishes by battling against the devil, the wisdom of this world, and the imaginations of the flesh; how many victories he wins; how he puts down error and prevents heresy. For he must strive and fight against the gates of hell (Matt. 16:18) and overcome the devil. This too is not his own doing; it is accomplished by his office and his word. These are the innumerable and unspeakable works and miracles of the preaching office. In a word, if we would praise God to the uttermost, we must praise his word and preaching; for the office and the word are his.

Now even if you were a king, you should not think you are too good to give your son and to train him for this office and work, even at the cost of all that you have. Is not the money and the labor you expend on such a son so highly honored, so gloriously blessed, so profitably invested that it counts in God's sight as better than any kingdom or empire? A man ought to be willing to crawl on his hands and knees to the ends of the earth to be able to invest his money so gloriously well. Yet right there in your own house and on your own lap you have that in which you can make such an investment. Shame, shame, and shame again upon our blind and despicable ingratitude that we should fail to see what extraordinary service we could render to God, indeed, how distinguished we could be in his sight with just a little application of effort and our own money and property. . . .

<hr />

ULRICH STADLER

Cherished Instructions on Sin, Excommunication, and the Community of Goods

Ulrich Stadler (d. 1540) was a leader among the Hutterites, an Anabaptist group in Moravia, just north of Austria, named after another of their leaders, Jacob Hutter (d. 1536). Like other Anabaptists, the Hutterites withdrew from the wider society in order to form a community of pure Christians. They baptized only adults who committed themselves to the community's discipline and rebaptized those who had been baptized as infants on the grounds that such an act, done without any decision on the part of the infant baptized, did not really count as baptism. All Anabaptists were pacifists; the Hutterites also lived communally and shared their

<hr />

Ulrich Stadler, *Cherished Instructions on Sin, Excommunication, and the Community of Goods*, in *Spiritual and Anabaptist Writers*, ed. George Huntston Williams (Philadelphia: Westminster, 1957), 277-82.

goods. They survived in spite of severe persecution, and some migrated to North America, where the chronicle of their history, kept in the community since the early 1500s, was discovered by astonished scholars in a small South Dakota Hutterite community in the early twentieth century. Stadler's *Cherished Instructions*, probably written about 1537, captures the kind of commitment to life in a community of set-apart Christians to which the Hutterites felt called.

The True Community of the Saints

There is one communion [*gmain*] of all the faithful in Christ and one community [*gmainschaft*] of the holy children called of God. They have one Father in heaven, one Lord Christ; all are baptized and sealed in their hearts with one Spirit. They have one mind, opinion, heart, and soul as having all drunk from the same Fountain, and alike await one and the same struggle, cross, trial, and, at length, one and the same hope in glory. But it, that is, such a community [*gmain*], must move about in this world, poor, miserable, small, and rejected of the world, of whom, however, the world is not worthy. Whoever strives for the lofty things (of this world) does not belong. Thus in this community everything must proceed equally, all things be one and communal, alike in the bodily gifts of their Father in heaven, which he daily gives to be used by his own according to his will. For how does it make sense that all who have here in this pilgrimage to look forward to an inheritance in the Kingdom of their Father should not be satisfied with their bodily goods and gifts? Judge, O ye saints of God, ye who are thus truly grafted into Christ, with him deadened to the world, to sin, and to yourselves, that you never hereafter live for the world or yourselves but rather for him who died for you and arose, namely, Christ. [They] have also yielded themselves and presented themselves to him intimately, patiently, of their own free will, naked and uncovered, to suffer and endure his will and, moreover, to fulfill it and thereafter also to devote themselves in obedience and service to all the children of God. Therefore, they also live with one another where the Lord assigns a place to them, peaceably, united, lovingly, amicably, and fraternally, as children of one Father. In their pilgrimage they should be satisfied with the bodily goods and gifts of their Father, since they should also be altogether as one body and members one toward another.

Now if, then, each member withholds assistance from the other, the whole thing must go to pieces. The eyes won't see, the hands won't take hold. Where, however, each member extends assistance equally to the whole body, it is built up and grows and there is peace and unity, yea, each member takes care for the other. In brief, equal care, sadness and joy, and peace [are] at hand. It is just the same in the spiritual body of Christ. If the deacon of the community will never serve, the teacher will not teach, the young brother will not be obedient, the strong will not work for the community but for himself and each one wishes to take care of himself; and if once in a while someone withdraws without profit to himself, the whole body is divided. In brief, *one, common* builds the Lord's house and is pure; but *mine, thine, his, own* divides the Lord's house and is impure. Therefore, where there is ownership and one has it, and it is his, and one does not wish to be one [*gmainsam*] with Christ and his own in living and dying, he is outside of Christ and his communion [*gmain*] and has thus no Father in heaven. If he says so, he lies. That is the life of the pilgrims of the Lord, who has purchased them in Christ, namely, the elect, the called, the holy ones in this life. These are his fighters and heralds, to whom also he will give the crown of life on the Day of his righteousness.

Secondly, such a community of the children of God has ordinances here in their pilgrimage. These should constitute the polity [*policeien*] for the whole world. But the wickedness of men has spoiled everything. For as the sun with its shining is common to all, so also the use of all creaturely things. Whoever appropriates them for himself and encloses them is a thief and steals what is not his. For everything has been created free in common [*in die gmain*]. Of such thieves the whole world is full. May God guard his own from them. To be sure, according to human law, one says: That is mine, but not according to divine law. Here in this ordinance [in our community] it [the divine law] is to be heeded [*gilt es aufsehens*] in such a way that unbearable burdens be not laid upon the children of the Lord, but rather ones which God, out of his grace, has put upon us, living according to which we may be pleasing to him. Thus only as circumstances dictate will the children of God have either many or few houses, institute faithful house managers and stewards, who will faithfully move among the children of God and conduct themselves in a mild and fatherly manner and pray to God for wisdom therein.

Ordinances of the Saints in Their Community and Life Here Together in the Lord with the Goods of Their Father

In order to hold in common all the gifts and goods which God gives and dispenses to his own, there must be free, unhampered [*ledige*], patient [*gelassene*], and full hearts in Christ, yea, hearts that truly believe and trust and in Christ are utterly devoted. Whoever is thus free, unhampered, and resigned in the Lord from everything, [ready] to give over all his goods and chattels, yea, to lay it up for distribution among the children of God — it is God's grace in Christ which prepares men for it. Being willing and ready — that makes one free and unhampered. But whoever is not thus at liberty to give over and lay up in Christ the Lord, as indicated, should nevertheless not hold back, nor conceal, nor disavow anything but instead be willing and ready to give even when there is nothing at hand, yea, even to let the deacons in to collect in order that [at least] they might have free access in the Lord to them and at all times to find a willing, open heart ready to share. The house managers who have devoted themselves to the Lord and his people with body and substance in the service of, and obedience to, the Lord in his community should not be changed where they are recognized as fitted for the work and found faithful, nor the [management of] the necessities withdrawn from them in the Lord, as long as they deal faithfully. Where, however, avarice or selfishness is detected, it should not be permitted. They must also be more community-minded with all the wretched of the Lord.

[As] deacons of welfare, true men should be ordained who take care that everything proceeds equally in the whole house of the Lord, everywhere in all the households, lest one have and another want. They also should be fatherly with all the little children of God; and also do all the buying and selling for the community.

The children of God should group themselves and hold together here in misery after they have been driven out in the worst sort of way — if they can achieve this, for it is good and purposeful; however, if it [can be managed] without hardship, they should not make big concentrations but rather, as opportunity affords, they should have many or at least a few [separated] houses. In brief, it belongs to all the children of God to live, to serve, to work, to seek not their own benefit but that of another, since we are all of the Lord. [Such] is their behavior on their pilgrimage.

Again, the brethren ought not to do business with each other, buy and sell like the heathen, each being rather in the Lord the Lord's own. Finally, everything should be arranged for the good of the saints of God in the church of the Lord according to time, place, propriety, and opportunity, for one cannot set up a specific instruction for everything. The hearts which are free, willing, unhampered, patient, [ready] to serve all the children of God, to have everything in common with them, yea, to persevere loyally and constantly in their service, shall remain always in the Lord. Where such hearts of grace exist, everything is soon ordered in the Lord. But whoever goes about in the congregation and the community of the saints with cunning and deception, untruth or lies, the Lord will bring to ruin . . . , however long postponed — [also him] who seeks himself or does not work faithfully as for the Lord himself or as with the goods of the Lord, and does not rightly go about in the fear of the Lord.

Now follow the counterarguments.

Someone says that it is better, because of bickering and complaining, to be separate from each other, and that if everyone takes care of and lives unto himself, it stays more peaceful.

Answer: The complainer and grumbler, of course, who have never mortified the flesh, who do not control their desires and lusts, who have indeed abandoned the patience and the true love of God (whoever has this love of God in his heart is long-suffering and patient along with the rest of the pious here in these troubled times lest he lose himself too far in the world), yea, because of these things it is difficult or even impossible [for them] to live along with and in the midst of the others — [for them] who seek themselves, [who seek] to maintain their own life here comfortably, and to cultivate their body, as they have since childhood learned and been accustomed to doing according to the perverse manner [of the world]. Indeed, for such unmortified, carnal, natural men without the Spirit, it certainly is a heavy, bitter, unbearable life. Such persons seek freedom only to dwell someplace unto themselves in order that they might live pleasantly according to the flesh and unto their corruption. Otherwise they would surely be captured by the snares of blessedness and love. Those who had not been constrained to love within their hearts would nevertheless endure it in order not to become obvious, but upon such as these, God's severity should be visited.

Secondly, it is said that the children of God cannot all dwell in the same place. They cannot all be even in one land; nor is this really necessary, for the whole earth is the Lord's, and it makes no difference where one dwells, so long as it is in the fear of God.

Answer: This is indeed true, but as far as it can be had and achieved, it is very good and purposeful to be together as well as can be so that all is possessed as by sojourners who seek another habitation. For to wander in the world and to have much to do with it and still to keep from being unsullied is possible for only a few and very hazardous. But whoever likes danger very likely comes to disaster thereby, especially in these times, which are much more full of danger than ever before. In this time a place has been given to the bride of the Lamb in which to dwell amid the wasteland of this world, there to put on the beautiful bright linen garment and thus to await the Lord until he leads her after him here in tribulation and afterward receives her with eternal joy. The time is now. Whoever has ears to hear, let him hear.

〜〜〜

JOHN CALVIN

Institutes of the Christian Religion

John Calvin (1509-1564) grew up in France, where he joined the Protestant cause in his early twenties. Passing through the Swiss city of Geneva in 1536, he was recruited to provide religious leadership for its newly born Protestantism; what had been intended to be an overnight stay occupied all but three years of the rest of his life. Calvin's goal was to make the whole city of Geneva what medieval monasteries had been at their best — a foretaste of God's kingdom. This selection comes from his greatest work, *Institutes of the Christian Religion,* originally published in 1536 but constantly revised — these selections come from the 1559 edition. Calvin sets out the basic principles of the Christian life and then turns to what he has to say about calls.

Most later Protestants distinguished between our "general calling" to be a Christian and our "special calling" to some particular vocation. Calvin used the same terms but in a different way — the "general calling" was the word that anyone could hear in preaching, inviting them to faith; a "special calling" worked only in the hearts of the elect, to bring them to that faith. Here and elsewhere, Calvin thus tied his understanding of vocation to his clear doctrine of predestination: God predestines some to salvation regardless of their merit and leaves others to their sins and damnation. To many of his critics, this has always seemed deeply unfair, but he insisted that it was the only way to credit God with our salvation in gratitude, rather than claiming in pride that we had somehow earned it.

═══

John Calvin, *Institutes of the Christian Religion,* ed. John T. McNeill and trans. Ford Lewis Battles (Philadelphia: Westminster, 1967), 1:689-92, 695, 720-21, 723-25; 2:974, 975-76.

Book 3, Chapter 7
The Sum of the Christian Life: The Denial of Ourselves

I. We Are Not Our Own Masters, but Belong to God

... the duty of believers is "to present their bodies to God as a living sacrifice, holy and acceptable to him," and in this consists the lawful worship of him (Rom. 12:1). From this is derived the basis of the exhortation that "they be not conformed to the fashion of this world, but be transformed by the renewal of their minds, so that they may prove what is the will of God" (Rom. 12:2). Now the great thing is this: we are consecrated and dedicated to God in order that we may thereafter think, speak, meditate, and do, nothing except to his glory. For a sacred thing may not be applied to profane uses without marked injury to him.

If we, then, are not our own (1 Cor. 6:19) but the Lord's, it is clear what error we must flee, and whither we must direct all the acts of our life.

We are not our own: let not our reason nor our will, therefore, sway our plans and deeds. We are not our own: let us therefore not set it as our goal to seek what is expedient for us according to the flesh. We are not our own: in so far as we can, let us therefore forget ourselves and all that is ours.

Conversely, we are God's: let us therefore live for him and die for him. We are God's: let his wisdom and will therefore rule all our actions. We are God's: let all the parts of our life accordingly strive toward him as our only lawful goal (Rom. 14:8; cf. 1 Cor. 6:19). O, how much has that man profited who, having been taught that he is not his own, has taken away dominion and rule from his own reason that he may yield it to God! For, as consulting our self-interest is the pestilence that most effectively leads to our destruction, so the sole haven of salvation is to be wise in nothing and to will nothing through ourselves but to follow the leading of the Lord alone. . . .

2. Self-Denial through Devotion to God

From this also follows this second point: that we seek not the things that are ours but those which are of the Lord's will and will serve to advance his glory. This is also evidence of great progress: that, almost forgetful of ourselves, surely subordinating our self-concern, we try faithfully to devote our zeal to God and his commandments. For when Scripture bids us leave off self-concern, it not only erases from our minds the yearning to possess, the desire for power, and the favor of men, but it also uproots ambition and all craving for human glory and other more secret plagues. Accordingly, the Christian must surely be so disposed and minded that he feels within himself it is with God he has to deal throughout his life. In this way, as he will refer all he has to God's decision and judgment, so will he refer his whole intention of mind scrupulously to Him. For he who has learned to look to God in all things that he must do, at the same time avoids all vain thoughts. This, then, is that denial of self which Christ enjoins with such great earnestness upon his disciples at the outset of their service (cf. Matt. 16:24). When it has once taken possession of their hearts, it leaves no place at all first either to pride, or arrogance, or ostentation; then either to avarice, or desire, or lasciviousness, or effeminacy, or to other evils that our self-love spawns (cf. 2 Tim. 3:2-5). . . .

5. Self-Renunciation Leads to Proper Helpfulness toward Our Neighbors

Now, in seeking to benefit one's neighbor, how difficult it is to do one's duty! Unless you give up all thought of self and, so to speak, get out of yourself, you will accomplish nothing here. For how can you perform those works which Paul teaches to be the works of love, unless you renounce yourself, and give yourself wholly to others? "Love," he says, "is patient and kind, not jealous or boastful, is not envious or puffed up, does not seek its own, is not irritable," etc. (1 Cor. 13:4-5). If this is the one thing required — that we seek not what is our own — still we shall do no little violence to nature, which so inclines us to love of ourselves alone that it does not easily allow us to neglect ourselves and our possessions in order to look after another's good, nay, to yield willingly what is ours by right and resign it to another. But Scripture, to lead us by the hand to this, warns that whatever benefits we obtain from the Lord have been entrusted to us on this condition: that they be applied to the common good of the church. And therefore the lawful use of all benefits consists in a liberal and kindly sharing of them with others. No surer rule and no more valid exhortation to keep it could be devised than when we are taught that all the gifts we possess have been bestowed by God and entrusted to us on condition that they be distributed for our neighbors' benefit (1 Pet. 4:10).

But Scripture goes even farther by comparing them to the powers with which the members of the human body are endowed (1 Cor. 12:12). No member has this power for itself nor applies it to its own private use; but each pours it out to the fellow members. Nor does it take any profit from its power except what proceeds from the common advantage of the whole body. So, too, whatever a godly man can do he ought to be able to do for his brothers, providing for himself in no way other than to have his mind intent upon the common upbuilding of the church. Let this, therefore, be our rule for generosity and beneficence: We are the stewards of everything God has conferred on us by which we are able to help our neighbor, and are required to render account of our stewardship. Moreover, the only right stewardship is that which is tested by the rule of love. Thus it will come about that we shall not only join zeal for another's benefit with care for our own advantage, but shall subordinate the latter to the former. . . .

Chapter 10, 2. The Main Principle

Let this be our principle: that the use of God's gifts is not wrongly directed when it is referred to that end to which the Author himself created and destined them for us, since he created them for our good, not for our ruin. Accordingly, no one will hold to a straighter path than he who diligently looks to this end. Now if we ponder to what end God created food, we shall find that he meant not only to provide for necessity but also for delight and good cheer. Thus the purpose of clothing, apart from necessity, was comeliness and decency. In grasses, trees, and fruits, apart from their various uses, there is beauty of appearance and pleasantness of odor (cf. Gen. 2:9). For if this were not true, the prophet would not have reckoned them among the benefits of God, "that wine gladdens the heart of man, that oil makes his face shine" (Ps. 104:15). Scripture would not have reminded us repeatedly in commending his kindness, that he gave all such things to men. And the natural qualities themselves of things demonstrate sufficiently to what end and extent we may enjoy them. Has the Lord clothed the flowers with the great beauty that greets our eyes, the sweetness of smell that is wafted upon our nostrils, and yet will it be unlawful for our eyes to be affected by that beauty, or our sense of smell by the sweetness of that odor? What? Did he not so distinguish colors as to make some more lovely than others? What? Did he not endow gold and silver, ivory and marble, with a loveliness that renders them more precious than other metals or stones? Did he not, in short, render many things attractive to us, apart from their necessary use? . . .

5. Frugality, Earthly Possessions Held in Trust

The second rule will be: they who have narrow and slender resources should know how to go without things patiently, lest they be troubled by an immoderate desire for them. If they keep this rule of moderation, they will make considerable progress in the Lord's school. So, too, they who have not progressed, in some degree at least, in this respect have scarcely anything to prove them disciples of Christ. For besides the fact that most other vices accompany the desire for earthly things, he who bears poverty impatiently also when in prosperity commonly betrays the contrary disease. This is my point: who is ashamed of mean clothing will boast of costly clothing; he who, not content with a slender meal, is troubled by the desire for a more elegant one, will also intemperately abuse those elegances if they fall to his lot. He who will bear reluctantly, and with a troubled mind, his deprivation and humble condition if he be advanced to honors will by no means abstain from arrogance. To this end, then, let all those for whom the pursuit of piety is not a pretense strive to learn, by the Apostle's example, how to be filled and to hunger, to abound and to suffer want (Phil. 4:12).

Besides, Scripture has a third rule with which to regulate the use of earthly things. Of it we said something when we discussed the precepts of love. It decrees that all those things were so given to us by the kindness of God, and so destined for our benefit, that they are, as it were, entrusted to us, and we must one day render account of them. Thus, therefore, we must so arrange it that this saying may continually resound in our ears: "Render account of your stewardship" (Luke 16:2). At the same time let us remember by whom such reckoning is required: namely, him who has greatly commended abstinence, sobriety, frugality, and moderation, and has also abominated excess, pride, ostentation, and vanity; who approves no other distribution of good things than one joined with love; who has already condemned with his own lips all delights that draw man's spirit away from chastity and purity, or befog his mind.

6. The Lord's Calling a Basis of Our Way of Life

Finally, this point is to be noted: the Lord bids each one of us in all life's actions to look to his calling. For he knows with what great restlessness human nature flames, with what fickleness it is borne hither and thither, how its ambition longs to embrace various things at once. Therefore, lest through our stupidity and rashness everything be turned topsy-turvy, he has appointed duties for every man in his particular way of life. And that no one may thoughtlessly transgress his limits, he has named these various kinds of living "callings." Therefore each individual has his own kind of living assigned to him by the Lord as a sort of sentry post so that he may not heedlessly wander about throughout life. Now, so necessary is this distinction that all our actions are judged in his sight by it, often indeed far otherwise than in the judgment of human and philosophical reason. No deed is considered more noble, even among philosophers, than to free one's country from tyranny. Yet a private citizen who lays his hand upon a tyrant is openly condemned by the heavenly judge (1 Sam. 24:7, 11; 26:9).

But I will not delay to list examples. It is enough if we know that the Lord's calling is in everything the beginning and foundation of well-doing. And if there is anyone who will not direct himself to it, he will never hold to the straight path in his duties. Perhaps, sometimes, he could contrive something laudable in appearance; but whatever it may be in the eyes of men, it will be rejected before God's throne. Besides, there will be no harmony among the several parts of his life. Accordingly, your life will then be best ordered when it is directed to this goal. For no one, impelled by his own rashness, will attempt more than his calling will permit, because he will know that it is not lawful to exceed its bounds. A man of obscure station will lead a private life ungrudgingly so as not to leave the rank in which he has been placed by God. Again, it will be no slight relief from cares, labors, troubles, and other burdens for a man to know that God is his guide in all these things. The magistrate will discharge his functions more willingly; the head of the household will confine himself to his duty; each man will bear and swallow the discomforts, vexations, weariness, and anxieties in his way of life, when he has been persuaded that the burden was laid upon him by God. From this will arise also a singular consolation: that no task will be so sordid and base, provided you obey your calling in it, that it will not shine and be reckoned very precious in God's sight. . . .

Chapter 24, 8. General and Special Calling (Matt. 22:2ff.)

The statement of Christ "Many are called but few are chosen" (Matt. 22:14) is, in this manner, very badly understood. Nothing will be ambiguous if we hold fast to what ought to be clear from the foregoing: that there are two kinds of call. There is the general call, by which God invites all equally to himself through the outward preaching of the word — even those to whom he holds it out as a savor of death (2 Cor. 2:16), and as the occasion for severer condemnation. The other kind of call is special, which he deigns for the most part to give to the believers alone, while by the inward illumination of his Spirit he causes the preached Word to dwell in their hearts. Yet sometimes he also causes those whom he illumines only for a time to partake of it; then he justly forsakes them on account of their ungratefulness and strikes them with even greater blindness. . . .

9. *The Example of Judas Is No Counterevidence*

The same reason applies to the exception raised just above, where Christ says that "no one perished but the son of perdition" (John 17:12); this is indeed an inexact expression but not at all obscure; for he was counted among Christ's sheep not because he truly was one but because he occupied the place of one. The Lord's assertion in another passage that he was chosen by him with the apostles is made only with reference to the ministry. "I have chosen twelve," he said, "and one of them is a devil" (John 6:70). That is, he had chosen him for the apostolic office. But when he speaks of election unto salvation, he banishes him far from the number of the elect: "I am not speaking of you all; I know whom I have chosen" (John 13:18). If anyone confuses the word "election" in the two passages, he will miserably entangle himself; if he notes their difference, nothing is plainer. Consequently, when Gregory (Pope Gregory I) teaches that we are aware only of our call but unsure of our election, he is badly and dangerously in error. From this notion he exhorts all men to fear and trembling, making use of this reason: that even though we may know what we are today, we know not what we shall be. But in this passage he sufficiently declares how he tripped on this stone. For, inasmuch as he made election depend upon the merits of works, he supplied ample reason for men's minds to become dejected; he could not strengthen them, for he did not transfer them from themselves to a trust in God's goodness.

From this believers have some taste of what we set out at the beginning: predestination, rightly understood, brings no shaking of faith but rather its best confirmation. Yet I do not deny that the Spirit sometimes accommodates the utterance to the measure of our understanding — for instance, when he says: "They shall not be in the secret of my people, or be enrolled in the register of my servants" (Ezek. 13:9). It is as if God were beginning to write in the book of life those whom he reckons among the number of His people, although we know, as Christ bears witness (Luke 10:20), that the names of the children of God have been written in the book of life from the beginning (Phil. 4:3). But these words simply express the casting away of those who seemed the chief among the elect, as the Psalm had it: "Let them be blotted out of the book of life; let them not be enrolled among the righteous" (Ps. 69:28; cf. Rev. 3:5).

IGNATIUS LOYOLA

The Spiritual Exercises

Ignatius Loyola (1491 or 1495-1556), son of a Spanish noble family, pursued the life of a soldier until he was seriously wounded in battle. Forced to reflection during a long convalescence, he turned to a life of severe asceticism and then set about getting an education. Some fellow students attracted by his passion and insight began the Society of Jesus, or Jesuits. Once approved as a new order by the Pope, they quickly became leading missionaries and intellectuals of the church. Parts of Ignatius's *Spiritual Exercises* have no more literary elegance than a cookbook, but, particularly when used by a spiritual director to guide a month-long retreat, the *Exercises* have been profoundly influential in shaping many lives. In contrast to Calvin's arguments for God's absolute sovereignty and predestination, Ignatius thinks of salvation as achieved by a combination of God's grace and human free will.

Introduction to Making a Choice of a Way of Life

In every good choice, in so far as it depends upon us, the direction of our intention should be simple. I must look only to the end for which I am created, that is, for the praise of God our Lord and for the salvation of my soul.

The Spiritual Exercises of St. Ignatius, trans. Anthony Mottola (Garden City, N.Y.: Image Books, 1964), 82-87.

Therefore, whatever I choose must have as its purpose to help me to this end. I must not shape or draw the end to the means, but the means to the end. Many, for example, first choose marriage, which is a means, and secondarily to serve God our Lord in the married state, which service of God is the end. Likewise there are others who first desire to have benefices (church offices with a guaranteed income), and afterward to serve God in them. These individuals do not go straight to God, but want God to come straight to their inordinate attachments. Acting thus, they make a means of the end, and an end of the means, so that what they ought to seek first, they seek last. My first aim, then, should be my desire to serve God, which is the end, and after this, to seek a benefice or to marry, if it is more fitting for me, for these things are but means to the end. Thus, nothing should move me to use such means or to deprive myself of them except it be only the service and praise of God our Lord and the eternal salvation of my soul.

A Consideration to Obtain Information on the Matters in Which a Choice Should Be Made

This contains four points and a note:

First point: All matters in which we wish to make a choice must be either indifferent or good in themselves. They must meet with the approbation of our Holy Mother, the hierarchical Church, and not be bad or repugnant to her.

Second point: There are some things that are the objects of an immutable choice, such as the priesthood, matrimony, etc. There are others in which the choice is not immutable, as, for example, accepting or relinquishing a benefice, accepting or renouncing temporal goods.

Third point: Once an immutable choice has been made there is no further choice, for it cannot be dissolved, as is true with marriage, the priesthood, etc. It should be noted only that if one has not made this choice properly, with due consideration, and without inordinate attachments, he should repent and try to lead a good life in the choice that he has made. Since this choice was ill considered and improperly made, it does not seem to be a vocation from God, as many err in believing, wishing to interpret an ill-considered or bad choice as a divine call. For every divine call is always pure and clean without any admixture of flesh or other inordinate attachments.

Fourth point: If one has made a proper and well-considered choice that is mutable, and has not been influenced either by the flesh or the world, there is no reason why he should make a new choice. But he should perfect himself as much as possible in the choice he has made.

Note

It is to be noted that if this mutable choice is not well considered and sincerely made, then it will be profitable to make the choice anew in the proper manner, if one wishes to bring forth fruits that are worthwhile and pleasing to God our Lord.

Three Occasions When a Wise and Good Choice Can Be Made

The first occasion is when God our Lord moves and attracts the will so that the devout soul, without question and without desire to question, follows what has been manifested to it. St. Paul and St. Matthew did this when they followed Christ our Lord.

The second occasion is present when one has developed a clear understanding and knowledge through the experience of consolations and desolations and the discernment of diverse spirits.

The third occasion is in a time of tranquility. Here one considers first for what purpose man is born, which is to praise God our Lord and to save his soul. Since he desires to attain this end, he chooses some life or state within the bounds of the church that will help him in the service of God our Lord and the salvation of his soul. I said "a time of tranquility," when the soul is not agitated by diverse spirits, and is freely and calmly making use of its natural powers.

If a Choice Has Not Been Made on the First or Second Occasion, Below Are Given Two Methods of Making It during the Third Occasion

The first method of making a wise and good choice contains six points:

The first point: To place before my mind's eye the thing on which I wish to make a choice. It may be an office or a benefice to be accepted or refused, or anything else that is the object of a mutable choice.

The second point: I must have as my aim the end for which I am created, which is the praise of God our Lord and the salvation of my soul. At the same time I must remain indifferent and free from any inordinate attachments so that I am not more inclined or disposed to take the thing proposed than to reject it, nor to relinquish it rather than to accept it. I must rather be like the equalized scales of balance, ready to follow the course which I feel is more for the glory and praise of God our Lord and the salvation of my soul.

The third point: I must ask God our Lord to deign to move my will and to reveal to my spirit what I should do to best promote His praise and glory in the matter of choice. After examining the matter thoroughly and faithfully with my understanding, I should make my choice in conformity with His good pleasure and His most holy will.

The fourth point: I will use my reason to weigh the many advantages and benefits that would accrue to me if I held the proposed office or benefice solely for the praise of God our Lord and the salvation of my soul. I will likewise consider and weigh the disadvantages and dangers that there are in holding it. I will proceed in like manner with the other alternative, that is, examine and consider the advantages and benefits as well as the disadvantages and dangers in not holding the proposed office or benefice.

The fifth point: After having thus weighed the matter and carefully examined it from every side, I will consider which alternative appears more reasonable. Acting upon the stronger judgment of reason and not on any inclination of the senses, I must come to a decision in the matter that I am considering.

The sixth point: After such a choice or decision has been reached I should turn with great diligence to prayer in the presence of God our Lord and offer Him this choice that His Divine Majesty may deign to accept and confirm it, if it be to His greater service and praise.

The second method of making a wise and good choice contains four rules and a note:

The first rule is that the love which moves me and causes me to make this choice should come from above, that is, from the love of God, so that before I make my choice I will feel that the greater or lesser love that I have for the thing chosen is solely for the sake of my Creator and Lord.

The second rule is to consider some man that I have never seen or known, and in whom I wish to see complete perfection. Now I should consider what I would tell him to do and choose for the greater glory of God our Lord and the greater perfection of his soul. I will act in like manner myself, keeping the rule that I have proposed for another.

The third rule is to consider that if I were at the point of death, what form and procedure I would wish to have observed in making this present choice. Guiding myself by this consideration, I will make my decision on the whole matter.

The fourth rule is to examine and consider how I shall be on the day of judgment, to think how I shall then wish to have made my decision in the present matter. The rule which I should then wish to have followed, I will now follow, that I may on that day be filled with joy and delight.

Note

Taking the above-mentioned rules as my guide for eternal salvation and peace, I will make my choice and offer myself to God our Lord, following the sixth point of the first method of making a choice.

Directions for Amending and Reforming One's Life and State

It is to be observed that those who hold ecclesiastical office or who are married (whether they are rich in worldly possessions or not), when they do not have an opportunity to make a decision or are not very willing to do so regarding things that are subject to choice, that instead of having them make a choice it is very profitable to give to each a form and method of amending and reforming his own life and state. This may be done by placing before him the purpose of his creation, life and state, which is the glory and praise of God our Lord and the salvation of his own soul.

If he wishes to attain and fulfill this end he should consider and examine thoroughly, using the Exercises and the methods of making a choice, explained above, how large a house and establishment he should maintain; how he should manage and govern it; how he should guide it by word and example. He ought also to consider what portion of his means he should use for his family and household, and how much should be given to the poor and to other pious works. In all these works he should desire and seek nothing but the greatest praise and glory of God our Lord. For each one must realize that he will make progress in all spiritual matters in proportion to his flight from self-love, self-will, and self-interest.

TERESA OF ÁVILA

The Life of Saint Teresa of Ávila by Herself

Teresa of Ávila (1515-1582) joined the Carmelite order of nuns in 1535; twenty years later she began to receive visions and voices from God. The Carmelite order for men had been founded in 1154; that for women, in 1452. The extreme asceticism of the early Carmelites had been considerably modified over the years, and Teresa sought, in the face of considerable opposition, to restore its earlier rigor. In 1562, shortly after completing her autobiography, she founded a convent at Ávila for the "barefoot Carmelites." She continued the rest of her life expanding this reformed order and writing about her mystical experiences. As with many religious autobiographies, the text probably exaggerates the author's wickedness.

1. How the Lord Began to Rouse Her Soul in Childhood to a Love of Virtue, and What a Help It Is in This Respect to Have Good Parents

If I had not been so wicked, the possession of devout and God-fearing parents, together with the favor of God's grace, would have been enough to make me good. My father was fond of reading holy books, and had some in Spanish so that his children might read them too. These, and the pains my mother took in teaching us to pray and educating us in devotion to Our Lady and certain Saints, began to rouse me at the age, I think, of six or seven. It was a help to me that I never saw my parents inclined to anything but virtue, and many virtues they had. My father was most charitable to the poor, and most compassionate to the sick, also to his servants; so much so that he could never be persuaded to keep slaves. He felt such pity for them that

The Life of Saint Teresa of Ávila by Herself, trans. J. M. Cohen (New York: Penguin, 1957), 23-31, 32-38.

when a slave-girl of his brother's was, on one occasion, staying in his house, he treated her like one of his own children. He said that he could not bear the pain of seeing her not free. He was an extremely truthful man, and was never heard to swear or speak slander. He was also most rigid in his chastity.

My mother too was a woman of many virtues, who endured a life of great sickness, and was extremely modest. Although she possessed remarkable beauty, she never showed the least signs of setting any store by it. Although she died at thirty-three, she already dressed like a woman advanced in years. She was very calm, and of great understanding. Throughout her life she endured severe sufferings, and she died in a most Christian manner.

We were three sisters and nine brothers, and all, by God's mercy, took after our parents in virtue, except myself, though I was my father's favorite. And before I began to sin against God I think he had some reason to cherish me particularly. Indeed, it saddens me to remember the good propensities with which the Lord endowed me, and what bad use I managed to make of them. For my brothers and sisters never stood in the way of my serving God.

I had one brother almost of my own age, whom I loved best, though I was very fond of them all and they of me. We used to read the lives of the Saints together, and when I read of the martyrdoms which they suffered for the love of God, I used to think that they had bought their entry into God's presence very cheaply. Then I fervently longed to die like them, not out of any conscious love for Him, but in order to attain as quickly as they had those joys which, as I read, are laid up in Heaven. I used to discuss with my brother ways and means of becoming martyrs, and we agreed to go together to the land of the Moors, begging our way for the love of God, so that we might be beheaded there. I believe that our Lord had given us courage enough even at that tender age, if only we could have seen a way. But our having parents seemed to us a very great hindrance.

We were astonished when we were told that pain and bliss will last forever; and very often we would discuss this saying. We took great pleasure in repeating over and over again: "For ever, for ever and ever." Through this constant repetition it pleased the Lord that the way of truth should be impressed upon my mind even in my earliest childhood.

As soon as I saw that it was impossible to go anywhere where I should be put to death for God's sake, we decided to become hermits; and we used to try very hard to build hermits' cells in an orchard belonging to the house. We used to pile up heaps of small stones, but they immediately tumbled down again, and so we found no way of achieving our desires. But even now it puts me into a state of devotion to see how early God gave me what I subsequently lost through my own fault. I gave alms, to the small extent of my powers. I contrived to be alone, in order to say my prayers, which were many. I was especially fond of telling my beads, a favorite practice of my mother's in which we naturally imitated her. When I was with other girls I especially enjoyed playing at nunneries, and pretending to be nuns; and I think I wanted to be one, though not so much as I wanted the other things I have mentioned.

I remember that when my mother died I was a little under twelve; and when I began to realize my loss, I went in my distress to an image of Our Lady and, weeping bitterly, begged her to be my mother. Though I did this in my simplicity, I believe that I benefited by it. For whenever I have turned to the supreme Virgin I have always been conscious of her aid, and in the end she brought me back to herself. It distresses me now to see that I did not persist in the good desires with which I began, and also to reflect on the reasons.

O my Lord, since You seem determined that I shall be saved — and may it be Your Majesty's pleasure that I am — and since You seem resolved to grant me as many graces as You have done, might You not have found it good — not for my gain but for Your own honor — that this habitation in which You have had to dwell for so long, should have been less greatly defiled? It distresses me, Lord, even to say this, since I know that all the blame has been mine. I do not think that You left anything undone to make me Yours entirely, even from my youth.

Nor could I complain of my parents, even if I felt inclined to do so. For I saw nothing in them that was not entirely good and devoted to my welfare. But as I grew older and began to be aware of the natural graces with which the Lord had endowed me — and people said that they were many — instead of giving Him thanks for them, I began to use them all, as I shall now relate, to offend against Him.

2. How She Came Gradually to Lose These Virtues, and of the Importance of Associating in Childhood with Good People

What I am about to describe is something which, I believe, began to do me great harm. I sometimes think how wrong it is of parents not to contrive that their children shall always and in every way see only what is good. For though my mother was, as I have said, extremely good herself, when I came to the age of reason I did not imitate her goodness as much as I might have done — indeed, I hardly did so at all — and evil things did me a great deal of harm. She was very fond of books of chivalry, and this amusement did not have the bad effect on her that it came to have on me, because she never neglected her duties for it. But we were always making time for reading, and she let us, perhaps in order to distract her mind from her great sufferings, or perhaps merely for the sake of amusing her children and keeping them from pursuing other wickednesses. This habit of ours so annoyed my father that we had to take care he never saw us with our books. But I began to become addicted to this reading, and this little fault, which I had observed in my mother, began to chill my desires and to lead me astray in other respects as well. It did not seem wicked to me to waste many hours of the day and the night on this vain occupation, even though I had to keep it secret from my father; and I was so enthralled by it that I do not believe I was ever happy if I had not a new book.

I began to wear finery, and to wish to charm by my appearance. I took great care of my hands and my hair, using perfumes and all the vanities I could obtain — and I obtained plenty of them, for I was very persistent. I had no bad intentions, for I should never have wished anyone to sin against God because of me. This excessive care for my appearance, together with other practices which I did not think wicked, lasted for many years, and now I see how wrong they must have been. I had some cousins, who were the only people allowed to enter my father's house. He was very careful about this, and would to God he had been careful about them too. For I now see the danger of conversation, at an age when the virtues should be beginning to grow, with those who do not recognize the vanity of the world, but encourage one to give oneself up to it. They were about my own age, or a little older. We always went about together, and they were very fond of me. I kept conversing with them about everything that pleased them, and I heard their accounts of their affections and follies, which were anything but edifying. What was worse, my soul became exposed to what has been the cause of all its troubles.

If parents were to ask me for advice, I would tell them to take great care what people their children consort with at this age. For great harm comes of bad company, since we are inclined by nature to follow the worse rather than the better. So it was with me. I had a sister many years older than I, from whose modesty and goodness — of which she had plenty — I learnt nothing, whereas from a relative who often visited us I learnt every kind of evil. Her conversation was so frivolous that my mother had tried her hardest to prevent her coming to the house. She seems to have realized what harm this person might do me. But there were so many pretexts for these visits that my mother was powerless. I loved the company of this person. I often talked and gossiped with her, for she helped me to get all the amusements I was so fond of, and even introduced me to some others. She also told me about her friends and own pastimes. Until I knew her, and I was then a little more than fourteen — I mean until we became friends and she took me into her confidence — I do not believe that I had ever turned away from God in mortal sin, or lost my fear of Him. But I was much more afraid for my good name, and this last fear gave me strength enough never entirely to forfeit it. Indeed, I do not think that I should have wavered in this resolution for anything in the world, or that there was anyone in the world for whom I felt such love that I could have been persuaded to surrender it. So since my natural inclination led me to defend everything that seemed to touch my good name, I might have had strength enough not to smirch the honor of God. But I did not see that I was losing my honor in quite a different way. In my vain anxiety to protect it I went to great extremes. Yet I took none of the steps necessary for its preservation. All that really concerned me was that I should not altogether ruin my good name.

My father and sister were most upset by this friendship, and very often took me to task. But as they could not prevent this person from coming to the house their efforts were of no avail, for I was clever at doing what was wrong. I am sometimes astonished at the harm which a single bad companion can do, and if I had no experience in the matter I should never believe it. This is particularly so when one is young, for then the evil effects are worst. I wish that parents would take warning by me, and consider this very carefully. As a result of my intercourse with this person, I was so changed that I lost nearly all my soul's natural disposition to virtue, so influenced was I by her and by another who was given to the same kind of amusements. . . .

I could not have been pursuing these vanities for more than three months when they took me to a convent in the city where I lived, in which girls like myself were educated, though there were none there as depraved as I. The reason for this move was, however, so disguised that it was known only to one or two of my relatives and myself. They waited for a moment when it would arouse no surprise; and this came after my sister's wedding, when it would not have been right for me to stay at home without a mother.

So great was my father's love for me and so complete my dissimulation that he could not believe me to be so wicked, and so I was never in disgrace with him. It had been going on for such a short time that although something had leaked out nothing could be said with certainty; as I was so afraid for my reputation, I had taken every care to be secret. But I did not see that I could conceal nothing from Him who sees all things. O my God, what evil is done in the world by forgetfulness of this, and in the belief that anything done against You can be concealed! I am certain that great evils could be avoided if we could understand that our business is not to be on our guard against men but against displeasing You.

For the first week I suffered greatly, but more from the suspicion that my frivolities were known than from my being in a convent. For I was now weary of wrong-doing, and had never ceased to be much afraid of God even when I sinned against Him; and I had always contrived to make a speedy confession. At first I was very restless, but in a week, or rather less, I felt much happier than in my father's house. All the sisters were pleased with me, for the Lord gave me the grace of pleasing wherever I might be. So I was made much of, and though I was then bitterly averse to taking the habit, yet I was delighted to see nuns who were so good. For they were all very good in that convent, most pure and observant and modest in their behavior. . . . There was a nun who slept with us seculars, and through her, it seems, the Lord chose to give me the beginnings of light, as I shall now relate.

3. How Good Company Reawakened Her Desires, and How God Began to Shed Some Light for Her on the Illusions under Which She Labored

As I began to enjoy this nun's good and holy conversation, I was gladdened by the eloquent way in which she spoke of God, for she was a very sensible and saintly woman. I think that there was never an occasion when I did not delight to listen to her. She began by telling me how she had come to be a nun, merely through reading the words of the Gospel: "Many are called but few chosen" (Matt. 22:14). She spoke to me of the reward which the Lord gives to those who forsake everything for Him. Her good company began to dispel the habits which bad company had formed in me, to bring back to my mind the desire for eternal things, and somewhat to rid me of my antipathy towards taking the veil, which had been very great indeed. If I saw anyone weep as she prayed, or show any other sign of a good state, I envied her extremely. For my heart was so hard in this respect that even if I had read the whole Passion through I should not have shed a tear; and this was a grief to me.

I stayed in this nunnery for a year and a half, and was much the better for it. I began to recite frequent prayers, and to ask everyone to pray to God for me, that He might put me in that place where I might serve Him. But I was still most anxious not to be a nun, for God had not yet been pleased to give me this desire, though I was afraid of marriage also. However, at the end of my stay there I was more inclined to take the veil, though not in that house, on account of certain devotional practices which prevailed there. I observed these during the latter part of my stay, and they seemed to me altogether excessive. Some of the younger sisters encouraged me in this feeling; if all the nuns had been of the same mind, it would have been greatly to my profit. But I had also a close friend in another convent, and this made me decide that, if I was to be a nun, it should be nowhere but in the house where she was. I was more intent on the gratification of my senses and my vanity than on the good of my soul. These good thoughts of entering religion came to me every now and then, and quickly departed. I could not make up my mind to act on them. . . .

I had now become subject to severe fainting fits attended by fever, for I had always had very poor health. But I got fresh life from my continued fondness for good books. I would read the Epistles of Saint Jerome, which gave me such courage that I resolved to speak to my father of my resolve, which was almost like taking the habit. For I set such store by my word that I should never, I believe, on any account have turned back, once I had announced my intention. My father, however, was so fond of me that I was quite unable to obtain his consent; nor were the entreaties of others, whom I asked to speak to him, of the least avail. The most that I could get from him was that I could do as I liked after his death. I now began to distrust myself and my own weakness, and to fear that I might turn back. This delay seemed to me dangerous, and so I achieved my aims in another way, as I shall now relate.

4. How the Lord Helped Her to Force Herself to Take the Habit, and of the Many Illnesses Which His Majesty Began to Send Her

. . . When I took the habit the Lord immediately showed me how He favors those who do violence to themselves in order to serve Him. No one saw what I endured, or thought that I acted out of anything but pure desire. At the moment of my entrance into this new state I felt a joy so great that it has never failed me even to this day; and God converted the dryness of my soul into a very great tenderness. All the details of the religious life delighted me. In fact sometimes when I used to sweep the house at hours that I had once spent on my indulgence and adornment, the memory that I was now free from these things gave me a fresh joy, which surprised me, for I could not understand where it came from.

When I remember this freedom, there is no task, however hard, that I would hesitate to do if it were put before me. For now I know from plentiful experience that if I resolutely persist in a purpose from the beginning, and it is done for God only, His Majesty rewards me even in this life in ways which only one who has known their joys can understand. In such cases, even before we begin, it is His will that the soul, for the increase of its merits, shall be afraid. Then the greater the fear, the greater and the sweeter the subsequent reward will be if we succeed. This I know from experience, as I have said, on many very serious occasions; and so if ever I were to be asked for an opinion, I would recommend anyone to whom a good inspiration repeatedly comes, never to neglect it out of fear. If he turns nakedly to God alone, he need not be afraid of failure, since God is all-powerful. May He be blessed for ever! Amen. . . .

The change in my life and diet affected my health; and even though I was very happy, that was not enough. My fainting fits began to become more frequent, and I suffered from such pains in the heart that everyone who saw them was alarmed. I had also many other ailments. I spent my first year, therefore, in a very bad state of health, though I do not think I offended God much during that time. As my condition was so serious that I was usually semi-conscious and sometimes lost consciousness altogether, my father took great pains to find some remedy; and as the local doctors could offer none, he arranged for me to be taken to a town that had a great reputation for the curing of other diseases, and where they said that mine could be cured too. The friend whom I spoke of as being in the house, and who was one of the elder nuns, was able to go with me, since we were under no vow of enclosure. I stayed in that town for almost a year, and for three months of it suffered the greatest tortures from the remedies they applied to me, which were so drastic that I do not know how I endured them. In fact, though I did endure them, they were too much for my constitution, as I shall relate. My cure was to start at the beginning of summer, and I had left the convent as winter set in. The intervening time I spent with that sister of whom I have spoken, in her house in the country, waiting for the month of April. For she lived only a short distance from that town, and I did not want to go away and come back again.

On my way I visited that uncle of mine whom I have mentioned, whose house was on the road, and he gave me a book, called *The Third Alphabet*, which contains lessons in the prayer of recollection. Although in my first year I had read good books — indeed, I would not touch any others, since I knew what harm they had done me — I did not know how to practice prayer or how to recollect myself. So I was delighted with this book, and decided to follow its instructions with all my strength. Since the Lord had already given me the gift of tears and I liked reading, I began to spend time in solitude, to confess frequently, and to start on the way of prayer, with this book as my guide. For I found no other guide — no confessor I mean — who understood me, though I sought one for the next twenty years. This did me great harm, for I very often fell back and might have been utterly lost, and a guide would at least have helped me to avoid the frequent risks I ran of offending God.

In these early days His Majesty began to grant me such great favors that, at the end of my time there, which amounted to some nine months of solitude, although I was not so free of sin against God as the book demanded, nevertheless I passed that over. Utter scrupulousness seemed to me almost impossible. I guarded against committing any mortal sin — and would to God I had always done so — but I paid little attention to venial sins, and that was what undid me. Still the Lord began to be so gracious to me on this path as to raise me sometimes to the prayer of quiet, and occasionally to that of union [supernaturally given states in which one turns away entirely from the senses and dies to the world in order to live in God], though I did not understand what either of these was, or how highly I should have valued them. If I had understood this, I think it would have been a great blessing to me. It is true that my experience of union lasted only for a short time; I do not know whether it was even for the length of an Ave Maria. But it left such an effect behind that, although I was not then twenty, I seemed to feel the world far below me, and I remember pitying those who followed its ways even on their lawful pursuits. I tried as hard as I could to bring the presence of Jesus Christ, our Lord and our Good, into my heart; and this was my method of prayer. If I thought of any incident of His life, I represented it to myself within me, though what still gave me most pleasure was the reading of good books, which was my only recreation. For the Lord did not give me a talent for intellectual meditation or for making use of the imagination. My imagination is so sluggish that however hard I tried to think of or picture Our Lord's human presence — and I tried very hard — I never succeeded.

Now although, if they persevere, men may arrive more quickly at contemplation along this road where they cannot work with the intellect, it is a very laborious and painful one. For if the will is left without employment, and love has no present object to occupy it, the soul remains without support or activity, solitude and dryness give great pain, and stray thoughts attack most fiercely. People who are made like this need a greater purity of consciousness than those who can work with the intellect. If a man can reflect on the nature of the world, on his debt to God, on Our Lord's great sufferings, on his own small service in return, and on what He gives to those who love Him, he gets material with which to defend himself against stray thoughts, also against perils and occasions for sin. But anyone who cannot make use of this method runs a far greater risk, and should frequently resort to reading, since he can get help in no other way. Indeed, inability to get this help is so very painful that if the master directing him forbids him to read, and thus help himself towards recollection, he will still need to make some small use of books as a substitute for mental prayer, which he is unable to practice. But if the director insists on his spending great periods at prayer without the aid of reading, he will not be able to persist for long. His health would suffer if he were to do so, for this is a most painful process.

It seems to me now that it was by God's providence that I did not find anyone to teach me. For I believe it would have been impossible for me to persevere for the eighteen years during which I suffered this trial and these great aridities, through not being able, as I have said, to meditate. All that time, except immediately after taking Communion, I never ventured to start praying without a book. My soul was as much afraid to engage in prayer without one, as if it had to fight against a host. With this protection, which was like a companion and a shield on which to take the blows of my many thoughts, I found comfort, for I was not generally in aridity. But always when I was without a book, my soul would at once become disturbed, and my thoughts wandered. As I read, I began to call them together again and, as it were, laid a bait for my soul. Very often I had to do no more than open a book. Sometimes I read a little, sometimes much, according to the favor which the Lord showed me. . . .

I have often reflected with amazement on God's great goodness, and my soul has rejoiced in the thought of His magnificence and His mercy. May He be blessed for all this, for as I clearly see, He has never failed to reward me, even in this life, for any good desire. Poor and imperfect as my works have been, this Lord of mine has improved and perfected them, and has increased their value. As for my wickednesses and sins, He has immediately hidden them away. He has even allowed the eyes of those who have seen them to be blind to them, and has expunged them from their memory. He gilds my faults and makes some virtue shine that He himself has given me, almost compelling me to possess it.

I must now return to what I have been commanded. But, indeed, if I had to relate in detail the way in which the Lord dealt with me in those early days, I should need a better understanding than my own, with which to appreciate what I owe Him for this, also my own ingratitude and wickedness; all of which I have forgotten. May He be blessed for ever who has endured so much from me! Amen.

SOR JUANA INÉS DE LA CRUZ

Reply to Sor Philothea

Sor Juana (1648 or 1651-1695) was born into the most unpromising of circumstances, the illegitimate daughter of a Spanish soldier in a small town
in colonial Mexico. Her love of learning brought her as a child prodigy to
the court of the Viceroy in Mexico City. Lacking a dowry and thus any pros-
pects for marriage, she entered a convent there, where she continued to
write — poems, plays, essays. The Archbishop of Mexico disapproved of
plays, of a theological critique she had written, and indeed of women devoting themselves to scholarship at all. His opposition led to this defense
of her sense of calling, written in 1691 to her friend the Bishop of Puebla.
(The customs of the time made it inappropriate for her to write such a letter to a man, so the letter is cast as to another nun.) But she was forced
into public repentance and then silence. She died a few years later of the
plague, contracted when nursing her sick sisters in the convent.

I have never written of my own accord, but only when pressured by others. I
could truthfully say to them: *Vos me coegistis* ["You have compelled me"
(2 Cor. 12:11)]. What is true and I will not deny (first because it is public
knowledge and then — even if this counts against me — because God, in
His goodness, has favored me with a great love of the truth) is that from my
first glimmers of reason, my inclination to letters was of such power and ve-
hemence, that neither the reprimands of others — and I have received many
— nor my own considerations — and there have been not a few of these —
have succeeded in making me abandon this natural impulse which God has
implanted in me — only His Majesty knows why and wherefore, and His
Majesty also knows that I have prayed to Him to extinguish the light of my

A Sor Juana Anthology, trans. Alan S. Trueblood (Cambridge, Mass.: Harvard University Press,
1988), 210-14, 216-19, 224-26. I am indebted to Nicholas Myers for suggesting this reading.

mind, only leaving sufficient to keep His Law, since any more is overmuch, so some say, in a woman, and there are even those who say it is harmful. His Majesty also knows that, not succeeding in this, I have tried to inter my name along with my mind and sacrifice it to Him alone who gave it to me; and that this was precisely my motivation in taking the veil, even though the exercises and shared life which a community entails were repellent to the independence and tranquility which my inclination to study needed. And once in the community, the Lord God knows and, in the world, he knows who alone had the right to know it, how hard I tried to conceal my name, and that he did not allow this, saying that it was temptation, which no doubt it was. If I could repay you some part of what I owe you, my Lady, I think I would be paying you simply by relating this, for it has never escaped my lips before, except when addressed to one who had the right to know it. But I want you to know that, in throwing wide open to you the gates of my heart, exposing to your gaze its most tightly guarded secrets, my justification for the liberty I am taking is the great debt I owe to your venerable person and overly generous favors.

To go on with the account of this strong bent of mine, about which I want you to be fully informed, let me say that when I was not yet three, my mother sent a sister of mine, older than I, to learn to read in one of those establishments called *Amigas* [girls' elementary schools], at which point affection and mischievousness on my part led me to follow her. Seeing that she was being given lessons, I became so inflamed with the desire to learn to read that I tricked the mistress — or so I thought — by telling her that my mother had directed her to give me lessons. This was not believable and she did not believe me, but falling in with my little trick, she did give me lessons. I continued attending and she went on teaching me, no longer as a joke, since the event opened her eyes. I learned to read in so short a time that I already knew how when my mother found out, for the mistress kept it from her in order to give her a pleasant surprise and receive her recompense all at one time. I kept still, since I thought I would be whipped for having acted on my own initiative. The person who taught me is still alive (may God preserve her) and can attest to this.

I remember that at this period, though I loved to eat, as children do at that age, I refrained from eating cheese, because someone had told me it made you stupid, and my urge to learn was stronger than my wish to eat, powerful as this is in children. Afterward, when I was six or seven and already knew how to read and write, along with all the sewing skills and needlework that women learn, I discovered that in the City of Mexico there was a university with schools where the different branches of learning could be studied, and as soon as I learned this I began to deluge my mother with urgent and insistent pleas to change my manner of dress and send me to stay with relatives in the City of Mexico so that I might study and take courses at the university. She refused, and rightly so; nevertheless, I found a way to read many different books my grandfather owned, notwithstanding the punishments and reproofs this entailed, so that when I went to the City of Mexico people were astonished, not so much at my intelligence as at the memory and store of knowledge I had at an age at which it would seem I had scarcely had time to learn to speak.

I began to study Latin, in which I do not believe I had twenty lessons in all, and I was so intensely studious that despite the natural concern of women — especially in the flower of their youth — with dressing their hair, I used to cut four or five fingers' width from mine, keeping track of how far it had formerly reached, and making it my rule that if by the time it grew back to that point, I did not know such-and-such a thing which I had set out to learn as it grew, I would cut it again as a penalty for my dullness. Thus it would happen that it would grow back and I still would not know what I had set myself to learn, because my hair grew rapidly, whereas I was a slow learner, and I did indeed cut it as a punishment for my slowness, for I did not consider it right that a head so bare of knowledge should be dressed with hair, knowledge being the more desirable ornament. I became a nun because, although I knew that that way of life involved much that was repellent to my nature — I refer to its incidental, not its central aspects — nevertheless given my total disinclination to marriage, it was the least unreasonable and most becoming choice I could make to assure my ardently desired salvation. To which first consideration, as most important, all the other small frivolities of my nature yielded and gave way, such as my wish to live alone, to have no fixed occupation which might curtail my freedom to study, nor the noise of a community to interfere with the tranquil stillness of my books. This made me hesitate a little before making up my mind, until, enlightened by learned persons that hesitation was temptation, I overcame it by the grace of God and entered upon the life I now pursue so unworthily. I thought I was escaping from myself, but, alas for me, I had brought myself along. In this propensity I brought my greatest enemy, given me by Heaven whether as a boon or a punishment I cannot decide, for, far from dying out or being hindered by all the exercises religion entails, it exploded like gunpowder. *Privatio est causa appetitus* [Privation arouses the appetite] had its confirmation in me.

I went back (I misspeak: I had never stopped); I went on with the studious pursuit (in which I found relaxation during all the free time remaining from my obligations) of reading and more reading, study and more study, with no other teacher than books themselves. One can readily imagine how hard it is to study from those lifeless letters, lacking a teacher's live voice and explanations. Still I happily put up with all those drawbacks, for the sheer love of learning. Oh, if it had only been for the love of God, which would have been the sound way, what merit would have been mine! . . .

In this way I went on, continually directing the course of my study, as I have said, toward the eminence of sacred theology. To reach this goal, I considered it necessary to ascend the steps of human arts and sciences, for how can one who has not mastered the style of the ancillary branches of learning hope to understand that of the queen of them all? How, lacking logic, was I to understand the general and specific methodologies of which Holy Scripture is composed? How, without rhetoric, could I understand its figures, tropes, and locutions? How, without physics, all the natural questions concerning the nature of sacrificial animals, which symbolize so many things already explicated, and so many others? How, whether Saul's being cured by the sound of David's harp (1 Sam. 16:23) came about by virtue of the natural power of music, or through supernatural powers which God was pleased to bestow on David? How, lacking arithmetic, could one understand such mysterious computations of years, days, months, hours, weeks, as those of Daniel and others, for the intelligence of which one needs to know the natures, concordances, and properties of numbers? How, without geometry, could one measure the sacred ark of the covenant and the holy city of Jerusalem, whose mysterious measurements form a cube in all its dimensions, and the marvelous proportional distribution of all its parts? How, without a knowledge of architecture, is one to understand Solomon's great temple, of which God Himself was the artificer who provided the arrangement and layout, the wise king being only the overseer who carried it out? In it, no column's base was without its mystery, no column without its symbolic sense, no cornice without allusiveness, no architrave without meaning, and so on with all its parts, not even the most miniscule fillet serving solely as support or complement to the design of the whole, but rather itself symbolizing greater things. How will one understand the historical books without a full knowledge of the principles and divisions of which history consists? Those recapitulations in the narrative which postpone what actually occurred first? How will one understand the legal books without a complete acquaintance with both codes of law? How, without a great deal of erudition, all the matters of secular history mentioned in Holy Writ, all the customs of the Gentiles, the rites, the ways of speaking? How, without many rules and much reading of the Church Fathers, will one be able to understand the prophets' obscure forms of expression? . . .

For my own part I can attest that what I do not understand in an author writing on one subject, I can usually understand in one writing on another seemingly far removed from it, and that authors, in developing their thought, will come up with metaphorical examples from other fields, as when the logicians say that the middle term is to the two other terms as a measuring rod is to two distant bodies, with respect to determining whether they are equidistant and that the logician's sentence proceeds in a straight line, taking the shortest way, while the rhetorician's moves in a curve, taking the longest, but that the two end up at the same point; and when it is said that expositors are like an open hand and scholastics like a closed fist. Thus I am not excusing myself, nor do I mean to, for having studied different things, since they are in fact mutually supportive. I am simply stating that my failure to progress in them has been due to my ineptitude and poor mind and has not been caused by such diversity.

What I might point out in self-justification is how severe a hardship it is to work not only without a teacher but also without fellow students with whom to compare notes and try out what has been studied. Instead I have had nothing but a mute book as teacher, an unfeeling inkwell as fellow student, and, in place of explanation and exercises, many hindrances, arising not only from my religious duties (it goes without saying that these occupy one's time most profitably and beneficially) but also from things implicit in the life of a religious community — such as when I am reading, those in a neighboring cell take it upon themselves to play music and sing. Or when I am studying and two maids quarrel and come to me to settle their dispute. Or when I am writing and a friend comes to visit, doing me a great disservice with the best of intentions, whereupon I not only must put up with the bother but act grateful for the injury. This goes on all the time, because, since the times I devote to my studies are those remaining when the regular duties of the community are over, the others are also free then to come and bother me. Only those who have experienced communal religious life can know how true this is. Only the strength of my vocation allows my nature to take pleasure in it — this and the great bond of love between me and my beloved sisters, for since love is union, there are no poles too distant for it. . . .

As I owe to God, among other good things, so gentle and accommodating a nature, and the nuns are so fond of me on account of it (and kindly overlook my faults) and thus greatly enjoy my company, it would often happen that, aware of this and spurred on by my great love for them (more understandable than theirs for me), during the free time we both had, I would go and comfort them and relax in their company. I realized that at such times I was neglecting my study and so made a vow not to enter a single cell unless obedience or charity required it of me. For, in the absence of a curb as harsh as this, love would have broken through a control arising from mere resolve. Knowing my frailty, I would make this vow for a month or a fort-night and then, allowing myself a recess of a day or two, I would renew it. The free day was intended not so much to give me a rest as to prevent their considering me unbending, withdrawn, and unappreciative of the unde-served affection of those dearest sisters.

This shows only too clearly the strength of my inclination. Blessed be God for his will to direct it toward learning and not toward some vice or other that would have proved all but irresistible to me. And one can easily deduce how very much against the stream my poor studies have had to row — or rather to founder. Well, the most arduous part of the difficulties still remains to be told, for those related up to now have been simply necessary or incidental annoyances which are such only indirectly. Still to come are the outright ones which have worked directly to hinder and to prohibit my pursuit of learning. Who could fail to believe, in view of such widespread plaudits, that I have sailed with a following wind on a glassy sea to the enco-miums of general acclaim? Well, the Lord knows that it has hardly been so, for amidst the bouquets of that very acclaim, asps of such invidiousness and relentlessness as I could never describe have stirred and reared up. Those most harmful and painful to me are not the persons who have pursued me with open hatred and ill will, but those who, while loving me and wishing me well (and being possibly very meritorious in God's eyes for their good intentions), have mortified and tortured me much more than the others, with their: "This study is incompatible with the blessed ignorance to which you are bound. You will lose your way, at such heights your head will be turned by your very perspicacity and sharpness of mind." What have I not gone through to hold out against this? Strange sort of martyrdom, in which I was both the martyr and my own executioner!

Why, for the ability (doubly infelicitous in my case) to compose verse, even when it was sacred verse, what nastiness have I not been subjected to, what unpleasantness has not come my way! I must say, Madam, that some-times I stop and reflect that anyone who stands out — or whom God singles out, for He alone can do so — is viewed as everyone's enemy, because it seems to some that he is usurping the applause due them or deflecting the admiration which they have coveted, for which reason they pursue him.

That politically barbarous law of the Athenians, whereby anyone emi-nent in natural endowments and virtues was to be exiled from their republic so that he might not tyrannize public liberty [in ancient Athens the assem-bly could vote to "ostracize" any citizen; even if he had committed no crime, he was then exiled for ten years; sometimes citizens were ostracized because their very superiority to everyone else was seen to threaten democracy], still holds, and is still observed in our day, although the reasoning of the Athenians no longer applies. There is a different consideration, however, no less efficacious though less well grounded, for it might be a maxim of that godless Machiavelli: hate anyone who stands out because he tarnishes the luster of others. So it goes, so it has always gone.

What, if not this, was the cause of that furious hatred the Pharisees conceived for Christ, when they had so many reasons to feel just the opposite? For if we consider His person, what trait could be more worthy of love than His divine beauty? Which more capable of stealing men's hearts? If human beauty of any sort holds sway over men's minds and is able to enthrall them with mild and welcome violence, what must have been the power of Christ's, with all its prerogatives and supreme gifts? How efficacious, how moving that unfathomable beauty must have been, with the radiance of Godhead showing through the beautiful face as through smooth, polished glass! How could that countenance fail to be moving when over and above perfections of a human order it displayed glimmers of the divine? . . .

As there is no created thing, no matter how lowly, in which one cannot recognize the *me fecit Deus* [God made me], there is none that does not confound the mind once it stops to consider it. Thus, I repeat, I looked and marveled at all of them, so much so that simply from the person with whom I spoke, and from what that person said to me, countless reflections arose in my mind. What could be the origin of so great a variety of characters and minds, when all belonged to one species? Which humors and hidden qualities could bring this about? If I saw a figure, I at once fell to working out the relationship of its lines, measuring it with my mind and recasting it along different ones. Sometimes I would walk back and forth across the front of a sleeping-room of ours — a very large one — and observe how, though the lines of its two sides were parallel and its ceiling horizontal, one's vision made it appear as if the lines inclined toward each other and the ceiling were lower at the far end, from which I inferred that visual lines run straight but not parallel, tending rather toward a pyramidal figure. And I asked myself whether this could be the reason the ancients questioned whether the world was spherical or not. Because, although it appears to be, this could be an optical illusion, and show concavities where there might in fact be none.

This type of observation would occur to me about everything and still does, without my having any say in the matter; indeed, it continually irritates me because it tires my mind. I thought the same thing occurred in everyone's case, and with writing verse as well, until experience proved me wrong. This turn, or habit, of mind is so strong that I can look upon nothing without reflecting on it. . . . What could I not tell you, my Lady, of the secrets of Nature which I have discovered in cooking! That an egg hangs together and fries in fat or oil, and that, on the contrary, it disintegrates in syrup. That, to keep sugar liquid, it suffices to add the tiniest part of water in which a quince or some other tart fruit has been. That the yolk and white of the same egg are so different in nature, that when eggs are used with sugar, the yolks must be used separately from the whites, never together with them. I do not wish to tire you with such trivia, which I relate only to give you a full picture of my native turn of mind, which will, no doubt, make you laugh. But, Madam, what is there for us women to know, if not bits of kitchen philosophy? As Lupercio Leonardo [Spanish poet and playwright, 1559-1613] said: One can perfectly well philosophize while cooking supper. And I am always saying, when I observe these small details: If Aristotle had been a cook, he would have written much more.

But to continue with the workings of my mind, let me say that this line of thought is so constant with me that I have no need of books. On one occasion when, owing to some serious stomach trouble, the doctor forbade my studying, I obeyed for several days, but then I pointed out that allowing me books would be much less harmful, since my mental activity was so vigorous, so vehement, that it used up more spirits in a quarter of an hour than studying from books did in four days. So they agreed reluctantly to allow me to read. And not only that, my Lady: even my sleep was not free from this constant activity of my brain. In fact, it seems to go on during sleep with all the more freedom and lack of restraint, putting together the separate images it has carried over from waking hours with greater clarity and tranquility, debating with itself, composing verses, of which I could draw up a whole catalogue for you, including certain thoughts and subtleties I have arrived at more easily while asleep than while awake, which I won't go into, not wishing to bore you. What has been said suffices for your own acumen and high-mindedness to grasp with clarity and full understanding my native disposition of mind and the origin, methods, and present state of my studies.

Even if these studies were to be viewed, my Lady, as to one's credit (as I see they are indeed celebrated in men), none would be due me, since I pursue them involuntarily. If they are seen as reprehensible, for the same reason I do not think I should be blamed. Still, though, I am so unsure of myself, that neither in this nor in anything do I trust my own judgment. Hence I leave the decision up to your supreme talent, and will abide by whatever it decrees, with no antagonism and no reluctance, for this has been nothing more than a simple account of my inclination to letters.

WILLIAM PERKINS

A Treatise of the Vocations

William Perkins (1558-1602) spent much of his life as a student and then a teacher at Cambridge University; he came to be recognized as one of the leading Puritan theologians, and this is the first, classic Puritan discussion of vocation in systematic form. Unlike Calvin, Perkins uses "general" and "particular" calling in what would become their standard meanings: "general" for the call to become a Christian, "particular" for the call to some particular vocation. He analyzes vocations in terms of two of the kinds of cause first defined by Aristotle: the "efficient cause" is the source of a thing's being or motion; the "final cause" is the purpose or goal for which it was made. Thus, the carpenter who built it would be the efficient cause of a cowshed, and housing the cows would be its final cause. An increasing use of Aristotle's philosophy in thinking about theology was characteristic of Protestants in the time after the Reformation; Luther, who mistrusted philosophy in general and Aristotle in particular, would have been horrified.

1 Cor. 7, verse 20: "Let every man abide in that calling, wherein he was called."

First, I will show what Vocation or Calling is. Secondly, I will set down the parts and kinds thereof. Thirdly, the holy and lawful use of every man's particular calling: all which are in some sort touched in the words of my Text.

For the first: *A vocation or calling is a certain kind of life, ordained and imposed on man by God for the common good.* First of all I say, it is a *certain condition or kind of life*: that is, a certain manner of leading our lives in this world. For ex-

William Perkins, *A Treatise of the Vocations* (London: John Haviland, 1631), 750-51, 752, 754-60, 775-76. Spelling and punctuation substantially modernized.

ample, the life of a King is to spend his time in the governing of his subjects, and that is his calling; and the life of a Subject is to live in obedience to the Magistrate, and that is his calling. The state and condition of a Minister is to lead his life in preaching of the Gospel and word of God, and that is his calling. A master of a family is to lead his life in the government of his family, and that is his calling. In a word, that particular and honest manner of conversation, wherunto every man is called and set apart, that is (I say) his calling.

Now in every calling we must consider two causes. First, the efficient [cause] and author thereof. Secondly, the final and proper end. The author of every calling is God himself: and therefore Paul says: *As God has called every man, let him walk* (1 Cor. 7:17). And for this cause, the order and manner of living in this world is called a *Vocation;* because every man is to live as he is called of God. For look as in the camp, the General appoints to every man his place and standing: one place for the horseman and another for the footman, and to every particular soldier likewise his office and standing, in which he is to abide against the enemy, and therein to live and die. Even so it is in human societies: God is the General appointing to every man his particular calling, and as it were his standing, and in that calling he assigns unto him his particular office, in performance whereof he is to live and die. And as in a camp, no soldier can depart his standing without the leave of the general; no more may any man leave his calling, except he receive liberty from God. Again, in a clock, made by the art and handy-work of man, there be many wheels, and every one has his several motion, some turn this way, some that way, some go softly, some apace: and they are all ordered by the motion of the watch. Behold here a notable resemblance of God's special providence over mankind, which is the watch of the great world, allotting to every man his motion and calling, and in that calling his particular office and function. Therefore it is true that I say, that God himself is the author and beginning of callings. . . .

Now as God is the Author of every calling; so he hath two actions therein. First, he ordains the calling itself. And secondly, he imposes it on the man called, and therefore I say, *vocation is a certain kind of life, ordained and imposed by God.* For the first, God ordains a calling, when he prescribes and commands the same, in and by his word: and those callings and states of life, which have no warrant from God's word, are unlawful. Now God in his word ordains callings two ways. First, by commanding and prescribing them particularly, as he does the most weighty callings in the family, Church, or Commonwealth. Secondly, by appointing and setting down certain laws and commandments generally, whereby we may easily gather that he does either approve, or not approve of them, though they be not particularly prescribed in the Word.

The second action of God, which is the imposition of callings, is when he does particularly set apart any man to any particular calling, and this must be understood of all callings in the world. Now God does this two ways. First, by himself immediately, without the help of any creature. Thus in the beginning was *Adam* called and appointed to dress the garden of Eden. Thus *Abraham* was called from the idolatry of his forefathers, and received into the covenant of grace. Thus was *Moses* called to be a Prince over the Israelites, to guide them out of Egypt into the promised land. And in the New Testament, thus were the Apostles called to preach the Gospel. Secondly, God calls mediately by means, which be of two sorts, men and Angels. By an Angel was *Philip*, being a Deacon, called to be an Evangelist; and the set or appointed callings in Church and Commonwealth are ordinarily disposed by men, who are in this matter the instruments of God. And therefore men lawfully called by them are truly called of God. Thus the Elders of Ephesus, called by the Apostles and the rest of the Church, are said to be called by the Holy Ghost. And thus we see how God is the author of every calling.

The final cause or end of every calling, I note in the last words of the description: *for the common good*, that is, for the benefit and good estate of mankind. In man's body there be sundry parts and members, and every one has his several use and office, which it performs not for itself, but for the good of the whole body; as the office of the eye is to see, of the ear to hear, and the foot to go. Now all societies of men are bodies, a family is a body, and so is every particular Church a body, and the Commonwealth also; and in these bodies there be several members, which are men walking in several callings and offices, the execution whereof must tend to the happy and good estate of the rest, yea of all men everywhere, as much as possible is. The common good of men stands in this, not only that they live, but that they live well, in righteousness and holiness, and consequently in true happiness. And for the attainment hereunto, God has ordained and disposed all callings, and in his providence designed the persons to bear them. Here then we must in general know that he abuses his calling, whosoever he be that against the end thereof employs it for himself, seeking wholly his own and not the common good. And that common saying, *Every man for himself, and God for us all*, is wicked, and is directly against the end of every calling or honest kind of life. . . .

Now follow the parts and kinds of Vocations; and they are of two sorts: General or Particular. The general calling is the calling of Christianity, which is common to all that live in the Church of God. The particular is that special calling that belongs to some particular men: as the calling of a Magistrate, the calling of a Minister, the calling of a Master, of a father, of a child, of a servant, of a subject, or any other calling that is common to all. And *Paul* acknowledges this distinction of *Callings* when he says, *Let every man abide in that calling, wherein he is called* (1 Cor. 7:20), that is, in that particular and personal calling, in which he was called to be a Christian. Of these two in order.

The general Calling is that whereby a man is called out of the world to be a child of God, a member of Christ, and heir of the kingdom of Heaven. . . .

. . . Now follows the second kind of calling, and that is personal. A personal calling is the execution of some particular office, arising of that distinction which God makes between man and man in every society. First I say, it is *the execution of some particular office,* as, for example, the calling of a Magistrate is to execute the office of government over his subjects, the office of a Minister is to execute the duty of teaching his people, the calling of a Master is to execute the office of authority and government over his servants, the office of a Physician is to put in practice the good means whereby life and health are preserved. In a word, in every estate the practice and execution of that particular office, wherein any man is placed, is his personal calling.

Secondly, I add, that it arises from that distinction which God makes between man and man in every society to show what is the foundation and ground of all personal callings. And it is a point to be considered of us, which I thus explain: God in his word has ordained the society of man with man, partly in the Commonwealth, partly in the Church, and partly in the family; and it is not the will of God that man should live and converse alone by himself. Now for the maintaining of society, he has ordained a certain bond to link men together, which Saint *Paul* calls *the bond of peace* (Eph. 4:3), and the bond of perfection, namely, love. And howsoever he has ordained societies, and the bond of them all, yet has he appointed that there should still remain a distinction between man and man, not only in regard of person, but also in other respects; for as the whole body is not the hand, nor the foot, nor the eye, but the hand one part, the foot another, and the eye another; and howsoever in the body one part is linked to another, yet there is a distinction between the members, whereby it comes to pass, that the hand is the hand, not the foot, and the foot, the foot, not the hand, nor the eye, so it is in societies; there is a distinction in the members thereof, and that in two respects; first, in regard of the inward gifts which God bestowed on every man, giving to several men several gifts according to his good pleasure. Of this distinction in regard of inward gifts, *Paul* entreats at large (1 Cor. 12), through the whole chapter, where he shows the diversity of gifts that God bestows on his Church, and so proportionally in every society. Now look as the inward gifts of men are divided, so are the persons distinguished in their societies accordingly. Secondly, persons are distinguished by order, whereby God has appointed, that in every society one person should be above or under another; not making all equal, as though the body should be all head and nothing else; but even in degree and order, he hath set a distinction, that one should be above another. And by reason of this distinction of men, partly in respect of gifts, partly in respect of order, come personal callings. For if all men had the same gifts, and all were in the same degree and order, then should all have one and the same calling; but in as much as God gives diversity of gifts inwardly, and distinction of order outwardly, hence proceed diversity of personal callings, and therefore I added, that personal callings arise from that distinction which God makes between man and man in every society. And thus we see what is a personal calling. Now before I come to entreat of parts thereof, there be other general Rules to be learned, which concern all personal callings whatsoever.

I. Rule

Every person, of every degree, state, sex, or condition without exception, must have some personal and particular calling to walk in. This appears plainly by the whole word of God. *Adam,* so soon as he was created, even in his integrity had a personal calling assigned him by God, which was, to dress and keep the garden. And after *Adam's* fall, the Lord gives a particular commandment to him and all his posterity, which binds all men to walk in some calling, either in the Church or Commonwealth, saying, *Gen. 3:19, In the sweat of thy brow shalt thou eat thy bread.* Again, in the renewing of the law in Mount Sinai, the fourth commandment does not only permit labor on six days, but also enjoins the same (as I take it) to us all. For God's example is there propounded for us to follow, that as he rested the seventh day, so must also we, and consequently, as he spent six days in the work of creation, so should we in our personal callings. And St. Paul gives this rule, *Eph. 4:28, Let him that stole steal no more, but let him rather work with his hands the thing that is good, that he may have to give to him that needs.* Christ the head of men, lived with *Joseph* in the calling of a Carpenter, till the time of his baptism, and hereupon it was that the Jews said, *Is not this the Carpenter, the son of Mary?* (Mark 6:3), and after he was baptized and was as it were solemnly admitted into the office of a Mediator, the work of our Redemption was then his calling, in which he both lived and died. Yea, the Angels of God have their particular callings, in that they do his *commandments in obeying the voice of his word* (Ps 103:20). And therefore all that descend of *Adam* must needs have some calling to walk in, either public or private, whether it be in the Church, or Commonwealth, or family.

Hence we may learn sundry points of instruction; first of all, that it is a foul disorder in any Commonwealth, that there should be suffered rogues, beggars, vagabonds; for such kind of persons commonly are of no civil society or corporation, nor of any particular Church, and are as rotten legs and arms that drop from the body. Again, to wander up and down from year to year to this end, to seek and procure bodily maintenance, is no calling, but the life of a beast, and consequently a condition or state of life flat against the rule that everyone must have a particular calling. And therefore the Statute made the last Parliament for the restraining of beggars and rogues is an excellent Statute, and being in substance the very law of God, is never to be repealed.

Again, hereby is overthrown the condition of Monks and Friars who challenge to themselves that they live in a state of perfection, because they live apart from the societies of men in fasting and prayer; but contrariwise, this Monkish kind of living is damnable, for besides the general duties of fasting and prayer which appertain to all Christians, every man must have a particular and personal calling, that he may be a good and profitable member of some society and body. And the ancient Church condemned all Monks for thieves and robbers, that besides the general duties of prayer and fasting, did not withal employ themselves in some other calling for their better maintenance.

Thirdly, we learn by this, that miserable and damnable is the estate of those that, being enriched with great livings and revenues, do spend their days in eating and drinking, in sports and pastimes, not employing themselves in service for Church or Commonwealth. It may perhaps be thought that such Gentlemen have happy lives, but it is far otherwise, considering everyone, rich or poor, man or woman, is bound to have a personal calling in which they must perform some duties for the common good, according to the measure of the gifts that God hath bestowed upon them.

Fourthly, hereby also it is required that such as we commonly call serving men should have, beside the office of waiting, some other particular calling, unless they tend on men of great place and state: for only to wait and give attendance is not a sufficient calling, as common experience tells, for waiting servants, by reason they spend the most of their time in eating and drinking, sleeping and gaming after dinner and after supper, do prove the most unprofitable members both in Church and Commonwealth. For when either their good Masters die or they be turned out of their office for some misdemeanor, they are fit for no calling, being unable to labor; and thus they give themselves either to beg or steal. The waiting man of *Cornelius* that Centurion (Acts 10) was also by calling a soldier, and it were to be wished nowadays that Gentlemen would make choice of such servants that might not only tend on their persons, but also tend upon some other convenient office. It is good for every man to have two strings to his bow.

II. Rule

Every man must judge that particular calling, in which God hath placed him, to be the best of all callings for him: I say not simply best, but best for him. This rule is set forth unto us in the example of *Paul, I have learned* [says he] *in whatsoever state I am, to be content and well pleased* (Phil. 4:11). The practice of this duty is the stay and foundation of the good estate both of Church and Commonwealth, for it makes every man to keep his own standing, and to employ himself painfully within his calling; but when we begin to mislike the wise disposition of God, and to think other men's callings better for us than our own, then follows confusion and disorder in every society. When *Absalom*, a child and subject of King *David*, was not content with his estate, but fought his Father's kingdom, and said, *O that I were judge among you* (2 Sam. 15:4), many contentions and hurliburlies followed in the Commonwealth of the Jews all his days. And the sons of *Zebedee*, not contenting themselves with the calling of Disciples, but being inflamed with desire of honor and dignity, fought for the two principal offices in Christ's kingdom, which (as they deemed) should be a civil and worldly kingdom. Hence arose envy and heart-burning among the Disciples, and further evils would have ensued, unless the wisdom of our Savior Christ had cut them off. The Bishops of the Church of Rome, not contented with their Ecclesiastical estate, affected the honor of the Empire, and by this means brought havoc and ruin upon the whole Church. . . .

III. Rule

Every man must join the practice of his personal calling with the practice of the general calling of Christianity, before described. More plainly: Every particular calling must be practiced in and with the general calling of a Christian. It is not sufficient for a man in the Congregation and in common conversation to be a Christian, but in his very personal calling he must show himself to be so. As, for example, a Magistrate must not only in general be a Christian, as every man is, but he must be a Christian Magistrate, in executing the office of a Magistrate in bearing the sword. A Master of a family must not only be a Christian abroad in the Town and in the Congregation, in the sight of strangers, but also in the administration and regiment of his particular family, towards wife, children, and servants. It is not enough for a woman to be virtuous openly to strangers; but her virtue must privately show itself in her subjection and obedience to her own husband. A Schoolmaster must not only be a Christian in the assembly, when he hears the Word and receives the Sacraments, but he must also show himself to be a Christian in the office of teaching. And thus must every man behave himself in his particular calling. . . .

Some man will say perchance, "What, must we not labor in our callings to maintain our families?" I answer, this must be done, but this is not the scope and end of our lives. The true end of our lives is to do service to God in serving of man; and for a recompense of this service, God sends his blessings on men's travails, and he allows them to take for their labors. Secondly, by this we learn how men of mean place and calling may comfort themselves. Let them consider that in serving of men by performance of poor and base duties they serve God, and therefore that their service is not base in his sight, and though their reward from men be little, yet the reward at God's hand shall not be wanting. For seeing they serve God in serving of men, they may justly look for reward from both. And thus may we reap marvelous content in any kind of calling, though it be but to sweep the house or keep sheep, if we can thus in practice unite our callings. . . .

Again, this rule serves to teach all men the right way to reform their lives. If you would lead a life unblameable both before God and man, you must first of all bethink yourself, what is your particular calling, and then proceed to practice duties of the Moral Law, and all other duties of Christianity, in that very calling. And if you would have signs and tokens of your election and salvation, you must fetch them from the constant practice of your two callings jointly together; sever them in your life, and you shall find no comfort, but rather shame and confusion of face, unless you repent.

IV. Rule

Such as bear public callings, must first reform themselves in private. When *Moses* went from Midian to Egypt, to be a Governor of the Israelites, the Lord withstood him in the way, by reason of fault in his private family, that his child was not circumcised according to the law of God. How shall he order public matters for the common good, that cannot order his own private estate?

V. Rule

A particular calling must give place to the general calling of a Christian, when they cannot both stand together. As, for example, a servant is bound to his master to obey him, either because he is a vassal, or at the least because he is hired to serve for wages; the said master, being a zealous Papist, threatens his servant, being a Protestant, that unless he condescend to hear Mass, he shall either burn at a stake, or carry a faggot [that is, bring a piece of wood to help build the fire to burn someone else]. Now the servant, seeing the malicious purpose of his master, and not finding himself able to bear the brunt of a trial in this case, he departs and withdraws himself for a time. And the question is, whether he does well or no? The answer is, he does, and in such a case, he may lawfully fly from his Master; for a servant that by personal calling is bound to an earthly Master is further, by a general calling, bound unto God. And the particular calling of any man is inferior to the general calling of a Christian, and when they cannot both stand together, the particular calling must give place; because we are bound unto God, and so far only as we may withal keep our bond with God. . . .

For better direction in the choice of an honest calling, this general ground must be observed: Every calling that serves to uphold and maintain the three several estates and societies, namely, the estate of the Church, or the estate of the Commonwealth, or the estate of the family, is grounded upon the moral law, and therefore lawful, and consequently may be had, used, and enjoyed with good conscience. On the contrary, if it be a hindrance to any of these three estates, in whole or in part, it is an unlawful calling.

II. Rule

Every man must choose a fit calling to walk in; that is, every calling must be fitted to the man, and every man be fitted to his calling. This rule is as necessary as the former, for when men are out of their proper callings in any society, it is as much as if a joint were out of the place in the body. Now in the choice of callings, two sorts of men must be considered, men of years, and children. Men of years make choice of fit callings for themselves when they try, judge, and examine themselves to what things they are apt and fit, and to what things they are not. And every man must examine himself of two things: first, touching his affection, secondly, touching his gifts. For his affection, he must search what mind he has to any calling, and in what calling he desires most of all to glorify God. For his gifts he must examine for and to what calling they are fittest. Having thus tried both his affection and gifts, finding also the calling to which they tend with one consent, he may say, that is his calling; because he likes it best, and is every way the fittest to it. As, for example, one brought up in the schools of learning desires to know what ought to be his calling; well, he examines his affections or desire, and finds it most of all inclined to the ministry of the Gospel; he examines his gifts also, and finds both knowledge and utterance fit for the same. Now such a one may safely say that the ministry is the calling to which he is set apart. And the like may any other man in any other calling say for himself. Yet, because many men are partial in judging of their inclination and gifts, the best way for them is to use the advice and help of others that are able to give direction herein, and to discern better than themselves.

Now touching children, it is the duty of parents to make choice of fit callings for them before they apply them to any particular condition of life. And that they may the better judge aright for what callings their children are fit, they must observe two things in them: first, their inclination; secondly, their natural gifts. Touching inclination, every child, even in his first years, does affect some one particular calling more than another; as some are affected more with music than others, some with merchandise, some with a more liberal kind of learning, some with this, some with that. And by this may the parents something judge of their inclination and towardness. This was practiced among the Athenians, who before they placed their children in any calling, did first bring them into a public place, where instruments of all sorts were laid, and they observed with what kind of instrument they took delight, and to the like art did they afterwards apply them with good success. And it will not be amiss for Christians to be followers of the Heathen in this, or any other commendable practice. Secondly, the natural gifts which parents are to observe in their children are either in their bodies or in their minds. And those children which excel in the gifts of the body are to be brought up in callings performed by the labor of the body, as in Mechanical Arts. And such as excel in the gifts of mind are to be applied to those sciences that are performed by wit and learning. The notes of a child that is fit for learning are these: a love of learning, a love of labor, a love of praise, and a wit neither too quick nor too dull. . . . And thus we see in some sort, how parents may judge to what calling every child is fit.

And here all parents must be warned, that the neglect of this duty is a great and common sin; for the care of most people is that their children may live, nothing regarding whether they live well, and do service to God in a fit calling or no. And the truth is, parents cannot do greater wrong to their children and the society of men, than to apply them unto unfit callings, as when a child is fit for learning, to apply him to a trade or other bodily service; contrariwise, to apply him to learning, when he is fittest for trade; for this is as much as if a man should apply his toes to feeling, and not his fingers; and to go on his hands, and not his feet, and to set the members of the body out of their proper places. . . .

A change of calling is a lawful going from one calling to another. It is not the Apostle's meaning to bar men to divert from this or that calling, but he gives them an item to keep them from changing upon every light conceit and every sudden occasion. And that changes may lawfully be made, it appears thus: *Amos* by calling was first a Herdsman, but after a Prophet, and the Disciples were first fishermen, and afterwards Apostles. Our Savior Christ himself was by calling a Carpenter, in his first and private life, till he was thirty years old; yet after his baptism, he showed himself to be the Messiah and Savior of the world. Nevertheless, a change may not be made, but upon urgent and weighty causes, and they are two especially: *Private necessity* and the *common good*. *Private necessity* is when men cannot maintain themselves and theirs by the callings in which they are; for then they may betake themselves to other callings. Thus a merchant may become a husbandman, and a husbandman, a merchant. Thus a physician may become a minister of the Gospel. And *Paul* the Apostle, upon private necessity, returned to the calling of a tentmaker; yet so as he performed his ministry, when occasion was offered.

The second cause of making change lawful is *the public good*. Thus may a private man become a magistrate. And it must be remembered, that as often as we change, it must be to better and more excellent callings, in which we may glorify God more, and bring greater benefit to the Church and Commonwealth. Thus *Paul* bids the Corinthians to seek for the best gifts, which might serve for the best callings. And here the fault of some is to be reproved, that having notable gifts of nature and learning, because they would attain to worldly wealth, make themselves merchants, or agents to merchants, or servingmen to great persons; whereas for their gifts, they might do God better service in the greatest callings of the Church. And thus much of constancy.

The consideration of this, that we are bound to be constant in duties of our particular callings, must teach us much more to be constant in the general duties of Christianity. And therefore let us all be careful, not only to profess the true religion for the present time, but to continue constant in this profession unto the end. Our general calling admits no vacation nor change as our particular callings do. Well then, in that we profess ourselves to be members of Christ, in these our happy days of peace let us arm ourselves against the evil days to come, that we may be faithful to the end.

GEORGE HERBERT

The Temple, or The Country Parson

George Herbert (1593-1633) attended Cambridge, where his success promised an important career in the Church of England. But he took a job as priest at a small church and remained there until the time of his death. He wrote both reflections on his life as a pastor and some of the great religious poetry of the English language; this essay reflects not only on callings in general but on the particular calling of a pastor.

Chapter 1. Of a Pastor

A Pastor is the deputy of Christ for the reducing of man to the obedience of God. This definition is evident, and contains the direct steps of pastoral duty

The Works of George Herbert (London: Bickers and Son, 1873), 157-58, 160-62, 239-45, modernized.

and Authority. For first, man fell from God by disobedience. Secondly, Christ is the glorious instrument of God for the revoking of man. Thirdly, Christ being not to continue on earth, but after he had fulfilled the work of reconciliation, to be received up into heaven, he constituted deputies in his place, and these are priests. And therefore St. *Paul* in the beginning of his Epistles, professes this, and in *Colossians* 1:24 plainly avouches that he *fills up that which is behind of the afflictions of Christ in his flesh, for his Body's sake, which is the Church.* Wherein is contained the complete definition of a minister. Out of this charter of the priesthood may be plainly gathered both the dignity thereof, and the duty: the dignity, in that a priest may do that which Christ did, and by his authority and as his Vicegerent; the duty, in that a priest is to do that which Christ did, and after his manner, both for doctrine and life....

Chapter 3. The Parson's Life

The country parson is exceeding exact in his life, being holy, just, prudent, temperate, bold, grave in all his ways. And because the two highest points of life, wherein a Christian is most seen, are patience and mortification, patience in regard of afflictions, mortification in regard of lusts and affections and the stupefying and deadening of all the clamorous powers of the soul, therefore he hath thoroughly studied these, that he may be an absolute master and commander of himself, for all the purposes which God hath ordained him. Yet in these points he labors most in those things which are most apt to scandalize his parish. And first, because country people live a hard life, and therefore as feeling their own sweat, and consequently knowing the price of money, are offended much with any who by hard usage increase their travail, the country parson is very circumspect in avoiding all covetousness, neither being greedy to get, nor niggardly to keep, nor troubled to lose any worldly wealth; but in all his words and actions slighting and disesteeming it, even to wondering that the world should so much value wealth, which in the day of wrath hath not one dram of comfort for us.

Secondly, because luxury is a very visible sin, the parson is very careful to avoid all the kinds thereof, but especially that of drinking, because it is the most popular vice; into which if he come, he prostitutes himself both to shame and sin, and by having fellowship with the unfruitful works of darkness, he disables himself of authority to reprove them. For sins make all equal, whom they find together; and then they are worst, who ought to be best. Neither is it for the servant of Christ to haunt inns, or taverns, or alehouses, to the dishonor of his person and office. The parson doth not so, but orders his life in such a fashion that when death takes him, as the Jews and Judas did Christ, he may say as He did, *I sat daily with you teaching in the Temple* (Matt. 26:55).

Thirdly, because country people (as indeed all honest men) do much esteem their word, it being the life of buying and selling and dealing in the world; therefore the parson is very strict in keeping his word, though it be to his own hindrance, as knowing, that if he be not so, he will quickly be discovered and disregarded. Neither will they believe him in the pulpit, whom they cannot trust in his conversation. As for oaths, and apparel, the disorders thereof are also very manifest. The Parson's yea is yea, and nay nay; and his apparel plain, but reverend and clean, without spots, or dust, or smell; the purity of his mind breaking out, and dilating itself even to his body, clothes, and habitation. . . .

Chapter 32. The Parson's Surveys

The Country Parson hath not only taken a particular survey of the faults of his own parish, but a general also of the diseases of the time, so that, when his occasions carry him abroad, or bring strangers to him, he may be the better armed to encounter them. The great and national sin of this land he esteems to be idleness, great in itself, and great in consequence. For when men have nothing to do, then they fall to drink, to steal, to whore, to scoff, to revile, to all sorts of gamings. Come, say they, we have nothing to do, let's go to the tavern, or to the stews [houses of prostitution], or what not. Wherefore the parson strongly opposes this sin, wheresoever he goes. And because idleness is twofold, the one in having no calling, the other in walking carelessly in our calling, he first represents to everybody the necessity of a vocation. The reason of this assertion is taken from the nature of man, wherein God hath placed two great instruments, reason in the soul and a hand in the body, as engagements of working: So that even in Paradise man had a calling, and how much more out of Paradise, when the evils which he is now subject unto, may be prevented or diverted by reasonable employment. Besides, every gift or ability is a talent to be accounted for and to be improved to our Master's advantage. Yet is it also a debt to our country to have a calling, and it concerns the Commonwealth that none should be idle, but all busied. Lastly, riches are the blessing of God, and the great instrument of doing admirable good; therefore all are to procure them honestly and seasonably, when they are not better employed. Now this reason crosses not our Savior's precept of selling what we have, because when we have sold all and given it to the poor, we must not be idle, but labor to get more, that we may give more, according to St. Paul's rule (Eph. 4:28; 1 Thess. 4:11, 12). So that our Savior's selling is so far from crossing Saint Paul's working that it rather establishes it, since they that have nothing are fittest to work. Now because the only one opposed to this doctrine is the gallant, who is witty enough to abuse both others and himself, and who is ready to ask if he shall mend shoes, or what he shall do? Therefore the parson unmoved, shows that ingenuous and fit employment is never wanting to those that seek it. But if it should be, the assertion stands thus: All are either to have a calling or prepare for it. He that hath or can have yet no employment, if he truly and seriously prepare for it, he is safe and within bounds. Wherefore all are either presently to enter into a calling, if they be fit for it, and it for them, or else to examine with care and advice what they are fittest for, and to prepare for that with all diligence.

But it will not be amiss in this exceedingly useful point to descend to particulars: for exactness lies in particulars. Men are either single or married: the married and house-keeper hath his hands full, if he do what he ought to do. For there are two branches of his affairs: first, the improvement of his family, by bringing them up in the fear and nurture of the Lord; and secondly, the improvement of his grounds, by drowning, or draining, or stocking, or fencing, and ordering his land to the best advantage both of himself and his neighbors. . . .

Now, for single men, they are either heirs or younger brothers. The heirs are to prepare in all the fore-mentioned points against the time of their practice. . . . As for younger brothers, those whom the parson finds loose and not engaged into some profession by their parents, whose neglect in this point is intolerable and a shameful wrong both to the Commonwealth and their own house: to them, after he hath showed the unlawfulness of spending the day in dressing, complimenting, visiting, and sporting, he first commends the study of the civil law, as a brave and wise knowledge, the Professors whereof were much employed by Queen Elizabeth, because it is the key of commerce and discovers the rules of foreign nations. Secondly, he commends mathematics as the only wonder-working knowledge, and therefore requiring the best spirits. After the several knowledge of these, he advises to insist and dwell chiefly on the two noble branches thereof, of fortification, and navigation, the one being useful to all countries, and the other especially to hands. But if the young gallant think these courses dull and phlegmatic, where can he busy himself better than in those new plantations and discoveries, which are not only a noble, but also as they may be handled, a religious employment? Or let him travel into Germany and France, and observing the artifices and manufactures there, transplant them hither, as diverse men have done lately, to our country's advantage.

***

GEORGE HERBERT

The Collar

The previous excerpt might leave Herbert seeming unnervingly self-satisfied as he lays out the rules of callings. This poem expresses his frustrations with, but finally acceptance of, his own calling. The title evokes not only the clergyman's collar, but the yoke or collar which ties an animal to its work, "choler" (anger), and "caller" (the God who calls).

I Struck the board, and cry'd, No more. I will abroad.
What? shall I ever sigh and pine?
My lines and life are free; free as the rode; Loose as the winde,
    as large as store.
Shall I be still in suit?
Have I no harvest but a thorn
To let me bloud, and not restore
What I have lost with cordiall fruit?
Sure there was wine
Before my sighs did drie it: there was corn
Before my tears did drown it.
Is the yeare onely lost to me?
Have I no bayes to crown it?
No flowers, no garlands gay? all blasted? All wasted?
Not so, my heart: but there is fruit,
    And thou hast hands.

The Poetical Works of George Herbert (New York: D. Appleton, 1858), 194-95.

Recover all thy sigh-blown age
On double pleasures: leave thy cold dispute
Of what is fit, and not. Forsake thy cage,
Thy rope of sands,
Which pettie thoughts have made, and made to thee
Good cable, to enforce and draw,
And be thy law,
While thou didst wink and wouldst not see.
Away; take heed:
I will abroad.
Call in thy death's head there: tie up thy fears.
He that forbears
To suit and serve his need,
Deserves his load.
But as I rav'd and grew more fierce and wilde
At every word,
Me thoughts I heard one calling, *Child!*
And I reply'd, *My Lord.*

RICHARD BAXTER

Directions about Our Labor and Callings

Richard Baxter (1615-1691) maintained a moderate Puritanism throughout the political changes in England during his life. By the end of the 1630s he had rejected the idea that the church should have bishops; this put him on the side of the "nonconformists" against the established Church of England. He joined the parliamentary army against the king in the English Civil War but was critical of the government the parliamentary forces established under Oliver Cromwell. In the midst of conflicts among Episco-

Richard Baxter, *The Practical Works of the Rev. Richard Baxter* (London: James Duncan, 1830), 577-87. Spelling and punctuation modernized.

palians, Presbyterians, and Independents, Baxter tried to find grounds for cooperation and mutual respect. His dissatisfaction with the parliamentary government led him to support the return of Charles II as king in 1660, but he still opposed having bishops, and so he was persecuted as disloyal to the reestablished Church of England. Near the end of his life, he supported replacing James II (Charles II's brother) with the more moderate rulers William and Mary. This excerpt shows his characteristic moderation and common sense.

Chapter X: Directions for the Government of the Body

Title 1. Directions for the Right Choice
of Our Calling and Ordinary Labor. . . .

Direction 1: "Understand how necessary a life of labor is, and the reasons of the necessity."

Question 1: "Is Labor necessary to all? Or to whom if not to all?" *Answer:* It is necessary (as a duty) to all that are able to perform it, but to the unable it is not necessary: as to infants and sick persons, or distracted persons that cannot do it, or to prisoners, or any that are restrained or hindered unavoidably by others, or to people that are disabled by age or by anything that makes it naturally impossible. . . .

Question 3: "May not religion excuse men from all other labor, save prayer and contemplation?" *Answer:* Religion is our obligation to obey God. God binds us to do all the good we can to others. Some men that have ability, opportunity, and a call may be excused by religion from worldly labors, as ministers; but not from such spiritual labors for others which they can perform. He that under pretence of religion withdraws from converse and forbears to do good to others and only lives to himself and his own soul, doth make religion a pretence against charity and the works of charity, which are a great part of religion: for "pure religion and undefiled before God and the Father is this, to visit the fatherless and widows in their affliction, and to keep himself unspotted from the world" (James 1:27). Even when sickness, imprisonment, or persecution makes us unable to do any more for others, we must pray for them. But while we can do more, we must.

Question 4: "Will not riches excuse one from laboring in a calling?" *Answer:* No, but rather bind them to it the more, for he that has most wages from God should do him most work. Though they have no outward want to urge them, they have as great a necessity of obeying God and doing good to others as any other men have that are poor.

Question 5: "Why is labor thus necessary to all that are able?" *Answer*: 1. God hath strictly commanded it to all, and his command is reason enough to us. "For even when we were with you, this we commanded you, that if any would not work, neither should he eat. For we hear that there are some which walk among you disorderly, working not at all, but are busy-bodies. Now them that are such, we command and exhort by our Lord Jesus Christ, that with quietness they work and eat their own bread" (2 Thess. 3:10-11). "We beseech you, brethren — that ye study to be quiet, and to do your own business, and work with your hands as we commanded you, that ye may walk honestly (or decently) towards them that are without, and that ye may have lack of nothing" (1 Thess. 4:10-12). "In the sweat of thy face shall thou eat bread, till thou return unto the ground" (Gen. 3:19). And in the fourth Commandment: "Six days shall thou labor" (Exod. 20:9). So Ephesians 4:28, Proverbs 31:33.

2. Naturally, action is the end of all our powers; and the power were vain, but in respect to the act. To be able to understand, to read, to write, to go, &c. were little worth, if it were not that we may do the things that we are enabled to.

3. It is for action that God maintains us and our abilities: work is the moral as well as the natural end of power. It is to act by the power that is commanded us.

4. It is action that God is most served and honored by, not so much by our being able to do good, but by our doing it. Who will keep a servant that is able to work, and will not? Will his mere ability answer your expectation?

5. The public welfare or the good of many is to be valued above our own. Every man therefore is bound to do all the good he can to others, especially for the church and commonwealth. And this is not done by idleness, but by labor! As the bees labor to replenish their hive, so man, being a sociable creature, must labor for the good of the society which he belongs to, in which his own is contained as a part.

6. Labor is necessary for the preservation of the faculties of the mind. (1.) The labor of the mind is necessary hereto, because unexercised abilities will decay, as iron not used will consume with rust. Idleness makes men fools and dullards, and spoils that little ability which they have. (2.) And the exercise of the body is ordinarily necessary, because of the mind's dependence on the body, and, acting according to its temperature and disposition, it is exceedingly helped or hindered by the body.

7. Labor is needful to our health and life: the body itself will quickly fall

into mortal diseases without it (except in some very few persons of extraordinary soundness). Next to abstinence, labor is the chief preserver of health. It stirs up the natural heat and spirits, which perform the chief offices for the life of man; it is the proper bellows for this vital fire; it helps all the concoctions of nature. . . . For want of bodily labor a multitude of the idle gentry, and rich people, and young people that are slothful, do heap up in the secret receptacles of the body a dunghill of unconcocted, excrementitious filth, and vitiate all the mass of humors which should be the fuel and oil of life, and die by thousands of untimely deaths (of fevers, palsies, convulsions, apoplexies, dropsies, consumptions, gout, &c.) more miserably than if thieves had murdered them by the highway, because it is their own doing, and by their sloth they kill themselves. For want of bodily exercise and labor interposed, abundance of students and sedentary persons fill themselves with diseases, and hasten their death, and causelessly blame their hard studies for that which was caused by their bodily sloth. . . .

8. Labor and diligence do keep the mind upon a lawful employment, and therefore keeps out many dangerous temptations and keeps the thoughts from vanity and sin, and also keeps out vain words, and preserves the soul from many sins, which a life of idleness and sloth doth cherish. It helps even unlearned persons more effectually to restrain their thoughts and words from sin than the greatest knowledge and diligent watchfulness can do in an idle kind of life.

9. Diligent labor mortifieth the flesh, and keeps under its luxurious inclinations, and subdues that pride and lust and brutish sensuality which is cherished by an idle life.

10. Lastly, it is God's appointed means for the getting of our daily bread, and as it is a more real honor to get our bread ourselves than to receive it by the gift of our friends or parents, so is it more comfortable to a well-informed mind. We may best believe that we have our food and provisions in mercy, and that they shall be blest to us, when we have them in God's appointed way, who hath said, "If any man will not work, neither should he eat."

Direction 2: "As labor is thus necessary, so understand how needful a stated calling is for the right performance of your labors."

A calling is a stated, ordinary course of labor. This is very needful for these reasons: 1. Outside of a calling a man's labors are but occasional, or inconstant, and so more time is spent in idleness than in labor. 2. A man is best skilled in that which he is used to. 3. And he will be best provided for it, with instruments and necessaries. 4. Therefore he doth it better than he could do another work, and so wrongs not others, but attains more the ends of his labor. 5. And he does it more easily; when a man unused, and un-skilled, and unfurnished, toils himself much in doing little. 6. And he will do his work more orderly, when another is continual confusion, and his business knows not its time and place, but one part contradicts another. Therefore some certain calling or trade of life is best for every man.

Question 1: "May not a man have a calling consisting of occasional, uncertain works? *Answer:* He that can have no better may do thus; so be it they are consistent works which he is able for: as a footman may go on various errands and a day-laborer may do many sorts of works. But great variety will be a great inconvenience to him.

Question 2: "May a man have diverse trades or callings at once?" *Answer:* Yes, no doubt, if it be for the common good or for his own and no injury to any other; nor so inconsistent, as that one shall make him unfaithful in the other: then God forbids it not. . . .

Direction 3: "Think not that a calling can be lawful, when the work of it is sin; nor that you, or your labor, or your gain in an unlawful calling shall be blest."

An unlawful act is bad enough, but an unlawful calling is a life of sin. To make sin a man's trade, and work, and living is a most horrid, desperate course of life. As mercenary soldiers, that for their pay will fight against authority, right or innocence, and murder men for half a crown a day; and those that live by cheating, stealing, oppressing, whoring or by resetting such, or upon the sin of such or of drunkards, gamesters, or other sensual vices, which they knowingly and willingly maintain.

Direction 4: "Think not that because a work is lawful, that therefore it is lawful to make a calling of it."

It is lawful to jest in time and measure, but not lawful to be a jester as a trade of life. If in some cases it should prove lawful to act a comedy or tragedy, it will not follow that therefore it is lawful to be by trade a stage-player; if a game at cards or dice may be in some cases lawful, it follows not that it is lawful to be a gamester by trade. The like I may say of many others.

Direction 5: "It is not enough that the work of your calling be lawful, nor that it be necessary, but you must take special care also that it be safe, and not very dangerous to your souls."

The calling of a vintner and ale-seller is lawful and needful; and yet it is so very dangerous that (unless it be in extraordinary place or case) a man that loves his soul should be loath to meddle with it, if he can have a safer way to get his bread by. They get so little by sober people, and their gain depends so much upon men's sin, that it is a constant temptation to them to be the maintainers of it. And frail man, that can so hardly stand on firm ground, should be loath for a little money to walk still upon the ice and to venture his soul in a life of such temptations; for it is twenty to one but they will prevail.

Direction 6: *"The principal thing to be intended in the choice of a trade or calling for yourselves or children, is the service of God, and the public good, and therefore (caeteris paribus [other things being equal]) that calling which most conduceth to the public good is to be preferred."*

The callings most useful to the public good are the magistrates, the pastors, and teachers of the church, schoolmasters, physicians, lawyers, husbandmen (ploughmen, graziers, and shepherds); and next to them are mariners, clothiers, booksellers, tailors, and such others that are employed about things most necessary to mankind. Some callings are employed about matters of so little use (as tobacco and lace-sellers, feather-makers, periwig-makers, and many more such) that he that may choose better should be loath to take up with one these, though possibly in itself it may be lawful. It is a great satisfaction to an honest mind to spend his life in doing the greatest good he can; and a prison and constant calamity to be tied to spend one's life in doing little good at all to others, though he should grow rich by it himself.

Direction 7: *"When two callings equally conduce to the public good, and one of them hath the advantage of riches, and the other is more advantageous to your souls, the latter must be preferred, and next to the public good, the soul's advantage must guide your choice."*

As suppose that a lawyer were as profitable to the public good as a divine, and it is the way to far more wealth and honor; yet the sacred calling is much more desirable for the benefit of your souls, because it is an exceeding great help, as we are engaged in our calling to have the word and doctrine of Christ still before us and in our minds and mouths, when others must be glad to be now and then exercised in it when their hearts are cooled by the frequent and long diversions of their worldly business, so that our calling and work is to an honest heart a recreation and preserving and edifying help to grace. So a schoolmaster's calling is usually but poor and very painful, requiring much close attendance, but yet it is of so great use to the common good, and allows the mind so much leisure and advantage to improve itself in honest studies that it is fitter to be chosen and delighted in by a well-tempered mind, than richer and more honored employments. It is sweet to be all day doing so much good.

Direction 8: "If it be possible, choose a calling which so exercises the body as not to overwhelm you with cares and labor and deprive you of all leisure for the holy and noble employments of the mind, and which so exercises your mind as to allow you some exercise for the body also."

1. That calling so takes up body and mind as neither to allow you commixed thoughts of greater things nor convenient intermissions for them is a constant snare and prison to the soul, which is the case of many who plunge themselves into more and greater business than they can otherwise dispatch and yet are contented to be thus continually alienated in their minds from God and heaven, to get more of the world. Many poor laborers (as clothiers, tailors, and other such) can work with their hands and meditate or discourse of heavenly things without any hindrance of their work, when many men of richer means have scarce room for a thought or word of God or heaven all day.

2. On the contrary, if the body have not also its labor as well as the mind, it will ruin your health, and body and mind will both grow useless.

Direction 9: "It is lawful and meet to look at the commodity of your calling in the third place (that is, after the public good, and after your personal good of soul and bodily health)."

Though it is said, "Labor not to be rich," the meaning is, that you make not riches your chief end; riches for our fleshly ends must not ultimately be intended or sought. But in subordination to higher things they may: that is, you may labor in that manner as tends most to your success and lawful gain. You are bound to improve all your master's talents, but then your end must be that you may be the better provided to do God service and may do the more good with what you have. If God show you a way in which you may lawfully get more than in another way (without wrong to your soul, or to any other), if you refuse this, and choose the less gainful way, you cross one of the ends of your calling, and you refuse to be God's steward and to accept his gifts and use them for him when he requires it; you may labor to be rich for God, though not for the flesh and sin.

Direction 10: "It is not enough that you consider what calling and labor is most desirable, but you must also consider what you or your children are fittest for, both in mind and body."

For that calling may be one man's blessing which would be another's misery and undoing. A weak body cannot undergo those labors that require strength, and a dull and heavy mind and wit cannot do the works which require great judgment and ingenuity. It hath been the calamity of the church, and undoing of many ministers themselves, that well-meaning parents out of love to the sacred work of God have set their children to be ministers that were unfit for it; and many self-conceited persons themselves are ready to thrust themselves into that holy office when they have some inconsiderable smattering of knowledge and some poor measure of gifts, overvalued by themselves, that know not what is required to so great a work. Be sure that you first look to the natural ingenuity of your children (or yourselves) and then to their grace and piety, and see that none be devoted to the ministry that have not naturally a quickness of understanding and a freedom of expression, unless you would have him live upon the ruin of souls and wrong of the church and work of God and turn an enemy to the best of his flock, when he sees that they value him but as he deserves; and let none be so unwise as to be a preacher of that faith and love and holiness which he never had himself. And even to the calling of a physician none should be designed that have not a special ingenuity, and sagacity, and natural quickness of apprehension, unless he should make a trade of killing men, for it is a calling that requires a quick and strong conjecturing ability, which no study will bring a man that hath not a natural acuteness and aptitude thereto. Thus also as to all other callings; you must consider not only the will of the child or parents, but their natural fitness of body and mind.

Direction 11: "Choose no calling (especially if it be of public consequence) without the advice of some judicious, faithful persons of that calling."

For they are best able to judge in their own profession. Never resolve on the sacred ministry without the advice of able ministers; resolve not to be a physician but by the counsel of physicians, and so of the rest; for abundance of persons ignorantly conceit themselves sufficient that are utterly insufficient, and so live all their days as wrongs and burdens unto others, and in sin and misery to themselves.

Direction 12: "If thou be called to the poorest laborious calling, do not carnally complain of it because it is wearisome to the flesh, nor imagine that God accepts the less of thy work and thee; but cheerfully follow it, and make it the matter of thy pleasure and joy that thou art still in thy heavenly Master's service, though it be about the lowest things, and that he who knows what is best for thee, hath chosen this for thy good, and tries and values thy obedience to him the more, by how much the meaner work thou stoopest to at his command."

But see that thou do it all in obedience to God, and not merely for thy own necessity; thus every servant must serve the Lord in serving their masters, and from God expect their chief reward.

JOHN BUNYAN

The Pilgrim's Progress

John Bunyan (1628-1688), born of a poor family, seems to have mostly educated himself by reading the Bible. From age seventeen to eighteen he served in the parliamentary army in the English Civil War. Afterwards he struggled with questions of what to believe and how to live until he joined a Baptist congregation; he soon became a Baptist lay preacher. When the monarchy was restored under Charles II in 1660, Bunyan, along with many other religious "dissenters," was thrown into jail, where he remained for eleven years and began writing *Pilgrim's Progress*, his best-known book. Its publication in 1678 soon made him famous. Even up to the American Civil War, other than the Bible, *Pilgrim's Progress* was probably the most widely read book in the United States.

As I walked through the wilderness of this world, I lighted on a certain place where was a den [a reference to Bunyan's jail cell], and I laid me down in that place to sleep, and as I slept I dreamed a dream. I dreamed and behold I saw a man clothed with rags (Isa. 64:6), standing in a certain place, with his face from his own house, a book in his hand, and a great burden upon his back (Ps. 38:4). I looked, and saw him open the book, and read therein; and as he read he wept and trembled, and not being able longer to contain, he brake out with a lamentable cry, saying, "'What shall I do?" (Acts 16:30-31).

In this plight therefore he went home and restrained himself as long as he could that his wife and children should not perceive his distress; but he could not be silent long, because that his trouble increased. Wherefore at length he brake his mind to his wife and children; and thus he began to talk to them, "O my dear wife," said he, "and you, the children of my bowels, I your dear friend am in myself undone, by reason of a burden that lieth hard

John Bunyan, *The Pilgrim's Progress* (New York: Signet, 1964), 17-21, 22, 92-96.

upon me; moreover, I am for certain informed that this our city will be burned with fire from heaven, in which fearful overthrow both myself, with thee, my wife, and you, my sweet babes, shall miserably come to ruin; except (the which, yet I see not) some way of escape can be found, whereby we may be delivered." At this his relations were sore amazed; not for that they believed that what he said to them was true, but because they thought that some frenzy distemper had got into his head; therefore, it drawing towards night, and they hoping that sleep might settle his brains, with all haste they got him to bed. But the night was as troublesome to him as the day; wherefore instead of sleeping, he spent it in sighs and tears. So when the morning was come, they would know how he did, and he told them worse and worse. He also set to talking to them again, but they began to be hardened. They also thought to drive away his distemper by harsh and surly carriages to him: sometimes they would deride; sometimes they would chide; and sometimes they would quite neglect him. Wherefore he began to retire himself to his chamber to pray for and pity them, and also to condole his own misery; he would also walk solitarily in the fields, sometimes reading, and sometimes praying, and thus for some days he spent his time.

Now, I saw upon a time when he was walking in the fields that he was (as he was wont) reading in his book and greatly distressed in his mind; and as he read, he burst out, as he had done before, crying, "What shall I do to be saved?"

I saw also that he looked this way and that way, as if he would run; yet he stood still, because, as I perceived, he could not tell which way to go. I looked then and saw a man named Evangelist coming to him and asked, "Wherefore dost thou cry?" He answered, "Sir, I perceive, by the book in my hand, that I am condemned to die and after that to come to judgment; and I find that I am not willing to do the first, nor able to do the second."

Then said the Evangelist, "Why not willing to die, since this life is attended with so many evils?" The man answered, "Because I fear that this burden that is upon my back will sink me lower than the grave, and I shall fall into Tophet [hell]. And, sir, if I be not fit to go to prison, I am not fit (I am sure) to go to judgment and from thence to execution; and the thoughts of these things make me cry."

Then said Evangelist, "If this be thy condition, why standest thou still?" He answered, "Because I know not whither to go." Then he gave him a parchment roll, and there was written within, "Fly from the wrath to come" (Matt. 3:7).

The man therefore read it, and looking upon Evangelist very carefully, said, "Whither must I fly?" Then said Evangelist, pointing with his finger over a very wide field, "Do you see yonder wicket-gate?" (Matt. 7:13, 14). The man said, "No." Then said the other, "Do you see yonder shining light?" (Ps. 119:105; 2 Pet. 1:19). He said, "I think I do." Then said Evangelist, "Keep that light in your eye, and go up directly thereto; so shalt thou see the gate, at which, when thou knockest, it shall be told thee what thou shalt do."

So I saw in my dream that the man began to run. Now he had not run far from his own door, but his wife and children perceiving it, began to cry after him to return. But the man put his fingers in his ears and ran on crying, "Life, life, eternal life." So he looked not behind him, but fled towards the middle of the plain (Gen. 19:17).

The neighbors also came out to see him run, and as he ran, some mocked, others threatened, and some cried after him to return. Now among those that did so, there were two that were resolved to fetch him back by force. The name of the one was Obstinate and the name of the other Pliable. Now by this time the man was got a good distance from them; but, however, they were resolved to pursue him, which they did and in little time they overtook him. Then said the man, "Neighbors, wherefore are you come?" They said, "To persuade you to go back with us." But he said, "That can by no means be. You dwell," said he, "in the City of Destruction [Isa. 19:18] (the place also where I was born). I see it to be so, and dying there, sooner or later, you will sink lower than the grave, into a place that burns with fire and brimstone. Be content, good neighbors, and go along with me."

"What!" said Obstinate, "and leave our friends and our comforts behind us!"

"Yes," said Christian (for that was his name), "because, all that which you shall forsake is not worthy to be compared with a little of that that I am seeking to enjoy, and if you will go along with me, and hold it, you shall fare as I myself; for there where I go is enough and to spare. Come away and prove my words."

> OBST. "What are the things you seek, since you leave all the world to find them?"
>
> CHR. "I seek an 'inheritance, incorruptible, undefiled, and that fadeth not away' (1 Pet. 1:4), and it is laid up in Heaven, and fast there, to be bestowed at the time appointed on them that diligently seek it. Read it so, if you will, in my book."
>
> OBST. "Tush," said Obstinate, "away with your book; will you go back with us or no?"
>
> CHR. "No, not I," said the other, "because I have laid my hand to the plow" (Luke 9:62).

OBST. "Come, then, neighbor Pliable, let us turn again, and go home without him; there is a company of these crazed-headed coxcombs, that when they take a fancy by the end are wiser in their own eyes than seven men that can render a reason" (Prov. 26:16).

PLI. Then said Pliable, "Don't revile; if what the good Christian says is true, the things he looks after are better than ours; my heart inclines to go with my neighbor."

OBST. "What! more fools still? Be ruled by me and go back; who knows whither such a brain-sick fellow will lead you? Go back, go back, and be wise."

CHR. "Come with me, neighbor Pliable; there are such things to be had which I spoke of and many more glories besides; if you believe not me, read here in this book, and for the truth of what is expressed therein, behold all is confirmed by the blood of him that made it."

PLI. "Well, neighbor Obstinate," said Pliable, "I begin to come to a point; I intend to go along with this good man and to cast in my lot with him. But, my good companion, do you know the way to this desired place?"

CHR. "I am directed by a man whose name is Evangelist to speed me to a little gate that is before us, where we shall receive instruction about the way."

PLI. "Come then, good neighbor, let us be going." Then they went both together.

OBST. "And I will go back to my place," said Obstinate. "I will be no companion of such misled fantastical fellows."

Now I saw in my dream that when Obstinate was gone back, Christian and Pliable went talking over the plain, and thus they began their discourse.

CHR. "Come, neighbor Pliable, how do you do? I am glad you are persuaded to go along with me, and had even Obstinate himself but felt what I have felt of the powers and terrors of what is yet unseen, he would not thus lightly have given us the back."

PLI. "Come, neighbor Christian, since there is none but us two here, tell me now further, what the things are and how to be enjoyed, whither we are going."

CHR. "I can better conceive of them with my mind than speak of them with my tongue. But yet since you are desirous to know, I will read of them in my book."

PLI. "And do you think that the words of your book are certainly true?"

CHR. "Yes, verily, for it was made by him that cannot lie" (Tit. 1:2).

PLI. "Well said; what things are they?"

CHR. "There is an endless kingdom to be inhabited and everlasting life to be given us, that we may inhabit that kingdom forever."

PLI. "Well said, and what else?"

CHR. "There are crowns of glory to be given us, and garments that will make us shine like the sun in the firmament of heaven."

PLI. "This is excellent, and what else?"

CHR. "There shall be no more crying, nor sorrow; for He that is owner of the place will wipe all tears from our eyes" (Rev. 21:4). . . .

Now I saw in my dream, that just as they had ended this talk, they drew near to a very miry slough that was in the midst of the plain, and they, heedless, did both fall suddenly into the bog. The name of the slough was Despond. Here therefore they wallowed for a time, being grievously bedaubed with the dirt; and Christian, because of the burden that was on his back, began to sink in the mire.

PLI. Then said Pliable, "Ah, neighbor Christian, where are you now?"

CHR. "Truly," said Christian, "I do not know."

PLI. At that Pliable began to be offended and angrily said to his fellow, "Is this the happiness you have told me all this while of? If we have such ill speed at our first setting out, what may we expect, 'twixt this and our journey's end? May I get out again with my life, you shall possess the brave country alone for me." And with that he gave a desperate struggle or two and got out of the mire, on that side of the slough which was next to his own house. So away he went, and Christian saw him no more.

Wherefore Christian was left to tumble in the slough of Despond alone; but still he endeavored to struggle to that side of the slough that was still further from his own house and next to the wicket-gate; the which he did, but could not get out, because of the burden that was upon his back. But I beheld in my dream that a man came to him, whose name was Help, and asked him what he did there.

CHR. "Sir," said Christian, "I was bid go this way by a man called Evangelist, who directed me also to yonder gate, that I might escape the wrath to come. And as I was going thither, I fell in here." . . .

[Rescued by Help, Christian finds a first companion in Faithful, who is killed by the evil people of Vanity Fair. He finds another companion in Hopeful.]

Now I saw in my dream that Christian went not forth alone, for there was one whose name was Hopeful (being made so by the beholding of Christian and Faithful in their words and behavior, in their sufferings at the fair) who joined himself unto him, and entering into a brotherly covenant, told him that he would be his companion. Thus one died to make testimony to the truth, and another rises out of his ashes to be a companion with Christian. This Hopeful also told Christian that there were many more of the men in the fair that would take their time and follow after.

So I saw that quickly after they were got out of the fair, they overtook one that was going before them, whose name was By-ends [secret, selfish motives]; so they said to him, "What countryman, sir? And how far go you this way?" He told them that he came from the town of Fair-speech and he was going to the Celestial City (but told them not his name).

"From Fair-speech," said Christian, "is there any that be good live there?"

BY-ENDS. "Yes," said By-ends, "I hope."

CHR. "Pray, sir, what may I call you?" said Christian.

BY-ENDS. "I am a stranger to you, and you to me; if you be going this way, I shall be glad of your company; if not, I must be content."

CHR. "This town of Fair-speech," said Christian, "I have heard of it, and, as I remember, they say it's a wealthy place."

BY-ENDS. "Yes, I will assure you that it is, and I have very many rich kindred there."

CHR. "Pray who are your kindred there, if a man may be so bold."

BY-ENDS. "Almost the whole town; and in particular, my Lord Turn-about, my Lord Time-server, my Lord Fair-speech (from whose ancestors that town first took its name). Also Mr. Smooth-man, Mr. Facing-bothways, Mr. Anything, and the parson of our parish, Mr. Two-tongues, was my mother's own brother by father's side. And to tell you the truth, I am become a gentleman of good quality; yet my great-grandfather was but a waterman, looking one way, and rowing another; and I got most of my estate by the same occupation."

CHR. "Are you a married man?"

BY-ENDS. "Yes, and my wife is a very virtuous woman, the daughter of a virtuous woman. She was my Lady Feigning's daughter; therefore she came of a very honorable family, and is arrived to such a pitch of breeding that she knows how to carry it to all, even to prince and peasant. 'Tis true, we somewhat differ in religion from those of the stricter sort, yet but in two small points: first, we never strive against wind and tide. Secondly, we are always most zealous when religion goes in his silver slippers; we love much to walk with him in the street, if the sun shines and the people applaud it."

Then Christian stepped a little aside [to speak] to this fellow Hopeful, saying, "It runs in my mind that this is one By-ends, of Fair-speech, and if it be he, we have as very a knave in our company as dwelleth in all these parts." Then said Hopeful, "Ask him; methinks he should not be ashamed of his name." So Christian came up with him again, and said, "Sir, you talk as if you knew something more than all the world doth, and if I take not my mark amiss, I deem I have half a guess of you. Is not your name Mr. By-ends of Fair-speech?"

BY-ENDS. "That is not my name, but indeed it is a nickname that is given me by some that cannot abide me, and I must be content to bear it as a reproach, as other good men have borne theirs before me."

CHR. "But did you never give an occasion to men to call you by this name?"

BY-ENDS. "Never, never! The worst that ever I did to give them an occasion to give me this name was that I had always the luck to jump in my judgment with the present way of the times, whatever it was, and my chance was to get thereby; but if things are thus cast upon me, let me count them a blessing, but let not the malicious load me therefore with reproach."

CHR. "I thought indeed that you were the man that I had heard of, and to tell you what I think, I fear this name belongs to you more properly than you are willing we should think it doth."

BY-ENDS. "Well, if you will thus imagine, I cannot help it. You shall find me a fair company-keeper, if you will still admit me your associate."

CHR. "If you will go with us, you must go against wind and tide, the which, I perceive, is against your opinion. You must also own religion in his rags, as well as when in his silver slippers, and stand by him, too, when bound in irons, as well as when he walketh the streets with applause."

BY-ENDS. "You must not impose, nor lord it over my faith; leave me to my liberty, and let me go with you."

CHR. "Not a step further, unless you will do in what I propound, as we."

Then said By-ends, "I shall never desert my old principles, since they are harmless and profitable. If I may not go with you, I must do as I did before you overtook me, even go by myself, until some overtake me that will be glad of my company."

Now I saw in my dream that Christian and Hopeful forsook him and kept their distance before him, but one of them looking back saw three men following Mr. By-ends, and behold, as they came up with him, he made them a very low congee [bow], and they also gave him a compliment. The men's names were Mr. Hold-the-World, Mr. Money-love, and Mr. Save-all, men that Mr. By-ends had formerly been acquainted with; for in their minority they were schoolfellows, and were taught by one Mr. Gripe-man, a school-master in Love-gain, which is a market town in the county of Coveting in the north. This school-master taught them the art of getting, either by violence, cozenage [fraud], flattery, lying or by putting on a guise of religion, and these four gentlemen had attained much of the art of their master, so that they could each of them have kept such a school themselves.

Well, when they had, as I said, thus saluted each other, Mr. Money-love said to Mr. By-ends, "Who are they upon the road before us?" for Christian and Hopeful were yet within view.

BY-ENDS. "They are a couple of far countrymen, that after their mode are going on pilgrimage."

MONEY-LOVE. "Alas, why did they not stay that we might have had their good company, for they and we and you, sir, I hope, are all going on pilgrimage."

BY-ENDS. "We are so indeed, but the men before us are so rigid and love so much their own notions and do also so lightly esteem the opinions of others that let a man be never so godly, yet if he jumps not with them in all things, they thrust him quite out of their company."

MR. SAVE-ALL. "That's bad. But we read of some that are righteous overmuch and such men's rigidness prevails with them to judge and condemn all but themselves. But I pray what and how many were the things wherein you differed?'

BY-ENDS. "Why, they after their headstrong manner conclude that it is duty to rush on their journey all weathers, and I am for waiting for wind and tide. They are for hazarding all for God at a clap, and I am for taking all advantages to secure my life and estate. They are for holding their notions, though all other men are against them, but I am for religion in what, and so far as the times, and my safety will bear it. They are for religion, when in rags and contempt, but I am for him when he walks in his golden slippers in the sunshine and with applause."

———

GEORGE FOX

Journal

George Fox (1624-1691), the son of a weaver, already as a teenager found all the church groups he encountered unsatisfactory in various ways. After much searching, he eventually concluded that only the Inner Light of the living Christ provides a reliable guide to religious truth. That light was available to everyone within themselves — rich or poor, clergy or laity, men or women — and it spoke to Fox directly in the revelations he called "openings." He insisted that the church was the people who had seen the light, and did not need to rely on priests or the buildings he refused to call "churches" but described as "steeple-houses." Repeatedly arrested and persecuted, Fox founded the Society of Friends or "Quakers" (so called from the way they shook when in the midst of prayer). This passage from his *Journal* shows how directly and immediately Fox understood himself to be directed by calls from God.

About the beginning of the year 1646 . . . as I was walking in a field on a First-day morning, the Lord opened to me that being bred at Oxford or Cambridge was not enough to fit and qualify men to be ministers of Christ; and I stranged [wondered] at it, because it was the common belief of people. But I saw it clearly as the Lord opened it to me, and was satisfied, and admired the goodness of the Lord who had opened this thing unto me that morning. This struck at priest Stephens' ministry, namely, that to be bred at Oxford or Cambridge was not enough to make a man fit to be a minister of

George Fox, *Journal* (London: J. M. Dent, 1924), 5-7, 14-17, 39-40. Spelling slightly modernized.

Christ. But my relations were much troubled that I would not go with them to hear the priest; for I would get into the orchard, or the fields, with my Bible by myself. I asked them, "Did not the apostle say to believers, that 'they needed no man to teach them, but as the anointing teacheth them'?" (1 John 2:27). And though they knew this was Scripture, and that it was true, yet they would be grieved because I could not be subject in this matter, to go to hear the priest with them. I saw that to be a true believer was another thing than they looked upon it to be. So neither them, nor any of the Dissenting people, could I join with, but was as a stranger to all, relying wholly upon the Lord Jesus Christ.

At another time it was opened in me that God, who made the world, did not dwell in temples made with hands. This, at the first, seemed a strange word because both priests and people used to call their temples or churches dreadful places, holy ground, and the temples of God. But the Lord showed me, so that I did see clearly, that He did not dwell in these temples which men had commanded and set up, but in people's hearts: for both Stephen and the apostle Paul bore testimony, that He did not dwell in temples made with hands, not even in that which He had once commanded to be built, since He put an end to it; but that His people were His temple, and He dwelt in them. This opened in me as I walked in the fields to my relations' house. When I came there, they told me that Nathaniel Stephens, the priest, had been there, and told them he was afraid of me, for going after new lights. I smiled in myself knowing what the Lord had opened in me concerning him and his brethren; but I told not my relations, who, though they saw beyond the priests, yet they went to hear them, and were grieved because I would not go also. But I brought them Scriptures and told them there was an anointing within man to teach him, and that the Lord would teach His people Himself. I had also great openings concerning the things written in the Revelations; and when I spoke of them, the priests and professors would say that was a sealed-up book, and would have kept me out of it: but I told them Christ could open the seals, and that they were the nearest things to us; for the Epistles were written to the saints that lived in former ages, but the Revelations were written of things to come. . . .

In Leicestershire, as I was passing through the fields, I was moved to go to Leicester, and when I came there I heard of a great meeting for a dispute, wherein Presbyterians, Independents, Baptists, and Common-prayer-men were said to be all concerned. The meeting was in a steeple-house; and thither I was moved by the Lord God to go, and be among them. I heard their discourse and reasonings, some being in pews and the priest in the pulpit; abundance of people being gathered together. At last one woman asked a question out of Peter, what that birth was, viz., a being "born again of incorruptible seed, by the Word of God, that liveth and abideth for ever" (1 Pet. 1:23). And the priest said to her, "I permit not a woman to speak in the church" (1 Tim. 2:12); though he had before given liberty for any to speak. Whereupon I was wrapped up, as in a rapture, in the Lord's power; and I stepped up in a place and asked the priest, "Dost thou call this place a church? Or dost thou call this mixed multitude a church?" For the woman asking a question, he ought to have answered it, having given liberty for any to speak. But, instead of answering me, he asked me what a church was? I told him the Church was the pillar and ground of Truth (1 Tim. 3:15), made up of living stones, living members, a spiritual household, which Christ was the head of: but He was not the head of a mixed multitude or of an old house made up of lime, stones and wood. This set them all on fire. The priest came down out of his pulpit and others out of their pews, and the dispute there was marred. But I went to a great inn, and there disputed the thing with the priests and professors of all sorts; they were all on a fire. But I maintained the true Church, and the true head thereof, over the heads of them all, till they all gave out and fled away. And there was one man that seemed and appeared for a while to join with me; but he soon turned against me, and joined with a priest in pleading for infants' baptism, though he himself had been a Baptist before; so left me alone. Howbeit, there were several convinced that day; and the woman that asked the question was convinced, and her family; and the Lord's power and glory shined overall.

After this I returned into Nottinghamshire again, and went into the Vale of Beavor [Belvoir]. As I went, I preached repentance to people; and there were many convinced in the Vale of Beavor, in many towns; for I stayed some weeks among them. And one morning, as I was sitting by the fire, a great cloud came over me, and a temptation beset me; but I sat still. And it was said, "All things come by nature"; and the elements and stars came over me, so that I was in a manner quite clouded with it. But inasmuch as I sat still and silent, the people of the house perceived nothing. And as I sat still under it, and let it alone, a living hope arose in me, and a true voice, which said, "There is a living God who made all." And immediately the cloud and temptation vanished away, and life rose over it all; my heart was glad, and I praised the living God. After some time, I met with some people who had such a notion that there was no God, but that all things came by nature. I had a great dispute with them and overturned them and made some of them confess that there is a living God. Then I saw that it was good that I had gone through that exercise. We had great meetings in those parts, for the power of the Lord broke though in that side of the country. Returning into Nottinghamshire, I found there a company of shattered Baptists, and others; and the Lord's power wrought mightily, and gathered many of them. Afterwards I went to Mansfield and thereaway, where the Lord's power was wonderfully manifested both at Mansfield and other neighboring towns. In Derbyshire the mighty power of God wrought in a wonderful manner. At Eaton, a town near Derby, there was a meeting of Friends, where there was such a mighty power of God that they were greatly shaken, and many mouths were opened in the power of the Lord God. Many were moved by the Lord to go to steeple-houses, to the priests and to the people, to declare the everlasting truth unto them.

At a certain time, when I was at Mansfield, there was a sitting of the justices about hiring of servants; and it was upon me from the Lord to go and speak to the justices, that they should not oppress the servants in their wages. So I walked towards the inn where they sat; but finding a company of fiddlers there, I did not go in, but thought to come in the morning when I might have a more serious opportunity to discourse them, not thinking that a seasonable time. But when I came again in the morning, they were gone, and I was struck even blind that I could not see. I inquired of the innkeeper where the justices were to sit that day; and he told me, "At a town eight miles off." My sight began to come to me again; and I went and ran thitherward as fast as I could. When I was come to the house where they were and many servants with them, I exhorted the justices not to oppress the servants in their wages, but to do that which was right and just to them; and I exhorted the servants to do their duties, and serve honestly, &c. They all received my exhortation kindly, for I was moved of the Lord therein.

Moreover, I was moved to go to several Courts and steeple-houses at Mansfield and other places, to warn them to leave off oppression and oaths, and to turn from deceit and to turn to the Lord, and do justly. Particularly at Mansfield, after I had been at a Court there, I was moved to go and speak to one of the wickedest men in the country, one who was a common drunkard, a noted whore-master, and a rhymemaker; and I reproved him in the dread of the mighty God for his evil courses. When I had done speaking and left him, he came after me, and told me that he was so smitten when I spoke to him that he had scarcely any strength left in him. So this man was convinced, and turned from his wickedness, and remained an honest, sober man, to the astonishment of the people who had known him before. Thus the work of the Lord went forward, and many were turned from the darkness to the light within the compass of these three years 1646, 1647 and 1648.

Divers meetings of Friends, in several places, were then gathered to God's teaching, by His light, spirit and power; for the Lord's power broke forth more and more wonderfully.

Now was I come up in spirit through the flaming sword, into the paradise of God. All things were new; and all the creation had another smell unto me than before, beyond what words can utter. I knew nothing but pureness, and innocency, and righteousness, being renewed up into the image of God by Christ Jesus, to the state of Adam, which he was in before he fell. The creation was opened to me; and it was showed me how all things had their names given them according to their nature and virtue. I was at a stand in my mind whether I should practise physic [medicine] for the good of mankind, seeing the nature and virtues of the creatures were so opened to me by the Lord. But I was immediately taken up in spirit, to see into another or more steadfast state than Adam's in innocency, even into a state in Christ Jesus that should never fall. And the Lord showed me that such as were faithful to Him, in the power and light of Christ, should come up into that state in which Adam was before he fell; in which the admirable works of the creation, and the virtues thereof, may be known through the openings of that divine Word of wisdom and power by which they were made. Great things did the Lord lead me into; and wonderful depths were opened unto me beyond what can by words be declared; but as people come into subjection to the Spirit of God, and grow up in the image and power of the Almighty, they may receive the word of wisdom that opens all things, and come to know the hidden unity in the Eternal Being.

(Fox has been imprisoned for a time on account of his teaching, but is eventually released.)

Thus being set at liberty again, I went on, as before, in the work of the Lord; and as I was walking in a close with several Friends, I lifted up my head and espied three steeple-house spires, and they struck at my life. I asked them what place that was; and they said, Lichfield. Immediately the word of the Lord came to me that thither I must go. So, being come to the house we were going to, I bid Friends that were with me to walk into the house from me, saying nothing to them whither I was to go. As soon as they were gone I stepped away, and went by my eye over hedge and ditch till I came within a mile of Lichfield, where, in a great field, there were shepherds keeping their sheep. I was commanded by the Lord, of a sudden, to untie my shoes and put them off. I stood still for it was winter, and the word of the Lord was like a fire in me, so I put off my shoes and was commanded to give them to the shepherds, and was to charge them to let no one have them except they paid for them. The poor shepherds trembled and were astonished. Then I walked on about a mile till I came into the town, and as soon as I was got within the town the word of the Lord came to me again, to cry, "Woe unto the bloody city of Lichfield!" So I went up and down the streets, crying with a loud voice, "Woe to the bloody city of Lichfield!" It being market-day, I went into the marketplace, and to and fro in the several parts of it, and made stands, crying as before, "Woe to the bloody city of Lichfield!" And no one laid hands on me; but as I went thus crying through the streets, there seemed to me to be a channel of blood running down the streets, and the marketplace appeared like a pool of blood.

And so at least some Friends and friendly people came to me and said, "Alack, George, where are thy shoes?" I told them it was no matter.

Now when I had declared what was upon me, and cleared myself, I came out of the town in peace; and returning to the shepherds, gave them some money, and took my shoes of them again. But the fire of the Lord was so in my feet, and all over me, that I did not matter to put on my shoes any more, and was at a stand whether I should or no, till I felt freedom from the Lord so to do; and as at last I came to a ditch and washed my feet, I put on my shoes again. After this a deep consideration came upon me, why, or for what reason, I should be sent to cry against that city, and call it the bloody city. For though the Parliament had the minster one while, and the King another, and much blood had been shed in the town during the wars between them, yet that could not be charged upon the town. But afterwards I came to understand, that in the Emperor Diocletian's time [around 300] a thousand Christians were martyred in Lichfield, and, so I must go in my stockings through the channel of their blood, and into the pool of their blood in the marketplace, that I might raise up the memorial to the blood of those martyrs which had been shed above a thousand years before, and lay cold in their streets. So the sense of this blood was upon me, and I obeyed the word of the Lord. Ancient records testify how many of the Christian Britons suffered there. Much I could write of the sense I had of the blood of the martyrs that had been slain in this nation for the name of Christ, both under the ten persecutions and since; but I leave it to the Lord and to His book, out of which all shall be judged; for His book is a most true record, and His Spirit a true recorder.

GERRARD WINSTANLEY

A *Declaration from the Poor Oppressed People of England*

Gerrard Winstanley (1609-1676) was a tradesman in London until he went bankrupt during the English Civil War. Sometime in the 1640s he became a Baptist lay preacher and then, finding even Independent Baptists too limiting, set off on his own religious journey. In April of 1649 he and perhaps half a dozen others began to dig up the soil and plant crops on the common land at St. George's Hill in Surrey, south of London. The "common land" was in principle available for the use of all the people, but had come to be used exclusively for grazing animals, and often only the animals of the local lord. So the activity of the "Diggers" (also called "Levellers," since they wanted to level out the various social classes) was radical and controversial.

By June 1, when this "Declaration" was issued, it had forty-five signatures, and Digger communes had sprung up elsewhere in England. A warrant was issued for Winstanley's arrest, but he seems never actually to have been arrested, and he continued Digger agitating until the mid-1650s. The course of his later life is hard to document, though it is known that he eventually became a Quaker. Amid those who were using religious ideas of vocation to support the current order of things, it is worth remembering that others found a Christian calling to try to make radical changes in the social order.

We whose names are subscribed, do in the name of all the poor oppressed people in England, declare unto you, that call yourselves Lords of Manors and Lords of the Land, that in regard the King of Righteousness, our Maker, hath enlightened our hearts so far as to see that the earth was not made pur-

Gerrard Winstanley, *The Works of Gerrard Winstanley*, ed. George H. Sabine (New York: Russell & Russell Inc., 1965), 269-72.

posely for you to be Lords of it, and we to be your slaves, servants, and beggars; but it was made to be a common livelihood to all, without respect of persons. And that your buying and selling of land and the fruits of it, one to another, is the cursed thing and was brought in by war, which hath, and still does establish murder and theft in the hands of some branches of mankind over others, which is the greatest outward burden and unrighteous power that the creation groans under. For the power of enclosing land and owning property was brought into the creation by your ancestors by the sword; which first did murder their fellow creatures, men, and after plunder or steal away their land, and left this land successively to you, their children. And therefore, though you did not kill or thieve, yet you hold that cursed thing in your hand by the power of the sword; and so you justify the wicked deeds of your fathers, and that sin of your fathers shall be visited upon the head of you and your children to the third and fourth generation, and longer too, till your bloody and thieving power be rooted out of the land.

And further, in regard the King of Righteousness hath made us sensible of our burdens, and the cries and groanings of our hearts are come before him. We take it as a testimony of love from him that our hearts begin to be freed from slavish fear of men, such as you are, and that we find resolutions in us, grounded upon the inward law of love, one towards another: to dig and plough up the commons and wastelands through England; and that our conversation shall be so unblameable that your laws shall not reach to oppress us any longer, unless you by your laws will shed the innocent blood that runs in our veins.

For though you and your ancestors got your property by murder and theft, and you keep it by the same power from us, that have an equal right to the land with you, by the righteous law of creation, yet we shall have no occasion of quarreling (as you do) about that disturbing devil, called particular property. For the earth, with all her fruits of corn, cattle, and such like, was made to be a common storehouse of livelihood to all mankind, friend and foe, without exception.

And to prevent all your scrupulous objections, know this: That we must neither buy nor sell. Money must not any longer (after our work of the earth's community is advanced) be the great god that hedges in some and hedges out others, for money is but part of the earth. And surely, the Righteous Creator who is King did never ordain that unless some of mankind do bring that mineral (silver and gold) in their hands to others of their own kind, that they should neither be fed nor be clothed; no, surely, for this was the project of Tyrant-flesh (which landlords are branches of) to set his image upon money. And they make this unrighteous law, that none should buy or sell, eat, or be clothed, or have any comfortable livelihood among men, unless they did bring his image stamped upon gold or silver in their hands....

For after our work of the earthly community is advanced, we must make use of gold and silver as we do of other metals, but not to buy and sell withal; for buying and selling is the great cheat that robs and steals the earth one from another. It is that which makes some Lords, others beggars; some rulers, others to be ruled; and makes great murderers and thieves to be imprisoners, and hangers of little ones, or of sincere-hearted men.

And while we are made to labor the earth together, with one consent and willing mind; and while we are made free, that everyone, friend and foe, shall enjoy the benefit of their creation, that is, to have food and raiment from the earth, their mother; and everyone subject to give account of those thoughts, words and actions to none, but to the one only righteous Judge and Prince of Peace, the Spirit of Righteousness that dwells, and that is now rising up to rule in every creature, and in the whole globe. We say, while we are made to hinder no man of his privileges given him in his creation, equal to one, as to another; what law then can you make to take hold upon us, but laws of oppression and tyranny that shall enslave or spill the blood of the innocent? And so yourselves, your judges, lawyers, and justices, shall be found to be the greatest transgressors, in and over mankind.

But to draw nearer to declare our meaning, what we would have, and what we shall endeavor to the uttermost to obtain, as moderate and righteous reason directs us, seeing we are made to see our privileges, given us in our creation, which have hitherto been denied to us and our fathers, since the power of the sword began to rule, and the secrets of the creation have been locked up under the traditional, parrot-like speaking, from the universities and colleges for scholars. And since the power of the murdering, and thieving sword, formerly, as well as now of late years, hath set up a government and maintains that government, for what are prisons and putting others to death by the power of the sword, to enforce people to that government which was got by conquest and sword, and cannot stand of itself, but by the same murdering power? . . .

And seeing further, the power of righteousness in our hearts, seeking the livelihood of others, as well as ourselves, hath drawn forth our bodies to begin to dig and plough in the commons and wasteland, for the reasons already declared, And seeing and finding ourselves poor, wanting food to feed upon while we labor the earth, to cast in seed and to wait till the first crop comes up, and wanting ploughs, carts, corn, and such materials to plant the commons withal, we are willing to declare our condition to you, and to all, that have the treasury of the earth locked up in your bags, chests, and barns, and will offer up nothing to this public treasury; but will rather see your fellow-creatures starve for want of bread, that have an equal right to it with yourselves, by the law of creation. But this by the way we only declare to you, and to all that follow the subtle art of buying and selling the earth with her fruits, merely to get the treasury thereof into their hands, to lock it up from them, to whom it belongs, that so, such covetous, proud, unrighteous, selfish flesh may be left without excuse in the day of judgment.

And therefore, the main thing we aim at, and for which we declare our resolutions to go forth and act, is this: To lay hold upon, and, as we stand in need, to cut and fell, and make the best advantage we can of the woods and trees that grow upon the commons; To be a stock for ourselves, and our poor brethren through the land of England; To plant the Commons withal and to provide us bread to eat, till the fruit of our labors in the earth bring forth increase; and we shall meddle with none of your Properties (but what is called Commonage) till the Spirit in you make you cast up your lands and goods, which were got, and still is kept in your hands by murder and theft, and then we shall take it from the Spirit that hath conquered you, and not from our swords, which is an abominable, and unrighteous power and a destroyer of the Creation. But the Son of Man comes not to destroy, but to save.

WILLIAM LAW

A Serious Call to a Devout and Holy Life

William Law (1686-1761) seemed destined to a successful academic career at Cambridge until he refused to take the oath of allegiance when George I came to the throne; "Non-jurors" like Law held that the descendents of the Stuart line going back to James II remained kings of England, and believed that taking the oath of allegiance to more recent kings violated an earlier oath. By this refusal Law came to be ineligible to hold any official position. He served for a time as a tutor to the son of a wealthy family and

William Law, *A Serious Call to a Devout and Holy Life* (London: Macmillan, 1898), 29-36.

then retired to his hometown, where he was eventually joined by two women in a small, informal religious community. They lived a life of great simplicity and gave most of their money to support local schools and other charities. Although Law was denied the right to preach, they faithfully attended their local parish. Law supplies an interesting corrective to the Puritan commitment to hard work in one's calling. One of his favorite devices was to invent imaginary characters whose behavior illustrated the flaws of a whole class of people — the discussion of "Calidus" in this excerpt is one example.

Chapter IV

We can please God in no state or employment of life, but by intending and devoting it all to His honor and glory.

Having in the first chapter stated the general nature of devotion, and shown that it implies not any form of prayer, but a certain form of life that is offered to God, not at any particular times or places, but everywhere and in everything; I shall now descend to some particulars, and show how we are to devote our labor and employment, our time and fortunes, unto God.

As a good Christian should consider every place as holy because God is there, so he should look upon every part of his life as a matter of holiness because it is to be offered unto God.

The profession of a clergyman is a holy profession because it is a ministration in holy things, an attendance at the altar. But worldly business is to be made holy unto the Lord, by being done as a service to Him, and in conformity to His Divine will.

For as all men, and all things in the world, as truly belong unto God, as any places, things, or persons that are devoted to Divine service, so all things are to be used, and all persons are to act in their several states and employments, for the glory of God.

Men of worldly business, therefore, must not look upon themselves as at liberty to live to themselves, to sacrifice to their own humors and tempers, because their employment is of a worldly nature. But they must consider, that, as the world and all worldly professions as truly belong to God, as persons and things that are devoted to the altar, so it is as much the duty of men in worldly business to live wholly unto God, as it is the duty of those who are devoted to Divine service.

As the whole world is God's, so the whole world is to act for God. As all men have the same relation to God, as all men have all their powers and faculties from God, so all men are obliged to act for God, with all their powers and faculties.

As all things are God's, so all things are to be used and regarded as the things of God. For men to abuse things on earth, and live to themselves, is the same rebellion against God, as for angels to abuse things in Heaven; because God is just the same Lord of all on earth, as He is the Lord of all in Heaven.

Things may, and must differ in their use, but yet they are all to be used according to the will of God.

Men may, and must differ in their employments, but yet they must all act for the same ends, as dutiful servants of God, in the right and pious performance of their several callings.

Clergymen must live wholly unto God in one particular way, that is, in the exercise of holy offices, in the ministration of prayers and sacraments, and a zealous distribution of spiritual goods.

But men of other employments are, in their particular ways, as much obliged to act as the servants of God, and live wholly unto Him in their several callings. This is the only difference between clergymen and people of other callings.

When it can be shown that men might be vain, covetous, sensual, worldly-minded, or proud in the exercise of their worldly business, then it will be allowable for clergymen to indulge the same tempers in their sacred profession. For though these tempers are most odious and most criminal in clergymen, who, besides their baptismal vow, have a second time devoted themselves to God, to be His servants, not in the common offices of human life, but in the spiritual service of the most holy sacred things, and who are therefore to keep themselves as separate and different from the common life of other men, as a church or an altar is to be kept separate from houses and tables of common use; yet as all Christians are by their baptism devoted to God, and made professors of holiness, so are they all in their several callings to live as holy and heavenly persons; doing everything in their common life only in such a manner as it may be received by God, as a service done to Him. For things spiritual and temporal, sacred and common, must, like men and angels, like Heaven and earth, all conspire in the glory of God.

As there is but one God and Father of us all, whose glory gives light and life to everything that lives, whose presence fills all places, whose power supports all beings, whose providence ruleth all events; so everything that lives, whether in Heaven or earth, whether they be thrones or principalities, men or angels, they must all, with one spirit, live wholly to the praise and glory of this one God and Father of them all. Angels as angels, in their heavenly ministrations; but men as men, women as women, bishops as bishops, priests as priests, and deacons as deacons; some with things spiritual, and some with things temporal, offering to God the daily sacrifice of a reasonable life, wise actions, purity of heart, and heavenly affections.

This is the common business of all persons in this world. It is not left to any women in the world to trifle away their time in the follies and impertinences of a fashionable life, nor to any men to resign themselves up to worldly cares and concerns; it is not left to the rich to gratify their passions in the indulgences and pride of life, nor to the poor to vex and torment their hearts with the poverty of their state; but men and women, rich and poor, must, with bishops and priests, walk before God in the same wise and holy spirit, in the same denial of all vain tempers, and in the same discipline and care of their souls; not only because they have all the same rational nature, and are servants of the same God, but because they all want the same holiness, to make them fit for the same happiness, to which they are all called. It is therefore absolutely necessary for all Christians, whether men or women, to consider themselves as persons that are devoted to holiness, and so order their common ways of life, by such rules of reason and piety, as may turn it into continual service unto Almighty God.

Now to make our labor or employment an acceptable service unto God, we must carry it on with the same spirit and temper that is required in giving of alms, or any work of piety. For, if "whether we eat or drink, or whatsoever we do," we must "do all to the glory of God" (1 Cor. 10:31); if "we are to use this world as if we used it not"; if we are to "present our bodies a living sacrifice, holy, acceptable to God" (Rom. 12:1); if "we are to live by faith, and not by sight," and to "have our conversation in heaven" (2 Cor. 5:7; Phil. 3:20); then it is necessary that the common way of our life, in every state, be made to glorify God by such tempers as make our prayers and adorations acceptable to Him. For if we are worldly or earthly-minded in our employments, if they are carried on with vain desires and covetous tempers, only to satisfy ourselves, we can no more be said to live to the glory of God than gluttons and drunkards can be said to eat and drink to the glory of God.

As the glory of God is one and the same thing, so whatever we do suitable to it must be done with one and the same spirit. That same state and temper of mind which makes our alms and devotions acceptable, must also make our labor or employment a proper offering unto God. If a man labors to be rich, and pursues his business, that he may raise himself to a state of figure and glory in the world, he is no longer serving God in his employ-ment; he is acting under other masters, and has no more title to a reward from God than he that gives alms that he may be seen, or prays that he may be heard of men. For vain and earthly desires are no more allowable in our employments than in our alms and devotions. For these tempers of worldly pride, and vain-glory, are not only evil, when they mix with our good works, but they have the same evil nature, and make us odious to God, when they enter into the common business of our employment. If it were allowable to indulge covetous or vain passions in our worldly employments, it would then be allowable to be vain-glorious in our devotions. But as our alms and devotions are not an acceptable service, but when they proceed from a heart truly devoted to God, so our common employment cannot be reckoned a service to Him, but when it is performed with the same temper and piety of heart.

Most of the employments of life are in their own nature lawful, and all those that are so may be made a substantial part of our duty to God, if we engage in them only so far, and for such ends, as are suitable to beings that are to live above the world, all the time that they live in the world. This is the only measure of our application to any worldly business, let it be what it will, where it will; it must have no more of our hands, our hearts, or our time than is consistent with a hearty, daily, careful preparation of ourselves for another life. For as all Christians as such have renounced this world, to prepare themselves by daily devotion, and universal holiness, for an eternal state of quite another nature, they must look upon worldly employments, as upon worldly wants and bodily infirmities; things not to be desired but only to be endured and suffered, till death and the resurrection have carried us to an eternal state of real happiness.

Now he that does not look at the things of this life in this degree of little-ness, cannot be said either to feel or believe the greatest truths of Christian-ity. For if he thinks anything great or important in human business, can he be said to feel or believe those Scriptures, which represent this life and the greatest things of life, as bubbles, vapors, dreams, and shadows?

If he thinks figure, and show, and worldly glory, to be any proper happi-ness of a Christian, how can he be said to feel or believe this doctrine, "Blessed are ye when men shall hate you, and when they shall separate you from their company, and shall reproach you, and cast out your name as evil, for the Son of man's sake" (Luke 6:22)? For surely, if there was any real hap-piness in figure, and show, and worldly glory; if these things deserved our thoughts and care; it could not be matter of the highest joy, when we are torn from them by persecutions and sufferings. If, therefore, a man will so live, as to show that he feels and believes the most fundamental doctrines of Christianity, he must live above the world; this is the temper that must enable him to do the business of life, and yet live wholly unto God, and to go through some worldly employment with a heavenly mind. And it is as necessary that people live in their employments with this temper, as it is necessary that their employment itself be lawful.

The husbandman that tills the ground is employed in an honest business that is necessary in life and very capable of being made an acceptable service unto God. But if he labors and toils, not to serve any reasonable ends of life, but in order to have his plough made of silver, and to have his horses harnessed in gold, the honesty of his employment is lost as to him, and his labor becomes his folly.

A tradesman may justly think that it is agreeable to the will of God for him to sell such things as are innocent and useful in life, such as help both himself and others to a reasonable support, and enable them to assist those that want to be assisted. But if, instead of this, he trades only with regard to himself, without any other rule than that of his own temper; if it be his chief end in it to grow rich, that he may live in figure and indulgence, and to be able to retire from business to idleness and luxury; his trade, as to him, loses all its innocence, and is so far from being an acceptable service to God that it is only a more plausible course of covetousness, self-love, and ambition. For such a one turns the necessities of employment into pride and covetousness, just as the drunk and epicure turn the necessities of eating and drinking into gluttony and drunkenness. Now he that is up early and late, that sweats and labors for these ends, that he may be some time or other rich, and live in pleasure and indulgence, lives no more to the glory of God than he that plays and games for the same ends. For though there is a great difference between trading and gaming, yet most of that difference is lost when men once trade with the same desires and tempers, and for the same ends, that others game. Charity and fine dressing are things very different; but if men give alms for the same reasons that others dress fine, only to be seen and admired, charity is then but like the vanity of fine clothes. In like manner, if the same motives make some people painful and industrious in their trades which make others constant at gaming, such pains are but like the pains of gaming.

Calidus [Law here invents a name for an imaginary typical character; the name means "eager" or "hasty" in Latin] has traded above thirty years in the greatest city of the kingdom; he has been so many years constantly increasing his trade and his fortune. Every hour of the day is with him an hour of business; and though he eats and drinks very heartily, yet every meal seems to be in a hurry, and he would say grace if he had time. Calidus ends every day at the tavern, but has not leisure to be there till near nine o'clock. He is always forced to drink a good hearty glass, to drive thoughts of business out of his head, and make his spirits drowsy enough for sleep. He does business all the time that he is rising, and has settled several matters before he can get to his counting-room. His prayers are a short ejaculation or two, which he never misses in stormy, tempestuous weather, because he has always something or other at sea. Calidus will tell you, with great pleasure, that he has been in this hurry for so many years, and that it must have killed him long ago, but that it has been a rule with him to get out of the town every Saturday, and make the Sunday a day of quiet, and good refreshment in the country.

He is now so rich that he would leave off his business, and amuse his old age with building, and furnishing a fine house in the country, but that he is afraid he should grow melancholy if he was to quit his business. He will tell you, with great gravity, that it is a dangerous thing for a man that has been used to get money, ever to leave it off. If thoughts of religion happen at any time to steal into his head, Calidus contents himself with thinking that he never was a friend to heretics, and infidels, that he has always been civil to the minister of his parish, and very often given something to the charity schools.

Now this way of life is at such a distance from all the doctrine and discipline of Christianity that no one can live in it through ignorance or frailty. Calidus can no more imagine that he is "born again of the Spirit" (John 3:6); that he is "in Christ a new creature"; that he lives here as a stranger and a pilgrim (1 Pet. 2:11); setting his affections on things above, and laying up treasures in heaven (Col. 3:1) — he can no more imagine this than he can think that he has been all his life an Apostle working miracles, and preaching the Gospel.

It must also be owned, that the generality of trading people, especially in great towns, are too much like Calidus. You see them all the week buried in business, unable to think of anything else; and then spending the Sunday in idleness and refreshment, in wandering into the country, in such visits and jovial meetings, as make it often the worst day of the week.

Now they do not live thus, because they cannot support themselves with less care and application to business; but they live thus because they want to grow rich in their trades, and to maintain their families in some such figure and degree of finery, as a reasonable Christian life has no occasion for. Take away but this temper, and then people of all trades will find themselves at leisure to live every day like Christians, to be careful of every duty of the Gospel, to live in a visible course of religion, and be every day strict observers both of private and public prayer.

Now the only way to do this is for people to consider their trade as something that they are obliged to devote to the glory of God, something that they are to do only in such a manner as that they may make it a duty to Him. Nothing can be right in business that is not under these rules. The Apostle commands servants to be obedient to their masters "in singleness of heart, as unto Christ. Not with eye-service, as men-pleasers; but as the servants of Christ, doing the will of God from the heart; with good will doing service, as unto the Lord, and not to men" (Eph. 6:5; Col. 3:22, 23).

JONATHAN EDWARDS

Personal Narrative

Jonathan Edwards (1703-1758) grew up on the New England frontier, the son of a Congregationalist minister. As pastor at Northampton, Massachusetts, he led a revival in 1734-1735 that anticipated the Great Awakening that would sweep the English colonies in North America in the 1740s. Edwards defended revivalism, as well as the absolute sovereignty of God (then under criticism from those who said that human free will must also play a part in our salvation), but he drew on new philosophical ideas from John Locke and Isaac Newton to do so. Few Christians have brought Edwards' level of psychological insight to the analysis of conversion. He believed in dramatic moments of transformation, but, as the account of his own life here indicates, he was also convinced that a Christian life usually involves more than one transforming experience.

Jonathan Edwards, *Personal Narrative*, in *Jonathan Edwards: Basic Writings*, ed. Ola Elizabeth Winslow (New York: Signet, 1966), 81-82, 83-86, 94-96. Punctuation updated somewhat.

I had a variety of concerns and exercises about my soul from my childhood; but had two more remarkable seasons of awakening, before I met with that change by which I was brought to those new dispositions, and that new sense of things, that I have since had. The first time was when I was a boy, some years before I went to college, at a time of remarkable awakening in my father's congregation. I was then very much affected for many months, and concerned about the things of religion, and my soul's salvation, and was abundant in duties. I used to pray five times a day in secret, and to spend much time in religious talk with other boys; and used to meet with them to pray together. I experienced I know not what kind of delight in religion. My mind was much engaged in it, and had much self-righteous pleasure; and it was my delight to abound in religious duties. I with some of my schoolmates joined together, and built a booth in a swamp, in a very retired spot, for a place of prayer. And besides, I had particular secret places of my own in the woods, where I used to retire by myself; and was from time to time much affected. My affections seemed to be lively and easily moved, and I seemed to be in my element when engaged in religious duties. And I am ready to think, many are deceived with such affections, and such a kind of delight as I then had in religion, and mistake it for grace.

But in process of time, my convictions and affections wore off; and I entirely lost all those affections and delights and left off secret prayer, at least as to any constant performance of it; and returned like a dog to his vomit, and went on in the ways of sin. Indeed, I was at times very uneasy, especially towards the latter part of my time at college, when it pleased God to seize me with a pleurisy; in which he brought me nigh to the grave, and shook me over the pit of hell. And yet, it was not long after my recovery before I fell again into my old ways of sin. But God would not suffer me to go on with any quietness; I had great and violent inward struggles till, after many conflicts with wicked inclinations, repeated resolutions, and bonds that I laid myself under by a kind of vows to God, I was brought wholly to break off all former wicked ways, and all ways of known outward sin; and to apply myself to seek salvation, and practice many religious duties; but without that kind of affection and delight which I had formerly experienced. My concern now wrought more by inward struggles and conflicts, and self-reflections. . . .

The first instance that I remember of that sort of inward, sweet delight in God and divine things that I have lived much in since, was on reading those words, 1 Timothy 1:17, *Now unto the King eternal, immortal, invisible, the only wise God, be honor and glory for ever and ever, Amen.* As I read the words, there came into my soul, and was as it were diffused through it, a sense of the glory of the Divine Being; a new sense, quite different from anything I ever experienced before. Never any words of scripture seemed to me as these words did. I thought with myself, how excellent a Being that was, and how happy I should be, if I might enjoy that God, and be rapt up to him in heaven, and be as it were swallowed up in him forever! I kept saying, and as it were singing over these words of scripture to myself; and went to pray to God that I might enjoy him, and prayed in a manner quite different from what I used to do, with a new sort of affection. But it never came into my thought that there was any thing spiritual, or of a saving nature in this.

From about that time, I began to have new kinds of apprehensions and ideas of Christ, and the work of redemption, and the glorious way of salvation by him. An inward, sweet sense of these things, at times, came into my heart; and my soul was led away in pleasant views and contemplations of them. And my mind was greatly engaged to spend my time in reading and meditating on Christ, on the beauty and excellency of his person, and the lovely way of salvation by free grace in him. I found no books so delightful to me, as those that treated of these subjects. Those words, Canticles [Song of Solomon] 2:1, used to be abundantly with me, *I am the Rose of Sharon, and the Lily of the valley.* The words seemed to me sweetly to represent the loveliness and beauty of Jesus Christ. The whole book of Canticles used to be pleasant to me, and I used to be much in reading it about that time; and found, from time to time, an inward sweetness that would carry me away in my contemplations. This I know not how to express otherwise, than by a calm, sweet abstraction of soul from all the concerns of this world; and sometimes a kind of vision, or fixed ideas and imaginations, of being alone in the mountains, or some solitary wilderness, far from all mankind, sweetly conversing with Christ, and wrapt and swallowed up in God. The sense I had of divine things would often of a sudden kindle up, as it were, a sweet burning in my heart; an ardor of soul that I know not how to express.

Not long after I first began to experience these things, I gave an account to my father of some things that had passed in my mind. I was pretty much affected by the discourse we had together; and when the discourse was ended, I walked abroad alone, in a solitary place in my father's pasture, for contemplation. And as I was walking there, and looking up on the sky and clouds, there came into my mind so sweet a sense of the glorious *majesty* and *grace* of God that I know not how to express. I seemed to see them both in a sweet conjunction, majesty and meekness joined together; it was a sweet, and gentle, and holy majesty; and also a majestic meekness; an awful sweetness; a high, and great, and holy gentleness.

After this my sense of divine things gradually increased, and became more and more lively, and had more of that inward sweetness. The appearance of every thing was altered; there seemed to be, as it were, a calm sweet cast, or appearance of divine glory, in almost every thing. God's excellency, his wisdom, his purity and love, seemed to appear in every thing; in the sun, moon, and stars; in the clouds and blue sky; in the grass, flowers, trees; in the water, and all nature; which used greatly to fix my mind. I often used to sit and view the moon for continuance; and in the day, spent much time in viewing the clouds and sky, to behold the sweet glory of God in these things; in the meantime, singing forth, with a low voice, my contemplations of the Creator and Redeemer. And scarce any thing, among all the works of nature, was so sweet to me as thunder and lightning; formerly, nothing had been so terrible to me. Before, I used to be uncommonly terrified with thunder, and to be struck with terror when I saw a thunder storm rising; but now, on the contrary, it rejoiced me. I felt God, so to speak, at the first appearance of a thunderstorm; and used to take the opportunity, at such times, to fix myself in order to view the clouds, and see the lightnings play, and hear the majestic and awful voice of God's thunder, which oftentimes was exceedingly entertaining, leading me to sweet contemplations of my great and glorious God. While thus engaged, it always seemed natural to me to sing or chant for my meditations; or, to speak my thoughts in soliloquies with a singing voice.

I felt then great satisfaction, as to my good state; but that did not content me. I had vehement longings of soul after God and Christ, and after more holiness, wherewith my heart seemed to be full, and ready to break; which often brought to my mind the words of the Psalmist, Psalm 119:28: *My soul breaketh for the longing it hath.* I often felt a mourning and lamenting in my heart, that I had not turned to God sooner, that I might have had more time to grow in grace. My mind was greatly fixed on divine things; almost perpetually in the contemplation of them. I spent most of my time in thinking of divine things, year after year; often walking alone in the woods, and solitary places, for meditation, soliloquy, and prayer, and converse with God; and it was always my manner, at such times, to sing forth my contemplations. I was almost constantly in ejaculatory prayer, wherever I was. Prayer seemed to be natural to me, as the breath by which the inward burnings of my heart had vent. The delights which I now felt in the things of religion were of an exceeding different kind from those before mentioned, that I had when a boy; and what I then had no more notion of, than one born blind has of pleasant and beautiful colors. They were of a more inward, pure, soul animating and refreshing nature. Those former delights never reached the heart; and did not arise from any sight of the divine excellency of the things of God; or any taste of the soul-satisfying and life-giving good there is in them. . . .

Often, since I lived in this town, I have had very affecting views of my own sinfulness and vileness; very frequently to such a degree as to hold me in a kind of loud weeping, sometimes for a considerable time together; so that I have often been forced to shut myself up. I have had a vastly greater sense of my own wickedness, and the badness of my heart, than ever I had before my conversion. It has often appeared to me, that if God should mark iniquity against me, I should appear the very worst of all mankind; of all that have been, since the beginning of the world to this time; and that I should have by far the lowest place in hell. When others, that have come to talk with me about their soul concerns, have expressed the sense they have had of their own wickedness, by saying that it seemed to them that they were as bad as the devil himself, I thought their expressions seemed exceeding faint and feeble to represent my wickedness.

My wickedness, as I am in myself, has long appeared to me perfectly ineffable, and swallowing up all thought and imagination; like an infinite deluge, or mountain over my head. I know not how to express better what my sins appear to me to be, than by heaping infinite upon infinite, and multiplying infinite by infinite. Very often, for these many years, these expressions are in my mind, and in my mouth, "Infinite upon infinite . . . Infinite upon infinite!" When I look into my heart, and take a view of my wickedness, it looks like an abyss infinitely deeper than hell. And it appears to me that, were it not for free grace, exalted and raised up to the infinite height of all the fullness and glory of the great Jehovah, and the arm of his power and grace stretched forth in all the majesty of his power, and in all the glory of his sovereignty, I should appear sunk down in my sins below hell itself; far beyond the sight of every thing but the eye of sovereign grace, that can pierce even down to such a depth. And yet it seems to me, that my conviction of sin is exceeding small, and faint; it is enough to amaze me, that I have no more sense of my sin. I know certainly, that I have very little sense of my sinfulness. When I have had turns of weeping and crying for my sins, I thought I knew at the time that my repentance was nothing to my sin.

I have greatly longed of late, for a broken heart, and to lie low before God; and, when I ask for humility, I cannot bear the thoughts of being no more humble than other Christians. It seems to me, that though their degrees of humility may be suitable for them, yet it would be a vile self-exaltation in me, not to be the lowest in humility of all mankind. Others speak of their longing to be "humbled to the dust"; that may be a proper expression for them, but I always think of myself, that I ought, and it is an expression that has long been natural for me to use in prayer, "to lie infinitely low before God." And it is affecting to think how ignorant I was when a young Christian, of the bottomless, infinite depths of wickedness, pride, hypocrisy and deceit, left in my heart.

I have a much greater sense of my universal, exceeding dependence on God's grace and strength, and mere good pleasure of late than I [had]; and have experienced more of an abhorrence of my own righteousness. The very thought of any joy arising in me, on any consideration of my own amiableness, performances, or experiences, or any goodness of heart or life, is nauseous and detestable to me. And yet I am greatly afflicted with a proud and self-righteous spirit, much more sensibly than I used to be formerly. I see that serpent rising and putting forth its head continually, every where, all around me.

Though it seems to me that, in some respects, I was a far better Christian for two or three years after my first conversion than I am now; and lived in a more constant delight and pleasure; yet of late years I have had a more full and constant sense of the absolute sovereignty of God, and a delight in that sovereignty, and have had more of a sense of the glory of Christ, as a Mediator revealed in the gospel. On one Saturday night, in particular, I had such a discovery of the excellency of the gospel above all other doctrines, that I could not but say to myself, "This is my chosen light, my chosen doctrine"; and of Christ, "This is my chosen Prophet." It appeared sweet, beyond all expression, to follow Christ, and to be taught, and enlightened, and instructed by him; to learn of him, and live to him. Another Saturday night (January 1739) I had such a sense, how sweet and blessed a thing it was to walk in the way of duty, to do that which was right and meet to be done and agreeable to the holy mind of God, that it caused me to break forth into a kind of loud weeping, which held me some time, so that I was forced to shut myself up, and fasten the doors. I could not but, as it were, cry out, "How happy are they which do that which is right in the sight of God! They are blessed indeed, they are the happy ones!" I had at the same time a very affecting sense, how meet and suitable it was that God should govern the world, and order all things according to his own pleasure; and I rejoiced in it, that God reigned, and that his will was done.

~~~~~

JOHN WESLEY

Journal

John Wesley (1703-1791), son of a rector in the Church of England, already while studying at Oxford gathered around him a group of friends who came to be called, among other things, "Methodists" because of their methodical approach to religious observance. They devoted themselves to systematic prayer and good works and became surprisingly controversial, in part because their high standard of piety constituted a critique of the rest of the Church of England.

After an unsuccessful missionary trip to Georgia, Wesley had a conversion experience in which he famously found his heart "strangely warmed" and began a remarkable career of preaching. When pastors refused to let him preach in their churches, he preached in the fields to the poor, achieving great success among classes the Church of England had generally ignored. Although Wesley himself never officially left the Church of England, the Methodist movement was already strong and widespread by the time of his death.

The introductory letter to Wesley's *Journals* contains the clearest account of the beginnings of the Methodist movement. The occasion for the letter (and its surprising opening) was the rumor that the fasting Wesley encouraged had contributed to the death of one already ill young man who had joined the movement. Worried at the damage the rumor might do his reputation, Wesley wrote the young man's father, and later included the letter as an introduction to the *Journals* to describe his time at Oxford, before the record of the *Journals* themselves begins. This selection is followed by excerpts from two characteristic sermons.

═══════

John Wesley, "Introductory Letter to the Journals," in *The Works of John Wesley* (Grand Rapids: Baker, 2002), 1:5-10, 11-12.

Introductory Letter

Oxford, Oct. 18th, 1732.

Sir,

The occasion of my giving you this trouble is of a very extraordinary nature. On Sunday last I was informed (as no doubt you will be ere long) that my brother and I had killed your son: That the rigorous fasting which he had imposed upon himself, by our advice, had increased his illness and hastened his death. Now though, considering it in itself, "it is a very small thing with me to be judged by man's judgment"; yet as being thought guilty of so mischievous an imprudence might make me the less able to do the work I came into the world for, I am obliged to clear myself of it, by observing to you, as I have done to others, that your son left off fasting about a year and a half since; and that it is not yet half a year since I began to practice it.

I must not let this opportunity slip of doing my part towards giving you a juster notion of some other particulars, relating both to him and myself, which have been industriously misrepresented to you. . . .

In November, 1729, at which time I came to reside at Oxford, your son, my brother, myself, and one more, agreed to spend three or four evenings in a week together. Our design was to read over the classics, which we had before read in private, on common nights, and on Sunday some book in divinity. In the summer following, Mr. M. told me he had called at the gaol [jail] to see a man who was condemned for killing his wife; and that, from the talk he had with one of the debtors, he verily believed it would do much good, if anyone would be at the pains of now and then speaking with them. This he so frequently repeated, that on the 24th of August, 1730, my brother and I walked with him to the castle [then used as a jail]. We were so well satisfied with our conversation there that we agreed to go thither once or twice a week; which we had not done long before he desired me to go with him to see a poor woman in the town who was sick. In this employment too, when we came to reflect upon it, we believed it would be worthwhile to spend an hour or two in a week; provided the Minister of the parish, in which any such person was, were not against it. . . .

In pursuance of these directions, I immediately went to Mr. Gerard, the Bishop of Oxford's Chaplain, who was likewise the person that took care of the prisoners when any were condemned to die. (At other times they were left to their own care.) I proposed to him our design of serving them as far as we could, and my own intention to preach there once a month, if the Bishop approved of it. He much commended our design, and said he would answer for the Bishop's approbation, to whom he would take the first opportunity of mentioning it. It was not long before he informed me he had done so, and that his Lordship not only gave his permission, but was greatly pleased with the undertaking, and hoped it would have the desired success. . . .

Upon this encouragement we still continued to meet together as usual; and to confirm one another, as well as we could, in our resolutions, to communicate as often as we had opportunity (which is here once a week); and do what service we could to our acquaintance, the prisoners, and two or three poor families in the town. But the outcry daily increasing, that we might show what ground there was for it, we proposed to our friends, or opponents, as we had opportunity, these or the like questions:

I. Whether it does not concern all men of all conditions to imitate Him, as much as they can, "who went about doing good" (Acts 10:38)?

Whether all Christians are not concerned in that command, "While we have time, let us do good to all men" (Gal. 6:10)?

Whether we shall not be more happy hereafter, the more good we do now?

Whether we can be happy at all hereafter, unless we have, according to our power, "fed the hungry, clothed the naked, visited those that are sick, and in prison" (Matt. 25:35-36); and made all these actions subservient to a higher purpose, even the saving of souls from death?

Whether it be not our bounden duty always to remember, that He did more for us than we can do for him, who assures us, "Inasmuch as ye have done it unto one of the least of these my brethren, ye have done it unto me"? (Matt. 25:45). . .

I do not remember that we met with any person who answered any of these questions in the negative; or who even doubted, whether it were not lawful to apply to this use that time and money which we should else have spent in other diversions. But several we met with who increased our little stock of money for the prisoners and the poor, by subscribing something quarterly to it; so that the more persons we proposed our designs to, the more we were confirmed in the belief of their innocence, and the more determined to pursue them, in spite of the ridicule, which increased fast upon us during the winter. . . .

Almost as soon as we had made our first attempts this way, some of the men of wit in Christ Church [this and Merton are colleges at Oxford] entered the lists against us; and, between mirth and anger, made pretty many reflections upon the Sacramentarians, as they were pleased to call us. Soon after, their allies at Merton changed our title, and did us the honor of styling us The Holy Club. But most of them being persons of well-known characters, they had not the good fortune to gain any proselytes from the sacrament, till a gentleman, eminent for learning, and well esteemed for piety, joining them, told his nephew, that if he dared to go to the weekly communion any longer, he would immediately turn him out of doors. That argument, indeed, had no success: The young gentleman communicated next week; upon which his uncle, having again tried to convince him that he was in the wrong way, by shaking him by the throat to no purpose, changed his method, and by mildness prevailed upon him to absent from it the Sunday following; as he has done five Sundays in six ever since. This much delighted our gay opponents, who increased their number apace.

〜〜〜

JOHN WESLEY

"Sermon 28: Sermon on the Mount-8"

> *"Lay not up for yourselves treasures upon earth, where moth and rust doth corrupt, and where thieves break through and steal;*
>
> *"But lay up for yourselves treasures in heaven, where neither moth nor rust doth corrupt, and where thieves do not break through nor steal;*
>
> *"For where your treasure is, there will your heart be also."*
>
> MATTHEW 6:19-21

. . . .

9. Therefore, "lay not up for yourselves treasures upon earth, where moth and rust doth corrupt, and where thieves break through and steal." If you do, it is plain your eye is evil; it is not singly fixed on God.

With regard to most of the commandments of God, whether relating to the heart or life, the Heathens of Africa or America stand much on a level with those that are called Christians. The Christians observe them (a few only being excepted) very near as much as the Heathens. For instance: The generality of the natives of England, commonly called Christians, are

John Wesley, "Sermon 28," in *The Works of John Wesley* (Grand Rapids: Baker, 2002), 3:365-68.

as sober and as temperate as the generality of the Heathens near the Cape of Good Hope. And so the Dutch or French Christians are as humble and as chaste as the Choctaw or Cherokee Indians. It is not easy to say, when we compare the bulk of the nations in Europe with those in America, whether the superiority lies on the one side or the other. At least, the American has not much the advantage. But we cannot affirm this with regard to the command now before us. Here the Heathen has far the pre-eminence. He desires and seeks nothing more than plain food to eat, and plain raiment to put on; and he seeks this only from day to day: He reserves, he lays up nothing; unless it be as much corn, at one season of the year, as he will need before that season returns. This command, therefore, the Heathens, though they know it not, do constantly and punctually observe. They "lay up for themselves no treasures upon earth"; no stores of purple or fine linen, of gold or silver, which either "moth or rust may corrupt, or thieves break through and steal." But how do the Christians observe what they profess to receive as a command of the most high God? Not at all! Not in any degree; no more than if no such command had ever been given to man. Even the good Christians, as they are accounted by others as well as themselves, pay no manner of regard thereto. It might as well be still hid in its original Greek, for any notice they take of it. . . . So that even these honest men do no more obey this command than a highwayman or a housebreaker. Nay, they never designed to obey it. From their youth up, it never entered into their thoughts. They were bred up by their Christian parents, masters, and friends, without any instruction at all concerning it; unless it were this — to break it as soon and as much as they could, and to continue breaking it to their lives' end.

10. There is no one instance of spiritual infatuation in the world, which is more amazing than this. Most of these very men read, or hear the Bible read — many of them every Lord's day. They have read or heard these words an hundred times, and yet never suspect that they are themselves condemned thereby, any more than by those which forbid parents to offer up their sons or daughters unto Moloch. O that God would speak to these miserable self-deceivers with his own voice, his mighty voice; that they may at last awake out of the snare of the devil, and the scales may fall from their eyes!

11. Do you ask what it is to "lay up treasures on earth"? It will be needful to examine this thoroughly. And let us, first, observe what is not forbidden in this command, that we may then clearly discern what is.

We are not forbidden in this command, First, to "provide things honest in the sight of all men," to provide wherewith we may render unto all their due — whatsoever they can justly demand of us. So far from it, that we are taught of God to "owe no man anything" (Rom. 13:8). We ought, therefore, to use all diligence in our calling, in order to owe no man anything; this being no other than a plain law of common justice, which our Lord came "not to destroy, but to fulfill" (Matt. 5:17).

Neither, Secondly, does he here forbid the providing for ourselves such things as are needful for the body; as of plain, wholesome food to eat, and clean raiment to put on. Yea, it is our duty, so far as God puts it into our power, to provide these things also; to the end we may eat our own bread, and be burdensome to no man.

Nor yet are we forbidden, Thirdly, to provide for our children, and for those of our own household. This also it is our duty to do, even upon principles of heathen morality. Every man ought to provide the plain necessaries of life, both for his own wife and children; and to put them into a capacity of providing these for themselves, when he is gone hence and is no more seen. I say, of providing *these;* the plain necessaries of life; not delicacies; not superfluities — and that by their diligent labor; for it is no man's duty to furnish them, any more than himself, with the means either of luxury or idleness. But if any man provide not thus far for his own children (as well as for the widows of his own house, of whom primarily St. Paul is speaking, in those well-known words to Timothy), he hath practically "denied the faith, and is worse than an infidel" (1 Tim. 5:8) or heathen.

Lastly we are not forbidden, in these words, to lay up, from time to time, what is needful for the carrying on our worldly business, in such a measure and degree as is sufficient to answer the foregoing purposes — in such a measure as, First, to owe no man anything; Secondly, to procure for ourselves the necessaries of life; and, Thirdly, to furnish those of our own house with them while we live, and with the means of procuring them when we are gone to God.

12. We may now clearly discern (unless we are unwilling to discern it) what that is which is forbidden here. It is, the designedly procuring more of this world's goods than will answer the foregoing purposes. The laboring after a larger measure of worldly substance, a larger increase of gold and silver — the laying up any more than these ends require — is what is here expressly and absolutely forbidden. If the words have any meaning at all, it must be this; for they are capable of no other. Consequently, whoever he is that, owing no man anything, and having food and raiment for himself and his household, together with a sufficiency to carry on his worldly business, so far as answers these reasonable purposes; whosoever, I say, being already in these circumstances, seeks a still larger portion on earth; he lives in an

open, habitual denial of the Lord that bought him. "He hath" practically "denied the faith, and is worse than" an African or American "infidel."

JOHN WESLEY

"Sermon 51: The Good Steward"

"Give an account of thy stewardship; for thou mayest be no longer steward."

LUKE 16:2

1. The relation which man bears to God, the creature to his Creator, is exhibited to us in the oracles of God under various representations. Considered as a sinner, a fallen creature, he is there represented as a debtor to his Creator. He is also frequently represented as a servant, which indeed is essential to him as a creature; insomuch that this appellation is given to the Son of God when in his state of humiliation: He "took upon him the form of a servant, being made in the likeness of men" (Phil. 2:7).

2. But no character more exactly agrees with the present state of man than that of a steward. Our blessed Lord frequently represents him as such; and there is a peculiar propriety in the representation. It is only in one particular respect, namely, as he is a sinner, that he is styled a debtor and when he is styled a servant, the appellation is general and indeterminate. But a steward is a servant of a particular kind; such a one as man is in all respects. This appellation is exactly expressive of his situation in the present world; specifying what kind of servant he is to God, and what kind of service his Divine Master expects from him.

It may be of use, then, to consider this point thoroughly, and to make our full improvement of it. In order to this, let us, First, inquire, in what respects we are now God's stewards. . . .

John Wesley, "Sermon 51," in *The Works of John Wesley* (Grand Rapids: Baker, 2002), 4:136-37, 139-40, 147.

I. 1. . . . . We are now indebted to Him for all we have. But although a debtor is obliged to return what he has received, yet until the time of payment comes he is at liberty to use it as he pleases. It is not so with a steward; he is not at liberty to use what is lodged in his hands as he pleases, but as his Master pleases. He has no right to dispose of anything which is in his hands, but according to the will of his Lord. For he is not the proprietor of any of these things, but barely entrusted with them by another; and entrusted on this express condition — that he shall dispose of all as his Master orders. Now, this is exactly the case of every man with relation to God. We are not at liberty to use what He has lodged in our hands as we please, but as He pleases who alone is the possessor of heaven and earth, and the Lord of every creature. . . .

2. On this condition he hath entrusted us with our souls, our bodies, our goods, and whatever other talents we have received: But in order to impress this weighty truth on our hearts, it will be needful to come to particulars. . . .

8. God has entrusted us, Fourthly, with several talents which do not properly come under any of these heads. Such is bodily strength; such are health, a pleasing person, an agreeable address; such are learning and knowledge, in their various degrees, with all the other advantages of education. Such is the influence which we have over others, whether by their love and esteem of us, or by power; power to do them good or hurt, to help or hinder them in the circumstances of life. Add to these, that invaluable talent of time with which God entrusts us from moment to moment. Add, Lastly, that on which all the rest depend, and without which they would all be curses, not blessings; namely, the grace of God, the power of his Holy Spirit, which alone works in us all that is acceptable in his sight.

II. 1. In so many respects are the children of men stewards of the Lord, the Possessor of heaven and earth: So large a portion of his goods, of various kinds, hath he committed to their charge. But it is not for ever, nor indeed for any considerable time: We have this trust reposed in us only during the short, uncertain space that we sojourn here below, only so long as we remain on earth, as this fleeting breath is in our nostrils. The hour is swiftly approaching; it is just at hand, when we "can be no longer stewards" (Luke 16:2)! The moment the body "returns to the dust as it was, and the spirit to God that gave it" (Eccl. 12:7), we bear that character no more; the time of our stewardship is at an end. Part of those goods wherewith we were before entrusted are now come to an end; at least, they are so with regard to us; nor are we longer entrusted with them: And that part which remains can no longer be employed or improved as it was before. . . .

6. Thy Lord will farther inquire, "Hast thou been a wise and faithful steward with regard to the talents of a mixed nature which I lent thee? Didst thou employ thy health and strength, not in folly or sin, not in the pleasures which perished in the using, 'not in making provision for the flesh, to fulfill the desires thereof' (Rom. 13:14); but in a vigorous pursuit of that better part which none could take away from thee? Didst thou employ whatever was pleasing in thy person or address, whatever advantages thou had by education, whatever share of learning, whatever knowledge of things or men, was committed to thee, for the promoting of virtue in the world, for the enlargement of my kingdom? Did thou employ whatever share of power thou had, whatever influence over others, by the love or esteem of thee which they had conceived, for the increase of their wisdom and holiness? Didst thou employ that inestimable talent of time, with wariness and circumspection, as duly weighing the value of every moment, and knowing that all were numbered in eternity? Above all, wast thou a good steward of my grace, preventing, accompanying, and following thee? Did thou duly observe and carefully improve all the influences of my Spirit? every good desire? every measure of light? all his sharp or gentle reproofs? How didst thou profit by 'the Spirit of bondage and fear,' which was previous to 'the Spirit of adoption' (Rom. 8:15)? And when thou were made a partaker of this Spirit, crying in thy heart, 'Abba, Father' (Rom. 8:15), didst thou stand fast in the glorious liberty wherewith I made thee free? Did thou from thenceforth present thy soul and body, all thy thoughts, thy words, and actions, in one flame of love, as a holy sacrifice, glorify me with thy body and thy spirit? Then 'well done, good and faithful servant! Enter thou into the joy of thy Lord' (Matt. 25:21)!"

And what will remain, either to the faithful or unfaithful steward? Nothing but the execution of that sentence which has been passed by the righteous Judge; fixing thee in a state which admits of no change through everlasting ages! It remains only that thou be rewarded, to all eternity, according to thy works.

4

Christian Callings in a
Post-Christian World, 1800-Present

Introduction

However liberating it may have been when the Reformers declared that almost any kind of work could be a vocation, many Christians today are nervous about defining their job as their vocation or calling. Much work today seems to be what Karl Marx called "alienated labor." Assembly-line workers tighten a single bolt on a product they never see completed; it is hard for them to feel pride in how well they do jobs that leave no room for achieving excellence.[1] The HMO medical assembly line replaces the family doctor. Lawyers write briefs on behalf of clients they never meet concerning cases that will never come to trial.[2] The list goes on. Can we honestly invite Christians to think of such tasks as their callings from God? Authors like Pope Leo XIII, Max Weber, and Walter Rauschenbusch were already worrying about such questions a hundred years ago, raising critical questions about the Reformation emphasis on job as vocation and exploring the possibility and character of meaningful work in an industrial society.

Jobs can seem not only meaningless but actually destructive of our lives as Christians. Store clerks and computer programmers miss church because they have to work Sundays. The promise that technology would lead to a shorter workweek has proven untrue; on average people work longer hours than they did a generation ago, and a long commute often adds to the length of the working day, with less time to spend with spouses and children, less time to be an active church member or an active community citizen. Corporate careers regularly involve multiple moves around the country: spouses change jobs, children change schools, parents and grandparents get left behind, to be visited only on rare occasions. In such a context, to urge people to think of their job as the call from God that gives their life meaning may be to push them in exactly the wrong direction, toward centering their lives ever more on jobs that already obsess them.

---

1. One need not read Marx to find the point made. See Adam Smith, *An Inquiry into the Nature and Causes of the Wealth of Nations* (New York: Random House, 1937), 734.

2. See Anthony T. Kronman, *The Lost Lawyer: Failing Ideals of the Legal Profession* (Cambridge, Mass.: Belknap Press of Harvard University Press, 1993).

Then too, not everyone has a job. Most people in the United States live a good many years after they retire. In economic downturns, some people cannot find work. Some people have amazing success in careers in spite of disabilities, but some sorts of disability really do seem to preclude meaningful jobs. Do we want to set apart Christians without a job as people to whose lives God has given no meaning?

In the light of these and other questions, some contemporary Christian writers want to get rid of the idea of job as vocation altogether. The twentieth-century French social theorist and theologian Jacques Ellul insisted, "Nothing in the Bible allows us to identify *work* with *calling*. When the terms that can be translated by the word 'vocation' or 'call from God' are encountered, they are always concerned with a summons to the specific service of God. . . . Work . . . is an imperative of survival, and the Bible remains realistic enough not to superimpose upon this necessity a superfluous spiritual decoration."[3] Our jobs, according to Ellul, do not give our lives meaning, and the Bible never claims that they do.

The American Baptist James Y. Holloway goes even a bit further. It is not just assembly-line workers for whom a job cannot be a vocation, he argues:

> Physician, lawyer, minister, teacher, priest, scientist, politician, administrator, and the divisions and subdivisions thereof — each seems trapped by what institutions and professions have been turned into by technique. Concern for one's fellow man through profession or institution is transformed into the dehumanizing goal of contemporary technology: efficiency.[4]

But this should not be a problem for a Christian understanding of vocation, Holloway writes, for the Bible never thought of job as calling anyway: "We do not know much about what the prophets or apostles did part-time to earn a living in a job or by a profession because it is not important to their *calling* from God. . . . work is *not* vocation."[5]

Work, the contemporary American ethicist and theologian Stanley Hauerwas concludes, provides "the means to survive, to be of service to others, and, perhaps most of all, work gives us a way to stay busy . . . a hedge against boredom. Attributing greater significance to work risks making it

---

3. Jacques Ellul, "Work and Calling," *Katallagete* 4.2-3 (1972): 8.
4. James Y. Holloway, "About This Issue of Calling and Jobs. . . ," *Katallagete* 4.2-3 (1972): 3.
5. Holloway, "About This Issue," 4.

demonic as work then becomes an idolatrous activity."[6] The theologian Miroslav Volf, born in Croatia and now teaching at Yale, agrees "that the dead hand of 'vocation' needed to be lifted from the Christian idea of work. It is both inapplicable to modern societies and theologically inadequate."[7]

Job as Vocation: One Option among Others?

I resist this impressive chorus of voices condemning the idea of job as vocation.[8] One reason, I am sure, is autobiographical. Unmarried and without children, I have found a richly rewarding life in college teaching — now in my thirtieth year at the same college. My abilities and even some of my faults seem to have contributed to doing my job well, and I think I have made a difference for good in a fair number of lives. I believe that this is what God wants me to be doing. I know nurses and priests and woodworkers and lawyers and first-grade teachers and ministers who feel the same. When Ellul and Holloway denounce the institutional bureaucratization that corrupts every kind of work in contemporary society,[9] I want to protest that things are not so bad for all of us.

Yet I recognize that I am lucky. There are lots of people who do not have jobs at all or do not feel about their jobs the way I feel about mine. There are many jobs that seem a more or less inevitable part of our mechanized, bureaucratized society to which I find it hard to imagine anyone feeling called by God. Some may be the kind of job a Christian should not take, but others are necessary but unavoidably dull and uninspiring. So — what should we do about the idea of job as vocation?

One lesson to be learned from the history of Christian ideas of vocation is that there is not just one account of what vocation means. Christians have felt called simply to be Christians, with all the risks that that has sometimes entailed. They have felt vocations to the monastic life, or the priesthood, or

6. Stanley Hauerwas, "Work as Co-Creation: A Critique of a Remarkably Bad Idea," in *Co-Creation and Capitalism: John Paul II's Laborem Exercens*, ed. J. W. Houck and O. F. Williams (Lanham, Md.: University Press of America, 1983), 48.

7. Miroslav Volf, *Work in the Spirit: Toward a Theology of Work* (New York: Oxford University Press, 1991), vii.

8. The strongest recent defense of job as vocation is Douglas J. Schuurman, *Vocation: Discerning Our Callings in Life* (Grand Rapids: William B. Eerdmans, 2004). Schuurman puts more emphasis on recovering the idea of job as calling than I would, and less on the variety of ways in which we can understand calling today.

9. See Ellul, "Work and Calling," 16.

secular jobs, or their roles in family life. We do not have to limit "vocation" or "calling" to one meaning and then vote it, in that sense, up or down. We can draw on the range of options the tradition offers us, or add some new ones. I think job as vocation should stay on the list, but not as the only possibility.

So we come back to where we started. Human beings generally want to know, "Does my life have some meaning, some purpose?" Christians assume that any answer to that question involves what the God we come to know in Jesus Christ wants us to do or be. For some of us, the center of the answer may lie in our jobs — from doctors curing patients to landscapers making the spaces in which people live a bit more beautiful. For others, our jobs will be meaningful primarily only in that they help us support our families, and it will be in the nurturing of a family that we find the core of our life's vocation. For still others, a hobby may create a community and reward not found in a paid job.[10] Still others may find the activities of their church the work that most gives meaning to their lives. Even on the job, some people may find the support and friendship they give their co-workers more significant than the doing of the job itself.

Indeed, in an age when once again committed Christians in Europe and North America may find themselves a minority voice in their society, simply being publicly a Christian, as in the early church, may itself be an important calling. Christians in other parts of the world, like those in the early church, are still today sometimes called to risk their lives for their faith. In Europe and North America we rarely confront such a dramatic demand. Yet Christians who stand up against racism, or resist the pressure to buy ever more consumer goods, or insist that their kids will not go to soccer practice if it is on Sunday morning can find themselves isolated from many neighbors as odd or strange in what some writers have come to call "post-Christian" societies. Perhaps that kind of witness is at least one aspect of their callings. These are not, moreover, brand new issues. Even in the nineteenth century, Christians like Søren Kierkegaard in Denmark and John Henry Newman in England were thinking about the challenge of how to introduce serious Christianity into a society that thought itself already Chris-

---

10. "The desire to do something well, whether it is sailing a boat — or building a boat — reflects a need that was previously met in the workplace. Competence was shown on the job — holidays were for messing around. . . . Technology has removed craft from most occupations. . . . For many, weekend free time has become not a chance to escape work but a chance to create work that is more meaningful . . . in order to realize the personal satisfactions that the workplace no longer offers." Witold Rybczynski, *Waiting for the Weekend* (New York: Viking, 1991), 223-24.

tian. In Russia Feodor Dostoevsky was defending traditional Orthodox understandings of freedom and the value of the monastic life against what he saw as a rising tide of modern secularism.

This chapter therefore contains the most varied readings. Traversing previous chapters has made it clear that the Christian tradition offers no one answer to how to think about "calling" or "vocation," though particular answers tended to dominate individual periods. But in our time every answer, including some new ones, seems a live option. Howard Thurman called African Americans to reflect on their vocations. Authors as diverse as Dietrich Bonhoeffer, Simone Weil, and Dorothy L. Sayers explored the idea of vocation during the darkness of World War II. Bonhoeffer emphasized obedience to Christ; Weil focused on cultivating attention for our prayer life; and Sayers offered the artist as a significant model of what it means to have a vocation.

After the war, Catholics came up with varied answers — Thomas Merton entered a Trappist monastery, while Dorothy Day devoted her life to serving the poor and protesting injustice. The great Protestant theologian Karl Barth looked back over the whole history of Christian reflection on vocation.

Some Common Themes Today

Thinking about vocation in our time has thus generated an unprecedented pluralism. In two other respects, however, we are now more uniform. First, in most previous times the story of calling was radically different for men and women. Men were far more likely to be out in a workplace away from their homes, women far more likely to be doing work at home, and that difference generated a long list of other differences. Men and women still do not have exactly the same place in the workforce or the home, but the differences are far less dramatic. Just about all the questions about vocation now apply to both sexes.

Second, for most of the centuries after the Reformation, Protestant and Catholic thinking about vocation diverged dramatically. Catholics retained the medieval ideal of "vocation" as a call to be a priest, a nun, or a monk; Protestants insisted that *any* job could equally be a vocation. Those sharp lines have recently grown fuzzier. Many Protestant denominations lack enough people going into ordained ministry and are looking for ways to emphasize that particular kind of vocation. Far more dramatically, on the Catholic side, in 1965 the Second Vatican Council declared that in "even the most ordinary everyday activities" people can "justly consider that by their labor they are unfolding the Creator's work, consulting the advantages of their brother men, and contributing by their personal industry to the realization in history of the divine plan. . . . Hence, the norm of human activity is this: that in accord with the divine plan and will, it should harmonize with the genuine good of the human race, and allow men as individuals and as members of society to pursue their total vocation and fulfill it."[11] More recently, Pope John Paul II wrote, "Work is a good thing for man — a good thing for his humanity — because through work man not only transforms nature, adapting it to his own needs, but he also achieves fulfillment as a human being and indeed in a sense becomes 'more a human being.'"[12] Such accounts of the place of the world of work in human life would previously have seemed obviously Protestant.

What should I do with my life? How can I know? Will I find something that gives my life a sense of purpose or meaning? Even though the context in which we ask such questions has grown ever more complex, the Christian tradition still provides us with a wide range of resources for thinking about how to answer them.

11. *Gaudium et spes: Pastoral Constitution on the Church in the Modern World* 34-35, *Documents of Vatican II*, ed. Walter M. Abbott (Chicago: Follett, 1966), 232-33.
12. John Paul II, *Laborem exercens* 9, 20-21.

SØREN KIERKEGAARD

Fear and Trembling

Søren Kierkegaard (1813-1855) grew up in a prosperous Danish family and was preparing to get married and studying for ordination as a Lutheran pastor. But he felt himself called to be a kind of Christian Socrates. Just as Socrates had challenged Athenians to realize how little they knew, so Kierkegaard challenged Danish Christians to realize how little faith they had. He faced, he wrote, the particularly difficult task of introducing real Christianity into a country where everyone thought they were already Christians — but they were far too comfortable, they thought faith far too easy. (Kierkegaard sometimes singled out for criticism the German philosopher Hegel, who had treated "faith" as an easy first step on the road to the higher level of philosophical knowledge.)

Kierkegaard found that pursuing his task led to social isolation. He felt he could not get married or ordained but had to devote his life to helping his fellow Danes realize that they were not Christians — a necessary preliminary to searching for what Christianity might really mean. He wrote a series of books, often under pseudonyms; *Fear and Trembling* appeared as written by "Johannes de Silentio." Johannes admits that he is not a Christian; he lacks faith. But, reading the story in Genesis 22 of how God called Abraham to sacrifice his son Isaac, Johannes at least recognizes that Abraham's kind of faith is an amazing thing, far beyond what he can understand. Faith — a faith that goes beyond resignation in the face of life's tragedies and may challenge basic ethical principles — may be the highest vocation of all.

Søren Kierkegaard, *Fear and Trembling*, trans. Howard V. Hong and Edna H. Hong (Princeton: Princeton University Press, 1983), 17-21, 28-30, 32-33, 37-41.

Exordium

Once upon a time there was a man who as a child had heard that beautiful story of how God tempted [*fristede*] Abraham and of how Abraham withstood the temptation [*fristede*], kept the faith, and, contrary to expectation, got a son a second time. When he grew older, he read the same story with even greater admiration, for life had fractured what had been united in the pious simplicity of the child. The older he became, the more often his thoughts turned to that story; his enthusiasm for it became greater and greater, and yet he could understand the story less and less. Finally, he forgot everything else because of it; his soul had but one wish, to see Abraham, but one longing, to have witnessed that event. His craving was not to see the beautiful regions of the East, not the earthly glory of the promised land, not that God-fearing couple whose old age God had blessed, not the venerable figure of the aged patriarch, not the vigorous adolescence God bestowed upon Isaac — the same thing could just as well have occurred on a barren heath. His craving was to go along on the three-day journey when Abraham rode with sorrow before him and Isaac beside him. His wish was to be present in that hour when Abraham raised his eyes and saw Mount Moriah in the distance, the hour when he left the asses behind and went up the mountain alone with Isaac — for what occupied him was not the beautiful tapestry of imagination but the shudder of the idea.

That man was not a thinker. He did not feel any need to go beyond faith; he thought that it must be supremely glorious to be remembered as its father, an enviable destiny to possess it, even if no one knew it.

That man was not an exegetical scholar. He did not know Hebrew; if he had known Hebrew, he perhaps would easily have understood the story and Abraham. . . .

By faith Abraham emigrated from the land of his fathers and became an alien in the promised land. He left one thing behind, took one thing along: he left behind his worldly understanding, and he took along his faith. Otherwise he certainly would not have emigrated but surely would have considered it unreasonable [*urimeligt*]. By faith he was an alien in the promised land, and there was nothing that reminded him of what he cherished, but everything by its newness tempted his soul to sorrowful longing. And yet he was God's chosen one in whom the Lord was well pleased! As a matter of fact, if he had been an exile, banished from God's grace, he could have better understood it — but now it was as if he and his faith were being mocked. There was also in the world one who lived in exile from the native land he loved. He is not forgotten, nor are his dirges of lamentation when he sorrowfully sought and found what was lost. There is no dirge by Abraham. It is human to lament, human to weep with one who weeps, but it is greater to have faith, more blessed to contemplate the man of faith.

By faith Abraham received the promise that in his seed all the generations of the earth would be blessed. Time passed, the possibility was there, Abraham had faith; time passed, it became unreasonable, Abraham had faith. There was one in the world who also had an expectancy. Time passed, evening drew near; he was not so contemptible as to forget his expectancy, and therefore he will not be forgotten, either. Then he sorrowed, and his sorrow did not disappoint him as life had done, it did everything it could for him; in the sweetness of his sorrow he possessed his disappointed expectancy. It is human to sorrow, human to sorrow with the sorrowing, but it is greater to have faith, more blessed to contemplate the man of faith. We have no dirge of sorrow by Abraham. As time passed, he did not gloomily count the days; he did not look suspiciously at Sarah, wondering if she was not getting old; he did not stop the course of the sun so she would not become old and along with her his expectancy; he did not soothingly sing his mournful lay for Sarah. Abraham became old, Sarah the object of mockery in the land, and yet he was God's chosen one and heir to the promise that in his seed all the generations of the earth would be blessed. Would it not have been better, after all, if he were not God's chosen? What does it mean to be God's chosen? Is it to be denied in youth one's youthful desire in order to have it fulfilled with great difficulty in one's old age? But had Abraham wavered, he would have given it up. He would have said to God, "So maybe it is not your will that this should be; then I will give up my wish. It was my one and only wish, it was my blessedness. My soul is open and sincere; I am hiding no secret resentment because you denied me this." He would not have been forgotten, he would have saved many by his example, but he still would not have become the father of faith, for it is great to give up one's desire, but it is greater to hold fast to it after having given it up; it is great to lay hold of the eternal, but it is greater to hold fast to the temporal after having given it up.

Then came the fullness of time. If Abraham had not had faith, then Sarah would surely have died of sorrow, and Abraham, dulled by grief, would not have understood the fulfillment but would have smiled at it as at a youthful dream. But Abraham had faith, and therefore he was young, for he who always hopes for the best grows old and is deceived by life, and he who is always prepared for the worst grows old prematurely, but he who has faith — he preserves an eternal youth. So let us praise and honor that story! For Sarah, although well advanced in years, was young enough to desire the pleasure of motherhood, and Abraham with his gray hairs was young enough to wish to be a father. Outwardly, the wonder of it is that it happened according to their expectancy; in the more profound sense, the wonder of faith is that Abraham and Sarah were young enough to desire and that faith had preserved their desire and thereby their youth. He accepted the fulfillment of the promise, he accepted it in faith, and it happened according to the promise and according to his faith. Moses struck the rock with his staff, but he did not have faith.

So there was joy in Abraham's house when Sarah stood as bride on their golden wedding day.

But it was not to remain that way; once again Abraham was to be tried. He had fought with that crafty power that devises all things, with that vigilant enemy who never dozes, with that old man who outlives everything — he had fought with time and kept his faith. Now all the frightfulness of the struggle was concentrated in one moment. "And God tempted Abraham and said to him, take Isaac, your only son, whom you love, and go to the land of Moriah and offer him as a burnt offering on a mountain that I shall show you" (Gen. 22:1-2).

So everything was lost, even more appallingly than if it had never happened! So the Lord was only mocking Abraham! He wondrously made the preposterous come true; now he wanted to see it annihilated. This was indeed a piece of folly, but Abraham did not laugh at it as Sarah did when the promise was announced. All was lost! Seventy years of trusting expectancy, the brief joy over the fulfillment of faith. Who is this who seizes the staff from the old man, who is this who demands that he himself shall break it! Who is this who makes a man's gray hairs disconsolate, who is this who demands that he himself shall do it! Is there no sympathy for this venerable old man, none for the innocent child? And yet Abraham was God's chosen one, and it was the Lord who imposed the ordeal. Now everything would be lost! All the glorious remembrance of his posterity, the promise in Abraham's seed — it was nothing but a whim, a fleeting thought that the Lord had had and that Abraham was now supposed to obliterate. That glorious treasure, which was just as old as the faith in Abraham's heart and many, many years older than Isaac, the fruit of Abraham's life, sanctified by prayer, matured in battle, the blessing on Abraham's lips — this fruit was now to be torn off prematurely and rendered meaningless, for what meaning would it have if Isaac should be sacrificed! That sad but nevertheless blessed hour when Abraham was to take leave of everything he held dear, when he once more would raise his venerable head, when his face would shine as the Lord's, when he would concentrate all his soul upon a blessing that would be so powerful it would bless Isaac all his days — this hour was not to come! For

Abraham would indeed take leave of Isaac, but in such a way that he himself would remain behind; death would separate them, but in such a way that Isaac would become its booty. The old man would not, rejoicing in death, lay his hand in blessing on Isaac, but, weary of life, he would lay a violent hand upon Isaac. And it was God who tested him! Woe to the messenger who brought such news to Abraham! Who would have dared to be the emissary of this sorrow? But it was God who tested Abraham.

Yet Abraham had faith, and had faith for this life. In fact, if his faith had been only for a life to come, he certainly would have more readily discarded everything in order to rush out of a world to which he did not belong. But Abraham's faith was not of this sort, if there is such a faith at all, for actually it is not faith but the most remote possibility of faith that faintly sees its object on the most distant horizon but is separated from it by a chasmal abyss in which doubt plays its tricks. But Abraham had faith specifically for this life — faith that he would grow old in this country, be honored among the people, blessed by posterity, and unforgettable in Isaac, the most precious thing in his life, whom he embraced with a love that is inadequately described by saying he faithfully fulfilled the father's duty to love the son, which is indeed stated in the command: the son, whom you love. Jacob had twelve sons, one of whom he loved; Abraham had but one, whom he loved.

But Abraham had faith and did not doubt; he believed the preposterous. If Abraham had doubted, then he would have done something else, something great and glorious, for how could Abraham do anything else but what is great and glorious! He would have gone to Mount Moriah, he would have split the firewood, lit the fire, drawn the knife. He would have cried out to God, "Reject not this sacrifice; it is not the best that I have, that I know very well, for what is an old man compared with the child of promise, but it is the best I can give you. Let Isaac never find this out so that he may take comfort in his youth." He would have thrust the knife into his own breast. He would have been admired in the world, and his name would never be forgotten; but it is one thing to be admired and another to become a guiding star that saves the anguished. . . .

The story about Abraham is remarkable in that it is always glorious no matter how poorly it is understood, but here again it is a matter of whether or not we are willing to work and be burdened. But we are unwilling to work, and yet we want to understand the story. We glorify Abraham, but how? We recite the whole story in clichés: "The great thing was that he loved God in such a way that he was willing to offer him the best." This is very true, but "the best" is a vague term. Mentally and orally we homologize Isaac and the best, and the contemplator can very well smoke his pipe while cogitating, and the listener may very well stretch out his legs comfortably. If that rich young man whom Jesus met along the way had sold all his possessions and given the money to the poor, we would praise him as we praise every great deed, even if we could not understand him without working, but he still would not become an Abraham, even though he sacrificed the best. What is omitted from Abraham's story is the anxiety, because to money I have no ethical obligation, but to the son the father has the highest and holiest. We forget it and yet want to talk about Abraham, talk and in the process of talking interchange the two terms, Isaac and the best, and everything goes fine. But just suppose that someone listening is a man who suffers from sleeplessness — then the most terrifying, the most profound, tragic, and comic misunderstanding is very close at hand. He goes home, he wants to do just as Abraham did, for the son, after all, is the best. If the preacher found out about it, he perhaps would go to the man, he would muster all his ecclesiastical dignity and shout, "You despicable man, you scum of society, what devil has so possessed you that you want to murder your son." And the pastor, who had not noticed any heat or perspiration when preaching about Abraham, would be surprised at himself, at the wrathful earnestness with which he thunders at the poor man. He would be pleased with himself, for he had never spoken with such emphasis and emotion. He would say to himself and his wife, "I am an orator — what was lacking was the occasion. When I spoke about Abraham on Sunday, I did not feel gripped at all." If the same speaker had a little superfluity of understanding to spare, I am sure he would have lost it if the sinner had calmly and with dignity answered: But, after all, that was what you yourself preached about on Sunday. How could the preacher ever get such a thing in his head, and yet it was so, and his only mistake was that he did not know what he was saying. And to think that there is no poet who could bring himself to prefer situations such as this to the nonsense and trumpery with which comedies and novels are stuffed. The comic and the tragic make contact here in absolute infinitude. By itself, the preacher's discourse was perhaps ludicrous enough, but it became infinitely ludicrous through its effect, and yet this was quite natural. Or suppose that the unprotesting sinner is convinced by the pastor's severe lecture, suppose that the zealous pastor goes home happy — happy in the consciousness that he not only was effective in the pulpit but above all had irresistible power as a spiritual counselor, inasmuch as on Sunday he inspired the congregation, while on Monday, like a cherub with a flaming sword, he placed himself in front of the person whose actions would give the lie to the old saying that things do not go in the world as the preacher preaches.

But if the sinner remains unconvinced, his situation is really tragic. Then he probably will be executed or sent to the madhouse. In short, in relation to so-called reality, he became unhappy; in another sense, I am sure, Abraham made him happy, for he who works does not perish.

How is a contradiction such as that of the speaker to be explained? Is it because Abraham has gained a prescriptive right to be a great man, so that what he does is great and when another man does the same thing it is a sin, an atrocious sin? In that case, I do not wish to participate in such empty praise. If faith cannot make it a holy act to be willing to murder his son, then let the same judgment be passed on Abraham as on everyone else. If a person lacks the courage to think his thought all the way through and say that Abraham was a murderer, then it is certainly better to attain this courage than to waste time on unmerited eulogies. The ethical expression for what Abraham did is that he meant to murder Isaac; the religious expression is that he meant to sacrifice Isaac — but precisely in this contradiction is the anxiety that can make a person sleepless, and yet without this anxiety Abraham is not who he is. . . .

Love indeed has its priests in the poets, and occasionally we hear a voice that knows how to honor it, but not a word is heard about faith. Who speaks to the honor of this passion? Philosophy goes further. Theology sits all rouged and powdered in the window and courts its favor, offers its charms to philosophy. It is supposed to be difficult to understand Hegel, but to understand Abraham is a small matter. To go beyond Hegel is a miraculous achievement, but to go beyond Abraham is the easiest of all. I for my part have applied considerable time to understanding Hegelian philosophy and believe that I have understood it fairly well; I am sufficiently brash to think that when I cannot understand particular passages despite all my pains, he himself may not have been entirely clear. All this I do easily, naturally, without any mental strain. Thinking about Abraham is another matter, however; then I am shattered. I am constantly aware of the prodigious paradox that is the content of Abraham's life, I am constantly repelled, and, despite all its passion, my thought cannot penetrate it, cannot get ahead by a hairsbreadth. I stretch every muscle to get a perspective, and at the very same instant I become paralyzed. . . .

This is the peak on which Abraham stands. The last stage to pass from his view is the stage of infinite resignation. He actually goes further and comes to faith. All those travesties of faith — the wretched, lukewarm lethargy that thinks: There's no urgency, there's no use in grieving beforehand; the despicable hope that says: One just can't know what will happen, it could just possibly be — those travesties are native to the paltriness of life, and infinite resignation has already infinitely disdained them.

Abraham I cannot understand; in a certain sense I can learn nothing from him except to be amazed. If someone deludes himself into thinking he may be moved to have faith by pondering the outcome of that story, he cheats himself and cheats God out of the first movement of faith — he wants to suck worldly wisdom out of the paradox. Someone might succeed, for our generation does not stop with faith, does not stop with the miracle of faith, turning water into wine — it goes further and turns wine into water.

Would it not be best to stop with faith, and is it not shocking that everyone wants to go further? Where will it all end when in our age, as declared in so many ways, one does not want to stop with love? In worldly shrewdness, in petty calculation, in paltriness and meanness, in everything that can make man's divine origin doubtful. Would it not be best to remain standing at faith and for him who stands to see to it that he does not fall, for the movement of faith must continually be made by virtue of the absurd, but yet in such a way, please note, that one does not lose the finite but gains it whole and intact. For my part, I presumably can describe the movements of faith, but I cannot make them. In learning to go through the motions of swimming, one can be suspended from the ceiling in a harness and then presumably describe the movements, but one is not swimming. In the same way I can describe the movements of faith. If I am thrown out into the water, I presumably do swim (for I do not belong to the waders), but I make different movements, the movements of infinity, whereas faith makes the opposite movements: after having made the movements of infinity, it makes the movements of finitude. Fortunate is the person who can make these movements! He does the marvelous, and I shall never weary of admiring him; it makes no difference to me whether it is Abraham or a slave in Abraham's house, whether it is a professor of philosophy or a poor servant girl — I pay attention only to the movements. But I do pay attention to them, and I do not let myself be fooled, either by myself or by anyone else. The knights of the infinite resignation are easily recognizable — their walk is light and bold. But they who carry the treasure of faith are likely to disappoint, for externally they have a striking resemblance to bourgeois philistinism, which infinite resignation, like faith, deeply disdains.

I honestly confess that in my experience I have not found a single authentic instance, although I do not therefore deny that every second person may be such an instance. Meanwhile, I have been looking for it for many years, but in vain. Generally, people travel around the world to see rivers and mountains, new stars, colorful birds, freakish fish, preposterous races of mankind; they indulge in the brutish stupor that gawks at life and thinks it has seen something. That does not occupy me. But if I knew where a knight of faith lived, I would travel on foot to him, for this marvel occupies me absolutely. I would not leave him for a second, I would watch him every minute to see how he made the movements; I would consider myself taken care of for life and would divide my time between watching him and practicing myself, and thus spend all my time in admiring him. As I said before, I have not found anyone like that; meanwhile, I may very well imagine him. Here he is. The acquaintance is made, I am introduced to him. The instant I lay eyes on him, I set him apart at once; I jump back, clap my hands, and say half aloud, "Good Lord, is this the man, is this really the one — he looks just like a tax collector!" But this is indeed the one. I move a little closer to him, watch his slightest movement to see if it reveals a bit of heterogeneous optical telegraphy from the infinite, a glance, a facial expression, a gesture, a sadness, a smile that would betray the infinite in its heterogeneity with the finite. No! I examine his figure from top to toe to see if there may not be a crack through which the infinite would peek. No! He is solid all the way through. His stance? It is vigorous, belongs entirely to finitude; no spruced-up burgher walking out to Fresberg on a Sunday afternoon treads the earth more solidly. He belongs entirely to the world; no bourgeois philistine could belong to it more. Nothing is detectable of that distant and aristocratic nature by which the knight of the infinite is recognized. He finds pleasure in everything, takes part in everything, and every time one sees him participating in something particular he does it with an assiduousness that marks the worldly man who is attached to such things. He attends to his job. To see him makes one think of him as a pen-pusher who has lost his soul to Italian bookkeeping, so punctilious is he. Sunday is for him a holiday. He goes to church. No heavenly gaze or any sign of the incommensurable betrays him; if one did not know him, it would be impossible to distinguish him from the rest of the crowd, for at most his hearty and powerful singing of the hymns proves that he has good lungs. In the afternoon, he takes a walk to the woods. He enjoys everything he sees, the swarms of people, the new omnibuses, the Sound. Encountering him on Strandveien, one would take him for a mercantile soul enjoying himself. He finds pleasure in this way, for he is not a poet, and I have tried in vain to lure the poetic incommensurability out of him. Toward evening he walks home, his gait goes as steady as a postman's. On the way, he thinks that his wife surely will have a special hot meal for him when he comes home — for example, roast lamb's head with vegetables. If he meets a kindred soul, he would go on talking all the way to Østerport about this delicacy with a passion befitting a restaurant operator. It so happens that he does not have four shillings to his name, and yet he firmly believes that his wife has this delectable meal waiting for him. If she has, to see him eat would be the envy of the elite and an inspiration to the common man, for his appetite is keener than Esau's. His wife does not have it — curiously enough, he is just the same. On the way he passes a building site and meets another man. They converse for a moment; in an instant he erects a building, and he himself has at his disposition everything required. The stranger leaves him thinking that he surely is a capitalist, while my admired knight thinks: Well, if it came right down to it, I could easily get it. He sits at an open window and surveys the neighborhood where he lives: everything that happens — a rat scurrying under a plank across the gutter, children playing — engages him with an equanimity akin to that of a sixteen-year-old girl. And yet he is no genius, for I have sought in vain to spy out the incommensurability of genius in him. In the evening, he smokes his pipe; seeing him, one would swear it was the butcher across the way vegetating in the gloaming. With the freedom from care of a reckless good-for-nothing, he lets things take care of themselves, and yet every moment of his life he buys the opportune time at the highest price, for he does not do even the slightest thing except by virtue of the absurd. And yet, yet — yes, I could be infuriated over it if for no other reason than envy — and yet this man has made and at every moment is making the movement of infinity. He drains the deep sadness of life in infinite resignation, he knows the blessedness of infinity, he has felt the pain of renouncing everything, the most precious thing in the world, and yet the finite tastes just as good to him as to one who never knew anything higher, because his remaining in finitude would have no trace of a timorous, anxious routine, and yet he has this security that makes him delight in it as if finitude were the surest thing of all. And yet, yet the whole earthly figure he presents is a new creation by virtue of the absurd. He resigned everything infinitely, and then he grasped everything again by virtue of the absurd. He is continually making the movement of infinity, but he does it with such precision and assurance that he continually gets finitude out of it, and no one ever suspects anything else. It is supposed to be the most difficult feat for a ballet dancer to leap into a specific posture in such a way that he never once strains for the posture but in the very leap assumes the posture. Perhaps there is no ballet dancer who can do it — but this knight does it. Most people live completely absorbed in worldly joys and sorrows; they are benchwarmers who do not take part in the dance. The knights of infinity are ballet dancers and have elevation. They make the upward movement and come down again, and this, too, is not an unhappy diversion and is not unlovely to see. But every time they come down, they are unable to assume the posture immediately, they waver for a moment, and this wavering shows that they are aliens in the world. It is more or less conspicuous according to their skill, but even the most skillful of these knights cannot hide this wavering. One does not need to see them in the air; one needs only to see them the instant they touch and have touched the earth — and then one recognizes them. But to be able to come down in such a way that instantaneously one seems to stand and to walk, to change the leap into life into walking, absolutely to express the sublime in the pedestrian — only that knight can do it, and this is the one and only marvel.

JOHN HENRY NEWMAN

Divine Calls

John Henry Newman (1801-1890) studied at Oxford, was ordained in the Church of England, and returned to Oxford to teach and preach. His sermons were deeply influential not only at the university but all over England. From 1833 to 1841, Newman and some of his friends wrote a series of articles called "Tracts for the Times," and the "Tractarian movement" or "Oxford Movement" they established argued for a "high church" interpretation of the beliefs of the Church of England — a more "Catholic" understanding of the Eucharist and more respect for saints, fasting, and the medieval church.

In 1845, Newman confirmed the suspicions of his critics in the Church of England, who had thought he was implicitly a Catholic all along, by converting to Roman Catholicism; his conversion was one of the big news stories of the time. He was made a cardinal in 1879. This sermon, preached at Oxford in the 1830s, when he was still a member of the Church of England, deals with the nature of faith and, in a very different way, with Kierkegaard's question: how can we receive a call to faith in a society where nearly everyone is brought up as a Christian?

John Henry Newman, *Parochial and Plain Sermons* (London: Longmans, Green, 1900), 11-15, 17-19.

"And the Lord came, and stood, and called as at other times,
Samuel, Samuel. Then Samuel answered, Speak; for Thy servant
heareth."

1 SAMUEL 3:10

In the narrative of which these words form part, we have a remarkable instance of a Divine call, and the manner in which it is our duty to meet it.
Samuel was from a child brought to the house of the Lord; and in due time
he was called to a sacred office, and made a prophet. He was called, and he
forthwith answered the call. God said, "Samuel, Samuel." He did not understand at first who called, and what was meant; but on going to Eli he learned
who spoke, and what his answer should be. So when God called again, he
said, "Speak, Lord; for Thy servant heareth." Here is prompt obedience.

Very different in its circumstances was St. Paul's call, but resembling
Samuel's in this respect, that, when God called, he, too, promptly obeyed.
When St. Paul heard the voice from heaven, he said at once, trembling and
astonished, "Lord, what wilt Thou have me to do?" This same obedient temper of his is stated or implied in the two accounts which he himself gives of
his miraculous conversion. In the 22nd chapter [of Acts] he says, "And I said,
What shall I do, Lord?" And in the 26th, after telling King Agrippa what the
Divine Speaker said to him, he adds what comes to the same thing, "Whereupon, O King Agrippa, I was not disobedient unto the heavenly vision."
Such is the account given us in St. Paul's case of that first step in God's gracious dealings with him, which ended in his eternal salvation. . . .

This, then, is the lesson taught us by St. Paul's conversion, promptly to
obey the call. If we do obey it, to God be the glory, for He it is works in us. If
we do not obey, to ourselves be all the shame, for sin and unbelief work in
us. Such being the state of the case, let us take care to act accordingly — being exceedingly alarmed lest we should not obey God's voice when He calls
us, yet not taking praise or credit to ourselves if we do obey it. This has been
the temper of all saints from the beginning — working out their salvation
with fear and trembling, yet ascribing the work to Him who wrought in
them to will and do of His good pleasure; obeying the call, and giving
thanks to Him who calls, to Him who fulfils in them their calling. So much
on the pattern afforded us by St. Paul.

Very different in its circumstances was Samuel's call, when a child in the
temple, yet resembling St. Paul's in this particular — that for our instruction
the circumstance of his obedience to it is brought out prominently even in
the words put into his mouth by Eli in the text. Eli taught him what to say,
when called by the Divine voice. Accordingly, when "the Lord came, and

stood, and called as at other times, Samuel, Samuel, then Samuel answered, Speak, Lord; for Thy servant heareth."

Such, again, is the temper of mind expressed by holy David in the 27th Psalm, "When Thou saidst, Seek ye My face, my heart said unto Thee, Thy face, Lord, will I seek."

And this temper, which in the above instances is illustrated in words spoken, is in the case of many other Saints in Scripture shown in word and deed; and, on the other hand, is illustrated negatively by being neglected in the case of others therein mentioned, who might have entered into life, and did not.

For instance, we read of the Apostles, that "Jesus, walking by the Sea of Galilee, saw two brethren, Simon called Peter, and Andrew his brother, casting a net into the sea; for they were fishers. And He saith unto them, Follow Me, and I will make you fishers of men. And they straightway left their nets and followed Him" (Mark 1:16-18). Again, when He saw James and John with their father Zebedee, "He called them; and they immediately left the ship, and their father, and followed Him" (Mark 1:19-20). And so of St. Matthew at the receipt of custom, "He said unto him, Follow Me; and he left all, rose up, and followed Him" (Mark 2:14). . . .

On the other hand, the young ruler shrank from the call, and found it a hard saying, "If thou wilt be perfect, go and sell that thou hast, and give to the poor, and thou shalt have treasure in heaven; and come, and follow Me. But when the young man heard that saying, he went away sorrowful, for he had great possessions." Others who seemed to waver, or rather who asked for some little delay from human feeling, were rebuked for want of promptitude in their obedience; time stays for no one; the word of call is spoken and is gone; if we do not seize the moment, it is lost. Christ was on His road heavenward. He walked by the sea of Galilee; He "passed forth"; He "passed by"; He did not stop; all men must join Him, or He would be calling on others beyond them. "He said to another, Follow Me. But he said, Lord, suffer me first to go and bury my father. Jesus said unto him, Let the dead bury their dead: but go thou and preach the kingdom of God. And another also said, Lord, I will follow Thee: but let me first go bid them farewell, which are at home at my house. And Jesus said unto him, No man, having put his hand to the plough, and looking back, is fit for the kingdom of God" (Luke 9:59-62). . . .

Such are the instances of Divine calls in Scripture, and their characteristic is this: to require instant obedience, and next to call us we know not to what; to call us on in the darkness. Faith alone can obey them.

But it may be urged, How does this concern us now? We were all called to serve God in infancy, before we could obey or disobey; we found ourselves called when reason began to dawn; we have been called to a state of salvation, we have been living as God's servants and children, all through our time of trial, having been brought into it in infancy through Holy Baptism, by the act of our parents. Calling is not a thing future with us, but a thing past.

This is true in a very sufficient sense; and yet it is true also that the passages of Scripture which I have been quoting do apply to us still — do concern us, and may warn and guide us in many important ways, as a few words will show.

For in truth we are not called once only, but many times; all through our life Christ is calling us. He called us first in Baptism; but afterwards also; whether we obey His voice or not, He graciously calls us still. If we fall from our Baptism, He calls us to repent; if we are striving to fulfill our calling, He calls us on from grace to grace, and from holiness to holiness, while life is given us. . . .

It were well if we understood this; but we are slow to master the great truth, that Christ is, as it were, walking among us, and by His hand, or eye, or voice, bidding us follow Him. We do not understand that His call is a thing which takes place now. We think it took place in the Apostles' days; but we do not believe in it, we do not look out for it in our own case. We have not eyes to see the Lord; far different from the beloved Apostle, who knew Christ even when the rest of the disciples knew Him not. When He stood on the shore after His resurrection, and bade them cast the net into the sea, "that disciple whom Jesus loved saith unto Peter, It is the Lord" (John 21:7).

Now what I mean is this: that they who are living religiously, have from time to time truths they did not know before, or had no need to consider, brought before them forcibly; truths which involve duties, which are in fact precepts, and claim obedience. In this and such like ways Christ calls us now. There is nothing miraculous or extraordinary in His dealings with us. He works through our natural faculties and circumstances of life. Still what happens to us in providence is in all essential respects what His voice was to those whom He addressed when on earth: whether He commands by a visible presence, or by a voice, or by our consciences, it matters not, so that we feel it to be a command. If it is a command, it may be obeyed or disobeyed; it may be accepted as Samuel or St. Paul accepted it, or put aside after the manner of the young man who had great possessions.

And these Divine calls are commonly, from the nature of the case, sudden now, and as indefinite and obscure in their consequences as in former times. The accidents and events of life are, as is obvious, one special way in which the calls I speak of come to us; and they, as we all know, are in their very nature, and as the word "accident" implies, sudden and unexpected. A man is going on as usual; he comes home one day, and finds a letter, or a message, or a person, whereby a sudden trial comes on him, which, if met religiously, will be the means of advancing him to a higher state of religious excellence. . . .

Perhaps it may be the loss of some dear friend or relative through which the call comes to us; which shows us the vanity of things below, and prompts us to make God our sole stay. We through grace do so in a way we never did before; and in the course of years, when we look back on our life, we find that that sad event has brought us into a new state of faith and judgment, and that we are as though other men from what we were. We thought, before it took place, that we were serving God, and so we were in a measure; but we find that, whatever our present infirmities may be, and however far we be still from the highest state of illumination, then at least we were serving the world under the show and the belief of serving God.

Or again, perhaps something occurs to force us to take a part for God or against Him. The world requires of us some sacrifice which we see we ought not to grant to it. Some tempting offer is made us; or some reproach or discredit threatened us; or we have to determine and avow what is truth and what is error. We are enabled to act as God would have us act; and we do so in much fear and perplexity. We do not see our way clearly; we do not see what is to follow from what we have done, and how it bears upon our general conduct and opinions: yet perhaps it has the most important bearings. That little deed, suddenly exacted of us, almost suddenly resolved on and executed, may be as though a gate into the second or third heaven — an entrance into a higher state of holiness, and into a truer view of things than we have hitherto taken.

Or again, we get acquainted with someone whom God employs to bring before us a number of truths which were closed on us before; and we but half understand them, and but half approve of them; and yet God seems to speak in them, and Scripture to confirm them. This is a case which not unfrequently occurs, and it involves a call "to follow on to know the Lord."

Or again, we may be in the practice of reading Scripture carefully, and trying to serve God, and its sense may, as if suddenly, break upon us, in a way it never did before. Some thought may suggest itself to us which is a key to a great deal in Scripture, or which suggests a great many other thoughts. A new light may be thrown on the precepts of our Lord and His Apostles. We may be able to enter into the manner of life of the early Christians, as recorded in Scripture, which before was hidden from us, and into the simple maxims on which Scripture bases it. We may be led to understand that it is very different from the life which men live now. Now knowledge is a call to action: an insight into the way of perfection is a call to perfection. . . .

To conclude. Nothing is more certain in matter of fact, than that some men do feel themselves called to high duties and works, to which others are not called. Why this is we do not know; whether it be that those who are not called forfeit the call from having failed in former trials, or have been called and have not followed; or that though God gives baptismal grace to all, yet He really does call some men by His free grace to higher things than others. But so it is; this man sees sights which that man does not see, has a larger faith, a more ardent love, and a more spiritual understanding. No one has any leave to take another's lower standard of holiness for his own. It is nothing to us what others are. If God calls us to greater renunciation of the world, and exacts a sacrifice of our hopes and fears, this is our gain, this is a mark of His love for us, this is a thing to be rejoiced in. Such thoughts, when properly entertained, have no tendency to puff us up; for if the prospect is noble, yet the risk is more fearful. While we pursue high excellence, we walk among precipices, and a fall is easy. Hence the Apostle says, "Work out your own salvation with fear and trembling, for it is God that worketh in you" (Phil. 2:12). Again, the more men aim at high things, the more sensitive perception they have of their own shortcomings; and this again is adapted to humble them especially. We need not fear spiritual pride, then, in following Christ's call, if we follow it as men in earnest. Earnestness has no time to compare itself with the state of other men; earnestness has too vivid a feeling of its own infirmities to be elated at itself. Earnestness is simply set on doing God's will. It simply says, "Speak, Lord, for Thy servant heareth"; "Lord, what wilt Thou have me to do?" Oh that we had more of this spirit! Oh that we could take that simple view of things, as to feel that the one thing which lies before us is to please God! What gain is it to please the world, to please the great, nay, even to please those whom we love, compared with this? What gain is it to be applauded, admired, courted, followed, compared with this one aim, of not being disobedient to a heavenly vision? What can this world offer comparable with that insight into spiritual things, that keen faith, that heavenly peace, that high sanctity, that ever-lasting righteousness, that hope of glory, which they have who in sincerity love and follow our Lord Jesus Christ?

Let us beg and pray Him day by day to reveal Himself to our souls more fully; to quicken our senses; to give us sight and hearing, taste and touch of the world to come; so to work within us that we may sincerely say, "Thou shalt guide me with Thy counsel, and after that receive me to glory. Whom have I in heaven but Thee? and there is none upon earth that I desire in comparison of Thee: my flesh and my heart faileth; but God is the strength of my heart, and my portion for ever" (Ps. 73:24-26).

———

FEODOR DOSTOEVSKY

The Brothers Karamazov

The riches of the work of Eastern Christian theologians are only now making a long overdue impact in Western Christianity. But many Protestant and Catholic theologians in the twentieth century have been influenced by reading the great Russian novelists, above all Feodor Dostoevsky (1821-1881). In this, his last and greatest novel, completed in 1880, Dostoevsky portrayed many of the issues that had concerned him most of his life in the contrast between two brothers — Alexey, the pious young novice monk, and Ivan, the cynical skeptic who believes that, "If God is dead, everything is permitted." The section from which this excerpt comes presents the thoughts of Alexey's mentor, the famous monk Father Zossima, on the dangers of Western ideas, the characteristic Russian virtues, and the true meaning of freedom.

═══════

Conversations and Exhortations of Father Zossima

(e) *The Russian Monk and His Possible Significance*

Fathers and teachers, what is the monk? In the cultivated world the word is nowadays pronounced by some people with a jeer, and by others it is used as a term of abuse, and this contempt for the monk is growing. It is true, alas, it is true, that there are many sluggards, gluttons, profligates and inso-

---

Feodor Dostoevsky, *The Brothers Karamazov,* trans. Constance Garnett (New York: Macmillan, 1916), 332-35.

lent beggars among monks. Educated people point to these: "You are idlers, useless members of society, you live on the labor of others, you are shameless beggars." And yet how many meek and humble monks there are, yearning for solitude and fervent prayer in peace. These are less noticed, or passed over in silence. And how surprised men would be if I were to say that from these meek monks, who yearn for solitary prayer, the salvation of Russia will come perhaps once more. For they are in truth made ready in peace and quiet "for the day and the hour, the month and the year." Meanwhile, in their solitude, they keep the image of Christ fair and undefiled, in the purity of God's truth, from the times of the Fathers of old, the Apostles and the martyrs. And when the time comes they will show it to the tottering creeds of the world. That is a great thought. That star will rise out of the East.

That is my view of the monk, and is it false? is it too proud? Look at the worldly and all who set themselves up above the people of God, has not God's image and His truth been distorted in them? They have science; but in science there is nothing but what is the object of sense. The spiritual world, the higher part of man's being, is rejected altogether, dismissed with a sort of triumph, even with hatred. The world has proclaimed the reign of freedom, especially of late, but what do we see in this freedom of theirs? Nothing but slavery and self-destruction. For the world says: "You have desires and so satisfy them, for you have the same rights as the most rich and powerful. Don't be afraid of satisfying them and even multiplying your desires." That is the modern doctrine of the world. In that they see freedom. And what follows from this right of multiplication of desires? In the rich, *isolation* and spiritual suicide; in the poor, envy and murder; for they have been given rights, but have not been shown the means of satisfying their wants. They maintain that the world is getting more and more united, more and more bound together in brotherly community, it overcomes distance and sets thoughts flying through the air. Alas, put no faith in such a bond of union. Interpreting freedom as the multiplication and rapid satisfaction of desires, men distort their *own* nature, for many senseless and foolish desires and habits and ridiculous fancies are fostered in them. They live only for mutual envy, for gluttony and ostentation. To have dinners, visits, carriages, rank and slaves to wait on one is looked upon as a necessity, for which life, honor and human feeling are sacrificed, and men even commit suicide if they are unable to satisfy it. We see the same thing among those who are not rich, while the poor drown their unsatisfied need and their envy in drunkenness. But soon they will drink blood instead of wine, they are being led on to it. I ask you, Is such a man free? I knew one "champion of freedom" who told me himself that, when he was deprived of tobacco in prison, he was so wretched at the privation that he almost went and betrayed his cause for the sake of getting tobacco again! And such a man says, "I am fighting for the cause of humanity." How can such a one fight, what is he fit for? He is capable perhaps of some action quickly over, but he cannot hold out long. And it's no wonder that instead of gaining freedom they have sunk into slavery, and instead of serving the cause of brotherly love and the union of humanity have fallen, on the contrary, into separation and isolation, as my mysterious visitor and teacher said to me in my youth. And therefore the idea of the service of humanity, of brotherly love and the solidarity of mankind, is more and more dying out in the world, and indeed this idea is sometimes treated with derision. For how can a man shake off his habits, what can become of him if he is in such bondage to the habit of satisfying the innumerable desires he has created for himself? He is isolated, and what concern has he with the rest of humanity? They have succeeded in accumulating a greater mass of objects, but the joy in the world has grown less.

The monastic way is very different. Obedience, fasting and prayer are laughed at, yet only through them lies the way to real, true freedom. I cut off my superfluous and unnecessary desires, I subdue my proud and wanton will and chastise it with obedience, and with God's help I attain freedom of spirit and with it spiritual joy. Who is more capable of conceiving a great idea and serving it — the rich man in his isolation or the man who has *freed himself* from the tyranny of material things and habits? The monk is reproached for his solitude, "You have secluded yourself within the walls of the monastery for your own salvation, and have forgotten the brotherly service of humanity!" But we shall see which will be most zealous in the cause of brotherly love. For it is not we, but they, who are in isolation, though they don't see that. Of old, leaders of the people came from among us, and why should they not again? The same meek and humble ascetics will rise up and go to work for the great cause. The salvation of Russia comes from the people. And the Russian monk has always been on the side of the people. We are isolated only if the people are isolated. The people believe as we do, and an unbelieving reformer will never do anything in Russia, even if he is sincere in heart and a genius. Remember that! The people will meet the atheist and overcome him, and Russia will be one and orthodox. Take care of the people and guard their hearts. Go on educating them quietly. That's your duty as monks, for this is a godfearing people.

(f) Of Masters and Servants, and of Whether It Is Possible for Them to Be Brothers in the Spirit

Of course, I don't deny that there is sin in the peasants too. And the fire of corruption is spreading visibly, hourly, working from above downwards. The spirit of isolation is coming upon the people too. Moneylenders and devourers of the commune are rising up. Already the merchant grows more and more eager for rank, and strives to show himself cultured though he has not a trace of culture, and to this end meanly despises his old traditions, and is even ashamed of the faith of his fathers. He visits princes, though he is only a peasant corrupted. The peasants are rotting in drunkenness and cannot shake off the habit. And what cruelty to their wives, to their children even! All from drunkenness! I've seen in the factories children of ten, frail, rickety, bent and already depraved. The stuffy workshop, the din of machinery, work all day long, the vile language and the drink, the drink — is that what a little child's heart needs? He needs sunshine, childish play, good examples all about him, and at least a little love. There must be no more of this, monks, nor more torturing of children, rise up and preach that, make haste, make haste! But God will save Russia, for though the peasants are corrupted and cannot renounce their filthy sin, yet they know it is cursed by God and that they do wrong in sinning. So that our people still believe in righteousness, have faith in God and weep tears of devotion.

It is different with the upper classes. They, following science, want to base justice on reason alone, but not with Christ, as before, and they have already proclaimed that there is no crime, that there is no sin. And that's consistent, for if you have no God, what is the meaning of crime? In Europe the people are already rising up against the rich with violence, and the leaders of the people are everywhere leading them to bloodshed, and teaching them that their wrath is righteous. But their "wrath is accursed, for it is cruel." But God will save Russia as He has saved her many times. Salvation will come from the people, from their faith and their meekness.

HORACE BUSHNELL

Every Man's Life a Plan of God

Horace Bushnell (1802-1876) spent most of his adult life as pastor of the North Congregational Church in Hartford, Connecticut. He was active in the early Sunday School movement, dedicated to the idea that children could grow steadily in Christian love and did not have to sink deep into sin before a dramatic conversion experience. Influenced in both content and style by the Romantic movement then important in theology, philosophy, literature, and the arts, Bushnell saw God's spirit at work in every aspect of both nature and history. He here sets out those views and goes on to give an account of how we are to know our callings.

Christ himself testifies to the girding of the Almighty when he says, "To this end was I born, and for this purpose came I into the world" (John 12:27). Abraham was girded for a particular work and mission, in what is otherwise denominated his call. Joseph, in Egypt, distinguishes the girding of God's hand, when he comforts his guilty brothers in the assurance, "So, it was not you that sent me hither, but God" (Gen. 45:8). Moses and Samuel were even called by name, and set to their great life-work, in the same manner. And what is Paul endeavoring, in all the stress and pressure of his mighty apostleship, but to perform the work for which God's Spirit girded him at his call, and to apprehend that for which he was apprehended of Christ Jesus. And yet these great master-spirits of the world are not so much distinguished, after all, by the acts they do, as by the sense itself of some mysterious girding of the Almighty upon them, whose behests they are set to fulfill. And all men may have this; for the humblest and commonest have a place and a work assigned them, in the same manner, and have it for their privilege to be always ennobled in the same lofty consciousness. God is girding

---

Horace Bushnell, *Sermons for the New Life* (New York: Scribner's, 1889), 9-17, 18, 21-23.

every man for a place and a calling, in which, taking it from him, even though it be internally humble, he may be as consciously exalted as if he held the rule of a kingdom. The truth I propose then for your consideration is this —

That God has a definite life-plan for every human person, girding him, visibly or invisibly, for some exact thing, which it will be the true significance and glory of his life to have accomplished.

Many persons, I am well aware, never even think of any such thing. They suppose that, for most men, life is a necessarily stale and common affair. What it means for them they do not know, and they scarcely conceive that it means anything. They even complain, venting heavy sighs, that, while some few are set forward by God to do great works and fill important places, they are not allowed to believe that there is any particular object in their existence. It is remarkable, considering how generally this kind of impression prevails, that the Holy Scriptures never give way to it, but seem, as it were, in all possible ways, to be holding up the dignity of common life, and giving a meaning to its appointments, which the natural dullness and lowness of mere human opinion cannot apprehend.

They not only show us explicitly, as we have seen, that God has a definite purpose in the lives of men already great, but they show us, how frequently, in the conditions of obscurity and depression, preparations of counsel going on, by which the commonest offices are to become the necessary first chapter of a great and powerful history. David among the sheep; Elisha following after the plough; Nehemiah bearing the cup; Hannah, who can say nothing less common than that she is the wife of Elkanah and a woman of a sorrowful spirit — who, that looks on these humble people, at their humble post of service, and discovers, at last, how dear a purpose God was cherishing in them, can be justified in thinking that God has no particular plan for him, because he is not signalized by any kind of distinction?

Besides, what do the scriptures show us, but that God has a particular care for every man, a personal interest in him and a sympathy with him and his trials, watching for the uses of his one talent as attentively and kindly and approving him as heartily, in the right employment of it, as if he had given him ten; and, what is the giving out of the talents itself, but an exhibition of the fact that God has a definite purpose, charge and work, be it this or that, for every man? They also make it the privilege of every man to live in the secret guidance of God; which is plainly nugatory, unless there is some chosen work, or sphere, into which he may be guided; for how shall God guide him, having nothing appointed or marked out for him to be guided into? no field opened for him, no course set down which is to be his wisdom?

God also professes in his Word to have purposes pre-arranged for all events; to govern by a plan which is from eternity even, and which, in some proper sense, comprehends every thing. And what is this but another way of conceiving that God has a definite place and plan adjusted for every human being? And, without such a plan, he could not even govern the world intelligently, or make a proper universe of the created system; for it becomes a universe only in the grand unity of reason, which includes it. Otherwise, it were only a jumble of fortuities, without counsel, end or law.

Turning, now, from the scriptures to the works of God, how constantly are we met here by the fact, everywhere visible, that ends and uses are the regulative reasons of all existing things. This we discover often, when we are least able to understand the speculative mystery of objects; for it is precisely the uses of things that are most palpable. These uses are to God, no doubt, as to us, the significance of his works. And they compose, taken together, a grand reciprocal system, in which part answers actively to part, constructing thus an all-comprehensive and glorious whole. And the system is, in fact, so perfect, that the loss or displacement of any member would fatally derange the general order. If there were any smallest star in heaven that had no place to fill, that oversight would beget a disturbance which no Leverrier [a distinguished French chemist and astronomer] could compute; because it would be a real and eternal, and not merely casual or apparent disorder. One grain, more or less, of sand would disturb, or even fatally disorder the whole scheme of the heavenly motions. So nicely balanced, and so carefully hung, are the worlds, that even the grains of their dust are counted, and their places adjusted to a correspondent nicety. There is nothing included in the gross, or total sum, that could be dispensed with. The same is true in regard to forces that are apparently irregular. Every particle of air is moved by laws of as great precision as the laws of the heavenly bodies, or, indeed, by the same laws; keeping its appointed place, and serving its appointed use. Every odor exhales in the nicest conformity with its appointed place and law. Even the viewless and mysterious heat, stealing through the dark centers and impenetrable depths of the worlds, obeys its uses with unfaltering exactness, dissolving never so much as an atom that was not to be dissolved. What now shall we say of man, appearing, as it were, in the center of this great circle of uses. They are all adjusted for him: has he, then, no ends appointed for himself? Noblest of all creatures, and closest to God, as he certainly is, are we to say that his Creator has no definite thoughts concerning him, no place prepared for him to fill, no use for him to serve, which is the reason of his existence?

There is, then, I conclude, a definite and proper end, or issue, for every man's existence; an end which, to the heart of God, is the good intended for him, or for which he was intended; that which he is privileged to become, called to become, ought to become; that which God will assist him to become and which he cannot miss, save by his own fault. Every human soul has a complete and perfect plan, cherished for it in the heart of God — a divine biography marked out, which it enters into life, to live. This life, rightly unfolded, will be a complete and beautiful whole, an experience led on by God and unfolded by his secret nurture, as the trees and the flowers, by the secret nurture of the world; a drama cast in the mould of a perfect art, with no part wanting; a divine study for the man himself, and for others; a study that shall forever unfold, in wondrous beauty, the love and faithfulness of God; great in its conception, great in the Divine skill by which it is shaped; above all, great in the momentous and glorious issues it prepares. What a thought is this for every human soul to cherish! What dignity does it add to life! What support does it bring to the trials of life! What instigations does it add to send us onward in everything that constitutes our excellence! We live in the Divine thought. We fill a place in the great everlasting plan of God's intelligence. We never sink below his care, never drop out of his counsel.

But there is, I must add, a single, but very important and even fearful qualification. Things all serve their uses, and never break out of their place. They have no power to do it. Not so with us. We are able, as free beings, to refuse the place and the duties God appoints; which, if we do, then we sink into something lower and less worthy of us. That highest and best condition for which God designed us is no more possible. We are fallen out of it, and it cannot be wholly recovered. And yet, as that was the best thing possible for us in the reach of God's original counsel, so there is a place designed for us now, which is the next best possible. God calls us now to the best thing left, and will do so till all good possibility is narrowed down and spent. And then, when he cannot use us anymore for our own good, he will use us for the good of others — an example of the misery and horrible desperation to which any soul must come, when all the good ends, and all the holy callings of God's friendly and fatherly purpose are exhausted. Or it may be now that, remitting all other plans and purposes in our behalf, he will henceforth use us, wholly against our will, to be the demonstration of his justice and avenging power before the eyes of mankind; saying over us, as he did over Pharaoh in the day of his judgments, "Even for this same purpose have I raised thee up, that I might show my power in thee, and that my name might be declared throughout all the earth" (Exod. 9:16). Doubtless, He had other and more genial plans to serve in this bad man, if only he could have accepted such; but, knowing his certain rejection of these, God turned his mighty counsel in him wholly on the use to be made of him as a reprobate. How many Pharaohs in common life refuse every other use God will make of them, choosing only to figure, in their small way, as reprobates; and descending, in that manner, to a fate that painfully mimics his.

God has, then, I conclude, a definite life-plan set for every man; one that, being accepted and followed, will conduct him to the best and noblest end possible. No qualification of this doctrine is needed, save the fearful one just named; that we, by our perversity, so often refuse to take the place and do the work he gives us.

It follows, in the same way, that, as God, in fixing on our end or use, will choose the best end or use possible, so he will appoint for us the best manner possible of attaining it; for, as it is a part of God's perfection to choose the best things, and not things partially good, so it will be in all the methods he prescribes for their attainment. And so, as you pass on, stage by stage, in your courses of experience, it is made clear to you that, whatever you have laid upon you to do or to suffer, whatever to want, whatever to surrender or to conquer, is exactly best for you. Your life is a school, exactly adapted to your lesson, and that to the best, last end of your existence.

No room for a discouraged or depressed feeling, therefore, is left you. Enough that you exist for a purpose high enough to give meaning to life, and to support a genuine inspiration. If your sphere is outwardly humble, if it even appears to be quite insignificant, God understands it better than you do, and it is a part of his wisdom to bring out great sentiments in humble conditions, great principles in works that are outwardly trivial, great characters under great adversities and heavy loads of encumbrance. The tallest saints of God will often be those who walk in the deepest obscurity, and are even despised or quite overlooked by man. Let it be enough that God is in your history and that the plan of your biography is his, the issue he has set for it is the highest and the best. Away, then, O man, with thy feeble complaints and feverish despondencies. There is no place left for this kind of nonsense. Let it fill thee with cheerfulness and exalted feeling, however deep in obscurity your lot may be, that God is leading you on, girding you for a work, preparing you to a good that is worthy of his Divine magnificence. If God is really preparing us all to become that which is the very highest and best thing possible, there ought never to be a discouraged or uncheerful being in the world. . . .

But, the inquiry will be made, supposing all this to be true, in the manner stated, how can we ever get hold of this life-plan God has made for us, or find our way into it? Here, to many if not all, will be the main stress of doubt and practical suspense. . . .

You are on the point of choosing, it may be, this or that calling, wanting to know where duty lies and what the course God himself would have you take. Beginning at a point most remote, and where the generality of truth is widest,

Consider (1) the character of God, and you will draw a large deduction from that; for all that God designs for you will be in harmony with his character. He is a being infinitely good, just, true. Therefore, you are to know that he can not really seek anything contrary to this in you. You may make yourselves contrary, in every attribute of character, to God; but he never made you to become any thing different from, or unworthy of, himself. A good being could not make another to be a bad being, as the proper issue and desired end of his existence; least of all could one infinitely good. A great many employments or callings are, by these first principles, forever cut off. No thought is permitted you, even for a moment, of any work or calling that does not represent the industry, justice, truth, beneficence, mercy of God.

(2) Consider your relation to him as a creature. All created wills have their natural center and rest in God's will. In him they all come into a play of harmony, and the proper harmony of being is possible only in this way. Thus, you know that you are called to have a will perfectly harmonized with God's and rested in his, and that gives you a large insight into what you are to be, or what is the real end of your being. In fact, nine-tenths of your particular duties may be settled, at once, by a simple reference in this manner to what God wills.

(3) You have a conscience, which is given to be an interpreter of his will and thus of your duty, and, in both, of what you are to become.

(4) God's law and his written Word are guides to present duty, which, if faithfully accepted, will help to set you in accordance with the mind of God and the plan he has laid for you. "I am a stranger in the earth," said one, "hide not thy commandments from me"; knowing that God's commandments would give him a clue to the true meaning and business of his life.

(5) Be an observer of Providence; for God is showing you ever, by the way in which he leads you, whither he means to lead. Study your trials, your talents, the world's wants, and stand ready to serve God now, in whatever he brings to your hand.

Again (6) consult your friends, and especially those who are most in the teaching of God. They know your talents and personal qualifications better, in some respects, than you do yourself. Ask their judgment of you and of the spheres and works to which you are best adapted.

Once more (7) go to God himself, and ask for the calling of God; for, as certainly as he has a plan or calling for you, he will somehow guide you into it. And this is the proper office and work of his Spirit. By this private teaching he can show us, and will, into the very plan that is set for us. And this is the significance of what is prescribed as our duty, viz., living and walking in the Spirit; for the Spirit of God is a kind of universal presence, or inspiration, in the world's bosom; an unfailing inner light, which if we accept and live in, we are guided thereby into a consenting choice, so that what God wills for us we also will for ourselves — settling into it as the needle to the pole. By this hidden union with God, or intercourse with him, we get a wisdom or insight deeper than we know ourselves; a sympathy, a oneness with the Divine will and love. We go into the very plan of God for us, and are led along in it by him, consenting, cooperating, answering to him, we know not how, and working out, with nicest exactness, that good end for which his unseen counsel girded us and sent us into the world. In this manner, not neglecting the other methods just named, but gathering in all their separate lights, to be interpreted in the higher light of the Spirit, we can never be greatly at a loss to find our way into God's counsel and plan. The duties of the present moment we shall meet as they rise, and these will open a gate into the next, and we shall thus pass on, trustfully and securely, almost never in doubt as to what God calls us to do. . . .

POPE LEO XIII

Rerum Novarum

The expansion of factories and industry in the nineteenth century created a class of wealthy owners, a class of industrial workers, and a host of new social problems. Socialists proposed that the state should take over the factories from private ownership. In this official papal statement, Leo XIII (1810-1903, pope from 1878 until his death) sought a middle ground, recognizing the oppression workers could suffer but rejecting the abolition of private property as a solution. In the Catholic tradition, Leo thinks of a job

Pope Leo XIII, "Rerum Novarum," *The Papal Encyclicals 1878-1903*, ed. Claudia Carlen Ihm (Raleigh, N.C.: McGrath, 1981), 241-47, 251-53.

primarily as a way to support one's family, not as a calling in itself — and this may be a more realistic approach to factory work. *Rerum Novarum* ("New things") is conservative on issues of the father's place in the family, but it was and is radical on issues of labor and capital.

———————

To Our Venerable Brethren the Patriarchs, Primates, Archbishops, Bishops, and Other Ordinaries of Places Having Peace and Communion with the Apostolic See.

1. That the spirit of revolutionary change, which has long been disturbing the nations of the world, should have passed beyond the sphere of politics and made its influence felt in the cognate sphere of practical economics is not surprising. The elements of the conflict now raging are unmistakable, in the vast expansion of industrial pursuits and the marvelous discoveries of science; in the changed relations between masters and workmen; in the enormous fortunes of some few individuals, and the utter poverty of the masses; in the increased self-reliance and closer mutual combination of the working classes; as also, finally, in the prevailing moral degeneracy. The momentous gravity of the state of things now obtaining fills every mind with painful apprehension; wise men are discussing it; practical men are proposing schemes; popular meetings, legislatures, and rulers of nations are all busied with it — actually there is no question which has taken a deeper hold on the public mind. . . .

3. In any case we clearly see, and on this there is general agreement, that some opportune remedy must be found quickly for the misery and wretchedness pressing so unjustly on the majority of the working class: for the ancient workingmen's guilds were abolished in the last century, and no other protective organization took their place. Public institutions and the laws set aside the ancient religion. Hence, by degrees it has come to pass that working men have been surrendered, isolated and helpless, to the hardheartedness of employers and the greed of unchecked competition. The mischief has been increased by rapacious usury, which, although more than once condemned by the Church, is nevertheless, under a different guise, but with like injustice, still practiced by covetous and grasping men. To this must be added that the hiring of labor and the conduct of trade are concentrated in the hands of comparatively few; so that a small number of very rich men have been able to lay upon the teeming masses of the laboring poor a yoke little better than that of slavery itself.

4. To remedy these wrongs the socialists, working on the poor man's envy of the rich, are striving to do away with private property, and contend

that individual possessions should become the common property of all, to be administered by the State or by municipal bodies. They hold that by thus transferring property from private individuals to the community, the present mischievous state of things will be set to rights, inasmuch as each citizen will then get his fair share of whatever there is to enjoy. But their contentions are so clearly powerless to end the controversy that were they carried into effect the working man himself would be among the first to suffer. They are, moreover, emphatically unjust, for they would rob the lawful possessor, distort the functions of the State, and create utter confusion in the community.

5. It is surely undeniable that, when a man engages in remunerative labor, the impelling reason and motive of his work is to obtain property, and thereafter to hold it as his very own. If one man hires out to another his strength or skill, he does so for the purpose of receiving in return what is necessary for the satisfaction of his needs; he therefore expressly intends to acquire a right full and real, not only to the remuneration, but also to the disposal of such remuneration, just as he pleases. Thus, if he lives sparingly, saves money, and, for greater security, invests his savings in land, the land, in such case, is only his wages under another form; and, consequently, a working man's little estate thus purchased should be as completely at his full disposal as are the wages he receives for his labor. But it is precisely in such power of disposal that ownership obtains, whether the property consist of land or chattels. Socialists, therefore, by endeavoring to transfer the possessions of individuals to the community at large, strike at the interests of every wage-earner, since they would deprive him of the liberty of disposing of his wages, and thereby of all hope and possibility of increasing his resources and of bettering his condition in life.

6. What is of far greater moment, however, is the fact that the remedy they propose is manifestly against justice. For every man has by nature the right to possess property as his own. This is one of the chief points of distinction between man and the animal creation, for the brute has no power of self-direction, but is governed by two main instincts, which keep his powers on the alert, impel him to develop them in a fitting manner, and stimulate and determine him to action without any power of choice. One of these instincts is self-preservation, the other the propagation of the species. Both can attain their purpose by means of things which lie within range; beyond their verge the brute creation cannot go, for they are moved to action by their senses only, and in the special direction which these suggest. But with man it is wholly different. He possesses, on the one hand, the full perfection of the animal being, and hence enjoys at least as much as the rest of the ani-

mal kind, the fruition of things material. But animal nature, however per-fect, is far from representing the human being in its completeness, and is in truth but humanity's humble handmaid, made to serve and to obey. It is the mind, or reason, which is the predominant element in us who are human creatures; it is this which renders a human being human, and distinguishes him essentially from the brute. And on this very account — that man alone among the animal creation is endowed with reason — it must be within his right to possess things not merely for temporary and momentary use, as other living things do, but to have and to hold them in stable and permanent possession; he must have not only things that perish in the use, but those also which, though they have been reduced into use, continue for further use in after time. . . .

13. That right to property, therefore, which has been proved to belong naturally to individual persons, must in like wise belong to a man in his ca-pacity of head of a family; nay, that right is all the stronger in proportion as the human person receives a wider extension in the family group. It is a most sacred law of nature that a father should provide food and all neces-saries for those whom he has begotten; and, similarly, it is natural that he should wish that his children, who carry on, so to speak, and continue his personality, should be by him provided with all that is needful to enable them to keep themselves decently from want and misery amid the uncer-tainties of this mortal life. Now, in no other way can a father effect this ex-cept by the ownership of productive property, which he can transmit to his children by inheritance. A family, no less than a State, is, as We have said, a true society, governed by an authority peculiar to itself, that is to say, by the authority of the father. Provided, therefore, the limits which are prescribed by the very purposes for which it exists be not transgressed, the family has at least equal rights with the State in the choice and pursuit of the things needful to its preservation and its just liberty. We say, "at least equal rights"; for, inasmuch as the domestic household is antecedent, as well in idea as in fact, to the gathering of men into a community, the family must necessarily have rights and duties which are prior to those of the community, and founded more immediately in nature. If the citizens, if the families on enter-ing into association and fellowship, were to experience hindrance in a com-monwealth instead of help, and were to find their rights attacked instead of being upheld, society would rightly be an object of detestation rather than of desire.

14. The contention, then, that the civil government should at its option intrude into and exercise intimate control over the family and the household is a great and pernicious error. True, if a family finds itself in exceeding dis-

tress, utterly deprived of the counsel of friends, and without any prospect of extricating itself, it is right that extreme necessity be met by public aid, since each family is a part of the commonwealth. In like manner, if within the precincts of the household there occur grave disturbance of mutual rights, public authority should intervene to force each party to yield to the other its proper due; for this is not to deprive citizens of their rights, but justly and properly to safeguard and strengthen them.

But the rulers of the commonwealth must go no further; here, nature bids them stop. Paternal authority can be neither abolished nor absorbed by the State; for it has the same source as human life itself. "The child belongs to the father," and is, as it were, the continuation of the father's personality; and speaking strictly, the child takes its place in civil society, not of its own right, but in its quality as member of the family in which it is born. And for the very reason that "the child belongs to the father" it is, as St. Thomas Aquinas says, "before it attains the use of free will, under the power and the charge of its parents." The socialists, therefore, in setting aside the parent and setting up a State supervision, act against natural justice, and destroy the structure of the home.

15. And in addition to injustice, it is only too evident what an upset and disturbance there would be in all classes, and to how intolerable and hateful a slavery citizens would be subjected. The door would be thrown open to envy, to mutual invective, and to discord; the sources of wealth themselves would run dry, for no one would have any interest in exerting his talents or his industry; and that ideal equality about which they entertain pleasant dreams would be in reality the leveling down of all to a like condition of misery and degradation.

Hence, it is clear that the main tenet of socialism, community of goods, must be utterly rejected, since it only injures those whom it would seem meant to benefit, is directly contrary to the natural rights of mankind, and would introduce confusion and disorder into the commonweal. The first and most fundamental principle, therefore, if one would undertake to alleviate the condition of the masses, must be the inviolability of private property. This being established, we proceed to show where the remedy sought for must be found. . . .

19. The great mistake made in regard to the matter now under consideration is to take up with the notion that class is naturally hostile to class, and that the wealthy and the working men are intended by nature to live in mutual conflict. So irrational and so false is this view that the direct contrary is the truth. Just as the symmetry of the human frame is the result of the suitable arrangement of the different parts of the body, so in a State is it or-

dained by nature that these two classes should dwell in harmony and agreement, so as to maintain the balance of the body politic. Each needs the other: capital cannot do without labor, nor labor without capital. Mutual agreement results in the beauty of good order, while perpetual conflict necessarily produces confusion and savage barbarity. Now, in preventing such strife as this, and in uprooting it, the efficacy of Christian institutions is marvelous and manifold. First of all, there is no intermediary more powerful than religion (whereof the Church is the interpreter and guardian) in drawing the rich and the working class together, by reminding each of its duties to the other, and especially of the obligations of justice.

20. Of these duties, the following bind the proletarian and the worker: fully and faithfully to perform the work which has been freely and equitably agreed upon; never to injure the property, nor to outrage the person, of an employer; never to resort to violence in defending their own cause, nor to engage in riot or disorder; and to have nothing to do with men of evil principles, who work upon the people with artful promises of great results, and excite foolish hopes which usually end in useless regrets and grievous loss. The following duties bind the wealthy owner and the employer: not to look upon their work people as their bondsmen, but to respect in every man his dignity as a person ennobled by Christian character. They are reminded that, according to natural reason and Christian philosophy, working for gain is creditable, not shameful, to a man, since it enables him to earn an honorable livelihood; but to misuse men as though they were things in the pursuit of gain, or to value them solely for their physical powers — that is truly shameful and inhuman. Again justice demands that, in dealing with the working man, religion and the good of his soul must be kept in mind. Hence, the employer is bound to see that the worker has time for his religious duties; that he be not exposed to corrupting influences and dangerous occasions; and that he be not led away to neglect his home and family, or to squander his earnings. Furthermore, the employer must never tax his work people beyond their strength, or employ them in work unsuited to their sex and age. His great and principal duty is to give everyone what is just. Doubtless, before deciding whether wages are fair, many things have to be considered; but wealthy owners and all masters of labor should be mindful of this — that to exercise pressure upon the indigent and the destitute for the sake of gain, and to gather one's profit out of the need of another, is condemned by all laws, human and divine. To defraud any one of wages that are his due is a great crime which cries to the avenging anger of Heaven. "Behold, the hire of the laborers . . . which by fraud has been kept back by you, crieth; and the cry of them hath entered into the ears of the Lord of Sabaoth" (James 5:4).

Lastly, the rich must religiously refrain from cutting down the workmen's earnings, whether by force, by fraud, or by usurious dealing; and with all the greater reason because the laboring man is, as a rule, weak and unprotected, and because his slender means should in proportion to their scantiness be accounted sacred.

Were these precepts carefully obeyed and followed out, would they not be sufficient of themselves to keep under all strife and all its causes?

21. But the Church, with Jesus Christ as her Master and Guide, aims higher still. She lays down precepts yet more perfect, and tries to bind class to class in friendliness and good feeling. The things of earth cannot be understood or valued aright without taking into consideration the life to come, the life that will know no death. Exclude the idea of futurity, and forthwith the very notion of what is good and right would perish; nay, the whole scheme of the universe would become a dark and unfathomable mystery. The great truth which we learn from nature herself is also the grand Christian dogma on which religion rests as on its foundation — that, when we have given up this present life, then shall we really begin to live. God has not created us for the perishable and transitory things of earth, but for things heavenly and everlasting; He has given us this world as a place of exile, and not as our abiding place. As for riches and the other things which men call good and desirable, whether we have them in abundance, or are lacking in them — so far as eternal happiness is concerned — it makes no difference; the only important thing is to use them aright. Jesus Christ, when He redeemed us with plentiful redemption, took not away the pains and sorrows which in such large proportion are woven together in the web of our mortal life. He transformed them into motives of virtue and occasions of merit; and no man can hope for eternal reward unless he follow in the blood-stained footprints of his Savior. "If we suffer with Him, we shall also reign with Him" (Rom. 8:17). Christ's labors and sufferings, accepted of His own free will, have marvelously sweetened all suffering and all labor. And not only by His example, but by His grace and by the hope held forth of everlasting recompense, has He made pain and grief more easy to endure; "for that which is at present momentary and light of our tribulation, worketh for us above measure exceedingly an eternal weight of glory" (2 Cor. 4:17).

22. Therefore, those whom fortune favors are warned that riches do not bring freedom from sorrow and are of no avail for eternal happiness, but rather are obstacles; that the rich should tremble at the threatenings of Jesus Christ — threatenings so unwonted in the mouth of our Lord — and that a most strict account must be given to the Supreme Judge for all we possess. The chief and most excellent rule for the right use of money is one the hea-

then philosophers hinted at, but which the Church has traced out clearly, and has not only made known to men's minds, but has impressed upon their lives. It rests on the principle that it is one thing to have a right to the possession of money and another to have a right to use money as one wills. Private ownership, as we have seen, is the natural right of man, and to exercise that right, especially as members of society, is not only lawful, but absolutely necessary. "It is lawful," says St. Thomas Aquinas, "for a man to hold private property; and it is also necessary for the carrying on of human existence." But if the question be asked: How must one's possessions be used? — the Church replies without hesitation in the words of the same holy Doctor: "Man should not consider his material possessions as his own, but as common to all, so as to share them without hesitation when others are in need. Whence the apostle saith, 'Command the rich of this world . . . to offer with no stint, to apportion largely'" (1 Tim. 6:17-18). True, no one is commanded to distribute to others that which is required for his own needs and those of his household; nor even to give away what is reasonably required to keep up becomingly his condition in life, "for no one ought to live other than becomingly." But when what necessity demands has been supplied, and one's standing fairly taken thought for, it becomes a duty to give to the indigent out of what remains over. "Of that which remaineth, give alms." It is duty, not of justice (save in extreme cases), but of Christian charity — a duty not enforced by human law. But the laws and judgments of men must yield place to the laws and judgments of Christ the true God, who in many ways urges on His followers the practice of almsgiving — "It is more blessed to give than to receive" (Acts 20:35); and who will count a kindness done or refused to the poor as done or refused to Himself — "As long as you did it to one of My least brethren you did it to Me" (Matt. 25:40). To sum up, then, what has been said: Whoever has received from the divine bounty a large share of temporal blessings, whether they be external and material, or gifts of the mind, has received them for the purpose of using them for the perfecting of his own nature, and, at the same time, that he may employ them, as the steward of God's providence, for the benefit of others. "He that hath a talent," said St. Gregory the Great, "let him see that he hide it not; he that hath abundance, let him quicken himself to mercy and generosity; he that hath art and skill, let him do his best to share the use and the utility thereof with his neighbor."

23. As for those who possess not the gifts of fortune, they are taught by the Church that in God's sight poverty is no disgrace, and that there is nothing to be ashamed of in earning their bread by labor. This is enforced by what we see in Christ Himself, who, "whereas He was rich, for our sakes became poor" (2 Cor. 8:9); and who, being the Son of God, and God Himself,

chose to seem and to be considered the son of a carpenter — nay, did not disdain to spend a great part of His life as a carpenter Himself. "Is not this the carpenter, the son of Mary?" (Mark 6:3). . . .

40. The working man, too, has interests in which he should be protected by the State; and first of all, there are the interests of his soul. Life on earth, however good and desirable in itself, is not the final purpose for which man is created; it is only the way and the means to that attainment of truth and that love of goodness in which the full life of the soul consists. It is the soul which is made after the image and likeness of God; it is in the soul that the sovereignty resides in virtue whereof man is commanded to rule the creatures below him and to use all the earth and the ocean for his profit and advantage. "Fill the earth and subdue it; and rule over the fishes of the sea, and the fowls of the air, and all living creatures that move upon the earth" (Gen. 1:28). In this respect all men are equal; there is here no difference between rich and poor, master and servant, ruler and ruled, "for the same Lord is Lord over all" (Rom. 10:12). No man may with impunity outrage that human dignity which God Himself treats with great reverence, nor stand in the way of that higher life which is the preparation of the eternal life of heaven. Nay, more; no man has in this matter power over himself. To consent to any treatment which is calculated to defeat the end and purpose of his being is beyond his right; he cannot give up his soul to servitude, for it is not man's own rights which are here in question, but the rights of God, the most sacred and inviolable of rights.

41. From this follows the obligation of the cessation from work and labor on Sundays and certain holy days. The rest from labor is not to be understood as mere giving way to idleness; much less must it be an occasion for spending money and for vicious indulgence, as many would have it to be; but it should be rest from labor, hallowed by religion. Rest (combined with religious observances) disposes man to forget for a while the business of his everyday life, to turn his thoughts to things heavenly, and to the worship which he so strictly owes to the eternal Godhead. It is this, above all, which is the reason and motive of Sunday rest; a rest sanctioned by God's great law of the Ancient Covenant — "Remember thou keep holy the Sabbath day" (Exod. 20:8), and taught to the world by His own mysterious "rest" after the creation of man: "He rested on the seventh day from all His work which He had done" (Gen. 2:2).

42. If we turn now to things external and material, the first thing of all to secure is to save unfortunate working people from the cruelty of men of greed, who use human beings as mere instruments for money-making. It is neither just nor human so to grind men down with excessive labor as to stu-

pefy their minds and wear out their bodies. Man's powers, like his general nature, are limited, and beyond these limits he cannot go. His strength is developed and increased by use and exercise, but only on condition of due intermission and proper rest. Daily labor, therefore, should be so regulated as not to be protracted over longer hours than strength admits. How many and how long the intervals of rest should be must depend on the nature of the work, on circumstances of time and place, and on the health and strength of the workman. Those who work in mines and quarries, and extract coal, stone and metals from the bowels of the earth, should have shorter hours in proportion as their labor is more severe and trying to health. Then, again, the season of the year should be taken into account; for not infrequently a kind of labor is easy at one time which at another is intolerable or exceedingly difficult. Finally, work which is quite suitable for a strong man cannot rightly be required from a woman or a child. And, in regard to children, great care should be taken not to place them in workshops and factories until their bodies and minds are sufficiently developed. For, just as very rough weather destroys the buds of spring, so does too early an experience of life's hard toil blight the young promise of a child's faculties, and render any true education impossible. Women, again, are not suited for certain occupations; a woman is by nature fitted for home-work, and it is that which is best adapted at once to preserve her modesty and to promote the good bringing up of children and the well-being of the family. As a general principle it may be laid down that a workman ought to have leisure and rest proportionate to the wear and tear of his strength, for waste of strength must be repaired by cessation from hard work.

In all agreements between masters and workpeople there is always the condition expressed or understood that there should be allowed proper rest for soul and body. To agree in any other sense would be against what is right and just; for it can never be just or right to require on the one side, or to promise on the other, the giving up of those duties which a man owes to his God and to himself.

43. We now approach a subject of great importance, and one in respect of which, if extremes are to be avoided, right notions are absolutely necessary. Wages, as we are told, are regulated by free consent, and therefore the employer, when he pays what was agreed upon, has done his part and seemingly is not called upon to do anything beyond. The only way, it is said, in which injustice might occur would be if the master refused to pay the whole of the wages, or if the workman should not complete the work undertaken; in such cases the public authority should intervene, to see that each obtains his due, but not under any other circumstances.

44. To this kind of argument a fair-minded man will not easily or entirely assent; it is not complete, for there are important considerations which it leaves out of account altogether. To labor is to exert oneself for the sake of procuring what is necessary for the various purposes of life, and chief of all for self-preservation. "In the sweat of thy face thou shalt eat bread." Hence, a man's labor necessarily bears two notes or characters. First of all, it is personal, inasmuch as the force which acts is bound up with the personality and is the exclusive property of him who acts, and, further, was given to him for his advantage. Secondly, man's labor is necessary; for without the result of labor a man cannot live, and self-preservation is a law of nature, which it is wrong to disobey. Now, were we to consider labor merely in so far as it is personal, doubtless it would be within the workman's right to accept any rate of wages whatsoever; for in the same way as he is free to work or not, so is he free to accept a small wage or even none at all. But our conclusion must be very different if, together with the personal element in a man's work, we consider the fact that work is also necessary for him to live: these two aspects of his work are separable in thought, but not in reality. The preservation of life is the bounden duty of one and all, and to be wanting therein is a crime. It necessarily follows that each one has a natural right to procure what is required in order to live, and the poor can procure that in no other way than by what they can earn through their work.

45. Let the working man and the employer make free agreements, and in particular let them agree freely as to the wages; nevertheless, there underlies a dictate of natural justice more imperious and ancient than any bargain between man and man, namely, that wages ought not to be insufficient to support a frugal and well-behaved wage-earner. If through necessity or fear of a worse evil the workman accept harder conditions because an employer or contractor will afford him no better, he is made the victim of force and injustice. In these and similar questions, however — such as, for example, the hours of labor in different trades, the sanitary precautions to be observed in factories and workshops, etc. — in order to supersede undue interference on the part of the State, especially as circumstances, times, and localities differ so widely, it is advisable that recourse be had to societies or boards such as We shall mention presently, or to some other mode of safeguarding the interests of the wage-earners; the State being appealed to, should circumstances require, for its sanction and protection.

46. If a workman's wages be sufficient to enable him comfortably to support himself, his wife, and his children, he will find it easy, if he be a sensible man, to practice thrift, and he will not fail, by cutting down expenses, to put by some little savings and thus secure a modest source of income. Na-

ture itself would urge him to this. We have seen that this great labor question cannot be solved save by assuming as a principle that private ownership must be held sacred and inviolable. The law, therefore, should favor ownership, and its policy should be to induce as many as possible of the people to become owners.

47. Many excellent results will follow from this; and, first of all, property will certainly become more equitably divided. For, the result of civil change and revolution has been to divide cities into two classes separated by a wide chasm. On the one side there is the party which holds power because it holds wealth; which has in its grasp the whole of labor and trade; which manipulates for its own benefit and its own purposes all the sources of supply, and which is not without influence even in the administration of the commonwealth. On the other side there is the needy and powerless multitude, sick and sore in spirit and ever ready for disturbance. If working people can be encouraged to look forward to obtaining a share in the land, the consequence will be that the gulf between vast wealth and sheer poverty will be bridged over, and the respective classes will be brought nearer to one another. A further consequence will result in the great abundance of the fruits of the earth. Men always work harder and more readily when they work on that which belongs to them; nay, they learn to love the very soil that yields in response to the labor of their hands, not only food to eat, but an abundance of good things for themselves and those that are dear to them. That such a spirit of willing labor would add to the produce of the earth and to the wealth of the community is self-evident. And a third advantage would spring from this: men would cling to the country in which they were born, for no one would exchange his country for a foreign land if his own afforded him the means of living a decent and happy life. These three important benefits, however, can be reckoned on only provided that a man's means be not drained and exhausted by excessive taxation. The right to possess private property is derived from nature, not from man; and the State has the right to control its use in the interests of the public good alone, but by no means to absorb it altogether. The State would therefore be unjust and cruel if under the name of taxation it were to deprive the private owner of more than is fair.

MAX WEBER

The Protestant Ethic and the Spirit of Capitalism

Max Weber (1864-1920) was a historian and sociologist rather than a theologian or preacher. This famous book, published in 1904-5, looks back to analyze what Protestant Christians had believed about work and vocation rather than making any proposals about what they ought to believe today. As history, moreover, it has been widely criticized as presenting far too simple a thesis. Yet Weber's approach — thinking about the relation between economics and religious belief — and his particular thesis — that the "asceticism" of many Protestants, their opposition to luxury and ostentation, and their dedication to hard work contributed to the birth of capitalism — have both been widely influential.

Remember that time *is* money. *He that can earn ten shillings a day by his labor, and goes abroad, or sits idle, one half of that day, though he spends but sixpence during his diversion or idleness, ought not to reckon that the only expense; he has really spent, or rather thrown away, five shillings besides. . . .*

Remember, that money is of the prolific, generating nature. Money can beget money, and its offspring can beget more, and so on. . . .

The most trifling actions that affect a man's credit are to be regarded. The sound of your hammer at five in the morning, or eight at night, heard by a creditor, makes him easy six months longer; but if he sees you at a billiard table, or hears your voice at a tavern, when you should be at work, he sends for his money the next day.

BENJAMIN FRANKLIN

Max Weber, *The Protestant Ethic and the Spirit of Capitalism* (Mineola, N.Y.: Dover, 2003), 47-48, 166, 168-72, 174-77, 178-79, 180-82.

. . . .

Let us now try to clarify the points in which the Puritan idea of calling and the premium it placed upon ascetic conduct was bound directly to influence the development of a capitalistic way of life. As we have seen, this asceticism turned with all its force against one thing: the spontaneous enjoyment of life and all it had to offer. . . .

Its attitude was thus suspicious and often hostile to the aspects of culture without any immediate religious value. It is not, however, true that the ideals of Puritanism implied a solemn, narrow-minded contempt of culture. Quite the contrary is the case at least for science, with the exception of the hatred of Scholasticism. Moreover, the great men of the Puritan movement were thoroughly steeped in the culture of the Renaissance. The sermons of the Presbyterian divines abound with classical allusions, and even the Radicals, although they objected to it, were not ashamed to display that kind of learning in theological polemics. Perhaps no country was ever so full of graduates as New England in the first generation of its existence. . . .

But the situation is quite different when one looks at non-scientific literature, and especially the fine arts. Here asceticism descended like a frost on the life of "Merrie old England." And not only worldly merriment felt its effect. The Puritan's ferocious hatred of everything which smacked of superstition, of all survivals of magical or sacramental salvation, applied to the Christmas festivities and the May Pole and all spontaneous religious art. . . .

The theatre was obnoxious to the Puritans, and with the strict exclusion of the erotic and of nudity from the realm of toleration, a radical view of either literature or art could not exist. The conceptions of idle talk, of superfluities, and of vain ostentation, all designations of an irrational attitude without objective purpose, thus not ascetic, and especially not serving the glory of God, but of man, were always at hand to serve in deciding in favor of sober utility as against any artistic tendencies. This was especially true in the case of decoration of the person, for instance clothing. That powerful tendency toward uniformity of life, which today so immensely aids the capitalistic interest in the standardization of production, had its ideal foundations in the repudiation of all idolatry of the flesh.

Of course we must not forget that Puritanism included a world of contradictions, and that the instinctive sense of eternal greatness in art was certainly stronger among its leaders than in the atmosphere of the Cavaliers. Moreover, a unique genius like Rembrandt, however little his conduct may have been acceptable to God in the eyes of the Puritans, was very strongly influenced in the character of his work by his religious environment. But that does not alter the picture as a whole. In so far as the development of the

Puritan tradition could, and in part did, lead to a powerful spiritualization of personality, it was a decided benefit to literature. But for the most part that benefit only accrued to later generations.

Although we cannot here enter upon a discussion of the influence of Puritanism in all these directions, we should call attention to the fact that the toleration of pleasure in cultural goods, which contributed to purely aesthetic or athletic enjoyment, certainly always ran up against one characteristic limitation: they must not cost anything. Man is only a trustee of the goods which have come to him through God's grace. He must, like the servant in the parable, give an account of every penny entrusted to him, and it is at least hazardous to spend any of it for a purpose which does not serve the glory of God but only one's own enjoyment. What person, who keeps his eyes open, has not met representatives of this viewpoint even in the present? The idea of a man's duty to his possessions, to which he subordinates himself as an obedient steward, or even as an acquisitive machine, bears with chilling weight on his life. The greater the possessions the heavier, if the ascetic attitude toward life stands the test, the feeling of responsibility for them, for holding them undiminished for the glory of God and increasing them by restless effort. The origin of this type of life also extends in certain roots, like so many aspects of the spirit of capitalism, back into the Middle Ages. But it was in the ethic of ascetic Protestantism that it first found a consistent ethical foundation. Its significance for the development of capitalism is obvious.

This worldly Protestant asceticism, as we may recapitulate up to this point, acted powerfully against the spontaneous enjoyment of possessions; it restricted consumption, especially of luxuries. On the other hand, it had the psychological effect of freeing the acquisition of goods from the inhibitions of traditionalistic ethics. It broke the bonds of the impulse of acquisition in that it not only legalized it, but (in the sense discussed) looked upon it as directly willed by God. . . .

. . . the outward forms of luxury . . . their code condemned as idolatry of the flesh, however natural they had appeared to the feudal mind. On the other hand, they approved the rational and utilitarian uses of wealth which were willed by God for the needs of the individual and the community. They did not wish to impose mortification on the man of wealth, but the use of his means for necessary and practical things. The idea of comfort characteristically limits the extent of ethically permissible expenditures. It is naturally no accident that the development of a manner of living consistent with that idea may be observed earliest and most clearly among the most consistent representatives of this whole attitude toward life. Over against the glitter and ostentation of feudal magnificence which, resting on an unsound economic basis, prefers a sordid elegance to a sober simplicity, they set the clean and solid comfort of the middle-class home as an ideal.

... And even more important: the religious valuation of restless, continuous, systematic work in a worldly calling, as the highest means to asceticism, and at the same time the surest and most evident proof of rebirth and genuine faith, must have been the most powerful conceivable lever for the expansion of that attitude toward life which we have here called the spirit of capitalism.

When the limitation of consumption is combined with this release of acquisitive activity, the inevitable practical result is obvious: accumulation of capital through ascetic compulsion to save. The restraints which were imposed upon the consumption of wealth naturally served to increase it by making possible the productive investment of capital. . . .

As far as the influence of the Puritan outlook extended, under all circumstances — and this is, of course, much more important than the mere encouragement of capital accumulation — it favored the development of a rational bourgeois economic life; it was the most important, and above all the only consistent influence in the development of that life. It stood at the cradle of the modern economic man.

To be sure, these Puritanical ideals tended to give way under excessive pressure from the temptations of wealth, as the Puritans themselves knew very well. With great regularity we find the most genuine adherents of Puritanism among the classes which were rising from a lowly status, the small bourgeois and farmers, while the *beati possidentes* ["blessed possessers"], even among Quakers, are often found tending to repudiate the old ideals. It was the same fate which again and again befell the predecessor of this worldly asceticism, the monastic asceticism of the Middle Ages. In the latter case, when rational economic activity had worked out its full effects by strict regulation of conduct and limitation of consumption, the wealth accumulated either succumbed directly to the nobility, as in the time before the Reformation, or monastic discipline threatened to break down, and one of its numerous reformations became necessary.

In fact the whole history of monasticism is in a certain sense the history of a continual struggle with the problem of the secularizing influence of wealth. The same is true on a grand scale of the worldly asceticism of Puritanism. The great revival of Methodism, which preceded the expansion of English industry toward the end of the eighteenth century, may well be compared with such a monastic reform. We may hence quote here a passage from John Wesley himself which might well serve as a motto for everything which has been said above. For it shows that the leaders of these ascetic movements understood the seemingly paradoxical relationships which we have here analyzed perfectly well, and in the same sense that we have given them. He wrote: "I fear, wherever riches have increased, the essence of religion has decreased in the same proportion. Therefore I do not see how it is possible, in the nature of things, for any revival of true religion to continue long. For religion must necessarily produce both industry and frugality, and these cannot but produce riches. But as riches increase, so will pride, anger, and love of the world in all its branches. How then is it possible that Methodism, that is, a religion of the heart, though it flourishes now as a green bay tree, should continue in this state? For the Methodists in every place grow diligent and frugal; consequently they increase in goods. Hence they proportionately increase in pride, in anger, in the desire of the flesh, the desire of the eyes, and the pride of life. So, although the form of religion remains, the spirit is swiftly vanishing away. Is there no way to prevent this — this continual decay of pure religion? We ought not to prevent people from being diligent and frugal; we must exhort all Christians to gain all they can, and to save all they can; that is, in effect, to grow rich."

There follows the advice that those who gain all they can and save all they can should also give all they can, so that they will grow in grace and lay up a treasure in heaven. It is clear that Wesley here expresses, even in detail, just what we have been trying to point out.

As Wesley here says, the full economic effect of those great religious movements, whose significance for economic development lay above all in their ascetic educative influence, generally came only after the peak of the purely religious enthusiasm was past. Then the intensity of the search for the Kingdom of God commenced gradually to pass over into sober economic virtue; the religious roots died out slowly, giving way to utilitarian worldliness. . . .

A specifically bourgeois economic ethic had grown up. With the consciousness of standing in the fullness of God's grace and being visibly blessed by Him, the bourgeois business man, as long as he remained within the bounds of formal correctness, as long as his moral conduct was spotless and the use to which he put his wealth was not objectionable, could follow his pecuniary interests as he would and feel that he was fulfilling a duty in doing so. The power of religious asceticism provided him in addition with sober, conscientious, and unusually industrious workmen, who clung to their work as to a life purpose willed by God. . . .

Now naturally the whole ascetic literature of almost all denominations is saturated with the idea that faithful labor, even at low wages, on the part

Max Weber

of those whom life offers no other opportunities, is highly pleasing to God. In this respect Protestant Asceticism added in itself nothing new. But it not only deepened this idea most powerfully, it also created the force which was alone decisive for its effectiveness: the psychological sanction of it through the conception of this labor as a calling, as the best, often in the last analysis the only means of attaining certainty of grace. And on the other hand it legalized the exploitation of this specific willingness to work, in that it also interpreted the employer's business activity as a calling. It is obvious how powerfully the exclusive search for the Kingdom of God only through the fulfillment of duty in the calling, and the strict asceticism which Church discipline naturally imposed, especially on the propertyless classes, was bound to affect the productivity of labor in the capitalistic sense of the word. The treatment of labor as a calling became as characteristic of the modern worker as the corresponding attitude toward acquisition of the business man. . . .

One of the fundamental elements of the spirit of modern capitalism, and not only of that but of all modern culture: rational conduct on the basis of the idea of the calling, was born — that is what this discussion has sought to demonstrate — from the spirit of Christian asceticism. One has only to re-read the passage from Franklin, quoted at the beginning of this essay, in order to see that the essential elements of the attitude which was there called the spirit of capitalism are the same as what we have just shown to be the content of the Puritan worldly asceticism, only without the religious basis, which by Franklin's time had died away. The idea that modern labor has an ascetic character is of course not new. Limitation to specialized work, with a renunciation of the Faustian universality of man which it involves, is a condition of any valuable work in the modern world; hence deeds and renunciation inevitably condition each other today. This fundamentally ascetic trait of middle-class life, if it attempts to be a way of life at all, and not simply the absence of any, was what Goethe wanted to teach, at the height of his wisdom, in the *Wanderjahren,* and in the end which he gave to the life of his *Faust.* For him the realization meant a renunciation, a departure from an age of full and beautiful humanity, which can no more be repeated in the course of our cultural development than can the flower of the Athenian culture of antiquity.

The Puritan wanted to work in a calling; we are forced to do so. For when asceticism was carried out of monastic cells into everyday life, and began to dominate worldly morality, it did its part in building the tremendous cosmos of the modern economic order. This order is now bound to the technical and economic conditions of machine production which today determine the lives of all the individuals who are born into this mechanism, not only those directly concerned with economic acquisition, with irresistible force. Perhaps it will so determine them until the last ton of fossilized is burnt. In Baxter's [Richard Baxter, 1615-1691, Puritan writer] view the care for external goods should only lie on the shoulders of the "saint like a light cloak, which can be thrown aside at any moment." But fate decreed that the cloak should become an iron cage.

Since asceticism undertook to remodel the world and to work out its ideals in the world, material goods have gained an increasing and finally an inexorable power over the lives of men as at no previous period in history. Today the spirit of religious asceticism — whether finally, who knows? — has escaped from the cage. But victorious capitalism, since it rests on mechanical foundations, needs its support no longer. The rosy blush of its laughing heir, the Enlightenment, seems also to be irretrievably fading, and the idea of duty in one's calling prowls about in our lives like the ghost of dead religious beliefs. Where the fulfillment of the calling cannot directly be related to the highest spiritual and cultural values, or when, on the other hand, it need not be felt simply as economic compulsion, the individual generally abandons the attempt to justify it at all. In the field of its highest development, in the United States, the pursuit of wealth, stripped of its religious and ethical meaning, tends to become associated with purely mundane passions, which often actually give it the character of sport.

<hr />

WALTER RAUSCHENBUSCH

Christianity and the Social Crisis

Walter Rauschenbusch (1861-1918), a Baptist pastor and theologian, spent eleven years serving a German congregation in the rough neighborhood of "Hell's Kitchen" in New York City before moving on to seminary teaching. The experience shaped his "theology of the social gospel." This book, pub-

Walter Rauschenbusch, *Christianity and the Social Crisis* (New York: Macmillan, 1907), 234, 235, 248-51, 271, 285, 349-52, 355-57.

lished in 1907, reflected on the impact of modern individualism and made him famous as a Christian committed to improving the lives of the urban poor.

———————————

A man's work is not only the price he pays for the right to fill his stomach. In his work he expresses himself. It is the output of his creative energy and his main contribution to the common life of mankind. The pride which an artist or professional man takes in his work, the pleasure which a housewife takes in adorning her home, afford a satisfaction that ranks next to human love in delightsomeness.

One of the gravest accusations against our industrial system is that it does not produce in the common man the pride and joy of good work. In many cases the surroundings are ugly, depressing, and coarsening. Much of the stuff manufactured is dishonest in quality, made to sell and not to serve, and the making of such cotton or wooden lies must react on the morals of every man that handles them. There is little opportunity for a man to put his personal stamp on his work. The medieval craftsman could rise to be an artist by working well at his craft. The modern factory hand is not likely to develop artistic gifts as he tends his machine.

It is a common and true complaint of employers that their men take no interest in their work. But why should they? What motive have they for putting love and care into their work? It is not theirs. Christ spoke of the difference between the hireling shepherd who flees and the owner who loves the sheep. Our system has made the immense majority of industrial workers mere hirelings. If they do conscientious work nevertheless, it is a splendid tribute to human rectitude. Slavery was cheap labor; it was also dear labor. In ancient Rome the slaves on the country estates were so wasteful that only the strongest and crudest tools could be given them. The more the wage worker approaches their condition, the more will the employer confront the same problem. The finest work is done only by free minds who put love into their work because it is their own. When a workman becomes a partner, he "hustles" in a new spirit. Even the small bonus distributed in profit-sharing experiments has been found to increase the carefulness and willingness of the men to such an extent that the bonus did not diminish the profits of the employers. The lowest motives for work are the desire for wages and the fear of losing them. Yet these are almost the only motives to which our system appeals. It does not even hold out the hope of promotion, unless a man unites managing ability to his workmanship. The economic loss to the community by this paralysis of the finer springs of human action is beyond computation. But the moral loss is vastly more threatening.

The demand for equality is often ridiculed as if it implied that all men were to be of identical wealth, wisdom, and authority. But social equality can coexist with the greatest natural differences. There is no more fundamental difference than that of sex, nor a greater intellectual chasm than that between an educated man and his little child, yet in the family all are equal. In a college community there are various gradations of rank and authority within the faculty, and there is a clearly marked distinction between the students and the faculty, but there is social equality. On the other hand, the janitor and the peanut vender are outside of the circle, however important they may be to it.

The social equality existing in our country in the past has been one of the chief charms of life here and of far more practical importance to our democracy than the universal ballot. After a long period of study abroad in my youth I realized on my return to America that life here was far poorer in music, art, and many forms of enjoyment than life on the continent of Europe; but that life tasted better here, nevertheless, because men met one another more simply, frankly, and wholesomely. In Europe a man is always considering just how much deference he must show to those in ranks above him, and in turn noting jealously if those below him are strewing the right quantity of incense due to his own social position.

That fundamental democracy of social intercourse, which is one of the richest endowments of our American life, is slipping from us. Actual inequality endangers the sense of equality. The rich man and the poor man can meet on a level if they are old friends, or if they are men of exceptional moral qualities, or if they meet under unusual circumstances that reduce all things to their primitive human elements. But as a general thing they will live different lives, and the sense of unlikeness will affect all their dealings. With women the spirit of social caste seems to be even more fatally easy than with men. It may be denied that the poor in our country are getting poorer, but it cannot well be denied that the rich are getting richer. The extremes of wealth and poverty are much farther apart than formerly, and thus the poor are at least relatively poorer. There is a rich class and a poor class, whose manner of life is wedged farther and farther apart, and whose boundary lines are becoming ever more distinct. The difference in housing, eating, dressing, and speaking would be a sufficient barrier. The dominant position of the one class in industry and the dependence of the other is even more decisive. The owners or managers of industry are rich or highly paid;

they have technical knowledge, the will to command, the habits of mind bred by the exercise of authority; they say "Go," and men go; they say "Do this," and an army of men obeys. On the other side is the mass who take orders, who are employed or dismissed at a word, who use their muscles almost automatically, and who have no voice in the conduct of their own shop. These are two distinct classes, and no rhetoric can make them equal. Moreover, such a condition is inseparable from the capitalistic organization of industry. As capitalism grows, it must create a proletariat to correspond. Just as militarism is based on military obedience, so capitalism is based on economic dependence.

We hear passionate protests against the use of the hateful word "class" in America. There are no classes in our country, we are told. But the hateful part is not the word, but the thing. If class distinctions are growing up here, he serves his country ill who would hush up the fact or blind the people to it by fine phrases. A class is a body of men who are so similar in their work, their duties and privileges, their manner of life and enjoyment, that a common interest, common conception of life, and common moral ideals are developed and cement the individuals. The business men constitute such a class. The industrial workers also constitute such a class. In old countries the upper class gradually adorned itself with titles, won special privileges in court and army and law, and created an atmosphere of awe and apartness. But the solid basis on which this was done was the feudal control of the land, which was then the great source of wealth. The rest was merely the decorative moss that grows up on the rocks of permanent wealth. With the industrial revolution a new source of wealth opened up; a new set of men gained control of it and ousted the old feudal nobility more or less thoroughly. The new aristocracy, which is based on mobile capital, has not yet had time to festoon itself with decorations, but likes to hasten the process by intermarriage with the remnants of the old feudal nobility. Whether it will ever duplicate the old forms in this country is immaterial, as long as it has the fact of power. In some way the social inequality will find increasing outward expression and will tend to make itself permanent. Where there are actual class differences, there will be a dawning class consciousness, a clear class interest, and there may be a class struggle.

Industry and commerce are good. They serve the needs of men. The men eminent in industry and commerce are good men, with the fine qualities of human nature. But the organization of industry and commerce is such that along with its useful service it carries death, physical and moral. Frederick Denison Maurice, one of the finest minds of England in the Victorian Age, said, "I do not see my way farther than this, Competition is put forth as the law of the universe; that is a lie." And his friend Charles Kingsley added, "Competition means death; cooperation means life." Every joint-stock company, trust, or labor union organized, every extension of government interference or government ownership, is a surrender of the competitive principle and a halting step toward cooperation. Practical men take these steps because competition has proved itself suicidal to economic welfare. Christian men have a stouter reason for turning against it, because it slays human character and denies human brotherhood. If money dominates, the ideal cannot dominate. If we serve mammon, we cannot serve the Christ.

In the last resort the only hope is in the moral forces which can be summoned to the rescue. If there are statesmen prophets, and apostles who set truth and justice above selfish advancement; if their call finds a response in the great body of the people; if a new tide of religious faith and moral enthusiasm creates new standards of duty and a new capacity for self-sacrifice; if the strong learn to direct their love of power to the uplifting of the people and see the highest self-assertion in self-sacrifice — then the intrenchments of vested wrong will melt away; the stifled energy of the people will leap forward; the atrophied members of the social body will be filled with a fresh flow of blood; and a regenerate nation will look with the eyes of youth across the fields of the future. . . .

In personal religion the first requirement is to repent and believe in the gospel. As long as a man is self-righteous and complacently satisfied with his moral attainments, there is no hope that he will enter into the higher development, and unless he has faith that a higher level of spiritual life is attainable, he will be lethargic and stationary.

Social religion, too, demands repentance for our social sins and faith in the possibility of a new social order. As long as a man sees in our present society only a few inevitable abuses and recognizes no sin and evil deep-seated in the very constitution of the present order, he is still in a state of moral blindness and without conviction of sin. Those who believe in a better social order are often told that they do not know the sinfulness of the human heart. They could justly retort the charge on the men of the evangelical school. When the latter deal with public wrongs, they often exhibit a curious unfamiliarity with the forms which sin assumes there, and sometimes reverently bow before one of the devil's spider-webs, praising it as one of the mighty works of God. Regeneration includes that a man must pass under the domination of the spirit of Christ, so that he will judge of life as Christ would judge of it. That means a revaluation of social values. Things that are now "exalted among men" must become "an abomination" to him because they are built on wrong and misery. Unless a man finds his judgment at least on some fundamental questions in opposition to the current ideas of the age, he is still a child of this world and has not "tasted the powers of the coming age." He will have to repent and believe if he wants to be a Christian in the full sense of the world.

No man can help the people until he is himself free from the spell which the present order has cast over our moral judgment. We have repeatedly pointed out that every social institution weaves a protecting integument of glossy idealization about itself like a colony of tent-caterpillars in an apple tree. For instance, wherever militarism rules, war is idealized by monuments and paintings, poetry and song. The stench of the hospitals and the maggots of the battle-field are passed in silence, and the imagination of the people is filled with waving plumes and the shout of charging columns. A Russian general thought Verestchagin's [Vassili Verestchagin, Russian artist, 1842-1904] pictures ought to be destroyed because they disenchanted the people. If war is ever to be relegated to the limbo of outgrown barbarism, we must shake off its magic. When we comprehend how few wars have ever been fought for the sake of justice or the people; how personal spite, the ambition of military professionals, and the protection of capitalistic ventures are the real moving powers; how the governing classes pour out the blood and wealth of nations for private ends and exude patriotic enthusiasm like a squid secreting ink to hide its retreat — then the mythology of war will no longer bring us to our knees, and we shall fail to get drunk with the rest when martial intoxication sweeps the people off their feet.

In the same way we shall have to see through the fictions of capitalism. We are assured that the poor are poor through their own fault; that rent and profits are the just dues of foresight and ability; that the immigrants are the cause of corruption in our city politics; that we cannot compete with foreign countries unless our working class will descend to the wages paid abroad. These are all very plausible assertions, but they are lies dressed up in truth. There is a great deal of conscious lying. Industrialism as a whole sends out deceptive prospectuses just like single corporations within it. But in the main these misleading theories are the complacent self-deception of those who profit by present conditions and are loath to believe that their life is working harm. It is very rare for a man to condemn the means by which he makes a living, and we must simply make allowance for the warping influence of self-interest when he justifies himself and not believe him entirely. In the early part of the nineteenth century, when tiny children in England were driven to the looms with whips, and women lost even the physical appearance of womanhood in the coal mines, the owners insisted that English industry would be ruined by the proposed reform laws, and doubtless they thought so. If men holding stock in traction companies assert that municipal ownership is un-American; if the express companies say that parcels cannot be carried below their own amazing rates; if Mr. Baer [George F. Baer, 1842-1914, president, Philadelphia and Reading Coal and Iron] in the midst of the coal strike assured a minister that "God in his infinite wisdom had given control of the property interests of the country" to him and his associates and they would do all things well — we must simply allow for the warping effect of self-interest and pass on to the order of the day. Macaulay [Thomas Babington Macaulay, 1800-1859, English historian and reformer] said that the doctrine of gravitation would not yet be accepted if it had interfered with vested interests.

The greatest contribution which any man can make to the social movement is the contribution of a regenerated personality, of a will which sets justice above policy and profit, and of an intellect emancipated from falsehood. Such a man will in some measure incarnate the principles of a higher social order in his attitude to all questions and in all his relations to men, and will be a well-spring of regenerating influences. If he speaks, his judgment will be a corrective force. If he listens, he will encourage the truthteller and discourage the peddler of adulterated facts and maxims. If others lose heart, he will stay them with his inspired patience. If any new principle is to gain power in human history, it must take shape and life in individuals who have faith in it. The men of faith are the living spirits, the channels by which new truth and power from God enter humanity. To repent of our collective social sins, to have faith in the possibility and reality of a divine life in humanity, to submit the will to the purposes of the kingdom of God, to permit the divine inspiration to emancipate and clarify the moral insight — this is the most intimate duty of the religious man who would help to build the coming Messianic era of mankind.

The older conception of religion viewed as religious only what ministered to the souls of men or what served the Church. When a man attended the services of the Church, contributed money to its work, taught in Sunday-school, spoke to the unconverted, or visited the sick, he was doing religious work. The conscientiousness with which he did his daily work also had a religious quality. On the other hand, the daily work itself, the ploughing, building, cobbling, or selling were secular, and the main output of his life was not directly a contribution to the kingdom of God, but merely the necessary method of getting a living for himself and his family. The ministry alone and a few allied callings had the uplifting consciousness of serving

God in the totality of daily work. A few professions were marked off as holy, just as in past stages of religion certain groves and temples were marked out as holy ground where God could be sought and served.

If now we could have faith enough to believe that all human life can be with divine purpose; that God saves not only the soul, but the whole of human life; that anything which serves to make men healthy, intelligent, happy, and good is a service to the Father of men; that the kingdom of God is not bounded by the Church, but includes all human relations — then all professions would be hallowed and receive religious dignity. A man making a shoe or arguing a law case or planting potatoes or teaching school, could feel that this was itself a contribution to the welfare of mankind, and indeed his main contribution to it.

But such a view of our professional life would bring it under religious scrutiny. (If a man's calling consisted in manufacturing or selling useless or harmful stuff, he would find himself unable to connect it with his religion.) In so far as the energy of business life is expended in crowding out competitors, it would also be outside of the sanction of religion, and religious men would be compelled to consider how industry and commerce could be reorganized so that there would be a maximum of service to humanity and a minimum of antagonism between those who desire to serve it. As soon as religion will set the kingdom of God before it as the all-inclusive aim, and will define it so as to include all rightful relations among men, the awakened conscience will begin to turn its searchlight on the industrial and commercial life in detail, and will insist on eliminating all professions which harm instead of helping, and on coordinating all productive activities to secure a maximum of service. That in itself would produce a quiet industrial revolution.

Scatter through all classes and professions a large number of men and women whose eyes have had a vision of a true human society and who have faith in it and courage to stand against anything that contradicts it, and public opinion will have a new swiftness and tenacity in judging on right and wrong. The murder of the Armenians, the horrors of the Congo Free State, the ravages of the liquor traffic in Africa, the peace movement, the protest against child labor in America, the movement for early closing of retail stores — all these things arouse only a limited number of persons to active sympathy; the rest are lethargic. It takes so long to "work up public sentiment," and even then it stops boiling as fast as a kettle of water taken off the fire. There are so many Christian people and such feeble sentiment on public wrongs. It is not because people are not good enough, but because their goodness has not been directed and educated in this direction. The multiplication of socially enlightened Christians will serve the body of society much as a physical organism would be served if a complete and effective system of ganglia should be distributed where few of them existed. The social body needs moral innervation; and the spread of men who combine religious faith, moral enthusiasm, and economic information, and apply the combined result to public morality, promises to create a moral sensitiveness never yet known.

The new evangel of the kingdom of God will have to be carried into the common consciousness of Christendom by the personal faith and testimony of the ordinary Christian qua man. It is less connected with the ministrations of the Church and therefore will be less the business of the professional ministry than the old evangel of the saved soul. It is a call to Christianize the everyday life, and the everyday man will have to pass on the call and make plain its meaning. But if the pulpit is willing to lend its immense power of proclamation and teaching, it will immeasurably speed the spread of the new conceptions. "With the assistance of the clergy everything in matters of social reforms is easy; without such help, or in spite of it, all is difficult and at times impossible."

HOWARD THURMAN

What Shall I Do with My Life?

Howard Thurman (1899-1981) grew up in poverty in Florida, raised by his grandmother, a former slave. Educated at Morehouse, Columbia, and Rochester Seminary, he served many years as pastor of the Church for the Fellowship of All Peoples in San Francisco and Dean of the Chapel at Boston University. His commitment to non-violence deeply influenced Martin Luther King, Jr., and other leaders of the civil rights movement. He gave this sermon, based on Matthew 4:1-11, many times, beginning in the 1920s; this particular version was preached to a student audience in 1939.

Howard Thurman, "What Shall I Do with My Life?" in *A Strange Freedom,* ed. Walter Earl Fluker and Catherine Tumber (Boston: Beacon, 1998), 30-34.

In the first temptation Jesus was hungry. The fact could have doubtless been duplicated all over Palestine with this important exception — many of his fellows were hungry through no choice of their own. They were hungry because necessity had confronted their universe with an invincible gesture. By their fellows they had been shut off from free and necessitous participation in the basic creature demands for survival. On the other hand, Jesus was hungry because he had foregone these demands under the impelling power of a great concentration. He was caught in the agonizing grip of a great challenge: What shall I do with my life? What must be for me an adequate disposition of my life?

Wrestling in the wilderness seemed strangely trivial and irrelevant. The quest in its practical bearing was this: How fundamentally important is bread, is feeding the hungry? It is true that man cannot live by bread alone. He must have bread. But should this be his major concern? Only a hungry man could face this question realistically. The danger for a hungry man in such a reflection is that the importance of food may be greatly overemphasized, for it is very natural to idealize possessions which we are denied.

With reference to the problem before him Jesus reached an amazingly significant conclusion. Man must live on bread but not bread alone. There is more besides, and it is this that reveals the true stature of the man. Man must have food, yes. But admitting this and seeing its practical significance in terms of actual survival, what then? He must let the bias of his life be on the side of those needs that cannot be adequately included in creature demands.

The problem for us is at once clear. I must not make the error of giving myself over to the meeting of these needs alone, but even as I recognize realistically the physical needs of men, I must let my bias be on the side of their deeper concerns; I must give priority to those of their desires and yearnings that can never be met by a full stomach or by all the economic security available in the world. The major emphasis must not be an either-or one but rather a both-and emphasis with a positive bias in favor of that which is deeper than food. My interests in creature needs must be genuine and practical, but I must see these needs as things which may stand clearly in the way of the realization of the higher ends of life. Feed the hungry? Yes, and always. But I must know that man is more than his physical body. There is something in him that calls for beauty and comradeship and righteousness. I love Jesus for the shaft of light that he throws across the pathway of those who seek to answer the question, What shall I do with my life?

In the second temptation Jesus is facing the problem of one of life's great illusions. The tempter suggests to him that if he were to go to the pinnacle of the temple and cast himself down, he would not be hurt; in other words, the operation of what we call natural law would be interrupted in his behalf and God would perform a miracle on the spot. For, the tempter quietly whispers, the world of nature is not really orderly.

Jesus' reply was very striking. He said in substance, "If I go to the pinnacle of the temple and cast myself down, I will break my neck. He who presumes to disregard the ordinary processes of nature tempts God." His choice here was on the side of the normal, natural working of the simple laws of life, demanding nothing of them that dared to stretch them out of shape. To do so would have been to deceive himself and to have created a spiritual problem for which no solution could have been found.

The bearing of this choice upon the lives of students is at once clear. I have had students who during an entire semester did not pay much attention to the simple, direct, natural operations of the classroom, who fulfilled none of the day-by-day requirements relative to their work. Then, when the day of judgment arrived, they came into the classroom, read the examination questions and expected, by some beyond-the-natural operation, to participate in complete knowledge and understanding of the questions raised. In other words, they expected a miracle. What they received was what they had rated — failure. It is a terrible truth that life does not have a habit of making exceptions in our case even though we may be good in general, even though our fathers may be great men and our reputations of outstanding merit. Let us not be deceived by the great illusions, but let us see the finger of God moving in the natural unfolding of antecedents and consequences. I love Jesus for the shaft of light that he throws across the pathway of those who seek to answer the question, What shall I do with my life?

In the third temptation the tempter strikes at the center of Jesus' dominant passion, to bring society under the acknowledged judgment of God and thereby insure its purification. More and more as he lived, Jesus became the embodiment of this great desire. He thought of himself as the example of the judgment and of the salvation of God. The tempter said to him, "Behold the kingdoms of the world. You want them to become the Kingdom of God. But they belong to me." It seems to me that the full realization of the tempter's thought came to Jesus with tremendous shock. His reasoning may have been, "God created me; God created the world of nature; God created all mankind. Therefore, God is the creator of the relationships that exist between men." At this point the devil suggested, "You may be logical, but you are not true. I made the relationships between men." In the awareness of the far-reaching significance of this fact, Jesus subsequently cautioned his disciples, "Behold, I send you out as lambs among wolves. You must be as wise as serpents and as harmless as doves." And again he said, "Rejoice when men persecute you for my sake, for it means that you are making inroads on territory that is foreign to the will of God."

It seems to me that experience reveals a potent half-truth; namely, that the world can be made good if all the men in the world as individuals become good men. After the souls of men are saved, the society in which they function will be a good society. This is only a half-truth. Many men have found that they are caught in a framework of relationships evil in design, and their very good deeds have developed into instrumentalities for evil. It is not enough to save the souls of men; the relationships that exist between men must be saved also.

To approach the problem from the other angle is to assume that once the relationships between men are saved, the individual men will thereby become instruments of positive weal. This is also a half-truth. The two processes must go on apace or else men and their relationships will not be brought under conscious judgment of God. We must, therefore, even as we purify our hearts and live our individual lives under the divine scrutiny, so order the framework of our relationships that good men can function in it to the glory of God. I love Jesus for the shaft of light that he throws across the pathway of those who seek to answer the question, What shall I do with my life?

> Give me the courage to live!
> Really live — not merely exist.
> Live dangerously,
> Scorning risk!
> Live honestly,
> Daring the truth —
> Particularly the truth of myself!
> Live resiliently —
> Ever changing, ever growing, ever adapting.
> Enduring the pain of change
> As though 'twere the travail of birth.
> Give me the courage to live,
> Give me the strength to be free
> And endure the burden of freedom
> And the loneliness of those without chains;
> Let me not be trapped by success,
> Nor by failure, nor pleasure, nor grief,
> Nor malice, nor praise, nor remorse!

Give me the courage to go on!
Facing all that waits on the trail —
Going eagerly, joyously on,
And paying my way as I go,
Without anger or fear or regret
Taking what life gives,
Spending myself to the full,
Head high, spirit winged, like a god —
On . . . on . . . till the shadows draw close.
Then even when darkness shuts down,
And I go out alone, as I came,
Naked and blind as I came —
Even then, gracious God, hear my prayer:
Give me the courage to live!

DIETRICH BONHOEFFER

The Cost of Discipleship

Dietrich Bonhoeffer (1906-1945) grew up in Berlin, the son of a prominent psychiatrist; his career in theology surprised his relatively secular family. He was active in the "Confessing Church," the German Protestants who were opposed to Hitler's efforts to control the churches, eventually teaching at the Confessing Church's more or less underground seminary. While visiting the United States just before the beginning of World War II, he was invited to stay here, but concluded that no one who avoided the hard times Germany was facing would have the moral authority to have influence in Germany after the war. So he went back and became peripherally involved in a plot to kill Hitler. He was arrested, imprisoned, and, shortly before the end of the war, executed. In this book, published in 1937, he ad-

Dietrich Bonhoeffer, *The Cost of Discipleship*, trans. R. H. Fuller (New York: Macmillan, 1959), 48-52, 53-55, 56-57, 60-66.

dressed the radical demands Christianity might make on one's life and the central importance of obedience to Jesus' call. In an earlier chapter he attacked the idea of "cheap grace," the notion that God's forgiveness leaves Christians free of tough ethical demands.

———————

And as he passed by he saw Levi, the son of Alphaeus, sitting at the place of toll, and he saith unto him, Follow me. And he arose and followed him.

MARK 2:14

The call goes forth, and is at once followed by the response of obedience. The response of the disciples is an act of obedience, not a confession of faith in Jesus. How could the call immediately evoke obedience? The story is a stumbling-block for the natural reason, and it is no wonder that frantic attempts have been made to separate the two events. By hook or by crook a bridge must be found between them. Something must have happened in between, some psychological or historical event. Thus we get the stupid question: Surely the publican must have known Jesus before, and that previous acquaintance explains his readiness to hear the Master's call. Unfortunately our text is ruthlessly silent on this point, and in fact it regards the immediate sequence of call and response as a matter of crucial importance. It displays not the slightest interest in the psychological reasons for a man's religious decisions. And why? For the simple reason that the cause behind the immediate following of call by response is Jesus Christ himself. It is Jesus who calls, and because it is Jesus, Levi follows at once. This encounter is a testimony to the absolute, direct, and unaccountable authority of Jesus. There is no need of any preliminaries, and no other consequence but obedience to the call. Because Jesus is the Christ, he has the authority to call and to demand obedience to his word. Jesus summons men to follow him not as a teacher or a pattern of the good life, but as the Christ, the Son of God. In this short text Jesus Christ and his claim are proclaimed to men. Not a word of praise is given to the disciple for his decision for Christ. We are not expected to contemplate the disciple, but only him who calls, and his absolute authority. According to our text, there is no road to faith or discipleship, no other road — only obedience to the call of Jesus.

And what does the text inform us about the content of discipleship? Follow me, run along behind me! That is all. To follow in his steps is something which is void of all content. It gives us no intelligible program for a

way of life, no goal or ideal to strive after. It is not a cause which human calculation might deem worthy of our devotion, even the devotion of ourselves. What happens? At the call, Levi leaves all that he has — but not because he thinks that he might be doing something worthwhile, but simply
for the sake of the call. Otherwise he cannot follow in the steps of Jesus. This
act on Levi's part has not the slightest value in itself, it is quite devoid of significance and unworthy of consideration. The disciple simply burns his
boats and goes ahead. . . .

When we are called to follow Christ, we are summoned to an exclusive
attachment to his person. The grace of his call bursts all the bonds of legal-
ism. It is a gracious call, a gracious commandment. It transcends the difference between the law and the gospel. Christ calls, the disciple follows; that is
grace and commandment in one. "I will walk at liberty, for I seek thy commandments" (Ps. 119:45). . . .

Discipleship without Jesus Christ is a way of our own choosing. It may
be the ideal way. It may even lead to martyrdom, but it is devoid of all promise. Jesus will certainly reject it.

> And they went to another village. And as they went in the way, a cer-
> tain man said unto him, I will follow thee whithersoever thou goest.
> And Jesus said unto him, The foxes have holes, and the birds of
> heaven have nests, but the Son of man hath not where to lay his head.
> And he said unto another, Follow me. But he said, Lord, suffer me
> first to go and bury my father. But he said unto him, Leave the dead to
> bury their dead, but go thou and publish abroad the kingdom of God.
> And another said, I will follow thee, Lord; but suffer me first to bid
> farewell to them that are at my house. But Jesus said unto him, No
> man, having put his hand unto the plough, and looking back, is fit for
> the kingdom of God (Luke 9:57-62).

The first disciple offers to follow Jesus without waiting to be called. Jesus damps his ardor by warning him that he does not know what he is doing. In fact he is quite incapable of knowing. That is the meaning of Jesus' answer — he shows the would-be disciple what life with him involves. We
hear the words of One who is on his way to the cross, whose whole life is
summed up in the Apostles' Creed by the word 'suffered'. No man can
choose such a life for himself. No man can call himself to such a destiny,
says Jesus, and his word stays unanswered. The gulf between a voluntary offer to follow and genuine discipleship is clear.

But where Jesus calls, he bridges the widest gulf. The second would-be disciple wants to bury his father before he starts to follow. He is held bound by the trammels of the law. He knows what he wants and what he must do. Let him first fulfill the law, and then let him follow. A definite legal ordinance acts as a barrier between Jesus and the man he has called. But the call of Jesus is stronger than the barrier. At this critical moment nothing on earth, however sacred, must be allowed to come between Jesus and the man he has called — not even the law itself. Now, if never before, the law must be broken for the sake of Jesus; it forfeits all its rights if it acts as a barrier to discipleship. Therefore Jesus emerges at this point as the opponent of the law, and commands a man to follow him. Only the Christ can speak in this fashion. He alone has the last word. His would-be follower cannot kick against the pricks. This call, this grace, is irresistible.

The third would-be disciple, like the first, thinks that following Christ means that he must make the offer on his own initiative as if it were a career he had mapped out for himself. There is, however, a difference between the first would-be disciple and the third, for the third is bold enough to stipulate his own terms. Unfortunately, however, he lands himself in a hopeless inconsistency, for although he is ready enough to throw in his lot with Jesus, he succeeds in putting up a barrier between himself and the Master. "Suffer me first." He wants to follow, but feels obliged to insist on his own terms. Discipleship to him is a possibility which can only be realized when certain conditions have been fulfilled. This is to reduce discipleship to the level of the human understanding. First you must do this and then you must do that. There is a right time for everything. The disciple places himself at the Master's disposal, but at the same time retains the right to dictate his own terms. But then discipleship is no longer discipleship, but a program of our own to be arranged to suit ourselves, and to be judged in accordance with the standards of a rational ethic. The trouble about this third would-be disciple is that at the very moment he expresses his willingness to follow, he ceases to want to follow at all. By making his offer on his own terms, he alters the whole position, for discipleship can tolerate no conditions which might come between Jesus and our obedience to him. Hence the third disciple finds himself at loggerheads not only with Jesus, but also with himself. His desires conflict not only with what Jesus wants, but also with what he wants himself. He judges himself, and decides against himself; and all this by saying, "Suffer me first." The answer of Jesus graphically proves to him that he is at variance with himself and that excludes discipleship. "No man, having put his hand to the plough and looking back, is fit for the kingdom of God."

If we would follow Jesus we must take certain definite steps. The first step, which follows the call, cuts the disciple off from his previous existence.... The first step places the disciple in the situation where faith is possible. If he refuses to follow and stays behind, he does not learn how to believe....

It is an extremely hazardous procedure to distinguish between a situation where faith is possible and one where it is not. We must first realize that there is nothing in the situation to tell us to which category it belongs. It is only the call of Jesus which makes it a situation where faith is possible. Secondly, a situation where faith is possible can never be demonstrated from the human side. Discipleship is not an offer man makes to Christ. It is only the call which creates the situation. Thirdly, this situation never possesses any intrinsic worth or merit of its own. It is only through the call that it receives its justification. Last, but not least, the situation in which faith is possible is itself only rendered possible through faith.

The idea of a situation in which faith is possible is only a way of stating the facts of a case in which the following two propositions hold good and are equally true: *only he who believes is obedient, and only he who is obedient believes.*

It is quite unbiblical to hold the first proposition without the second. We think we understand when we hear that obedience is possible only where there is faith. Does not obedience follow faith as good fruit grows on a good tree? First faith, then obedience. If by that we mean that it is faith which justifies, and not the act of obedience, all well and good, for that is the essential and unexceptionable presupposition of all that follows. If, however, we make a chronological distinction between faith and obedience, and make obedience subsequent to faith, we are divorcing the one from the other — and then we get the practical question, when must obedience begin? Obedience remains separated from faith. From the point of view of justification it is necessary thus to separate them, but we must never lose sight of their essential unity. For faith is only real when there is obedience, never without it, and faith only becomes faith in the act of obedience.

Since, then, we cannot adequately speak of obedience as the consequence of faith, and since we must never forget the indissoluble unity of the two, we must place the one proposition that only he who believes is obedient alongside the other, that only he who is obedient believes. In the one case faith is the condition of obedience, and in the other obedience the condition of faith. In exactly the same way in which obedience is called the consequence of faith, it must also be called the presupposition of faith. Only the obedient believe. If we are to believe, we must obey a concrete command. Without this preliminary step of obedience, our faith will only be pious humbug, and lead us to the grace which is not costly. Everything depends on the first step. It has a unique quality of its own. The first step of obedience makes Peter leave his nets, and later get out of the ship; it calls upon the young man to leave his riches. Only this new existence, created through obedience, can make faith possible. . . .

Once we are sure of this point, we must add at once that this step is, and can never be more than, a purely external act and a dead work of the law, which can never of itself bring a man to Christ. As an external act the new existence is no better than the old. Even at the highest estimate it can only achieve a new law of life, a new way of living which is poles apart from the new life with Christ. If a drunkard signs the pledge, or a rich man gives all his money away, they are both of them freeing themselves from their slavery to alcohol or riches, but not from their bondage to themselves. They are still moving in their own orbit, perhaps even more than they were before. They are still subject to the commandment of works, still as submerged in the death of the old life as they were before. Of course, the work has to be done, but of itself it can never deliver them from death, disobedience and ungodliness. If we think our first step is the pre-condition for faith and grace, we are already judged by our work, and entirely excluded from grace. Hence the term "external work" includes everything we are accustomed to call "disposition" or "good intention," everything which the Roman Church means when it talks of *facere quod in se est* [to do what is in one; Luther feared that he could never be sure that he had done everything that was in him to do]. If we take the first step with the deliberate intention of placing ourselves in the situation where faith is possible, even this possibility of faith will be nothing but a work. The new life it opens to us is still a life within the limits of our old existence, and therefore a complete misapprehension of the true nature of the new life. We are still in unbelief.

Nevertheless the external work must be done, for we have to find our way into the situation where faith is possible. We must take a definite step. What does this mean? It means that we can only take this step aright if we fix our eyes not on the work we do, but on the word with which Jesus calls us to do it. Peter knows he dare not climb out of the ship in his own strength — his very first step would be his undoing. And so he cries, "Lord, bid me come to thee upon the waters," and Jesus answers: "Come." Christ must first call him, for the step can only be taken at his word. This call is his grace, which calls him out of death into the new life of obedience. But when once Christ has called him, Peter has no alternative — he must leave the ship and come to him. In the end, the first step of obedience proves to be an act of faith in the word of Christ. But we should completely misunderstand the nature of grace if we were to suppose that there was no need to take the first step, because faith was already there. Against that we must boldly assert that the step of obedience must be taken before faith can be possible. Unless he obeys, a man cannot believe.

Are you worried because you find it so hard to believe? No one should be surprised at the difficulty of faith, if there is some part of his life where he is consciously resisting or disobeying the commandment of Jesus. Is there some part of your life which you are refusing to surrender at his behest, some sinful passion, maybe, or some animosity, some hope, perhaps your ambition or your reason? If so, you must not be surprised that you have not received the Holy Spirit, that prayer is difficult, or that your request for faith remains unanswered. Go rather and be reconciled with your brother, re-nounce the sin which holds you fast — and then you will recover your faith! If you dismiss the word of God's command, you will not receive his word of grace. How can you hope to enter into communion with him when at some point in your life you are running away from him? The man who disobeys cannot believe, for only he who obeys can believe. . . .

This brings us to the story of the rich young man.

> And behold, one came and said unto him, Good Master, what good things shall I do, that I may have eternal life? And he said unto him, Why callest thou me good? There is none good but one, that is, God: but if thou wilt enter into life, keep the commandments. He saith unto him, Which? Jesus said, Thou shalt do no murder, Thou shalt not commit adultery, Thou shalt not steal, Thou shalt not bear false witness, Honour thy father and thy mother, and, Thou shalt love thy neighbour as thyself. The young man saith unto him, All these things have I kept from my youth up. What lack I yet? Jesus said unto him, If thou wilt be perfect, go and sell all that thou hast, and give to the poor, and thou shalt have treasure in heaven, and come and follow me. But when the young man heard that saying, he went away sor-rowful, for he had great possessions (Matt. 19:16-22).

The young man's enquiry about eternal life is an enquiry about salva-tion, the only ultimate, serious question in the world. But it is not easy to formulate in the right terms. This is shown by the way the young man obvi-ously intends to ask one question, but actually asks another. By so doing he succeeds in avoiding the real issue. For he addresses his question to the "good master." He wants to hear the opinion and receive the advice of the good master, and consult the good teacher on this specific problem. He thus succeeds in giving himself away on two points. First, he feels this is such an important question that Jesus must have something significant to say about it. Secondly, what he expects from the good master and great teacher is a weighty pronouncement, but certainly not a direction from God which would make an absolute claim on his obedience. Eternal life is for him an academic problem which is worth discussing with a "good master." But the very first word of Jesus' answer is a rude shock to him: "Why callest thou me good? One there is who is good." The question has betrayed his real feelings. He wanted to speak about eternal life to a good rabbi. He now realizes he is talking not to a good master, but to God himself, and therefore the only answer he receives from the Son of God is an unmistakable pointer to the commandment of the One God. He will not receive the answer of "good master," a personal opinion to supplement the revealed will of God. Jesus points away from himself to God who alone is good and at once proves himself thereby to be the perfect Son of God. The questioner stands before God himself and is shown up as one who is trying to evade the revealed will of God, while all the time he knows that will already. The young man knows the commandments. But such is his situation that he cannot be satisfied with them but wants to go beyond them. Jesus sees through his question and knows it to be the question of a piety shaped by and centered in the self. Why does he pretend that he has for long been ignorant of the answer? Why does he accuse God of leaving him so long in ignorance of this fundamental problem of life? So already the young man is caught and summoned to the judgment seat of God. He is challenged to drop the academic question, and recalled to a simple obedience to the will of God as it has been revealed.

Once more the young man tries to evade the issue by posing a second question: "Which?" The very devil lurks beneath this question. The young man knew he was caught in a trap, and this was the only way out. Of course, he knows the commandments. But who can know, out of the abundance of commandments, which apply to him in his present situation? The revelation of the commandments is ambiguous, not clear, says the young man. Once again he does not see the commandments except in relation to himself and his own problems and conflicts. He neglects the unmistakable command of God for the very interesting but purely human concern of his own moral difficulties. His mistake lies not so much in his awareness of those difficulties as in his attempt to play them off against the commandments of God. In fact, the very purpose for which these commandments were given was to solve these difficulties. Moral difficulties were the first consequence of the Fall, and are themselves the outcome of "Man in Revolt" against God. The Serpent in Paradise put them into the mind of the first man by asking, "Hath God said?" Until then the divine command had been clear enough, and man was ready to observe it in childlike obedience. But that is now past, and moral doubts and difficulties have crept in. The command, suggests the Serpent, needs to be explained and interpreted. "Hath God said?" Man must decide for himself what is good by using his conscience and his knowledge of good and evil. The commandment may be variously interpreted, and it is God's will that it should be interpreted and explained: for God has given man a free will to decide what he will do.

But this means disobedience from the start. Doubt and reflection take the place of spontaneous obedience. The grown-up man with his freedom of conscience vaunts his superiority over the child of obedience. But he has acquired the freedom to enjoy moral difficulties only at the cost of renouncing obedience. In short, it is a retreat from the reality of God to the speculations of men, from faith to doubt. The young man's question shows him up in his true colors. He is — man under sin. The answer of Jesus completes his exposure. Jesus simply quotes the commandments of God as they are revealed in Scripture, and thus reaffirms them as the commandments of God. The young man is trapped once more. He had hoped to avoid committing himself to any definite moral obligations by forcing Jesus to discuss his spiritual problems. He had hoped Jesus would offer him a solution of his moral difficulties. But instead he finds Jesus attacking not his question but himself. The only answer to his difficulties is the very commandment of God, which challenges him to have done with academic discussion and to get on with the task of obedience. Only the devil has an answer for our moral difficulties, and he says: "Keep on posing problems, and you will escape the necessity of obedience." But Jesus is not interested in the young man's problems; he is interested in the young man himself. He refuses to take those difficulties as seriously as the young man does. There is one thing only which Jesus takes seriously, and that is, that it is high time the young man began to hear the commandment and obey it. Where moral difficulties are taken so seriously, where they torment and enslave man, because they do not leave him open to the freeing activity of obedience, it is there that his total godlessness is revealed. All his difficulties are shown to be ungodly, frivolous, and the proof of sheer disobedience. The one thing that matters is practical obedience. That will solve his difficulties and make him (and all of us) free to become the child of God. Such is God's diagnosis of man's moral difficulties.

The young man has now been twice brought face to face with the truth of the Word of God, and there is no further chance of evading his commandment. It is clear there is no alternative but to obey it. But he is still not satisfied. "All these things have I observed from my youth up: what lack I yet?" Doubtless he was just as convinced of his sincerity this time as he was before. But it is just here that his defiance of Jesus reaches its climax. He knows the commandment and has kept it, but now, he thinks, that cannot be all God wants of him, there must be something more, some extraordinary and unique demand, and this is what he wants to do. The revealed commandment of God is incomplete, he says, as he makes the last attempt to preserve his independence and decide for himself what is good and evil. He affirms the commandment with one hand and subjects it to a frontal attack on the other. "All these things have I observed from my youth up." St. Mark adds at this point: "and Jesus, looking upon him, loved him" (Mark 10:21). Jesus sees how hopelessly the young man has closed his mind to the living Word of God, how serious he is about it, and how heartily he rages against the living commandment and the spontaneous obedience it demands. Jesus wants to help the young man because he loves him. So now comes his last word: "If thou wouldest be perfect, go, sell all that thou hast and give to the poor, and thou shalt have treasure in heaven: and come, follow me." There are three points to notice here. First it is Jesus himself who now gives the commandment. The same Jesus who earlier had pointed the young man away from the good master to the God who alone is good, now takes up his claim to divine authority and pronounces the last word. The young man must realize that it is the very Son of God who stands before him. As the Son of God, though the young man knew it not, Jesus had pointed him away from the Son to the Father, with whom he was in perfect union. And now once more as the Son he utters the commandment of God himself. Jesus must make that commandment unmistakably clear at the moment when he calls the young man to follow him. Here is the sum of the commandments — to live in fellowship with Christ. This Christ now confronts the young man with his call. He can no longer escape into the unreal world of his moral difficulties. The commandment is plain and straightforward: "Follow me." The second point to be noticed is that even this command might be misunderstood and therefore it has to be explained. For the young man might still fall back into his original mistake, and take the commandment as an opportunity for moral adventure, a thrilling way of life, but one which might easily be abandoned for another if occasion arose. It would be just as wrong if the young man were to regard discipleship as the logical conclusion of his search for truth in which he had hitherto been engaged, as an addition, a clarification or a completion of his old life. And so to avoid all misunderstandings, Jesus has to create a situation in which there can be no retreat, an irrevocable situation. At the same time it must be made clear to him that this is in no sense a fulfillment of his past life. So he bids him embrace voluntary poverty. This is the "existential," pastoral side of the question, and its aim is to enable the young man to reach a final understanding of the true way of obedience. It springs from Jesus' love for the young man, and it represents the only link between the old life and the new. But it must be noted that the link is not identical with the new life itself; it is not even the first step in the right direction, though as an act of obedience it is the essential preliminary. First the young man must go and sell all that he has and give to the poor, and then come and follow. Discipleship is the end, voluntary poverty the means. The third point to be noticed is this. When the young man asks, "What lack I yet?" Jesus rejoins: "If thou wouldest be perfect. . . ." At first sight it would seem that Jesus is thinking in terms of an addition to the young man's previous life. But it is an addition which requires the abandonment of every previous attachment. Until now perfection had always eluded his grasp. Both his understanding and his practice of the commandment had been at fault. Only now, by following Christ, can he understand and practice it aright, and only now because it is Jesus Christ who calls him. In the moment he takes up the young man's question, Jesus wrenches it from him. He had asked the way to eternal life: Jesus answers: "I call thee, and that is all."

The answer to the young man's problem is — Jesus Christ. He had hoped to hear the word of the good master, but he now perceives that this word is the Man to whom he had addressed his question. He stands face to face with Jesus, the Son of God: it is the ultimate encounter. It is now only a question of yes or no, of obedience or disobedience. The answer is no. He went away sorrowful, disappointed and deceived of his hopes, unable to wrench himself from his past. He had great possessions. The call to follow means here what it had meant before — adherence to the person of Jesus Christ and fellowship with him. The life of discipleship is not the hero-worship we would pay to a good master, but obedience to the Son of God.

Simone Weil

───〜───

SIMONE WEIL

Reflections on the Right Use of School Studies with a View to the Love of God

Simone Weil (1909-1943), precociously brilliant, studied and taught philosophy, and then, involved in movements for workers' rights, worked in an auto factory and did farm labor. When the Germans occupied France, she joined the Resistance and later fled to England. As a gesture of solidarity with those still in France, she refused to eat more than the minimum ration allowed to them; malnourishment, along with tuberculosis, led to her death. She had grown up a Jew, but a series of mystical experiences brought her close to Catholicism, though, for characteristically complicated reasons, she refused to be baptized. She wrote this essay in 1942 for a group of Catholic schoolchildren.

───────

The key to a Christian conception of studies is the realization that prayer consists of attention. It is the orientation of all the attention of which the soul is capable towards God. The quality of the attention counts for much in the quality of the prayer. Warmth of heart cannot make up for it.

It is the highest part of the attention only which makes contact with God, when prayer is intense and pure enough for such a contact to be established; but the whole attention is turned towards God.

Of course school exercises only develop a lower kind of attention. Nevertheless they are extremely effective in increasing the power of attention which will be available at the time of prayer, on condition that they are carried out with a view to this purpose and this purpose alone. . . .

If we have no aptitude or natural taste for geometry, this does not mean

Simone Weil, *Waiting on God,* trans. Emma Gruafurd (London: Routledge and Kegan Paul, 1951), 51-57.

that our faculty for attention will not be developed by wrestling with a problem or studying a theorem. On the contrary it is almost an advantage.

It does not even matter much whether we succeed in finding the solution or understanding the proof, although it is important to try really hard to do so. Never in any case whatever is a genuine effort of the attention wasted. It always has its effect on the spiritual plane and in consequence on the lower one of the intelligence, for all spiritual light lightens the mind.

If we concentrate our attention on trying to solve a problem of geometry, and if at the end of an hour we are no nearer to doing so than at the beginning, we have nevertheless been making progress each minute of that hour in another more mysterious dimension. Without our knowing or feeling it, this apparently barren effort has brought more light into the soul. The result will one day be discovered in prayer. Moreover, it may very likely be felt besides in some department of the intelligence in no way connected with mathematics. Perhaps he who made the unsuccessful effort will one day be able to grasp the beauty of a line of Racine more vividly on account of it. But it is certain that this effort will bear its fruit in prayer. There is no doubt whatever about that. . . .

Students must therefore work without any wish to gain good marks, to pass examinations, to win school successes; without any reference to their natural abilities and tastes; applying themselves equally to all their tasks, with the idea that each one will help to form in them the habit of that attention which is the substance of prayer. When we set out to do a piece of work, it is necessary to wish to do it correctly, because such a wish is indispensable if there is to be true effort. Underlying this immediate objective, however, our deep purpose should aim solely at increasing the power of attention with a view to prayer; as, when we write, we draw the shape of the letter on paper, not with a view to the shape, but with a view to the idea we want to express. To make this the sole and exclusive purpose of our studies is the first condition to be observed if we are to put them to the right use.

The second condition is to take great pains to examine squarely and to contemplate attentively and slowly each school task in which we have failed, seeing how unpleasing and second-rate it is, without seeking any excuse or overlooking any mistake or any of our tutor's corrections, trying to get down to the origin of each fault. There is a great temptation to do the opposite, to give a sideways glance at the corrected exercise if it is bad, and to hide it forthwith. Most of us do this nearly always. We have to withstand this temptation. Incidentally, moreover, nothing is more necessary for academic success, because, despite all our efforts, we work without making much progress when we refuse to give our attention to the faults we have made and our tutor's corrections.

Above all it is thus that we can acquire the virtue of humility and that is a far more precious treasure than all academic progress. From this point of view it is perhaps even more useful to contemplate our stupidity than our sin. Consciousness of sin gives us the feeling that we are evil, and a kind of pride sometimes finds a place in it. When we force ourselves to fix the gaze, not only of our eyes but of our souls, upon a school exercise in which we have failed through sheer stupidity, a sense of our mediocrity is borne in upon us with irresistible evidence. No knowledge is more to be desired. If we can arrive at knowing this truth with all our souls, we shall be well established on the right foundation.

If these two conditions are perfectly carried out, there is no doubt that school studies are quite as good a road to sanctity as any other.

To carry out the second, it is enough to wish to do so. This is not the case with the first. In order really to pay attention, it is necessary to know how to set about it.

Most often attention is confused with a kind of muscular effort. If one says to one's pupils: "Now you must pay attention," one sees them contracting their brows, holding their breath, stiffening their muscles. If after two minutes they are asked what they have been paying attention to, they cannot reply. They have been concentrating on nothing. They have not been paying attention. They have been contracting their muscles.

We often expend this kind of muscular effort on our studies. As it ends by making us tired, we have the impression that we have been working. That is an illusion. Tiredness has nothing to do with work. Work itself is the useful effort, whether it is tiring or not. This kind of muscular effort in work is entirely barren, even if it is made with the best of intentions. Good intentions in such cases are among those that pave the way to hell. Studies conducted in such a way can sometimes succeed academically from the point of view of gaining marks and passing examinations, but that is in spite of the effort and thanks to natural gifts; moreover, such studies are never of any use.

Will power, the kind that, if need be, makes us set our teeth and endure suffering, is the principal weapon of the apprentice engaged in manual work. But, contrary to the usual belief, it has practically no place in study. The intelligence can only be led by desire. For there to be desire, there must be pleasure and joy in the work. The intelligence only grows and bears fruit in joy. The joy of learning is as indispensable in study as breathing is in running. Where it is lacking there are no real students, but only poor caricatures of apprentices who, at the end of their apprenticeship, will not even have a trade.

It is the part played by joy in our studies that makes of them a preparation for spiritual life, for desire directed towards God is the only power capable of raising the soul. Or rather, it is God alone who comes down and possesses the soul, but desire alone draws God down. He only comes to those who ask him to come; and he cannot refuse to come to those who implore him long, often and ardently.

Attention is an effort, the greatest of all efforts perhaps, but it is a negative effort. Of itself, it does not involve tiredness. When we become tired, attention is scarcely possible any more, unless we have already had a good deal of practice. It is better to stop working altogether, to seek some relaxation, and then a little later to return to the task; we have to press on and loosen up alternately, just as we breathe in and out.

Twenty minutes of concentrated, untired attention is infinitely better than three hours of the kind of frowning application which leads us to say with a sense of duty done: "I have worked well!"

But, in spite of all appearances, it is also far more difficult. There is something in our soul which has a far more violent repugnance for true attention than the flesh has for bodily fatigue. This something is much more closely connected with evil than is the flesh. That is why every time that we really concentrate our attention, we destroy the evil in ourselves. If we concentrate with this intention, a quarter of an hour of attention is better than a great many good works.

Attention consists of suspending our thought, leaving it detached, empty and ready to be penetrated by the object, it means holding in our minds, within reach of this thought, but on a lower level and not in contact with it, the diverse knowledge we have acquired which we are forced to make use of. Our thought should be in relation to all particular and already formulated thoughts, as a man on a mountain who, as he looks forward, sees also below him, without actually looking at them, a great many forests and plains. Above all our thought should be empty, waiting, not seeking anything, but ready to receive in its naked truth the object which is to penetrate it.

All wrong translations, all absurdities in geometry problems, all clumsiness of style and all faulty connection of ideas in compositions and essays, all such things are due to the fact that thought has seized upon some idea too hastily and being thus prematurely blocked, is not open to the truth. The cause is always that we have wanted to be too active; we have wanted to carry out a search. This can be proved every time, for every fault, if we trace it to its root. There is no better exercise than such a tracing down of our faults, for this truth is one of those which we can only believe when we have experienced it hundreds and thousands of times. This is the way with all essential truths.

We do not obtain the most precious gifts by going in search of them but by waiting for them. Man cannot discover them by his own powers, and if he sets out to seek for them he will find in their place counterfeits of which he will be unable to discern the falsity.

The solution of a geometry problem does not in itself constitute a precious gift, but the same law applies to it because it is the image of something precious. Being a little fragment of particular truth, it is a pure image of the unique, eternal and living Truth, the very Truth which once in a human voice declared, "I am the Truth."

Every school exercise, thought of in this way, is like a sacrament.

In every school exercise there is a special way of waiting upon truth, setting our hearts upon it, yet not allowing ourselves to go out in search of it. There is a way of giving our attention to the data of a problem in geometry without trying to find the solution, or to the words of a Latin or Greek text without trying to arrive at the meaning, a way of waiting, when we are writing, for the right word to come of itself at the end of our pen, while we merely reject all inadequate words.

Our first duty towards school-children and students is to make known this method to them, not only in a general way but in the particular form which bears on each exercise. It is not only the duty of those who teach them, but also of their spiritual guides. Moreover, the latter should bring out in a brilliantly clear light the correspondence between the attitude of the intelligence in each one of these exercises and the position of the soul, which, with its lamp well filled with oil, awaits the Bridegroom's coming with confidence and desire. May each loving adolescent, as he works at his Latin prose, hope through this prose to come a little nearer to the instant when he will really be the slave — faithfully waiting while the master is absent, watching and listening — ready to open the door to him as soon as he knocks. The master will then make his slave sit down and himself serve him with meat.

―――――――

DOROTHY L. SAYERS

"Vocation in Work"

Dorothy L. Sayers (1893-1957) studied medieval literature at Oxford, where she was one of the first women to receive a degree. Her writing ranged from detective novels about Lord Peter Wimsey to a translation of Dante's *Divine Comedy* to religious essays and plays. She wrote popular journalism both defending and constructively criticizing the Church of England.

―――――――

In December 1940, the leaders of the churches in Britain put forward as one of the points necessary for the reconstruction of society: "That the sense of Divine vocation must be restored to a man's daily work." By thus lifting the subject of labor out of the sphere of economics, and calling for a sacramental relation between man and his work, they were courageously grappling with a problem which too many "social planners" have scandalously neglected.

Since the break with the Catholic tradition in the fifteenth century, religious opinion in the Reformed Churches has relied for guidance chiefly upon the text of the Canonical Scriptures. Oddly enough, apart from one very noble passage in the Apocrypha, the Scriptures are not very explicit on the subject of work; and I think that our feeling about it may have been too strongly influenced by an unimaginative interpretation of the famous passage in Genesis about the curse of Adam. "Cursed is the ground for thy sake; thorns also and thistles shall it bring forth to thee: in the sweat of thy face shalt thou eat bread" (Gen. 3:17).

Work, it seemed, was a curse and a punishment; perhaps this encouraged men to feel that no blessing and no sacrament could be associated with

Dorothy L. Sayers, "Vocation in Work," in *A Christian Basis for the Post-War World*, ed. A. E. Baker (New York: Morehouse-Gorham, 1942), 89-99, 104-05. I am indebted to Professor Laura Simmons for suggesting and providing this text.

it. Yet the whole of Christian doctrine centers round the great paradox of redemption, which asserts that the very pains and sorrows by which fallen man is encompassed can become the instruments of his salvation, if they are accepted and transmuted by love. "O blessed sin," says the Ambrosian liturgy boldly, "that didst merit such and so great a Redeemer." The first Adam was cursed with labor and suffering; the redemption of labor and suffering is the triumph of the second Adam — the Carpenter nailed to the cross.

We ought, perhaps, to look a little more closely at that profound and poetic myth of the creation and fall of man. "God," says the writer, "made man in his own image — in the image of God created he him; male and female created he them" (Gen. 1:27). And the first thing he tells us about God, in whose image both man and woman were created, is that He was Himself a Creator. He made things. Not presumably, because He had to, but because He wanted to. He made light and water, and earth and birds, and fish and animals, and enjoyed what He had done. And then He made man "in his own image" — a creature in the image of a Creator. And there is indeed one thing which is quite distinctive about man: he makes things — not just one uniform set of necessary things, as a bee makes honeycomb, but an interminable variety of different and not strictly necessary things, because he wants to. Even in this fallen and unsatisfactory life, man is still so near His divine pattern that he continually makes things, as God makes things, for the fun of it. He is *homo faber* — man the craftsman — and this is the point from which I want to set out. Man is a maker, who makes things because he wants to, because he cannot fulfill his true nature if he is prevented from making things for the love of the job. He is made in the image of the Maker, and he must himself create or become something less than a man.

Can we really believe that the writer of Genesis supposed the unfallen happiness of Adam and Eve to consist in an interminable idleness? If so, a study of the tale itself will correct that idea — the poet imagined for man no such hell of unmitigated boredom. Adam was put in the garden of Eden "to dress and till it," and for intellectual occupation he had the surely very enjoyable task of naming all the animals. What, then, in the writer's mind, was the really operative part of the curse? The work was to be more difficult, certainly — there were to be thorns and thistles — but there was to be something else as well. Work was to be conditioned by economic necessity — that was the new and ominous thing. "In the sweat of thy face shalt thou eat bread." And here we may look at what the materialist dogma of Communism has said about man's nature: "Man is first man when he produces the means of livelihood." *The means of livelihood.* To the assertion, "Man is only man when he produces (or makes)," the Christian may readily assent: for that is the Adam made in the image of God. But when the words "the means of livelihood" are added, they rivet upon the essential nature of man the judgment of man's corruption: "economic man" is Adam under the curse. The economic factor in human society is, of course, a reality, as sin and pain and sorrow and every other human evil are realities; and it is the duty of Christians to accept and redeem those real evils. But to assume, as we have increasingly allowed ourselves to assume of late years — to assume, as so many well-intentioned architects of an improved society assume today — that economics is the sole basis of man's dealings with nature and with his fellow-men, is the very negation of all Christian principle. This assumption is rooted in a lie; it is a falsehood that runs counter to the law of human nature; and like everything that runs counter to the nature of things, it can only lead to the judgment of catastrophe. For this reason it is impossible that the economic situation should ever be rightly adjusted so long as it is looked upon as being merely an economic question. To get the economic situation dealt with we must lift it out of the economic sphere altogether and consider first what is the right relation between the work itself and the worker who is made in the image of the eternal Craftsman.

Now this point of view, which a few centuries ago would have been a commonplace, is today almost inconceivably remote from the ideas of the ordinary man. It appears to him to be a kind of theoretical luxury, out of all relation to the facts of life. He will ask, How can we indulge in any such high-falutin romance about work until we have gained a measure of economic security? And again, How can men hope to enjoy their work creatively when most of it is so distasteful that they can only be induced to do it by the necessity for earning a livelihood? The answer to this is one which it is almost impossible to get people to understand: namely, that it is precisely the concentration upon economic security which makes both security and enjoyment in work unattainable, because it is a setting up of the means to an end as an end-in-itself, so that the true end and object of work is lost and forgotten.

Let us for a moment consider a group of workers who have never — in spite of much incidental corruption — altogether abandoned the divine conception of what work ought to be. They are people whose way of life is, in essentials, so sharply distinguished from that of the ordinary worker that the designers of economic Utopias can find no place for them, and will scarcely allow them to be workers at all. Economic society has grown so far away from them that it views them with suspicion as mysterious aliens, does its best to push them out of the control of practical affairs, and is usually contemptuous and hostile at the very sound of their name. That these men and women have become, as it were, an enclosed community, cut off from the world, is bad for the world and bad for them. It is not that the working world does not see and hear plenty of them — as indeed it sees and hears and gossips about the animals in the Zoo; but always with the iron bars of misunderstanding set up between. This odd, alien community is that of the men and women who live by and for the works of the creative imagination — the people whom we lump together under the general name of "artists."

The great primary contrast between the artist and the ordinary worker is this: the worker works to make money, so that he may enjoy those things in life which are not his work and which his work can purchase for him; but the artist makes money by his work in order that he may go on working. The artist does not say: "I must work in order to live"; but "I must contrive to make money so that I may live to work." For the artist there is no distinction between work and living. His work is his life, and the whole of his life — not merely the material world about him, or the colors and sounds and events that he perceives, but also all his own personality and emotions, the whole of his Life — is the actual material of his work.

Consider the great barrier that this forges between himself and the economic worker, in quite practical and mundane ways. For example, it would be preposterous for a genuine artist to submit himself to strict trade-union rules. How could he agitate for an eight-hour day or keep to it if he got it? There is no moment in the twenty-four hours when he can truthfully say he is not working. The emotions, the memories, the sufferings, the dreams even of the periods when he is not actually at his desk or his easel — these are his stuff and his tools; and his periods of leisure are the periods when his creative imagination may be most actively at work. He cannot say, "Here work stops and leisure begins"; he cannot stop work unless he stops living. Or how could he, in his own financial interests or those of his fellows, adopt the policy of keeping his work, in speed or quality, down to the level of the slowest or stupidest of his colleagues. . . . Any limitation upon his right to work himself to death if he chooses, or to choose the kind of work he will do, that he will resist to his last breath, for to set fetters upon his work is to set fetters upon his life.

There is a price paid for the artist's freedom, as for all freedom. He, of all workers in the world, has the least economic security. The money value of his work is at the mercy of every wind of public opinion; and if he falls by the wayside he cannot claim unemployment benefit, or look to the State to pay doctor's bills, educate his children, and compensate him for injuries incurred in the exercise of his profession. If he falls off a cliff while painting a picture, if he loses his wits or suffers a failure of invention, society will not hold itself responsible; nor, if his publisher suddenly decides to be rid of him, can he sue the man for wrongful dismissal. Moreover, he is taxed with a singular injustice; while the world pays tribute to his unworldliness by expecting him to place a great deal of his time, energy, and stock-in-trade at the disposal of the community without payment. The artist puts up with these disabilities because his way of life is not primarily rooted in economics. True, he often demands high prices for his work — but he wants the money not in order that he may stop working and go away and do something different, but in order that he may indulge in the luxury of doing some part of his work for nothing. "Thank heaven," the artist will say, "I've made enough with that book, or play, or picture of mine, to take a couple of years off to do my own work" — by which he probably means some book or play or picture which will cost him an immense amount of labor and pains and which he has very little chance of selling. In fact, when the artist rejoices because he has been relieved from the pressure of economic necessity, he means that he has been relieved — not from the work, but from the money.

Now, this is not merely because the artist is his own master, working for himself and not for an employer. The same thing holds good of the actor, for example, who is quite literally an employed person — who can actually draw unemployment benefit. The actor, like other artists, passionately enjoys doing work for nothing or next to nothing if only he can afford to do it. And he never talks of himself as "employed"; if he is employed, he tells you that he is "working."

I think we can measure the distance we have fallen from the idea that work is a vocation to which we are called, by the extent to which we have come to substitute the word "employment" for "work." We say we must solve the "problem of unemployment" — we reckon up how many "hands" are "employed"; our social statistics are seldom based upon the work itself — whether the right people are doing it, or whether the work is worth doing. We have come to set a strange value on leisure for its own sake — not the leisure which enables a man to get on properly with his job, but the leisure which is a polite word for idleness. The commodities which it is easiest to advertise and sell are those which purport to "take the work out" of everything — the tinned foods that need no cooking — the clothes that wash themselves — the switches and gadgets that save time and make leisure. Which would be grand if we eagerly needed that extra time and leisure in order to make and do things. Alas, the commodities easiest to sell after the labor-saving gadgets are the inventions for saving us from the intolerable leisure we have produced, and for painlessly killing the time we have saved. The entertainment to which we can passively listen, the game we can watch without taking part in it, the occupation, however meaningless, which can relieve us from the trouble of thinking. As a result, far too many people in this country seem to go about only half alive. All their existence is an effort to escape from what they are doing. And the inevitable result of this is a boredom, a lack of purpose, a passivity which eats life away at the heart and a disillusionment which prompts men to ask what life is all about, and complain, with only too much truth, that they can "make nothing of it."

Now that the Churches are setting themselves to tackle this dislocation that has weakened our grip upon work, I think they will find in it the root cause of a great many other evils — evils that they have failed to cure directly because they were treating the symptoms rather than the disease. It is, for instance, passivity, lack of purpose, and a failure to discharge pent-up creative energy into daily work that drives a civilization into that bored and promiscuous sexuality which derives not from excess of vitality, but from lack of something better to do, and which is always the mark of a civilization which has lost sight of true purpose in its work.

Or again: the appearance of a parasitic and exploiting class is closely connected with a way of life deficient in opportunities for creative activity. In this connection, both churches and secular "planners" should give some attention to what is known as the "woman's question" — an important subject usually ignored in the schemes for a "new order."

In this war, as in the last, the women are being called upon to come out of their homes and do, as we say, "the men's work." They come, and they do it, and everybody says how splendid they are. But the offers of work to them are usually accompanied with the warning that after the war the men will have to come back to their jobs — and, indeed, I notice a very strong tendency, both on the Left and on the Right, to suggest that when the crisis is past the women are to be pushed out of the trades and professions and restored, as far as possible, to their homes, in the interests of "employment."

I see the men's point of view about this. I understand the resentment against the women who "take the men's jobs." But it should be realized that, under modern conditions, the opportunities for intelligent work afforded by the home are very greatly restricted compared with what they were, and that many of the women's traditional jobs have, since the age of mechanical industry began, been filched from them by the men. The baking industry, the whole of the nation's spinning, weaving, and dyeing, the breweries, the distilleries, the confectionery, the preserving, curing and pickling of food, the perfumery, the lace-making, the dairying, the cheese-making have been transferred from the home to the factory, and the control and management — the intelligent part of them — handed over to men. It was the commercial age that presented us with a class of really leisured women — pampered and exploiting women, with no creative job to which they might set hand and brain. It was then that the possession of an idle woman became the hallmark of a man's success; and it is dangerous when — through a vast reserve either of slave-labor as in ancient Rome or of machine-labor as in modern Europe — idleness becomes an ideal attainable by a vast mass of citizens. Because an idle and a bored class is bound to be a parasitic and exploiting class. Men cannot live for their work if they are harassed by an army of empty-minded women demanding that they should work in order to get money to support a decorative idleness. We cannot now, of course, restore to the home everything that machines and commerce have taken from it. But I ask the Churches, and I ask all social reformers, to take seriously this warning that they cannot have a society of creatively-working and unexploited men unless they can also arrange for a society of creatively working women without the temptation to become exploiters of men's labor.

At this point, of course, we come up against a really fundamental difficulty. It is all very well for the artist to talk like this, but his work is of a really creative and satisfying kind. That is why he doesn't want to get away from it. But how about the factory-hand whose work consists of endlessly and monotonously pushing a pin into a slot? How can he be expected to live for the sake of the work? Isn't he right to want to make money so as to get away from it as quickly as possible? Can you blame him for looking on work as "employment" — as something to be done grudgingly, with as little exertion as possible? Doesn't it correspond to the artist's necessary "pot-boiler," which has to be ground out in order that he may get away to "his own work"? It is useless and silly to say that machines and industry ought to be abolished. We can't turn time backwards. We have to cope with things as they are and make the best of them. This is what the worker will always retort when you talk to him about the sense of vocation in work. Well, that is so; and unless and until we can achieve a radical change in our whole attitude to work and money, we shall have to allow that a great deal of necessary work is in the nature of a pot-boiler, and that it ought to be arranged so as to boil the pot as quickly as possible and in such a way that nobody's pot remains without a fire to boil it. This is the task on which those reformers are engaged who try to deal with the question in purely economic terms. And while we have to deal with it along those lines, we may take the opportunity of trying to establish two things: First, that even work done for potboiling should be done as well and as conscientiously as possible. Secondly, that when the pot-boiling is done, the worker should be taught and encouraged to turn to "his own work" — to some creative and satisfying hobby at least; and not merely to an idle and soul-deadening killing of time. But these things are at best palliatives. They do not get to the root of the matter, which is the nation-wide and world-wide acceptance of a false scale of values about work, money, and leisure.

First of all, is there anything whatever that will not only reconcile the worker to even the most monotonous and soul-killing kind of toil, but also make him ready to undertake it with eagerness and a kind of passionate satisfaction?

The enthusiasm with which labor went to work after the Dunkirk disaster and during the "Tanks-for-Russia" week suggests that the power that enables men to work with enthusiasm is a real conviction of the worth of their work. They will endure much if, like the artist, they passionately desire to see the job completed and to know that it is very good. But what are we to say about a civilization which employs so many of its workers in doing work which has no worth at all, work which no living man with a soul in him could desire to see, work which has nothing whatever to justify it, *except* the manufacture of employment and the creation of profits? *That* is the real vicious circle in which we are all enclosed. *That* is the real indictment we have to bring against a commercial age. And it is one which we cannot meet by the adjustment of wages, or by the restriction of private enterprise, or by the transference of capital from the individual to the State. . . .

I do not think that when this war ends we shall enter upon a period of security and stability and prosperity. I do not see how we could — and I do not think it really desirable that we should. But I do think it essential that we should somehow contrive to enter upon a period of eager, and honest, and dedicated work. A period when we shall be prepared to live hard and rough so long as the work is done; when we shall forget to think about money and think first and foremost about the true needs of man and the right handling of material things. If, when the strains and stresses of war are over, we try to let up and sink back and rest, we shall destroy ourselves. In war, work has found its soul — this time we must not lose it again in peace. Instead of crying out for an "enduring peace," we might do well to hope, not exactly for an enduring war, but for the carrying over into the strenuous times that lie ahead of that meaning which war has taught us to give to work.

I will not, as some of our prophets do, offer the slightest hope of a secure and easy time "after the war." I think it will be a time when we must continue to adventure forth, "a fire on the one hand and a deep water on the other," working as we have never worked in our lives and looking to the end of the work.

———

DOROTHY DAY

Selected Writings

Dorothy Day (1897-1980) dropped out of the University of Illinois to write for socialist and pacifist newspapers. In 1917 she was arrested at the White House, protesting that women could not vote. Seeking a more practical way to serve, she trained as a nurse. Having had an abortion, when she was pregnant again she insisted on having the child, though the father was uninterested in marrying her. Day had been raised without any connection to a church. Now she joined the Catholic Church and had her daughter baptized. Shortly afterwards, she met Peter Maurin, a French former Christian Brother now dedicated to a Franciscan ideal of poverty. Together they founded the Catholic Worker Movement, involving first a newspaper and then a number of homes for the otherwise homeless. Day continued to write, protest, and serve the poor until her death. The first excerpt comes from the first issue of *The Catholic Worker*.

To Our Readers

For those who are sitting on park benches in the warm spring sunlight. For those who are huddling in shelters trying to escape the rain. For those who are walking the streets in the all but futile search for work.

For those who think that there is no hope for the future, no recognition of their plight — this little paper is addressed.

It is printed to call their attention to the fact that the Catholic Church

"To Our Readers," from the first issue of *The Catholic Worker*, May 1933; "A Note on *The Catholic Worker*," from Dorothy Day, *On Pilgrimage: The Sixties* (New York: Curtis Books, 1972), 13-14; "On Pilgrimage," from Dorothy Day, *On Pilgrimage* (Grand Rapids: William B. Eerdmans, 1999), 123-24, 125-26, 247-49, 249-50; "Postscript," from Dorothy Day, *Selected Writings*, ed. Robert Ellsberg (Maryknoll, N.Y.: Orbis, 1996), 362-63.

has a social program — to let them know that there are men of God who are working not only for their spiritual but for their material welfare.

*   *   *

It's time there was a Catholic paper printed for the unemployed. The fundamental aim of most radical sheets is the conversion of its readers to Radicalism and Atheism.

Is it not possible to be radical and not atheist?

Is it not possible to protest, to expose, to complain, to point out abuses and demand reforms without desiring the overthrow of religion?

In an attempt to popularize and make known the encyclicals of the Popes in regard to social justice and the program put forth by the Church for the "reconstruction of the social order," this news sheet, *The Catholic Worker,* is started.

It is not as yet known whether it will be a monthly, a fortnightly, or a weekly. It all depends on the funds collected for the printing and distribution. Those who can subscribe and those who can donate are asked to do so.

This first number of *The Catholic Worker* was planned, written, and edited in the kitchen of a tenement on Fifteenth Street, on subway platforms, on the El, the ferry. There is no editorial office; no overhead in the way of telephone or electricity; no salaries paid.

The money for the printing of the first issue was raised by begging small contributions from friends. A colored priest in Newark sent us ten dollars and the prayers of his congregation. A colored Sister in New Jersey, garbed also in holy poverty, sent us a dollar. Another kindly and generous friend sent twenty-five. The rest of it the editors squeezed out of their own earnings, and at that they were using money necessary to pay milk bills, gas bills, electric light bills.

By accepting delay the utilities did not know that they were furthering the cause of social justice. They were, for the time being, unwitting cooperators.

Next month someone may donate us an office. Who knows?

It is cheering to remember that Jesus Christ wandered this earth with no place to lay His head. The foxes have holes and the birds of the air their nests, but the Son of Man has no place to lay His head. And when we consider our fly-by-night existence, our uncertainty, we remember (with pride at sharing the honor) that the disciples supped by the seashore and wandered through cornfields picking the ears from the stalks wherewith to make their frugal meals.

A Note on *The Catholic Worker*

The Catholic Worker is an eight-page tabloid which appears nine times a year. It was first issued and sold in Union Square on May 1, 1933.

From a first printing of 3,000, the circulation rose to over one hundred thousand. At the time of the Spanish Civil War it was reduced to 40,000, when the churches and Catholic associations began to realize what the Sermon on the Mount meant to the editors in time of class war, race war, civil war and international war. *The Catholic Worker* professed itself pacifist and anarchist in principle, and those who did not like those terms used "personalist and communitarian."

Its editors are mostly Catholic, and if they are not, they agree that without brotherly love there can be no love of God. They profess voluntary poverty and sharing — living together in city and country with the poor and the wounded in spirit in what are now called communes, but which Peter Maurin, who was the theoretician of what has now come to be called the Catholic Worker Movement, termed "Houses of Hospitality."

Dorothy Day is editor and publisher of the paper. She spends some months of every year travelling and visiting readers of the paper, which now has subscribers and followers around the world.

The editors who live in C.W. houses receive no salaries, but room, board and clothing. The subscription price of the paper is twenty-five cents a year. However, many of the subscribers send more, so that the Catholic Workers have been able to buy some farms and houses. Many have been in prison for participating in demonstrations, for their conscientious objection to war and conscription, and for their refusal to pay taxes for war. The number of houses of hospitality and farming communes around the country vary in size and character from year to year, according to the age and vocational status of the young people who run them. In general, though, every house has a resemblance to a large and disorderly but loving family.

On Pilgrimage

Whenever I groan within myself and think how hard it is to keep writing about love in these times of tension and strife, which may at any moment become for us all a time of terror, I think to myself, "What else is the world interested in?" What else do we all want, each one of us, except to love and be loved, in our families, in our work, in all our relationships? God is Love. Love casts out fear. Even the most ardent revolutionist, seeking to change the world, to overturn the tables of the money changers, is trying to make a world where it is easier for people to love, to stand in that relationship to each other. We want with all our hearts to love, to be loved. And not just in the family but to look upon all as our mothers, sisters, brothers, children. It is when we love the most intensely and most humanly that we can recognize how tepid is our love for others. The keenness and intensity of love brings with it suffering, of course, but joy too, because it is a foretaste of heaven. I often think in relation to my love for little Becky, Susie, and Eric [her grandchildren]: "That is the way I must love every child and want to serve them, cherish them, and protect them." Even that relationship which is set off from other loves by that slight change in phraseology (instead of "loving," one is "in love") — the very change in terminology, denoting a living in love, a dwelling in love at all times, being bathed in love, so that every waking thought, word, deed, and suffering is permeated by that love — yes, that relationship above all should give us not only a taste of the love of God for us but the kind of love we should have for all.

When you love people, you see all the good in them, all the Christ in them. God sees Christ, His Son, in us and loves us. And so we should see Christ in others, *and nothing else*, and love them. There can never be enough of it. There can never be enough thinking about it. St. John of the Cross said that where there was no love, put love and you would take out love. The principle certainly works. I've seen my friend, Sister Peter Claver, with that warm friendliness of hers which is partly natural (she is half-Jew and half-Irish) but which is intensified and made enduring by grace, come into a place which is cold with tension and conflict, and warm the house with her love.

And this is not easy. Everyone will try to kill that love in you, even your nearest and dearest; at least they will try to prune it. "Don't you know this, that, and the other thing about this person? He or she did this. If you don't want to hear it, you must hear. It is for your good to hear it. It is my duty to tell you, and it is your duty to take recognition of it. You must stop loving, modify your loving, show your disapproval. You cannot possibly love — if you pretend you do, you are a hypocrite, and the truth is not in you. You are contributing to the delinquency of that person by your sentimental blindness. It is such people as you who add to the sum total of confusion and wickedness and soft appeasement and compromise and the policy of expediency in this world. You are to blame for communism, for industrial capitalism, and finally for hell on earth."

The antagonism often rises to a crescendo of vituperation, an intensification of opposition on all sides. You are quite borne down by it. And the only Christian answer is *love,* to the very end, to the laying down of your life. . . .

It is always a terrible thing to come back to Mott Street [one of the Catholic Worker houses in New York]. To come back in a driving rain, to men crouched on the stairs, huddled in doorways, without overcoats because they sold them perhaps the week before when it was warm, to satisfy hunger or thirst — who knows? Those without love would say, "It serves them right, drinking up their clothes." God help us if we got just what we deserved!

It is a terrible thing to see the ugliness and poverty of the cities, to see what man has made of man. I needed those few days at Newburgh to brace myself for work. Father Anthony, a young Benedictine from Newton, New Jersey, was with us that week, giving a retreat on the sacraments, and the conferences I was in time for continued what I had been pondering of the love of God for man and man for man. "From Genesis to Revelation," he said, in one conference, "it is the story of God's love for man. All the story of God's dealing with man is a love story. Some say the Old Testament tells of God's justice and the New of his love. But there is not a page but emphasizes God's folly in ever forgiving and drawing man back to him." I remembered the book of Hosea, the prophet and holy man who was commanded by God to love and marry a harlot, who had children by him, and who left him again and again, having children also by her lovers. And how Hosea again and again took her back. How he must have been scorned by his generation, he a holy man, so weak and uxorious, so soft-minded that again and again, "he allured her" to him, on one occasion even buying her back from her lover, even providing her, while she was with her lover, with corn and wine and oil. And God even commanded it so that down through the ages there would be this example of God's love for a faithless people, of the folly of love, a foretaste of the folly of the Cross. . . . If we could only learn to be such fools! God give us the strength to persist in trying to learn such folly. . . .

December

Love of brother means voluntary poverty, stripping one's self, putting off the old man, denying one's self, etc. It also means nonparticipation in those comforts and luxuries which have been manufactured by the exploitation of others. While our brothers suffer, we must compassionate them, suffer with them. While our brothers suffer from lack of necessities, we will refuse to enjoy comforts. These resolutions, no matter how hard they are to live up to, no matter how often we fail and have to begin over again, are part of the vision and the long-range view which Peter Maurin has been trying to give us these past years. . . . And we must keep this spirit in mind, recognize the truth of it, the necessity for it, even though we do not, cannot, live up to it. Like perfection. We are ordered to be perfect as our heavenly Father is perfect, and we aim at it, in our intention, though in our execution we may fall short of the mark over and over. St. Paul says, it is by little and by little that we proceed.

If these jobs do not contribute to the common good, we pray God for the grace to give them up. Have they to do with shelter, food, clothing? Have they to do with the works of mercy? Father Tompkins of Nova Scotia says that everyone should be able to place his job in the category of the works of mercy.

This would exclude jobs in advertising, which only increases people's useless desires. In insurance companies and banks, which are known to exploit the poor of this country and of others. Banks and insurance companies have taken over land and built huge collective farms, ranches, plantations, of 30,000, 100,000 acres, and have dispossessed the poor man. Loan and finance companies have further defrauded him. Movies [and] radio have further enslaved him. So that he has no time nor thought to give to his life, either of soul or body. Whatever has contributed to his misery and degradation may be considered a bad job and not to be worked at.

If we examine our conscience in this way, we would soon be driven into manual labor, into humble work, and so would become more like our Lord and our Blessed Mother.

Poverty means nonparticipation. It means what Peter calls regional living. This means fasting from tea, coffee, cocoa, grapefruit, pineapple, etc., from things not grown in the region in which one lives. One day last winter we bought broccoli which had the label on it of a corporation farm in Arizona or Texas, where we had seen men, women, and children working at two o'clock in the morning with miners' lamps on their foreheads, in order to avoid the terrible heat of the day, which often reached 125 degrees. These were homeless migrants, of which there are some million in the United States. Carey McWilliams' *Factories in the Fields,* which you can get at any library, tells of the conditions of these workers. For these there is "no room at the inn."

We ought not to eat food produced under such conditions. We ought not to smoke, not only because it is a useless habit but also because tobacco impoverishes the soil and pauperizes the farmer, and means women and children working in the fields. Poverty means having a bare minimum in the way of clothes and seeing to it that these are made under decent working conditions, proper wages and hours, etc. The union label tries to guarantee this. Considering the conditions in woolen mills, it would be better to raise one's own sheep and angora goats and rabbits, and spin and weave and make one's own blankets and stockings and suits. Many groups are trying to do these things throughout the country, both as a remedy for unemployment and for more abundant living. . . .

How far we all are from it! We do not even see our infirmities. Common sense tells us, "Why live in a slum? It is actually cheaper to live in a model housing project, have heat and hot water, a mauve or pink bath and toilet, etc. We can manage better; we have more time to pray, to meditate, study. We would have more money to give to the poor." Yes, this is true according to the candlelight of common sense, but not according to the flaming heat of the Sun of justice. Yes, we will have more time with modern conveniences, but we will not have more love. "The natural man does not perceive the things of the spirit." We need to be fools for Christ. What if we do have to buy coal by the bucket instead of by the ton? Let us squander money, be as lavish as God is with His graces, as He is with His fruits of the earth.

Let us rejoice in poverty, because Christ was poor. Let us love to live with the poor, because they are specially loved by Christ. Even the lowest, most depraved — we must see Christ in them and love them to folly. When we suffer from dirt, lack of privacy, heat and cold, coarse food, let us rejoice.

When we are weary of manual labor and think, "What foolishness to shovel out ashes, build fires, when we can have steam heat! Why sew when it can be better done on a machine? Why laboriously make bread when we can buy so cheaply?" Such thoughts have deprived us of good manual labor in our city slums and have substituted shoddy store-bought goods, clothes, and bread.

Poverty and manual labor — they go together. They are weapons of the spirit, and very practical ones, too. What would one think of a woman who refused to wash her clothes because she had no washing machine, or clean her house because she had no vacuum, or sew because she had no machine? In spite of the usefulness of the machine, and we are not denying it, there is still much to be done by hand. So much, one might say, that it is useless to multiply our tasks, go in for work for work's sake.

But we must believe in it for Christ's sake. We must believe in poverty and manual labor for love of Christ and for love of the poor. It is not true love if we do not know them, and we can only know them by living with them, and if we love with knowledge we will love with faith, hope, and charity.

Postscript

We were just sitting there talking when Peter Maurin came in.

We were just sitting there talking when lines of people began to form, saying, "We need bread." We could not say, "Go, be thou filled." If there were six small loaves and a few fishes, we had to divide them. There was always bread.

We were just sitting there talking, and people moved in on us. Let those who can take it, take it. Some moved out, and that made room for more. And somehow the walls expanded.

We were just sitting there talking and someone said, "Let's all go and live on a farm."

It was as casual as all that, I often think. It just came about. It just happened.

I found myself, a barren woman, the joyful mother of children. It is not easy always to be joyful, to keep in mind the duty of delight.

The most significant thing about the Catholic Worker is poverty, some say.

The most significant thing is community, others say. We are not alone anymore.

But the final word is love. At times it has been, in the words of Father Zossima, a harsh and dreadful thing, and our very faith in love has been tried through fire.

We cannot love God unless we love each other. We know Him in the breaking of bread, and we know each other in the breaking of bread, and we are not alone anymore. Heaven is a banquet and life is a banquet, too, even with a crust, where there is companionship.

We have all known the long loneliness, and we have learned that the only solution is love, and that love comes with community.

It all happened while we sat there talking, and it is still going on.

THOMAS MERTON

No Man Is an Island

Thomas Merton (1915-1968) grew up, the son of an artist, in France, England, and the United States. After studying at Columbia University in New York, he was writing poetry and very much living the life of a young bohemian until his conversion to Catholicism in 1938. In 1941 he joined the Trappist monastery at Gethsemani in Kentucky. Dedicated to a life of silence, the Trappists, an offshoot of the Cistercian order, are perhaps the most rigorous of monastic orders today. Merton's autobiography, *The Seven Storey Mountain*, published in 1948, became a best-seller, and he continued to write poems and essays, attacking racism, poverty, and nuclear armament as well as discussing the spiritual life. He died in Bangkok, where he had gone to a meeting between Catholic and Buddhist monks.

1. Each one of us has some kind of vocation. We are all called by God to share in His life and in His Kingdom. Each one of us is called to a special place in the Kingdom. If we find that place we will be happy. If we do not find it, we can never be completely happy. For each one of us, there is only one thing necessary: to fulfill our own destiny, according to God's will, to be what God wants us to be.

We must not imagine that we discover this destiny only by a game of hide-and-seek with Divine Providence. Our vocation is not a sphinx's riddle which we must solve in one guess or else perish. Some people find, in the end, that they have made many wrong guesses and that their paradoxical vocation is to go through life guessing wrong. It takes them a long time to find out that they are happier that way.

Thomas Merton, *No Man Is an Island* (New York: Harcourt, Brace, and World, 1955), 131-33, 140-48, 152-57.

In any case, our destiny is the work of two wills, not one. It is not an immutable fate, forced upon us without any choice of our own, by a divinity without heart.

Our vocation is not a supernatural lottery but the interaction of two freedoms, and, therefore, of two loves. It is hopeless to try to settle the problem of vocation outside the context of friendship and of love. We speak of Providence: that is a philosophical term. The Bible speaks of our Father in Heaven. Providence is, consequently, more than an institution, it is a person. More than a benevolent stranger, He is our Father. And even the term "Father" is too loose a metaphor to contain all the depths of the mystery: for He loves us more than we love ourselves, as if we were Himself. He loves us, moreover, with our own wills, with our own decisions. How can we understand the mystery of our union with God Who is closer to us than we are to ourselves? It is His very closeness that makes it difficult for us to think of Him. He Who is infinitely above us, infinitely different from ourselves, infinitely "other" than we, nevertheless dwells in our souls, watches over every movement of our life with as much love as if we were His own self. His love is at work bringing good out of all our mistakes and defeating even our sins.

In planning the course of our lives, we must remember the importance and the dignity of our own freedom. A man who fears to settle his future by a good act of his own free choice does not understand the love of God. For our freedom is a gift God has given us in order that He may be able to love us more perfectly, and be loved by us more perfectly in return.

2. Love is perfect in proportion to its freedom. It is free in proportion to its purity. We act most freely when we act purely in response to the love of God. But the purest love of God is not servile, not blind, not limited by fear. Pure charity is fully aware of the power of its own freedom. Perfectly confident of being loved by God, the soul that loves Him dares to make a choice of its own, knowing that its own choice will be acceptable to love.

At the same time pure love is prudent. It is enlightened with a clear-sighted discretion. Trained in freedom, it knows how to avoid the selfishness that frustrates its action. It sees obstacles and avoids or overcomes them. It is keenly sensitive to the smallest signs of God's will and good pleasure in the circumstances of its own life, and its freedom is conditioned by the knowledge of all these. Therefore, in choosing what will please God, it takes account of all the slightest indications of His will. Yet if we add all these indications together, they seldom suffice to give us absolute certitude that God wills one thing to the exclusion of every other. He Who loves us means by this to leave us room for our own freedom, so that we may dare to choose for ourselves, with no other certainty than that His love will be pleased by our intention to please Him. . . .

10. There is something in the depths of our being that hungers for wholeness and finality. Because we are made for eternal life, we are made for an act that gathers up all the powers and capacities of our being and offers them simultaneously and forever to God. The blind spiritual instinct that tells us obscurely that our own lives have a particular importance and purpose, and which urges us to find out our vocation, seeks in so doing to bring us to a decision that will dedicate our lives irrevocably to their true purpose. The man who loses this sense of his own personal destiny, and who renounces all hope of having any kind of vocation in life, has either lost all hope of happiness or else has entered upon some mysterious vocation that God alone can understand.

Most human vocations tend to define their purpose not only by placing the one called in a definite relation to God, but also by giving him a set place among his fellow men. The vocation of each one of us is fixed just as much by the need others have for us as by our own need for other men and for God. Yet when I speak here of a need, I do not mean to exclude the untrammeled exercise of spiritual freedom. If I am called to the priesthood, it may be because the Church has need of priests and, therefore, that she had need of me. And it may also happen that my own peace and spiritual balance and the happiness of my whole life may ultimately depend on my becoming a priest. But the Church is not determined to accept me as a priest simply because she needs priests, nor am I forced to become a priest by the pressure of my own spiritual condition.

The freedom that is exercised in the choice of priestly vocations is a mystery hidden in God, a mystery that reaches out of the obscurity of God's Providence to select, sometimes, unlikely men to be "other Christs" and sometimes to reject those who are, in the eyes of men, best fitted for such a vocation.

11. What is the function of a priest in the world? To teach other men? To advise them? To console them? To pray for them? These things enter into his life, but they can be done by anyone. Every man in the world is called to teach and to advise and to console some other man, and we are all bound to pray for one another that we may be saved. These actions require no special priesthood other than our baptismal participation in the priesthood of Christ, and they can be exercised even without this. Nor is the priest's distinctive vocation simply that he must be a man of God. The monk is a man of God, and he does not have to be a priest.

The priest is called to be another Christ in a far more particular and intimate sense than the ordinary Christian or the monk. He must keep alive in the world the sacramental presence and action of the Risen Savior. He is a visible human instrument of the Christ Who reigns in Heaven, Who teaches and sanctifies and governs the Church through His anointed priests. The words of the priest are not to be merely his own words or his own doctrine. They should always be the doctrine of the One Who sent him. The action of the priest upon souls should come from something more than his own poor human power to advise and to console. Human though his acts may be, poor and deficient in themselves, they must be supported by the sacramental action of Jesus Christ and vivified by the hidden working of the Divine Spirit.

The priest is just as much sanctified by the actions he performs in the course of his sacred ministry as are those souls for whom he performs them. The Mass is, indeed, normally more fruitful for the priest who celebrates it than for any of those who assist at it. Indeed, one might say that the priest's holiness should be as great as the cumulative holiness of all those to whom he administers the sacraments. In any case, his vocation is to keep alive in the world the sanctity and the sanctifying power of the One High Priest, Jesus Christ.

This explains at once the beauty and the terror of the priestly vocation. A man, weak as other men, imperfect as they are, perhaps less well endowed than many of those to whom he is sent, perhaps even less inclined to be virtuous than some of them, finds himself caught, without possibility of escape, between the infinite mercy of Christ and the almost infinite dreadfulness of man's sin. He cannot help but feel in the depths of his heart something of Christ's compassion for sinners, something of the eternal Father's hatred of sin, something of the inexpressible love that drives the Spirit of God to consume sin in the fires of sacrifice. At the same time he may feel in himself all the conflicts of human weakness and irresolution and dread, the anguish of uncertainty and helplessness and fear, the inescapable lure of passion. All that he hates in himself becomes more hateful to him, by reason of his close union with Christ. But also by reason of his very vocation he is forced to face resolutely the reality of sin in himself and in others. He is bound by his vocation to fight this enemy. He cannot avoid the battle. And it is a battle that he alone can never win. He is forced to let Christ Himself fight the enemy in him. He must do battle on the ground chosen not by himself but by Christ. That ground is the hill of Calvary and the Cross. For, to speak plainly, the priest makes no sense at all in the world except to perpetuate in it the sacrifice of the Cross, and to die with Christ on the Cross for the love of those whom God would have him save.

12. Then there is the monastic vocation.

If the priest can be in some sense defined by other men's need of his sanctifying action in the world, this is less obviously true of the monk. For although it is true that the presence of every holy man in the world exercises a sanctifying effect, the monk does not exist precisely in order that others may be holy.

That is why it would be a mistake to assume that the essence of the monastic vocation is public prayer. The monk does, indeed, pray for other men and for the whole Church. But that is not the sole or even the main reason for his existence. Still less does the monk justify his existence by teaching, by writing, by the study of Scripture or of Gregorian chant, or by farming and raising cattle. There are plenty of cows in the world without monks to raise them.

It is true that the monastic vocation bears witness to the infinite transcendence of God, because it proclaims to the whole world that God has a right to call some men apart in order that they may live for Him alone. But in entering the monastery the monk should think of something more than this. Indeed, it would not be good for him to be too conscious of the fact that his sacrifice may still have some meaning to other men. If he dwells too long on the fact that the world remembers him, his very consciousness will reestablish the ties that he is supposed to have cut beyond recovery. For the essence of the monastic vocation is precisely this leaving of the world and all its desires and ambitions and concerns in order to live not only for God, but by Him and in Him, not for a few years but forever.

The one thing that most truly makes a monk what he is, is this irrevocable break with the world and all that is in it, in order to seek God in solitude.

The world itself is even quicker to realize this fact than the monk who allows the purity of his vocation to be tarnished by concessions to the secular spirit. The first ones to condemn the monastery that has become infected with worldliness are those who, in the world, are themselves least monastic, for even those who have abandoned their religion often retain a high and exacting idea of religious perfection. St. Benedict saw that it was a matter of primary importance for the monk to "become a stranger to the ways of this world" — *a saeculi actibus se facere alienum*. But in establishing this principle, the Father of Western Monasticism was not simply thinking of public edification. He was thinking of the most urgent need of the monk's own soul. . . .

17. We would be better able to understand the beauty of the religious vocation if we remembered that marriage too is a vocation. The religious life is a special way of sanctity, reserved for comparatively few. The ordinary way to holiness and to the fullness of Christian life is marriage. Most men and women will become saints in the married state. And yet so many Christians

who are not called to religious life or to the priesthood say of themselves: "I have no vocation!" What a mistake! They have a wonderful vocation, all the more wonderful because of its relative freedom and lack of formality. For the "society" which is the family lives beautifully by its own spontaneous inner laws. It has no need of codified rule and custom. Love is its rule, and all its customs are the living expression of deep and sincere affection. In a certain sense, the vocation to the married state is more desirable than any other because of the fact that this spontaneity, this spirit of freedom and union in charity, is so easily accessible, for the ordinary man, in family life. The formalism and artificiality which creep into religious communities are with difficulty admitted into the circle of a family where powerful human values triumphantly resist the incursions of falsity.

Married people, then, instead of lamenting their supposed "lack of vocation," should highly value the vocation they have actually received. They should thank God for the fact that this vocation, with all its responsibilities and hardships, is a safe and sure way to become holy without being warped or shriveled up by pious conventionalism. The married man and the mother of a Christian family, if they are faithful to their obligations, will fulfill a mission that is as great as it is consoling: that of bringing into the world and forming young souls capable of happiness and love, souls capable of sanctification and transformation in Christ. Living in close union with God the Creator and source of life, they will understand better than others the mystery of His infinite fecundity, in which it is their privilege to share. Raising children in difficult social circumstances, they will enter perhaps more deeply into the mystery of divine Providence than others who, by their vow of poverty, ought ideally to be more directly dependent on God than they, but who in fact are never made to feel the anguish of insecurity.

18. All vocations are intended by God to manifest His love in the world. For each special calling gives a man some particular place in the Mystery of Christ, gives him something to do for the salvation of all mankind. The difference between the various vocations lies in the different ways in which each one enables men to discover God's love, appreciate it, respond to it, and share it with other men. Each vocation has for its aim the propagation of divine life in the world.

In marriage, God's love is made known and shared under the sacramentalized veils of human affection. The vocation to marriage is a vocation to a supernatural union which sanctifies and propagates human life and extends the Kingdom of God in the world by bringing forth children who will be members of the Mystical Christ. All that is most human and instinctive, all that is best in man's natural affections, is here consecrated to God and becomes a sign of divine love and an occasion of divine grace.

In married life, divine love is more fully incarnate than in the other vocations. For that reason it is easier to apprehend, easier to appreciate. But its extension, being less spiritual, is less wide. The sphere of action of the father and mother's love extends only to their own children and to their relatives and to a circle of friends and associates.

In order to extend the effectiveness of divine charity, the other vocations progressively spiritualize our human lives and actions in order to spread them over a wider and wider area. So, in the active religious life or in the secular priesthood the physical expression of human love is sacrificed, family life is given up, and the potentialities of love thus set free are extended to a whole parish or to a hospital or a school. In the active life instinctive human affections are consecrated to God more fully than in family life, and in a less incarnate fashion. But it is nevertheless still easy to see and appreciate the action of God's love in the corporal works of mercy — care of the sick and the poor, as well as in the tender care of homeless children, of the aged, and so on. Here too the labors and difficulties and sacrifices of the life bring with them a corresponding protection of human values in the soul of the one "called." In dealing with other people, one retains one's sense of relatedness and integration.

In the contemplative life the problems and difficulties are more interior and also much greater. Here divine love is less incarnate. We must apprehend it and respond to it in a still more spiritual way. Fidelity is much more difficult. The human affections do not receive much of their normal gratification in a life of silence and solitude. The almost total lack of self-expression, the frequent inability to "do things for" other people in a visible and tangible way can sometimes be a torture and lead to great frustration. That is why the purely contemplative vocation is not for the immature. One has to be very strong and very solid to live in solitude.

Fortunately, the monastic life is not so purely contemplative that it does not provide for a certain amount of activity and self-expression. Living and working together in the monastic community, the monks normally preserve their sense of relatedness and do not lose their humanity. On the contrary, if they are faithful to the spirit of their rule, they will find human affection deepened and spiritualized into a profound union of charity which is no longer dependent on personal moods and fancies. And then they will come to realize something of their mission to embrace the whole world in a spiritual affection that is not limited in time or in space.

19. The higher one ascends in the scale of vocations the more careful the

selection of the candidates must be. Normally, in the married life, selection takes care of itself: the will of God can be incarnate in a decision based on natural attraction. In the active life attraction and aptitude normally go together, and the one "called" can be accepted on the basis of his ability to do the required work in peace and with spiritual joy.

Normally, more than half the people who present themselves for admission to contemplative monasteries have no vocation. "Attraction" to the contemplative life is a much less serious criterion of vocation than attraction to the active life. The stricter and more solitary a contemplative Order may be, the greater will be the gap between "attraction" and "aptitude." That is especially true in a time like ours, in which men cannot find the normal amount of silence and solitude that human nature requires for its sound functioning. There are perhaps very many nuns and brothers in active Orders who have perfectly good active vocations, but who are so overworked and so starved for a normal life of prayer that they imagine they need to become Trappists or Carthusians. In some cases the solution may indeed be a transit to an enclosed Order, but more often all that is required is a proper adjustment in their own religious institute. The problem of such adjustments is too big even to be mentioned here.

The higher a man ascends in the scale of vocations the more he must be able to spiritualize and extend his affections. To live alone with God, he must really be able to live alone. You cannot live alone if you cannot stand loneliness. And you cannot stand loneliness if your desire for "solitude" is built on frustrated need for human affection. To put it in plain language, it is hopeless to try to live your life in a cloister if you are going to eat your heart out thinking that nobody loves you. You have to be able to disregard that whole issue, and simply love the whole world in God, embracing all your brethren in that same pure love, without seeking signs of affection from them and without caring whether or not you ever get any. If you think this is very easy, I assure you that you are mistaken.

KARL BARTH

Church Dogmatics

Karl Barth (1886-1968) moved in 1921 from serving as a pastor in his native Switzerland to teaching theology at a series of German universities. He eagerly supported the Confessing Church in its opposition to Nazi efforts to take control of the Protestant churches and in 1934 wrote the Barmen Declaration, the Confessing Church's basic statement of its faith. Refusing to take an oath to Hitler, he had to leave Germany, and taught theology back in Switzerland from 1935 until his retirement in 1962. His greatest work, the *Church Dogmatics,* unfinished after many long volumes, argued that Christianity must start with God as revealed in Christ, and nothing else. If Christians in a pleasant and tolerant culture let their culture become one of the starting points of their faith, Barth insisted, then they have no grounds on which to resist if, in a Nazi culture, the Nazis want to make their doctrines one of the starting points of Christian faith. This excerpt gives a remarkable overview of the history of Christian thinking about vocation.

We speak of the vocation of man confronting and corresponding to the divine calling. It is clear that in so doing we give the term a meaning which transcends its customary use in the narrower technical sense. Vocation in the usual sense means a particular position and function of a man in connection with the process of human work, i.e., his job; and then in the broader sense a whole group of such positions and functions. Now obviously it can also be part of what we understand as human vocation that a man has his "vocation" in this technical sense. For many men this will really be so. There are also men, however, who do not legitimately have a vocation in this technical sense.

Karl Barth, *Church Dogmatics* III:4 (Edinburgh: T&T Clark, 1985), 599-602, 641-42, 645-47, 522-29, 534.

It is of a piece with the rather feverish modern over-estimation of work and of the process of production that particularly at the climax of the 19th century, and even more so in our own, it should be thought essential to man, or more precisely to the true nature of man, to have a vocation in this sense. On such a view it is forgotten that there are children and the sick and elderly and others for whom vocation in this sense can be only the object either of expectation and preparation or of recollection. It is also forgotten that there are the unemployed, though these are certainly not without a vocation. Finally, it is forgotten that there are innumerable active women who do not have this kind of vocation. The ridiculous result has been that many mothers and housewives have wanted to have their activity as such fully honored as activity in vocation, as is often unthinkingly conceded even in official usage.

A vocation in the comprehensive sense in which we are now using the term is proper to all men inasmuch as all are destined to be recipients of the divine calling and hearers of the divine command. They do not have a vocation, therefore, only when they take up a "vocation" in the narrower sense.

We have to remember that for many men the center of vocation in the material and comprehensive sense is not to be found at the point of their vocation in the narrower sense. As we have seen, a man does not live to work; he works to live. This is basically true of all men, even of those who have the good fortune to have the center of their vocation in their profession, but much more so of those whose profession can be only the circumference of their vocation, so that the essential thing to which they are truly called is to be found elsewhere than in its discharge.

That a man's vocation is exhausted in his profession is no more true than that God's calling which comes to him is simply an impulsion to work. He will always live in widely different spheres if he receives the divine calling and is obedient to it.

When we call man's vocation the epitome of all that the man to whom the command of God comes already is and has behind him and brings with him, we say already that we cannot even remotely conceive of it in the wholeness corresponding to its reality. In its reality vocation is the whole of the particularity, limitation and restriction in which every man meets the divine call and command, which wholly claims him in the totality of his previous existence, and to which above all wholeness and therefore total differentiation and specification are intrinsically proper as God intends and addresses this man and not another. Precisely because it is a matter of the totality of particularity in which man as he faces God is this man and not another, it is materially impossible to conceive it at a glance. All that we can do is to try to draw a few of the innumerable lines within which the calling of man is actualized and by which he must orientate himself if he is to recognize and fulfill the command of God, if he is to become and be a free man within his limitations and at the place of his specific responsibility, if the new thing which God will have of him here and now and in this way is to become an event in his life. The place of his responsibility, i.e., his vocation, is for every man a special one, just as the divine calling is for every man a special calling. This is what makes the task of a complete exposition of human vocation unending and therefore impossible. Nevertheless, from the characteristics of human vocation which are the same in general form for all men we can mention at least the most important, and we can thus lay down a number of criteria which always call for attention in answering the question of obedience to the command of God.

Before applying ourselves to this task, we may briefly explain why we have adopted the present usage. . . . Our premise is that the word "vocation" is not known to the New Testament in its present meaning, i.e., in the narrower technical sense in which it denotes the definite area of man's work. In the New Testament *klēsis* always means quite unambiguously the divine calling, i.e., the act of the call of God issued in Jesus Christ by which a man is transplanted into his new state as a Christian, is made a participant in the promise (Eph. 1:18; 4:4) bound up with this new state, and assumes the duty (Eph. 4:1; 2 Pet. 1:10) corresponding to this state. This calling is holy (2 Tim. 1:9). It is heavenly (Heb. 3:1). It comes, therefore, from above (Phil. 3:14). . . . Its sovereignty in face of all human greatness is reflected in the fact that at Corinth only a few wise and mighty and noble and a majority of foolish, weak, lowly and despised persons have received it (1 Cor. 1:26f.). Hence its sovereignty in face of all differences in human origin and social position consists in the fact that we may and must become obedient to it whether we are circumcised or uncircumcised, slave or free, there being also no question of abandoning these human conditions on its account (1 Cor. 7:18f.). The divine calling comes from above into all these and other human spheres, cutting diagonally across them. Thus the New Testament *klēsis* has nothing to do with the divine confirmation of these spheres as such, nor with the direction to enter such a sphere, or more particularly to enter a special sphere of work.

This is the case even in 1 Cor. 7:20, "Let each of you remain in the vocation in which you were called." To be sure, Luther here translated *klēsis*, "vocation," as "*Beruf*," and took it to mean that each must keep to the divinely allotted sphere of work, recognising in it his vocation, and being obedient to God in it, with no thoughts of becoming a monk the better to serve God in a

Christian activity outside the secular sphere. This is how the word *Beruf* is understood in the Augsburg Confession (Art. 16 and 27), and it is in this sense that, with a religious pathos corresponding to its origin, it has passed over into modern thinking and usage. . . .

Karl Holl shows expressly in his essay that in the Early Church and right up to the end of the Middle Ages no one ever dreamed of taking the verse in this sense. Prior to the Reformation, apart from a few variant interpretations by German Mystics in the late Middle Ages, *klēsis, vocatio,* call, or vocation was taken in the basic New Testament sense of the special divine calling of man to become a Christian. The only trouble was that this calling was no longer that of the New Testament, i.e., his calling to that which makes every man a Christian, but rather — and it is here that we have the great break of monasticism from the universal Christianity orientated to the average man — the special calling of man, namely, of the dissatisfied church-goer, to full and strict obedience to the command of Christ, i.e., to the observance of the "evangelical counsels." To have practical knowledge of true Christianity thus became a matter of special technique, discipline and craft exercised and con-ceived by a Christian aristocracy on the basis of its reading of the New Testa-ment as a new law. And *klēsis,* vocation, meant the admission and transition of the *homo religiosus* [religious man] to this true and special Christianity, to the true *militia Christi* [soldier of Christ]. What happened to a man when he donned the monastic habit was called a second and new baptism. To be pre-cise, was it not his only real baptism on this view? Here at least he now re-ceived full remission of his sins. And *vocatio* was now understood only as this *vocatio.* Only as he was obedient to it was there concretely the putting on of Christ of Gal. 3:27. Only with this obedience did he concretely bring the complete sacrifice of his life which is due to God and which distinguishes the monk even from the crusader, but especially from the men of other pro-fessions who give themselves to secular work. According to the view preva-lent at the height of the Middle Ages, the latter only existed to free for the work of their profession those who were totally and exclusively occupied in rendering true obedience for the salvation of each and all. There could be no question of calling for Christians in other professions.

This narrowing of the sphere of Christian *klēsis,* this dismissal of most Christians from its scope, was the flagrant evil and perversion of pre-Reformation Christianity which cried urgently for redress. How could the Church be "one body and one spirit" calling upon the one Lord and living by the one faith on the basis of the one baptism, how could it be the Church of the one God and Father of all (Eph. 4:6), if it was not prepared to take seri-ously the "one hope of your calling" upon which it was founded? What were and are all external schisms compared with this schism which the Church allowed, willed, blessed and finally achieved within itself by making and teaching and institutionalizing the distinction between first-class Christians who have a *klēsis* and second-class Christians who have not?

Yet the damage could not be made good by a devaluation of the concept of Christian *klēsis* such as took place at the Reformation. It was an antithetical and unthinking and ultimately merciless concession to the supposed needs of the ordinary man when the aristocracy was removed and overthrown and *klēsis* was allowed to be issued again to all Christians as such. But its character as *klēsis* from above, the sovereignty with which according to the New Testament it comes into all human spheres and cuts right across them, was obscured and darkened past recognition when it was understood as the direction of every man, made by the Gospel and to be accepted in faith, into the specific sphere of work to which he was obligated by a law firmly established from a very different quarter, and when this sphere of work was declared to be his God-given vocation; or conversely, when his vocation, profession or office, in the form which it took in the framework of existing human society as ordered by God, was equated with his divine calling, and therefore his industrious and skilful work in this vocation with the required obedience to his calling. . . .

When we see the vocation of a man as his destiny already disclosed and imposed as the will and law of God, so that he needs only an inner call to recognize and apprehend it, to what purpose is the calling of God, Christ or the Gospel? What more can this be than his perhaps not absolutely necessary self-direction to vocation? Calling, then, shrinks necessarily to what Holl describes as "awareness of God's presence in every moment of life." What can this mean in practice, however, if there is opposed to it, itself as a divine imperative and to be understood in concert with it, a law of historical events and relationships? The co-ordination of calling with a voice of things themselves and their necessity, and therefore with a vocation which for its part is also to be regarded as imperative; the attempt to listen to a Word of God on the right hand and another word on the left, has always had the unfortunate result, as in Protestantism, that vocation has begun to take and has actually taken precedence over calling, so that the Word of God on the right hand has increasingly and finally to yield before that on the left, the Gospel before the Law. And what then remains? The Law of God, a Word of God on the left hand? No, but "the voice of things themselves and their necessity" interpreted by the voice of an inner call; a law of man's understanding of self and time; a conservative or liberal and eventually even national or social ideal of culture and society. And what man must do within this framework and for its fulfilment is supposed to be his vocation, or, to give the matter a Christian air, his divine calling. Protestantism successfully expelled monasticism by recalling the fact that *klēsis* is the presupposition of all Christian existence. But it lost sight of the divine grandeur and purity of this idea which were always in some sense retained even by monasticism. . . .

Emil Brunner, in *The Divine Imperative,* has rightly called attention to the fact that faithfulness in vocation must exclude any intention of radically reforming life. We must not think ourselves summoned to clean up the "places within the world" before we can decide to live in them. We must not become those for whom "no place in the world is good enough . . . until he has put something within it to rights." Brunner's prognosis in respect of this kind of man is right. "His whole life is spent in this ceaseless endeavor to alter conditions, the personal meaning of life is forgotten, a nervous haste takes possession of him, and finally, since he is forced to admit that all these reforms do not alter anything essential, he falls into a state of mind which is either one of cynical resignation or of irritated hostility to every thing and everyone. . . . The reform of life as a principle produces a way of living which ignores real life."

It is to be noted that in this matter of modesty the minister, especially of the Reformed Church, incurs a particular danger. We may leave it an open question whether Zwingli and Calvin did not sometimes expect too much of themselves, and therefore of those around, when they wanted to discuss and decide in all possible fields beyond their necessary ministry of preaching, teaching, tending and guiding the flock. There can be no doubt, however, that the man who is not a Zwingli or Calvin must not try to be a central monad in even the smallest village congregation. He must not try to be the one who sees and knows better about everything and anything, the one who is equipped and authorized to criticize and initiate as the village pundit, *le divin du village* [god of the village], not even on appeal to the sovereignty of Jesus Christ over all areas of life or to the "guardian office of the Church," nor in assertion of the universality of the kingdom of God. Let the minister proclaim this kingdom. But let him proclaim it as the kingdom of God! Let him not think himself the one who is summoned and able to make heaven and earth new with his knowledge and intuition! Otherwise there will probably be weakness in his sermon preparation, in his maintenance of discipline in the instruction of candidates for confirmation, in his essential visitation, and even in his punctuality in book-keeping and the payment of accounts. And he must not be surprised if in his desire always to have the first and last word he is not taken seriously as the universal fount of knowledge he imagines himself to be. . . .

. . . we now assume that a man has sought, chosen, entered and to the best of his ability filled his sphere of operation according to the plan and providence of God. The command of God has called him to this place, and according to this command he has now tried to work in it under the will and plan of the divine providence. He will remain in it so long and so far as the command of God summons him to do so. On this presupposition he must prove his faithfulness in this vocation. 1 Cor. 7:20 is relevant in this connection: "Let every man abide in the same calling wherein he was called." But what does it mean to abide in his calling? It certainly means that he must not glance aside at the callings of others. It certainly means that he must apply himself wholeheartedly to his own. It certainly means, therefore, that he must not allow this application to be challenged or disturbed by the thought of other desirable or very different callings. There is no other calling for any man. Each has his own calling. Nevertheless, the divine calling in which he is to remain, and to remain faithful, but in which he has always to become faithful afresh, might sometimes involve a change of his sphere of operation, the abandonment of one task and the adoption of another. What abides is the calling, the Word, the command of God, not the sphere of operation to which this has led him and in which it will now rule him. It is this sphere of operation only so long and so far as it is allotted to him by the calling of God, and he is thus bound to it by his calling, being laid under this specific obligation. The relation may not be reversed. In every case, to abide in one's calling is to remain in it with a readiness to be called elsewhere. There is no other law, whether outer or inner, to bind a man absolutely to this place. His calling alone can be his law. In obedience to it, it is always possible to make a change, not on the basis of one's own ideas and opinions or those of others, nor under the pressure of external circumstances or one's own rambling fancies, but in obedience to one's calling. When this demands such a change, one is obliged to follow. Did God err when He previously led me to this or that field and bade me work in it? Perhaps I myself erred. Perhaps I must now redress the error which I then committed. God, however, did not err. Irrespective of any possible error of mine, He perhaps put me there first that I might prove myself at that point. But now it is right that I am summoned to choose again: to choose what God has perhaps chosen afresh and differently for me; to decide whether I have still to prove myself at the first point and in the first way, or elsewhere and differently.

We are not to think here of what is usually called a change of vocation. This, too, can be commanded. It was Calvin — Luther would not have written this — who expressly said of 1 Cor. 7:20 that it might be fitting for a tailor to learn another trade, or a salesman to switch to farming, and therefore why should not a doctor become a minister or a minister a doctor or politician, a scholar a man of affairs or a man of affairs a scholar? Such later changes do occur in the life of a man, and they can do so in faithfulness to his one calling which makes them necessary even though so sharp a change is involved. Yet there may also be changes in the human sphere of operation which are no less radical, though less striking, within the same vocation. For example, every change of pastorate implies a tremendous break for the minister if he has taken his work seriously and is still prepared to do so. The same is true for every serious man taking up another post within his sphere of vocation, especially if it carries with it higher and greater responsibility. Even in the same post within the same vocation new tasks can mean a radical shift in the personal sphere of operation. Finally, sickness or age may bring with them quite unbidden the problem of finding and occupying new spheres of operation.

We have to realize that in every such transition the more serious and possibly all the problems which confronted us at the first choice of our way will be raised again in a new and perhaps even more urgent form. There will again be involved a human choice with all the possibilities of error and failure which this entails. The more serious the change in question, the more we have to ask ourselves whether it is really the calling of God and not just our own caprice that we think we must follow. . . .

We may again be confident in advance that this time, too, the providence of God will have both the first and the last word above, in and in spite of all the human error which may creep in, and that in view of this we may make the boldest ventures. When may we do so? We may do so when we have to do so, when we are again confronted by the command of God which we may not oppose or withstand. The less this is the case, the less we should make such ventures, and the more advised we are to be satisfied with the first choice and therefore *pacato animo* [in tranquility of soul] to continue where we have begun. . . .

We imply nothing derogatory to human work or culture if we say that in obedience to the divine command work can be done only incidentally, as a *parergon* [secondary work], in the context of the service to which man is truly and essentially called, as its indispensable presupposition in virtue of the fact that the one called is a man, and that therefore, if he is willing and ready for this service, he must be willing to be man, and to affirm, express and prove himself as such. In its incidental character, as this *parergon*, work has its dignity and is itself service. As he allows himself to be called to work, man seriously accepts the fact that as a human creature, and in his being as such, he must stand at the disposal of his Lord and Creator. In the true and essential service to which he is called, it is a matter of himself as a human being. Yet it is also a matter of proving himself to be such by his activity. For this reason, culture is certainly a problem and a task. Is there any other way in which it could be so stringently and imperiously demanded? Culture as an end in itself will always be an extra duty which man may accept or evade. But as a *parergon* of the *ergon* [work] which is truly and essentially required, it is an obligatory duty which no one who is prepared to obey the call of God can overlook or neglect. For no one can obey God without willing to be man and therefore without pulling himself together, without turning with whole-hearted loyalty to the earthly and creaturely work of this synthesis, and therefore without being prepared to work.

Let us frankly admit that there can be no other reason for work within the framework of Christian ethics. It is an advantage of Christian ethics that it can show that the work of man is in fact commanded by God in the context of his true and essential service as a Christian. It can demonstrate the meaning and necessity of work as a *parergon* of that *ergon*. Yet there is the corresponding disadvantage that it cannot show that work is commanded, or how far it is commanded, outside this context. No independent meaning of work, no intrinsic necessity, can be proved in the framework of Christian ethics. On the contrary, the idea of an independent value and existence of human culture, and the consequent requirement of work for work's sake, can only be dismissed. This means that, strictly speaking, it is only as a Christian, only as he is claimed for co-operation in the service of the Christian community and thus knows the meaning of work, that man finds himself summoned to it. Without faith and its obedience, man's work will always stand under the shadow of the most profound uncertainty. Why is it really and finally necessary? In this uncertainty some help might perhaps be found in an ideology of culture, but even this is unlikely in most cases. Man will just work without being able to give any decisive reason why he should, or to what end. At few points does it emerge so clearly how much he stands in need of the Gospel and what a liberation it means for him to be called by the community to the community, to come to faith and to be obedient in faith. It certainly makes a decisive difference whether a man is a Christian and may therefore know, or whether he is not a Christian and cannot know, the meaning and necessity of his work in connection with the true and essential service which he is under obligation to render as man.

We do not say this in depreciation of the work which is actually performed always and everywhere, and often very ably and very well, by people who do not see this connection. The connection which the Christian may see exists even where it is not yet or no longer seen by others. It does not rest upon the faith and obedience of Christians. It is established by divine providence. Irrespective of whether it is recognized and acknowledged by us men or not, it rests on the nexus of God's will, on the connection between creation and the covenant. It rests on the fact that God's sovereignty over the whole world and all men has its center and aim in the coming of His kingdom. The objective teleology of this connection is the basis of the fact that God has created man as man, that He has ordained and equipped him for human existence, for its active affirmation and therefore for work, and that as man and as worker, whether he recognizes it or not, man is already engaged in preparation for the true and essential service to which God wills to call him with the coming of His kingdom. It is the wisdom, goodness and power of God's providence that he does not even consider releasing man from the teleology in which He has created him. As certainly as God is the Creator and Lord, there is no human existence for its own sake nor work for work's sake. What appears as such is only sin as the flood of human uncertainty and illusion. But sin cannot alter the faithfulness with which God never ceases to acknowledge human existence as He has willed and created it. Nor can it alter the factual orientation of all human work on the service for which man is truly and essentially determined, on the work of faith and its obedience as the *opus proprium* [proper work] intended for man. When man affirms himself as such, and is thus at work, he may be entangled in great uncertainty and error regarding its meaning and necessity, but he is already accepted into this service. He is thus protected by the blessing of God, who knows what He has in view for him and does not withhold it because it is still concealed from him. No one can show this connection but God Himself in His own good time. Even Christian ethics can only indicate that it exists; it cannot demonstrate it. Hence the Christian knows that all work, even that of the non-Christian, has meaning and necessity as ordained by divine providence with a view to this goal. He regards the work of all men as their preparation for the service in which he is engaged as a Christian. Thus he can never dream of trying to depreciate the work of the non-Christian as such. For he knows the value which it possesses before God equally with his own. He will regard it exactly as he does his own, knowing that it, too, is done in that service and therefore under God's blessing. He will not be surprised if he must often acknowledge to his shame that, notwithstanding the utter absence of gratitude with which it is done, it is obviously better done than his own, and better adapted to prepare and make possible the true and essential thing which must be done. In face of it, he will be radically and unhesitatingly prepared to give it the respect and esteem which it deserves, and therefore to co-operate with it as may be required, because he believes in

God's effective rule over all creatures and understands this, too, as a human response to the divine action. Yet he cannot give any other explanation of its meaning and necessity than that it happens objectively in this connection. For the Christian there can be no question of an appreciation of work on the basis of a general concept of labor and culture, whether in respect of his own work or that of others. Such appreciation, then, can have no place in Christian ethics but can only be excluded in confidence that this is really in the best interests of work itself.

The restriction for which we contend in respect of the place to be assigned to work is suggested by the fact that the affirmation of human existence which is to be achieved in it has first and supremely the character of a simple act of self-preservation. It is true enough that work is culture, and that every act of work is an act of that significant synthesis corresponding in the terrestrial sphere to the structure of human being. It may also be true that a man selects and performs a particular work because it interests him, because he considers it important, because it is so important that he devotes himself to it. It may be true also that he does this because he thinks he is adapted to perform this task, because it promises to give free rein to his powers and inclinations. Yet first and generally and much more simply what is basically at issue in all fields of human work is the desire of men to "prolong" their own lives and those of their relatives, i.e., to maintain, continue, develop and mould them, to secure and hold at the common table of life a place in closest keeping with their desires and requirements, or, in less grandiose terms, to earn their daily bread and a little more. It is for this that soul and body, head and hand and heart and hand must meet and work together in various combinations in all the different departments of human work. It is with this in view that we find this or that type of work interesting and think that we are ordained and adapted to it. . . .

A sense of shame, and therefore the attempt to gloss over this basic motive in favor of a higher, can only be false in all cases. For what is there to be ashamed of? The active affirmation of human existence obviously means at bottom that man bestirs himself to do what he can to guarantee his existence. To be able to serve he must live, and therefore he must find a guarantee of his existence. Again, he cannot serve or give himself to service unless he belongs to himself and is thus independent. But to be independent he must do what he can, within the limits of what is possible, to guarantee his existence. The limits within which he can do this are narrowly defined. God alone can give man the decisive thing and most of the other things necessary for existence. Nor can he dispense with the goodwill and co-operation of his fellows. Nevertheless, at least in days of health and strength, there is a sphere in which he himself can seek to guarantee his existence and therefore to create the presupposition of his service as an independent man. The sphere is small, but large enough for the purpose. His dependence on God does not affect the independence which he needs and must secure and preserve. And if he is honestly bent on securing and preserving this independence because otherwise he cannot serve, then he will see no violation of it if he lets himself be aided and assisted by others. Indeed, his dependence on God would be an oppressive dominion, the help of others would mean servitude and degradation, and he himself would be incapable of service, if he were not interested in his independence and did not honestly do what he could to secure his existence. The small sphere which is left for him has to be filled, and its filling is the work required of him.

It is in this sense that Paul urges Christians to work. They are to study to be quiet, to do their own business, to work with their hands and to live honestly in face of the outside world, in order that they should not have to need or ask anything from it (1 Thess. 4). Paul insists that if they are unwilling to work, they should not eat. He has heard of the disorderly conduct of some among them. He cannot call this "work" but only "superfluous busy-ness." He thus commands "in the Lord Jesus" that they should labor in quietness and eat their bread (2 Thess. 3:10f.). Even more severely he can write: "Let him that stole steal no more: but rather let him labor, working with his hands the thing which is good, that he may have to give to him that needeth" (Eph. 4:28). It is to be noted that, apart from the places in which Paul speaks of his own work as an artisan, these are the only injunctions in the New Testament in which work is directly commended. It is also to be noted how soberly it is commended in these three passages. Man must work to live. For the sake of his inner and outer independence he is required not to busy himself in useless matters but to care for his life. Nor is he to live as an unlawful recipient, but as a free giver. It is for these reasons that the work of his hands is demanded.

Work, however, is not just any activity for the procuring of the various means of livelihood. Thus the command to live the active life implies far more than simply the requirement that man should go and play his part in some possible or suitable form to preserve, safeguard, develop and fashion his existence. . . .

The work required of man is the human form of prolonging life as distinct from many activities which may also, and very lucratively, serve to prolong life, which may also be "strenuous," but the humanity of which is highly questionable and perhaps rather more than questionable. We must now consider some of the criteria by which to define what is work in the serious sense because it is commanded and right.

I. We may begin with the formal but by no means unimportant criterion that work is the prolongation of life in the form of striving in which man sets himself certain ends and does his best to attain them. We shall return later to the problem of fixing these ends. There is no doubt that the world of human work is one of ends in which individually or in totality, ostensibly or in truth, seemingly or in reality, it is a question of the preservation, safeguarding, development and fashioning of human life. Man works as he integrates himself at some point into this world of ends and does his best to attain one of the ends envisaged in it. His own part, however, necessarily means his best if he does not merely seem to work, namely, his best for this particular end and as measured by it: not, then, a maximum or optimum of his capacity; not a gigantic effort; but the maximum effort corresponding to this end and necessary for its attainment. The synthesis in which he has to express his human nature thus takes on the form which it must have if this end is to be achieved. Man is not merely present in body and soul but is immersed in the matter in hand. We may thus call this criterion of the work demanded the criterion of objectivity.

The animal, too, strives for definite ends in its life. But it seems that it does so only as it lives according to its nature and follows fixed impulses. Objectivity is not a problem for it; it lies in its very nature. Man, however, sets ends for himself, and these are always new, or they are the same in a different way. In setting them, man binds and commits himself to them. And to attain them, he not only can but must immerse himself in these particular ends, orientating himself on them, allowing them fully to engage him, concentrating upon them. He must devote himself to them. Only then does he work in a serious sense, obeying the commandment according to which he should work. Human work in all its branches is rightly done if done with the appropriate objectivity. There will be differences in the various spheres of human work at the various times and stages of the history of the process of human labor and among the various workers. But the attainment of the particular ends demands from every worker the observance of a definite rule of the game. This rule will always present itself in new forms. It will always have to be discovered afresh by man. But it is objectively present in every purpose, claiming all who turn to it, demanding from them the complete subordination, the full surrender and yet also the total freedom of those who are totally committed, if they are to work seriously and not just for the sake of appearances. This criterion is as keen as a blade. If we really want to do something for the prolongation of life, and therefore to be present in the world of work, and consequently of ends, with the claim to a good place or seat at the table of life, yet we are not prepared to study the rules for the attainment of our chosen end, or do not care if we break them or substitute for them the rules for a very different end, then we do not do objective work but are dilettantes or bunglers and perhaps do not even work at all. The question of the work which is commanded and therefore right may thus be put in the sharper form: Does the ostensible worker know what he wills and will what he knows? At this point there is a legitimate place for the righteousness of works elsewhere suspect in theology. Right work is righteous work, i.e., work which to the best of its ability does justice to each specific task and end; whereas dilettante or botched work, however profitable or well meaning in other respects, and whatever the effort incurred, cannot possibly be right work. This is not the whole story. Yet the fact remains, with reservations in respect of our future positive deliberations but with none at all negatively, that all objective work, no matter what the object, has the advantage that it might be right work and therefore obedience to the divine command, whereas all dilettante or botched work, however high and noble its purposes and however rich its material profit, cannot possibly be right and is not therefore obedience.

I once had two experiences closely related in time. The first was on a Saturday evening when I attended a variety show which was perfect in all its items and therefore, so far as I could see, executed with a real righteousness of works. The second was on the following Sunday morning when I listened to an extremely poor sermon, a real piece of theological bungling. Could I resist the impression that, formally at least, the right thing had been done at the place of very secular amusement and not at the place where the Gospel is preached and worship offered? Vengeance is swift if we think that the service of the Christian community is not also a human activity, that it does not fall under the concept of work and the question of right work, and that theological and ecclesiastical work does not also possess its own distinctive orientation on an end and the resultant objectivity. . . .

It is clear that the distinction between objective and unobjective work does not lend itself to precise and comprehensive formulation in every conceivable instance. Not everything that looks like the strictest observance of the rules is really done objectively. Nor is every dilettante as such or in every respect a bungler. Here, too, the first might be last and the last first. God alone knows definitely and irrefutably who or when someone is or is not heart and soul in a thing. The fact that God does know, however, means that the distinction between objective and unobjective is drawn and must be taken into account. The reference is primarily to the technical aspect of work. Yet we cannot say that this is only a technical question. Precisely as such it can be the decisive ethical question. Whatever our work or its particular purpose, we are either usable or useless servants. We are either heart and soul in a thing or we take things easily. *Tertium non datur* [a third option is not given]. God knows perfectly well whether we are heart and soul in a matter, or whether we are merely playing at it.

As an instructive example, we may cite the verdict of August Bebel: "Strictly speaking, the worker who drains sewers to protect humanity from unhealthy miasmas is a very useful member of society, whereas the professor who teaches falsified history in the interests of the ruling class, or the theologian who seeks to befog the brain with supernatural, transcendental doctrines, is an extremely harmful individual." We must be careful not to be guilty of what is here stated to be the activity of theologians, and if we cannot do better than this we should make all haste to become good drainers of sewers. Similarly, if the professor of history cannot do better than teach history which is falsified in the interests of a class, to the sewers with him also!

Index

Aaron, 14

Abraham, 13, 18, 167, 169, 264, 333-40, 353

Absalom, 268

accountants, 8

actors, 282, 409. *See also* theater

Adam, 4, 136, 264, 266-67, 298, 405-7

advertising, 9, 418

almsgiving, 142-43, 162-63, 167, 183, 245, 306-8, 366

ambition, 90, 98, 101, 236-37, 268, 308, 352

Ambrose, 89, 92, 97, 164

Amos, 11, 272

Anabaptists, 208, 217, 227

Ananias, 20

Andrew (apostle), 18, 345

angels, 75-76, 79, 84, 137, 139, 267, 305-6; as means of calling, 13, 16-17, 19, 191, 193, 205, 264; priests as, 223-25

Anna (prophetess), 206

Antiochus, 180

Antony, 59-65, 76, 97, 100, 214

Apology (Tertullian), 51-58

Apostles, 8, 60, 167, 238, 264, 272, 328, 345-47

Aristides, Aelius, 27

Aristotle ("the Philosopher"), 36, 155-57, 162-63, 165-66, 168, 172, 262

art, 372, 379

artisans, 186, 440

artists, 331, 378, 382, 408-9, 411-12

asceticism, 24, 32, 59, 61-64, 74-78, 167, 239, 371-77

assembly line. *See* factories, work in

Athanasius, 59-65

atheism, 9, 351, 414

Athenians, customs of, 259-60, 271

Augsburg Confession, 432

Augustine, 11, 27, 29-30, 83-103, 108, 155-58, 164-65, 168-69

avarice, 142, 146, 174-75, 186, 215-16, 230, 259, 274, 301-3, 308, 360

banks, 418

baptism, 19-20, 94, 103, 123-24, 126, 305, 348, 423; adult, 208-9, 227; of Christ, 266, 272; deathbed, 85; infant, 346; one, 211-12

Baptists, 209, 286, 296-97, 300

Barak, 15

Barmen Declaration, 429

Barrett, Anthony A., 29n.11

445